Atomic Kotlin

Bruce Eckel and Svetlana Isakova

Atomic Kotlin

Bruce Eckel and Svetlana Isakova

ISBN 978-0-9818725-5-1

This is a Leanpub book. Leanpub empowers authors and publishers with the Lean Publishing process. Lean Publishing is the act of publishing an in-progress ebook using lightweight tools and many iterations to get reader feedback, pivot until you have the right book and build traction once you do.

© 2020 - 2021 Mindview LLC

Contents

Copyright 1

Section I: Programming Basics 5

Introduction 7

Why Kotlin? 13

Hello, World! 27

`var` & `val` 31

Data Types 35

Functions 39

`if` Expressions 43

String Templates 49

Number Types 51

Booleans 57

Repetition with `while` 61

Looping & Ranges 65

The `in` Keyword 71

Expressions & Statements	75
Summary 1	79

Section II: Introduction to Objects 93

Objects Everywhere	95
Creating Classes	99
Properties	103
Constructors	109
Constraining Visibility	113
Packages	119
Testing	123
Exceptions	129
Lists	135
Variable Argument Lists	143
Sets	149
Maps	153
Property Accessors	157
Summary 2	163

Section III: Usability 187

Extension Functions	189
Named & Default Arguments	193

Overloading 199

when Expressions 203

Enumerations 209

Data Classes 213

Destructuring Declarations 217

Nullable Types 223

Safe Calls & the Elvis Operator 227

Non-Null Assertions 231

Extensions for Nullable Types 235

Introduction to Generics 239

Extension Properties 245

break & continue 249

Section IV: Functional Programming 255

Lambdas 257

The Importance of Lambdas 263

Operations on Collections 269

Member References 275

Higher-Order Functions 281

Manipulating Lists 287

Building Maps 293

Sequences 301

Local Functions 309

Folding Lists 317

Recursion 321

Section V: Object-Oriented Programming . 329

Interfaces 331

Complex Constructors 339

Secondary Constructors 341

Inheritance 345

Base Class Initialization 351

Abstract Classes 357

Upcasting 365

Polymorphism 371

Composition 375

Inheritance & Extensions 381

Class Delegation 393

Downcasting 399

Sealed Classes 407

Type Checking 413

Nested Classes 425

Objects 433

Inner Classes 437

Companion Objects 447

Section VI: Preventing Failure 457

Exception Handling 459

Check Instructions 471

The Nothing Type 481

Resource Cleanup 487

Logging 491

Unit Testing 497

Section VII: Power Tools 507

Extension Lambdas 509

Scope Functions 521

Creating Generics 533

Operator Overloading 553

Using Operators 569

Property Delegation 575

Property Delegation Tools 585

Lazy Initialization 591

Late Initialization 595

Appendices 599

Appendix A: AtomicTest 601

Appendix B: Java Interoperability 605

Copyright

Atomic Kotlin

By Bruce Eckel, President, MindView, LLC, and Svetlana Isakova, JetBrains sro.

Copyright ©2021, MindView LLC
eBook ISBN 978-0-9818725-4-4
  Version 1.0: December 2020
  Version 1.1: November 2021
Print Book ISBN 978-0-9818725-5-1
  First printing: January 2021
  Second printing: November 2021

November 2021 updates include adjustments for Kotlin 1.5, and corrections.

The eBook ISBN covers the Leanpub and Stepik eBook distributions, both available through *www.AtomicKotlin.com*.

Please purchase this book through *www.AtomicKotlin.com*, to support its continued maintenance and updates.

All rights reserved. Printed in the United States of America. This publication is protected by copyright, and permission must be obtained from the publisher prior to any prohibited reproduction, storage in a retrieval system, or transmission in any form or by any means, electronic, mechanical, photocopying, recording, or likewise. For information regarding permissions, see *www.AtomicKotlin.com*.

Created in Crested Butte, Colorado, USA, and Munich, Germany.

Text printed in the United States.

Cover design by Daniel Will-Harris, www.Will-Harris.com[1]

Many of the designations used by manufacturers and sellers to distinguish their products are claimed as trademarks. Where those designations appear in this book, and the publisher was aware of a trademark claim, the designations are printed with initial capital letters or in all capitals.

The Kotlin trademark belongs to the Kotlin Foundation[2]. Java is a trademark or registered trademark of Oracle, Inc. in the United States and other countries. Windows is a registered trademark of Microsoft Corporation in the United States and other countries. All other product names and company names mentioned herein are the property of their respective owners.

The authors and publisher have taken care in the preparation of this book, but make no expressed or implied warranty of any kind and assume no responsibility for errors or omissions. No liability is assumed for incidental or consequential damages in connection with or arising out of the use of the information or programs contained herein.

Visit us at *www.AtomicKotlin.com*.

Source Code

All the source code for this book is available as copyrighted freeware, distributed via Github[3]. To ensure you have the most current version, this is the official code distribution site. You may use this code in classroom and other educational situations as long as you cite this book as the source.

The primary goal of this copyright is to ensure that the source of the code is properly cited, and to prevent you from republishing the code without permission. (As long as this book is cited, using examples from the book in most media is generally not a problem.)

In each source-code file you find a reference to the following copyright notice:

---

[1] http://www.Will-Harris.com
[2] https://kotlinlang.org/foundation/kotlin-foundation.html
[3] https://github.com/BruceEckel/AtomicKotlinExamples

// Copyright.txt
This computer source code is Copyright ©2021 MindView LLC.
All Rights Reserved.

Permission to use, copy, modify, and distribute this
computer source code (Source Code) and its documentation
without fee and without a written agreement for the
purposes set forth below is hereby granted, provided that
the above copyright notice, this paragraph and the
following five numbered paragraphs appear in all copies.

1. Permission is granted to compile the Source Code and to
include the compiled code, in executable format only, in
personal and commercial software programs.

2. Permission is granted to use the Source Code without
modification in classroom situations, including in
presentation materials, provided that the book "Atomic
Kotlin" is cited as the origin.

3. Permission to incorporate the Source Code into printed
media may be obtained by contacting:

MindView LLC, PO Box 969, Crested Butte, CO 81224
MindViewInc@gmail.com

4. The Source Code and documentation are copyrighted by
MindView LLC. The Source code is provided without express
or implied warranty of any kind, including any implied
warranty of merchantability, fitness for a particular
purpose or non-infringement. MindView LLC does not
warrant that the operation of any program that includes the
Source Code will be uninterrupted or error-free. MindView
LLC makes no representation about the suitability of the
Source Code or of any software that includes the Source
Code for any purpose. The entire risk as to the quality
and performance of any program that includes the Source
Code is with the user of the Source Code. The user
understands that the Source Code was developed for research
and instructional purposes and is advised not to rely
exclusively for any reason on the Source Code or any
program that includes the Source Code. Should the Source

Code or any resulting software prove defective, the user
assumes the cost of all necessary servicing, repair, or
correction.

5. IN NO EVENT SHALL MINDVIEW LLC, OR ITS PUBLISHER BE
LIABLE TO ANY PARTY UNDER ANY LEGAL THEORY FOR DIRECT,
INDIRECT, SPECIAL, INCIDENTAL, OR CONSEQUENTIAL DAMAGES,
INCLUDING LOST PROFITS, BUSINESS INTERRUPTION, LOSS OF
BUSINESS INFORMATION, OR ANY OTHER PECUNIARY LOSS, OR FOR
PERSONAL INJURIES, ARISING OUT OF THE USE OF THIS SOURCE
CODE AND ITS DOCUMENTATION, OR ARISING OUT OF THE INABILITY
TO USE ANY RESULTING PROGRAM, EVEN IF MINDVIEW LLC, OR
ITS PUBLISHER HAS BEEN ADVISED OF THE POSSIBILITY OF SUCH
DAMAGE. MINDVIEW LLC SPECIFICALLY DISCLAIMS ANY
WARRANTIES, INCLUDING, BUT NOT LIMITED TO, THE IMPLIED
WARRANTIES OF MERCHANTABILITY AND FITNESS FOR A PARTICULAR
PURPOSE. THE SOURCE CODE AND DOCUMENTATION PROVIDED
HEREUNDER IS ON AN "AS IS" BASIS, WITHOUT ANY ACCOMPANYING
SERVICES FROM MINDVIEW LLC, AND MINDVIEW LLC HAS NO
OBLIGATIONS TO PROVIDE MAINTENANCE, SUPPORT, UPDATES,
ENHANCEMENTS, OR MODIFICATIONS.

Please note that MindView LLC maintains a Web site which is
the sole distribution point for electronic copies of the
Source Code, where it is freely available under the terms
stated above:

  https://github.com/BruceEckel/AtomicKotlinExamples

If you think you've found an error in the Source Code,
please submit a correction at:
https://github.com/BruceEckel/AtomicKotlinExamples/issues

You may use the code in your projects and in the classroom (including your presentation materials) as long as the copyright notice that appears in each source file is retained.

Section I: Programming Basics

There was something amazingly enticing about programming—**Vint Cerf**

This section is for readers who are learning to program. If you're an experienced programmer, skip forward to *Summary 1* and *Summary 2*.

Introduction

This book is for dedicated novices and experienced programmers.

You're a novice if you don't have prior programming knowledge, but "dedicated" because we give you just enough to figure it out on your own. When you're finished, you'll have a solid foundation in programming and in Kotlin.

If you're an experienced programmer, skip forward to **Summary 1** and **Summary 2**, then proceed from there.

The "Atomic" part of the book title refers to atoms as the smallest indivisible units. In this book, we try to introduce only one concept per chapter, so the chapters cannot be further subdivided—thus we call them *atoms*.

Concepts

All programming languages consist of features. You apply these features to produce results. Kotlin is powerful—not only does it have a rich set of features, but you can usually express those features in numerous ways.

If everything is dumped on you too quickly, you might come away thinking Kotlin is "too complicated."

This book attempts to prevent overwhelm. We teach you the language carefully and deliberately, using the following principles:

1. **Baby steps and small wins**. We cast off the tyranny of the chapter. Instead, we present each small step as an *atomic concept* or simply *atom*, which looks like a tiny chapter. We try to present only one new concept per atom. A typical atom contains one or more small, runnable pieces of code and the output it produces.
2. **No forward references**. As much as possible, we avoid saying, "These features are explained in a later atom."

3. **No references to other programming languages**. We do so only when necessary. An analogy to a feature in a language you don't understand isn't helpful.
4. **Show don't tell**. Instead of verbally describing a feature, we prefer examples and output. It's better to see a feature in code.
5. **Practice before theory**. We try to show the mechanics of the language first, then tell why those features exist. This is backwards from "traditional" teaching, but it often seems to work better.

If you know the features, you can work out the meaning. It's usually easier to understand a single page of Kotlin than it is to understand the equivalent code in another language.

Where Is the Index?

This book is written in Markdown and produced with Leanpub. Unfortunately, neither Markdown nor Leanpub supports indexes. However, by creating the smallest-possible chapters (atoms) consisting of a single topic in each atom, the table of contents acts as a kind of index. In addition, the eBook versions allow for electronic searching across the book.

Cross-References

A reference to an atom in the book looks like this: **Introduction**, which in this case refers to the current atom. In the various eBook formats, this produces a hyperlink to that atom.

Formatting

In this book:

- *Italics* introduce a new term or concept, and sometimes emphasize an idea.

- `Fixed-width font` indicates program keywords, identifiers and file names. The code examples are also in this font, and are colorized in the eBook versions of the book.
- In prose, we follow a function name with empty parentheses, as in `func()`. This reminds the reader they are looking at a function.
- To make the eBook easy to read on all devices and allow the user to increase the font size, we limit our code listing width to 47 characters. At times this requires compromise, but we feel the results are worth it. To achieve these widths we may remove spaces that might otherwise be included in many formatting styles—in particular, we use two-space indents rather than the standard four spaces.

"Pause"

Occasionally you will see:

- -

This indicates a pause, or a kind of small reset. In this book it often appears before a brief summary of the current subsection, but where a "Summary" subhead would be overkill. Some books use a mechanism like this to indicate that an idea is complete and we are starting something new, but it's still within the same topic and not big enough to warrant a subsection or a new section. The markdown in Leanpub is quite limited, and using one or more dots (my original attempt) isn't possible. Putting two dashes in the markdown produces a dot and a dash. There might be a better way to do this but I haven't found it, so I settled on that.

Sample the Book

We provide a free sample of the electronic book at *AtomicKotlin.com*. The sample includes the first two sections in their entirety, along with several subsequent atoms. This way you can try out the book and decide if it's a good fit for you.

The complete book is for sale, both as a print book and an eBook. If you like what we've done in the free sample, please support us and help us continue our work by paying for what you use. We hope the book helps, and we appreciate your sponsorship.

In the age of the Internet, it doesn't seem possible to control any piece of information. You'll probably find the electronic version of this book in numerous places. If you are unable to pay for the book right now and you do download it from one of these sites, please "pay it forward." For example, help someone else learn the language once you've learned it. Or help someone in any way they need. Perhaps in the future you'll be better off, and then you can pay for the book.

Exercises and Solutions

Most atoms in *Atomic Kotlin* are accompanied by a handful of small exercises. To improve your understanding, we recommend solving the exercises immediately after reading the atom. Most of the exercises are checked automatically by the JetBrains IntelliJ IDEA integrated development environment (IDE), so you can see your progress and get hints if you get stuck.

You can find the following links at http://AtomicKotlin.com/exercises/[4].

To solve the exercises, install IntelliJ IDEA with the Edu Tools plugin by following these tutorials:

1. Install IntelliJ IDEA and the EduTools Plugin[5].
2. Open the Atomic Kotlin course and solve the exercises[6].

In the course, you'll find solutions for all exercises. If you're stuck on an exercise, check for hints or try peeking at the solution. We still recommend implementing it yourself.

If you have any problems setting up and running the course, please read The Troubleshooting Guide[7]. If that doesn't solve your problem, please contact the support team as mentioned in the guide.

---

[4]http://AtomicKotlin.com/exercises/
[5]https://www.jetbrains.com/help/education/install-edutools-plugin.html
[6]https://www.jetbrains.com/help/education/learner-start-guide.html?section=Atomic%20Kotlin
[7]https://www.jetbrains.com/help/education/troubleshooting-guide.html

If you find a mistake in the course content (for example, a test for a task produces the wrong result), please use our issue tracker to report the problem with this pre-filled form[8]. Note that you'll need to log in into YouTrack. We appreciate your time in helping to improve the course!

Seminars

You can find information about live seminars and other learning tools at *AtomicKotlin.com*.

Conferences

Bruce creates *Open-Spaces* conferences such as the Winter Tech Forum[9]. Join the mailing list at *AtomicKotlin.com* to stay informed about our activities and where we are speaking.

Support Us

This was a big project. It took time and effort to produce this book and accompanying support materials. If you enjoy this book and want to see more things like it, please support us:

- **Blog, tweet, etc. and tell your friends.** This is a grassroots marketing effort so everything you do will help.
- **Purchase an eBook or print version** of this book at *AtomicKotlin.com*.
- **Check** *AtomicKotlin.com* for other support products or events.

About Us

Bruce Eckel is the author of the multi-award-winning *Thinking in Java* and *Thinking in C++*, and a number of other books on computer programming including Atomic

---

[8]https://youtrack.jetbrains.com/newIssue?project=EDC&summary=AtomicKotlin%3A&c=Subsystem%20Kotlin&c=
[9]http://www.WinterTechForum.com

Scala[10]. He's given hundreds of presentations throughout the world and puts on alternative conferences and events like the Winter Tech Forum[11] and developer retreats. Bruce has a BS in applied physics and an MS in computer engineering. His blog is at www.BruceEckel.com[12] and his consulting, training and conference business is Mindview LLC[13].

Svetlana Isakova began as a member of the Kotlin compiler team, and is now a developer advocate for JetBrains. She teaches Kotlin and speaks at conferences worldwide, and is coauthor of the book *Kotlin in Action*.

Acknowledgements

- The Kotlin Language Design Team and contributors.
- The developers of Leanpub, which made publishing this book *so* much easier.
- James Ward for converting the Gradle build to Kotlin, and being generally awesome.

Dedications

For my beloved father, E. Wayne Eckel. April 1, 1924—November 23, 2016. You first taught me about machines, tools, and design.

For my father, Sergey Lvovich Isakov, who passed away so early and who we will always miss.

About the Cover

Daniel Will-Harris[14] designed the cover based on the Kotlin logo.

---

[10] http://www.atomicscala.com/
[11] http://www.WinterTechForum.com
[12] http://www.BruceEckel.com
[13] https://www.mindviewllc.com/
[14] http://www.will-harris.com

Why Kotlin?

> *Programs must be written for people to read, and only incidentally for machines to execute.*—**Harold Abelson**, coauthor, *Structure and Interpretation of Computer Programs.*

This atom is an overview of the historical development of programming languages so you can understand where Kotlin fits and why you might want to learn it. We introduce some topics which, if you are a novice, might seem too complicated right now. Feel free to skip this atom and come back to it after you've read more of the book.

Programming language design is an evolutionary path from serving the needs of the machine to serving the needs of the programmer.

A programming language is invented by a language designer and implemented as one or more programs that act as tools for using the language. The implementer is usually the language designer, at least initially.

Early languages focused on hardware limitations. As computers become more powerful, newer languages shift toward more sophisticated programming with an emphasis on reliability. These languages can choose features based on the psychology of programming.

Every programming language is a collection of experiments. Historically, programming language design has been a succession of guesses and assumptions about what will make programmers more productive. Some of those experiments fail, some are mildly successful and some are very successful.

We learn from the experiments in each new language. Some languages address issues that turn out to be incidental rather than essential, or the environment changes (faster processors, cheaper memory, new understanding of programming and languages) and that issue becomes less important or even inconsequential. If those ideas become obsolete and the language doesn't evolve, it fades from use.

The original programmers worked directly with numbers representing processor machine instructions. This approach produced numerous errors, and *assembly language* was created to replace the numbers with mnemonic *opcodes*—words that programmers could more easily remember and read, along with other helpful tools. However, there was still a one-to-one correspondence between assembly-language instructions and machine instructions, and programmers had to write each line of assembly code. In addition, each computer processor used its own distinct assembly language.

Developing programs in assembly language is exceedingly expensive. Higher-level languages help solve that problem by creating a level of abstraction away from low-level assembly languages.

Compilers and Interpreters

The instructions of an interpreted language are executed directly by a program called an *interpreter*. Kotlin is *compiled* rather than *interpreted*. The source code of a compiled language is converted into a different representation that runs as its own program, either directly on a hardware processor or on a *virtual machine* that emulates a processor:

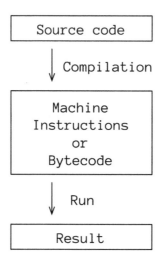

Languages such as C, C++, Go and Rust compile into *machine code* that runs directly on the underlying hardware *central processing unit* (CPU). Languages like Java and Kotlin compile into *bytecode* which is an intermediate-level format that doesn't run directly on the hardware CPU, but instead on a *virtual machine*, which is a program that executes bytecode instructions. Programs produced by the JVM version of Kotlin run on the *Java Virtual Machine* (JVM).

Portability is an important benefit of a virtual machine. The same bytecode can run on every computer that has a virtual machine. Virtual machines can be optimized for particular hardware and to solve speed problems. The JVM contains many years of such optimizations, and has been implemented on many platforms.

At *compile time*, the code is checked by the compiler to discover *compile-time errors*. (IntelliJ IDEA and other development environments highlight these errors when you input the code, so you can quickly discover and fix any problems). If there are no compile-time errors, the source code will be compiled into bytecode.

A *runtime error* cannot be detected at compile time, so it only emerges when you run the program. Typically, runtime errors are more difficult to discover and more expensive to fix. *Statically-typed languages* like Kotlin discover as many errors as possible at compile time, while *dynamic languages* perform their safety checks at runtime (some dynamic languages don't perform as many safety checks as they might).

Languages that Influenced Kotlin

Kotlin draws its ideas and features from many languages, and those languages were influenced by earlier languages. It's helpful to know some programming-language history to gain perspective on how we got to Kotlin. The languages described here are chosen for their influence on the languages that followed them. All these languages ultimately inspired the design of Kotlin, sometimes by being an example of what *not* to do.

FORTRAN: FORmula TRANslation (1957)

Designed for use by scientists and engineers, Fortran's goal was to make it easier to encode equations. Finely-tuned and tested Fortran libraries are still in use today, but they are typically "wrapped" to make them callable from other languages.

LISP: LISt Processor (1958)

Rather than being application-specific, LISP embodied essential programming concepts; it was the computer scientist's language and the first *functional* programming language (You'll learn about functional programming in this book). The tradeoff for its power and flexibility was efficiency: LISP was typically too expensive to run on early machines, and only in recent decades have machines become fast enough to produce a resurgence in the use of LISP. For example, the GNU Emacs editor is written entirely in LISP, and can be extended using LISP.

ALGOL: ALGOrithmic Language (1958)

Arguably the most influential of the 1950's languages because it introduced syntax that persisted in many subsequent languages. For example, C and its derivatives are "ALGOL-like" languages.

COBOL: COmmon Business-Oriented Language (1959)

Designed for business, finance, and administrative data processing. It has an English-like syntax, and was intended to be self-documenting and highly readable. Although this intent generally failed—COBOL is famous for bugs introduced by a misplaced period—the US Department of Defense forced widespread adoption on mainframe computers, and systems are still running (and requiring maintenance) today.

BASIC: Beginners' All-purpose Symbolic Instruction Code (1964)

BASIC was one of the early attempts to make programming accessible. While very successful, its features and syntax were limited, so it was only partly helpful for people who needed to learn more sophisticated languages. It is predominantly an interpreted language, which means that to run it you need the original code for the program. Despite that, many useful programs were written in BASIC, in particular as a scripting language for Microsoft's "Office" products. BASIC might even be thought of as the first "open" programming language, as people made numerous variations of it.

Simula 67, the Original Object-Oriented Language (1967)

A *simulation* typically involves many "objects" interacting with each other. Different objects have different characteristics and behaviors. Languages that existed at the time were awkward to use for simulations, so Simula (another "ALGOL-like" language) was developed to provide direct support for creating simulation objects. It turns out that these ideas are also useful for general-purpose programming, and this was the genesis of Object-Oriented (OO) languages.

Pascal (1970)

Pascal increased compilation speed by restricting the language so it could be implemented as a *single-pass compiler*. The language forced the programmer to structure their code in a particular way and imposed somewhat awkward and less-readable constraints on program organization. As processors became faster, memory cheaper, and compiler technology better, the impact of these constraints became too costly.

An implementation of Pascal, Turbo Pascal from Borland, initially worked on CP/M machines and then made the move to early MS-DOS (precursor to Windows), later evolving into the Delphi language for Windows. By putting everything in memory, Turbo Pascal compiled at lightning speeds on very underpowered machines, dramatically improving the programming experience. Its creator, Anders Hejlsberg, later went on to design both C# and TypeScript.

Niklaus Wirth, the inventor of Pascal, created subsequent languages: Modula, Modula-2 and Oberon. As the name implies, Modula focused on dividing programs into modules, for better organization and faster compilation. Most modern languages support *separate compilation* and some form of module system.

C (1972)

Despite the increasing number of higher-level languages, programmers were still writing assembly language. This is often called *systems programming*, because it is done at the level of the operating system, but it also includes embedded programming for dedicated physical devices. This is not only arduous and expensive (Bruce began his career writing assembly language for embedded systems), but it isn't portable—assembly language can only run on the processor it is written for. C was designed to be a "high-level assembly language" that is still close enough to the hardware that you rarely need to write assembly. More importantly, a C program runs on any processor with a C compiler. C decoupled the program from the processor, which solved a huge and expensive problem. As a result, former assembly-language programmers could be vastly more productive in C. C has been so effective that recent languages (notably Go and Rust) are still attempting to usurp it for systems programming.

Smalltalk (1972)

Designed from the beginning to be purely object-oriented, Smalltalk significantly moved OO and language theory forward by being a platform for experimentation and demonstrating rapid application development. However, it was created when languages were still proprietary, and the entry price for a Smalltalk system could be in the thousands. It was interpreted, so you needed a Smalltalk environment to run programs. Open-source Smalltalk implementations did not appear until after the programming world had moved on. Smalltalk programmers have contributed great insights benefitting later OO languages like C++ and Java.

C++: A Better C with Objects (1983)

Bjarne Stroustrup created C++ because he wanted a better C and he wanted support for the object-oriented constructs he had experienced while using Simula-67. Bruce was a member of the C++ Standards Committee for its first eight years, and wrote three books on C++ including *Thinking in C++*.

Backwards-compatibility with C was a foundational principle of C++ design, so C code can be compiled in C++ with virtually no changes. This provided an easy migration path—programmers could continue to program in C, receive the benefits of C++, and slowly experiment with C++ features while still being productive. Most criticisms of C++ can be traced to the constraint of backwards compatibility with C.

One of the problems with C was the issue of *memory management.* The programmer must first acquire memory, then run an operation using that memory, then release the memory. Forgetting to release memory is called a *memory leak* and can result in using up the available memory and crashing the process. The initial version of C++ made some innovations in this area, along with *constructors* to ensure proper initialization. Later versions of the language have made significant improvements in memory management.

Python: Friendly and Flexible (1990)

Python's designer, Guido Van Rossum, created the language based on his inspiration of "programming for everyone." His nurturing of the Python community has given it the reputation of being the friendliest and most supportive community in the programming world. Python was one of the first open-source languages, resulting in implementations on virtually every platform including embedded systems and machine learning. Its dynamism and ease-of-use makes it ideal for automating small, repetitive tasks but its features also support the creation of large, complex programs.

Python is a true "grass-roots" language; it never had a company promoting it and the attitude of its fans was to never push the language, but simply to help anyone learn it who wants to. The language continues to steadily improve, and in recent years its popularity has skyrocketed.

Python may have been the first mainstream language to combine functional and OO programming. It predated Java with automatic memory management using *garbage collection* (you typically never have to allocate or release memory yourself) and the ability to run programs on multiple platforms.

Haskell: Pure Functional Programming (1990)

Inspired by Miranda (1985), a proprietary language, Haskell was created as an open standard for pure functional programming research, although it has also been used for products. Syntax and ideas from Haskell have influenced a number of subsequent languages including Kotlin.

Java: Virtual Machines and Garbage Collection (1995)

James Gosling and his team were given the task of writing code for a TV set-top box. They decided they didn't like C++ and instead of creating the box, created the Java language. The company, Sun Microsystems, put an enormous marketing push behind the free language (still a new idea at the time) to attempt domination of the emerging Internet landscape.

This perceived time window for Internet domination put a lot of pressure on Java language design, resulting in a significant number of flaws (The book *Thinking in Java* illuminates these flaws so readers are prepared to cope with them). Brian Goetz at Oracle, the current lead developer of Java, has made remarkable and surprising improvements in Java despite the constraints he inherited. Although Java was remarkably successful, an important Kotlin design goal is to fix Java's flaws so programmers can be more productive.

Java's success came from two innovative features: a *virtual machine* and *garbage collection*. These were available in other languages—for example, LISP, Smalltalk and Python have garbage collection and UCSD Pascal ran on a virtual machine—but they were never considered practical for mainstream languages. Java changed that, and in doing so made programmers significantly more productive.

A virtual machine is an intermediate layer between the language and the hardware. The language doesn't have to generate machine code for a particular processor; it only needs to generate an intermediate language (bytecode) that runs on the virtual machine. Virtual machines require processing power and, before Java, were believed to be impractical. The *Java Virtual Machine* (JVM) gave rise to Java's slogan "write once, run everywhere." In addition, other languages can be more easily developed by targeting the JVM; examples include Groovy, a Java-like scripting language, and Clojure, a version of LISP.

Garbage collection solves the problem of forgetting to release memory, or if it's difficult to know when a piece of storage is no longer used. Projects have been significantly delayed or even cancelled because of memory leaks. Although garbage collection appears in some prior languages, it was believed to produce an unacceptable amount of overhead until Java demonstrated its practicality.

JavaScript: Java in Name Only (1995)

The original Web browser simply copied and displayed pages from a Web server. Web browsers proliferated, becoming a new programming platform that needed language support. Java wanted to be this language but was too awkward for the job. JavaScript began as LiveScript and was built into NetScape Navigator, one of the first Web browsers. Renaming it to JavaScript was a marketing ploy by NetScape, as the language has only a vague similarity to Java.

As the Web took off, JavaScript became tremendously important. However, the behavior of JavaScript was so unpredictable that Douglas Crockford wrote a book with the tongue-in-cheek title *JavaScript, the Good Parts*, where he demonstrated all the problems with the language so programmers could avoid them. Subsequent improvements by the ECMAScript committee have made JavaScript unrecognizable to an original JavaScript programmer. It is now considered a stable and mature language.

Web assembly (WASM) was derived from JavaScript to be a kind of bytecode for web browsers. It often runs much faster than JavaScript and can be generated by other languages. At this writing, the Kotlin team is working to add WASM as a target.

C#: Java for .NET (2000)

C# was designed to provide some of the important abilities of Java on the .NET (Windows) platform, while freeing designers from the constraint of following the Java language. The result included numerous improvements over Java. For example, C# developed the concept of *extension functions*, which are heavily used in Kotlin. C# also became significantly more functional than Java. Many C# features clearly influenced Kotlin design.

Scala: SCALAble (2003)

Martin Odersky created Scala to run on the Java virtual machine: To piggyback on the work done on the JVM, to interact with Java programs, and possibly with the idea that it might displace Java. As a researcher, Odersky and his team used Scala as a platform to experiment with language features, notably those not included in Java.

These experiments were illuminating and a number of them found their way into Kotlin, usually in a modified form. For example, the ability to redefine operators like + for use in special cases is called *operator overloading*. This was included in C++ but not Java. Scala added operator overloading but also allows you to invent new operators by combining any sequence of characters. This often produces confusing code. A limited form of operator overloading is included in Kotlin, but you can only overload operators that already exist.

Scala is also an object-functional hybrid, like Python but with a focus on pure functions and strict objects. This helped inspire Kotlin's choice to also be an object-functional hybrid.

Like Scala, Kotlin runs on the JVM but it interacts with Java far more easily than Scala does (see **Appendix B**). In addition, Kotlin targets JavaScript, the Android OS, and it generates native code for other platforms.

Atomic Kotlin evolved from the ideas and material in Atomic Scala[15].

Groovy: A Dynamic JVM Language (2007)

Dynamic languages are appealing because they are more interactive and concise than static languages. There have been numerous attempts to produce a more dynamic programming experience on the JVM, including Jython (Python) and Clojure (a dialect of Lisp). Groovy was the first to achieve wide acceptance.

At first glance, Groovy appears to be a cleaned-up version of Java, producing a more pleasant programming experience. Most Java code will run unchanged in Groovy, so Java programmers can be quickly productive, later learning the more sophisticated features that provide notable programming improvements over Java.

The Kotlin operators ?. and ?: that deal with the problem of emptiness first appeared in Groovy.

There are numerous Groovy features that are recognizable in Kotlin. Some of those features also appear in other languages, which probably pushed harder for them to be included in Kotlin.

Why Kotlin? (Introduced 2011, Version 1.0: 2016)

Just as C++ was initially intended to be "a better C," Kotlin was initially oriented towards being "a better Java." It has since evolved significantly beyond that goal.

---

[15]http://www.AtomicScala.com

Kotlin pragmatically chooses only the most successful and helpful features from other programming languages—after those features have been field-tested and proven especially valuable.

Thus, if you are coming from another language, you might recognize some features of that language in Kotlin. This is intentional: Kotlin maximizes productivity by leveraging tested concepts.

Readability

Readability is a primary goal in the design of the language. Kotlin syntax is concise—it requires no ceremony for most scenarios, but can still express complex ideas.

Tooling

Kotlin comes from JetBrains, a company that specializes in developer tooling. It has first-class tooling support, and many language features were designed with tooling in mind.

Multi-Paradigm

Kotlin supports multiple programming paradigms, which are gently introduced in this book:

- Imperative programming
- Functional programming
- Object-oriented programming

Multi-Platform

Kotlin source code can be compiled to different target platforms:

- **JVM**. The source code compiles into JVM bytecode (`.class` files), which can then be run on any Java Virtual Machine (JVM).

- **Android**. Android has its own runtime called ART[16] (the predecessor was called Dalvik). The Kotlin source code is compiled into *Dalvik Executable Format* (`.dex` files).
- **JavaScript**, to run inside a web browser.
- **Native Binaries** by generating machine code for specific platforms and CPUs.

This book focuses on the language itself, using the JVM as the only target platform. Once you know the language, you can apply Kotlin to different application and target platforms.

Two Kotlin Features

This atom does not assume you are a programmer, which makes it hard to explain most of the benefits of Kotlin over the alternatives. There are, however, two topics which are very impactful and can be explained at this early juncture: Java interoperability and the issue of indicating "no value."

Effortless Java Interoperability

To be "a better C," C++ must be backwards compatible with the syntax of C, but Kotlin does not have to be backwards compatible with the syntax of Java—it only needs to work with the JVM. This frees the Kotlin designers to create a much cleaner and more powerful syntax, without the visual noise and complication that clutters Java.

For Kotlin to be "a better Java," the experience of trying it must be pleasant and frictionless, so Kotlin enables effortless integration with existing Java projects. You can write a small piece of Kotlin functionality and slip it in amidst your existing Java code. The Java code doesn't even know the Kotlin code is there—it just looks like more Java code.

Companies often investigate a new language by building a standalone program with that language. Ideally, this program is beneficial but nonessential, so if the project fails it can be terminated with minimal damage. Not every company wants to spend the kind of resources necessary for this type of experimentation. Because Kotlin

[16]https://source.android.com/devices/tech/dalvik

seamlessly integrates into an existing Java system (and benefits from that system's tests), it becomes very cheap or even free to try Kotlin to see whether it's a good fit.

In addition, JetBrains, the company that creates Kotlin, provides IntelliJ IDEA in a "Community" (free) version, which includes support for both Java and Kotlin along with the ability to easily integrate the two. It even has a tool that takes Java code and (mostly) rewrites it to Kotlin.

Appendix B covers Java interoperability.

Representing Emptiness

An especially beneficial Kotlin feature is its solution to a challenging programming problem.

What do you do when someone hands you a dictionary and asks you to look up a word that doesn't exist? You could guarantee results by making up definitions for unknown words. A more useful approach is just to say, "There's no definition for that word." This demonstrates a significant problem in programming: How do you indicate "no value" for a piece of storage that is uninitialized, or for the result of an operation?

The *null reference* was invented in 1965 for ALGOL by Tony Hoare, who later called it "my billion-dollar mistake." One problem was that it was too simple—sometimes being told a room is empty isn't enough. You might need to know, for example, *why* it is empty. This leads to the second problem: the implementation. For efficiency's sake, it was typically just a special value that could fit in a small amount of memory, and what better than the memory already allocated for that information?

The original C language did not automatically initialize storage, which caused numerous problems. C++ improved the situation by setting newly-allocated storage to all zeroes. Thus, if a numerical value isn't initialized, it is simply a numerical zero. This didn't seem so bad but it allowed uninitialized values to quietly slip through the cracks (newer C and C++ compilers often warn you about these). Worse, if a piece of storage was a *pointer*—used to indicate ("point to") another piece of storage—a null pointer would point at location zero in memory, which is almost certainly not what you want.

Java prevents accesses to uninitialized values by reporting such errors at runtime. Although this discovers uninitialized values, it doesn't solve the problem because the only way you can verify that your program won't crash is by running it. There are swarms of these kinds of bugs in Java code, and programmers waste huge amounts of time finding them.

Kotlin solves this problem by preventing operations that might cause null errors at compile time, *before the program can run*. This is the single-most celebrated feature by Java programmers adopting Kotlin. This one feature can minimize or eliminate Java's null errors, saving your project significant amounts of time and money.

An Abundance of Benefits

The two features we were able to explain here (without requiring more programming knowledge) make a huge difference whether or not you're a Java programmer. If Kotlin is your first language and you end up on a project that needs more programmers, it is much easier to recruit one of the many existing Java programmers into Kotlin.

Kotlin has many other benefits, which we cannot explain until you know more about programming. That's what the rest of the book is for.

- -

Languages are often selected by passion, not reason... I'm trying to make Kotlin a language that is loved for a reason.—Andrey Breslav, Kotlin Lead Language Designer.

Hello, World!

"Hello, world!" is a program commonly used to demonstrate the basic syntax of programming languages.

We develop this program in several steps so you understand its parts.

First, let's examine an empty program that does nothing at all:

```
// HelloWorld/EmptyProgram.kt

fun main() {
  // Program code here ...
}
```

The example starts with a *comment*, which is illuminating text that is ignored by Kotlin. `//` (two forward slashes) begins a comment that goes to the end of the current line:

```
// Single-line comment
```

Kotlin ignores the `//` and everything after it until the end of the line. On the following line, it pays attention again.

The first line of each example in this book is a comment starting with the name of the the subdirectory containing the source-code file (Here, `HelloWorld`) followed by the name of the file: `EmptyProgram.kt`. The example subdirectory for each atom corresponds to the name of that atom.

keywords are reserved by the language and given special meaning. The keyword `fun` is short for *function*. A function is a collection of code that can be executed using that function's name (we spend a lot of time on functions throughout the book). The function's name follows the `fun` keyword, so in this case it's `main()` (in prose, we follow the function name with parentheses).

`main()` is actually a special name for a function; it indicates the "entry point" for a Kotlin program. A Kotlin program can have many functions with many different names, but `main()` is the one that's automatically called when you execute the program.

The *parameter list* follows the function name and is enclosed by parentheses. Here, we don't pass anything into `main()` so the parameter list is empty.

The *function body* appears after the parameter list. It begins with an opening brace (`{`) and ends with a closing brace (`}`). The function body contains *statements* and *expressions*. A statement produces an effect, and an expression yields a result.

`EmptyProgram.kt` contains no statements or expressions in the body, just a comment.

Let's make the program display "Hello, world!" by adding a line in the `main()` body:

```
// HelloWorld/HelloWorld.kt

fun main() {
  println("Hello, world!")
}
/* Output:
Hello, world!
*/
```

The line that displays the greeting begins with `println()`. Like `main()`, `println()` is a function. This line *calls* the function, which executes its body. You give the function name, followed by parentheses containing one or more parameters. In this book, when referring to a function in the prose, we add parentheses after the name as a reminder that it is a function. Here, we say `println()`.

`println()` takes a single parameter, which is a `String`. You define a `String` by putting characters inside quotes.

`println()` moves the cursor to a new line after displaying its parameter, so subsequent output appears on the next line. You can use `print()` instead, which leaves the cursor on the same line.

Unlike some languages, you don't need a semicolon at the end of an expression in Kotlin. It's only necessary if you put more than one expression on a single line (this is discouraged).

For some examples in the book, we show the output at the end of the listing, inside a *multiline comment*. A multiline comment starts with a `/*` (a forward slash followed by an asterisk) and continues—including line breaks (which we call *newlines*)—until a */ (an asterisk followed by a forward slash) ends the comment:

```
/* A multiline comment
Doesn't care
about newlines */
```

It's possible to add code on the same line *after* the closing */ of a comment, but it's confusing, so people don't usually do it.

Comments add information that isn't obvious from reading the code. If comments only repeat what the code says, they become annoying and people start ignoring them. When code changes, programmers often forget to update comments, so it's good practice to use comments judiciously, mainly for highlighting tricky aspects of your code.

Exercises and solutions can be found at *www.AtomicKotlin.com*.

var & val

> When an identifier holds data, you must decide whether it can be reassigned.

You create *identifiers* to refer to elements in your program. The most basic decision for a data identifier is whether it can change its contents during program execution, or if it can only be assigned once. This is controlled by two keywords:

- var, short for *variable*, which means you can reassign its contents.
- val, short for *value*, which means you can only initialize it; you cannot reassign it.

You define a var like this:

```
var identifier = initialization
```

The var keyword is followed by the identifier, an equals sign and then the initialization value. The identifier begins with a letter or an underscore, followed by letters, numbers and underscores. Upper and lower case are distinguished (so thisvalue and thisValue are different).

Here are some var definitions:

```
// VarAndVal/Vars.kt

fun main() {
  var whole = 11              // [1]
  var fractional = 1.4        // [2]
  var words = "Twas Brillig"  // [3]
  println(whole)
  println(fractional)
  println(words)
}
/* Output:
11
1.4
Twas Brillig
*/
```

In this book we mark lines with commented numbers in square brackets so we can refer to them in the text like this:

- **[1]** Create a var named `whole` and store 11 in it.
- **[2]** Store the "fractional number" 1.4 in the var `fractional`.
- **[3]** Store some text (a String) in the var `words`.

Note that `println()` can take any single value as an argument.

As the name *variable* implies, a var can vary. That is, you can change the data stored in a var. We say that a var is *mutable*:

```
// VarAndVal/AVarIsMutable.kt

fun main() {
  var sum = 1
  sum = sum + 2
  sum += 3
  println(sum)
}
/* Output:
6
*/
```

The assignment `sum = sum + 2` takes the current value of `sum`, adds two, and assigns the result back into `sum`.

The assignment `sum += 3` means the same as `sum = sum + 3`. The `+=` operator takes the previous value stored in `sum` and increases it by 3, then assigns that new result back to `sum`.

Changing the value stored in a var is a useful way to express changes. However, when the complexity of a program increases, your code is clearer, safer and easier to understand if the values represented by your identifiers cannot change—that is, they cannot be reassigned. We specify an unchanging identifier using the `val` keyword instead of var. A val can only be assigned once, when it is created:

```
val identifier = initialization
```

The val keyword comes from *value*, indicating something that cannot change—it is *immutable*. Choose val instead of var whenever possible. The Vars.kt example at the beginning of this atom can be rewritten using vals:

```
// VarAndVal/Vals.kt

fun main() {
  val whole = 11
  // whole = 15 // Error   // [1]
  val fractional = 1.4
  val words = "Twas Brillig"
  println(whole)
  println(fractional)
  println(words)
}
/* Output:
11
1.4
Twas Brillig
*/
```

- **[1]** Once you initialize a `val`, you can't reassign it. If we try to reassign `whole` to a different number, Kotlin complains, saying "Val cannot be reassigned."

Choosing descriptive names for your identifiers makes your code easier to understand and often reduces the need for comments. In `Vals.kt`, you have no idea what `whole` represents. If your program is storing the number 11 to represent the time of day when you get coffee, it's more obvious to others if you name it `coffeetime` and easier to read if it's `coffeeTime` (following Kotlin style, we make the first letter lowercase).

- -

`var`s are useful when data must change as the program is running. This sounds like a common requirement, but turns out to be avoidable in practice. In general, your programs are easier to extend and maintain if you use `val`s. However, on rare occasions it's too complex to solve a problem using only `val`s. For that reason, Kotlin gives you the flexibility of `var`s. However, as you spend more time with `val`s you'll discover that you almost never need `var`s and that your programs are safer and more reliable without them.

Exercises and solutions can be found at www.AtomicKotlin.com.

Data Types

Data can have different *types*.

To solve a math problem, you write an expression:

```
5.9 + 6
```

You know that adding those numbers produces another number. Kotlin knows that too. You know that one is a fractional number (5.9), which Kotlin calls a `Double`, and the other is a whole number (6), which Kotlin calls an `Int`. You know the result is a fractional number.

A *type* (also called *data type*) tells Kotlin how you intend to use that data. A type defines the set of values an expression of that type may produce. A type also defines the operations that can be performed on the data, the meaning of the data, and how values of that type can be stored.

Kotlin uses types to verify that your expressions are correct. In the above expression, Kotlin creates a new value of type `Double` to hold the result.

Kotlin tries to adapt to what you need. If you ask it to do something that violates type rules, it produces an error message. For example, try adding a `String` and a number:

```
// DataTypes/StringPlusNumber.kt

fun main() {
  println("Sally" + 5.9)
}
/* Output:
Sally5.9
*/
```

Types tell Kotlin how to use them correctly. In this case, the type rules tell Kotlin how to add a number to a `String`: by appending the two values and creating a `String` to hold the result.

Now try multiplying a `String` and a `Double` by changing the + in StringPlusNumber.kt to a *:

```
"Sally" * 5.9
```

Combining types this way doesn't make sense to Kotlin, so it gives you an error.

In *var & val*, we stored several types. Kotlin figured out the types for us, based on how we used them. This is called *type inference*.

We can be more verbose and specify the type:

```
val identifier: Type = initialization
```

You start with the val or var keyword, followed by the identifier, a colon, the type, an =, and the initialization value. So instead of saying:

```
val n = 1
var p = 1.2
```

You can say:

```
val n: Int = 1
var p: Double = 1.2
```

We've told Kotlin that n is an Int and p is a Double, rather than letting it infer the type.

Here are some of Kotlin's basic types:

```
// DataTypes/Types.kt

fun main() {
  val whole: Int = 11                  // [1]
  val fractional: Double = 1.4         // [2]
  val trueOrFalse: Boolean = true      // [3]
  val words: String = "A value"        // [4]
  val character: Char = 'z'            // [5]
  val lines: String = """Triple quotes let
you have many lines
in your string"""                      // [6]
  println(whole)
  println(fractional)
  println(trueOrFalse)
  println(words)
  println(character)
```

```
  println(lines)
}
/* Output:
11
1.4
true
A value
z
Triple quotes let
you have many lines
in your string
*/
```

- [1] The Int data type is an *integer*, which means it only holds whole numbers.
- [2] To hold fractional numbers, use a Double.
- [3] A Boolean data type only holds the two special values true and false.
- [4] A String holds a sequence of characters. You assign a value using a double-quoted String.
- [5] A Char holds one character.
- [6] If you have many lines and/or special characters, surround them with triple-double-quotes (this is a *triple-quoted String*).

Kotlin uses type inference to determine the meaning of mixed types. When mixing Ints and Doubles during addition, for example, Kotlin decides the type for the resulting value:

```
// DataTypes/Inference.kt

fun main() {
  val n = 1 + 1.2
  println(n)
}
/* Output:
2.2
*/
```

When you add an Int to a Double using type inference, Kotlin determines that the result n is a Double and ensures that it follows all the rules for Doubles.

Kotlin's type inference is part of its strategy of doing work for the programmer. If you leave out the type declaration, Kotlin can usually infer it.

Exercises and solutions can be found at www.AtomicKotlin.com.

Functions

> A *function* is like a small program that has its own name, and can be executed (*invoked*) by calling that name from another function.

A function combines a group of activities, and is the most basic way to organize your programs and to re-use code.

You pass information into a function, and the function uses that information to calculate and produce a result. The basic form of a function is:

```
fun functionName(p1: Type1, p2: Type2, ...): ReturnType {
  lines of code
  return result
}
```

`p1` and `p2` are the *parameters*: the information you pass into the function. Each parameter has an identifier name (`p1`, `p2`) followed by a colon and the type of that parameter. The closing parenthesis of the parameter list is followed by a colon and the type of result produced by the function. The lines of code in the *function body* are enclosed in curly braces. The expression following the `return` keyword is the result the function produces when it's finished.

A parameter is how you define what is passed into a function—it's the placeholder. An argument is the actual value that you pass into the function.

The combination of name, parameters and return type is called the *function signature*.

Here's a simple function called `multiplyByTwo()`:

```
// Functions/MultiplyByTwo.kt

fun multiplyByTwo(x: Int): Int {  // [1]
  println("Inside multiplyByTwo") // [2]
  return x * 2
}

fun main() {
  val r = multiplyByTwo(5)         // [3]
  println(r)
}
/* Output:
Inside multiplyByTwo
10
*/
```

- **[1]** Notice the fun keyword, the function name, and the parameter list consisting of a single parameter. This function takes an Int parameter and returns an Int.
- **[2]** These two lines are the body of the function. The final line returns the value of its calculation x * 2 as the result of the function.
- **[3]** This line *calls* the function with an appropriate argument, and captures the result into val r. A function call mimics the form of its declaration: the function name, followed by arguments inside parentheses.

The function code is executed by calling the function, using the function name multiplyByTwo() as an abbreviation for that code. This is why functions are the most basic form of simplification and code reuse in programming. You can also think of a function as an expression with substitutable values (the parameters).

println() is also a function call—it just happens to be provided by Kotlin. We refer to functions defined by Kotlin as *library functions*.

If the function doesn't provide a meaningful result, its return type is Unit. You can specify Unit explicitly if you want, but Kotlin lets you omit it:

```
// Functions/SayHello.kt

fun sayHello() {
  println("Hallo!")
}

fun sayGoodbye(): Unit {
  println("Auf Wiedersehen!")
}

fun main() {
  sayHello()
  sayGoodbye()
}
/* Output:
Hallo!
Auf Wiedersehen!
*/
```

Both sayHello() and sayGoodbye() return Unit, but sayHello() leaves out the explicit declaration. The main() function also returns Unit.

If a function is only a single expression, you can use the abbreviated syntax of an equals sign followed by the expression:

```
fun functionName(arg1: Type1, arg2: Type2, ...): ReturnType = expression
```

A function body surrounded by curly braces is called a *block body*. A function body using the equals syntax is called an *expression body*.

Here, multiplyByThree() uses an expression body:

```
// Functions/MultiplyByThree.kt

fun multiplyByThree(x: Int): Int = x * 3

fun main() {
  println(multiplyByThree(5))
}
/* Output:
15
*/
```

This is a short version of saying `return x * 3` inside a block body.

Kotlin infers the return type of a function that has an expression body:

```
// Functions/MultiplyByFour.kt

fun multiplyByFour(x: Int) = x * 4

fun main() {
  val result: Int = multiplyByFour(5)
  println(result)
}
/* Output:
20
*/
```

Kotlin infers that `multiplyByFour()` returns an `Int`.

Kotlin can *only* infer return types for expression bodies. If a function has a block body and you omit its type, that function returns `Unit`.

- -

When writing functions, choose descriptive names. This makes the code easier to read, and can often reduce the need for code comments. We can't always be as descriptive as we would prefer with the function names in this book because we're constrained by line widths.

Exercises and solutions can be found at www.AtomicKotlin.com.

`if` Expressions

> An *if expression* makes a choice.

The `if` keyword tests an expression to see whether it's `true` or `false` and performs an action based on the result. A true-or-false expression is called a *Boolean*, after the mathematician George Boole who invented the logic behind these expressions. Here's an example using the > (greater than) and < (less than) symbols:

```
// IfExpressions/If1.kt

fun main() {
  if (1 > 0)
    println("It's true!")
  if (10 < 11) {
    println("10 < 11")
    println("ten is less than eleven")
  }
}
/* Output:
It's true!
10 < 11
ten is less than eleven
*/
```

The expression inside the parentheses after the `if` must evaluate to `true` or `false`. If `true`, the following expression is executed. To execute multiple lines, place them within curly braces.

We can create a Boolean expression in one place, and use it in another:

```
// IfExpressions/If2.kt

fun main() {
  val x: Boolean = 1 >= 1
  if (x)
    println("It's true!")
}
/* Output:
It's true!
*/
```

Because `x` is `Boolean`, the `if` can test it directly by saying `if(x)`.

The Boolean `>=` operator returns `true` if the expression on the left side of the operator is *greater than or equal* to that on the right. Likewise, `<=` returns `true` if the expression on the left side is *less than or equal* to that on the right.

The `else` keyword allows you to handle both `true` and `false` paths:

```
// IfExpressions/If3.kt

fun main() {
  val n: Int = -11
  if (n > 0)
    println("It's positive")
  else
    println("It's negative or zero")
}
/* Output:
It's negative or zero
*/
```

The `else` keyword is only used in conjunction with `if`. You are not limited to a single check—you can test multiple combinations by combining `else` and `if`:

```
// IfExpressions/If4.kt

fun main() {
  val n: Int = -11
  if (n > 0)
    println("It's positive")
  else if (n == 0)
    println("It's zero")
  else
    println("It's negative")
}
/* Output:
It's negative
*/
```

Here we use == to check two numbers for equality. != tests for inequality.

The typical pattern is to start with if, followed by as many else if clauses as you need, ending with a final else for anything that doesn't match all the previous tests. When an if expression reaches a certain size and complexity you'll probably use a when expression instead. when is described later in the book, in *when Expressions*.

The "not" operator ! tests for the opposite of a Boolean expression:

```
// IfExpressions/If5.kt

fun main() {
  val y: Boolean = false
  if (!y)
    println("!y is true")
}
/* Output:
!y is true
*/
```

To verbalize if(!y), say "if not y."

The entire if is an expression, so it can produce a result:

```
// IfExpressions/If6.kt

fun main() {
  val num = 10
  val result = if (num > 100) 4 else 42
  println(result)
}
/* Output:
42
*/
```

Here, we store the value produced by the entire if expression in an intermediate identifier called result. If the condition is satisfied, the first branch produces result. If not, the else value becomes result.

Let's practice creating functions. Here's one that takes a Boolean parameter:

```
// IfExpressions/TrueOrFalse.kt

fun trueOrFalse(exp: Boolean): String {
  if (exp)
    return "It's true!"          // [1]
  return "It's false"            // [2]
}

fun main() {
  val b = 1
  println(trueOrFalse(b < 3))
  println(trueOrFalse(b >= 3))
}
/* Output:
It's true!
It's false
*/
```

The Boolean parameter exp is passed to the function trueOrFalse(). If the argument is passed as an expression, such as b < 3, that expression is first evaluated and the result is passed to the function. trueOrFalse() tests exp and if the result is true, line **[1]** is executed, otherwise line **[2]** is executed.

- **[1]** return says, "Leave the function and produce this value as the function's result." Notice that return can appear anywhere in a function and does not have to be at the end.

Rather than using return as in the previous example, you can use the else keyword to produce the result as an expression:

```
// IfExpressions/OneOrTheOther.kt

fun oneOrTheOther(exp: Boolean): String =
  if (exp)
    "True!" // No 'return' necessary
  else
    "False"

fun main() {
  val x = 1
  println(oneOrTheOther(x == 1))
  println(oneOrTheOther(x == 2))
}
/* Output:
True!
False
*/
```

Instead of two expressions in trueOrFalse(), oneOrTheOther() is a single expression. The result of that expression is the result of the function, so the if expression becomes the function body.

Exercises and solutions can be found at www.AtomicKotlin.com.

String Templates

A *String template* is a programmatic way to generate a `String`.

If you put a `$` before an identifier name, the `String` template will insert that identifier's contents into the `String`:

```
// StringTemplates/StringTemplates.kt

fun main() {
  val answer = 42
  println("Found $answer!")    // [1]
  println("printing a $1")     // [2]
}
/* Output:
Found 42!
printing a $1
*/
```

- **[1]** `$answer` substitutes the value of `answer`.
- **[2]** If what follows the `$` isn't recognizable as a program identifier, nothing special happens.

You can also insert values into a `String` using concatenation (+):

```
// StringTemplates/StringConcatenation.kt

fun main() {
  val s = "hi\n" // \n is a newline character
  val n = 11
  val d = 3.14
  println("first: " + s + "second: " +
    n + ", third: " + d)
}
/* Output:
first: hi
second: 11, third: 3.14
*/
```

Placing an expression inside ${} evaluates it. The return value is converted to a String and inserted into the resulting String:

```
// StringTemplates/ExpressionInTemplate.kt

fun main() {
  val condition = true
  println(
    "${if (condition) 'a' else 'b'}")  // [1]
  val x = 11
  println("$x + 4 = ${x + 4}")
}
/* Output:
a
11 + 4 = 15
*/
```

- **[1]** if(condition) 'a' else 'b' is evaluated and the result is substituted for the entire ${} expression.

When a String must include a special character, such as a quote, you can either escape that character with a \ (*backslash*), or use a String literal in triple quotes:

```
// StringTemplates/TripleQuotes.kt

fun main() {
  val s = "value"
  println("s = \"$s\".")
  println("""s = "$s".""")
}
/* Output:
s = "value".
s = "value".
*/
```

With triple quotes, you insert a value of an expression the same way you do it for a single-quoted String.

Exercises and solutions can be found at www.AtomicKotlin.com.

Number Types

Different types of numbers are stored in different ways.

If you create an identifier and assign an integer value to it, Kotlin infers the `Int` type:

```
// NumberTypes/InferInt.kt

fun main() {
  val million = 1_000_000   // Infers Int
  println(million)
}
/* Output:
1000000
*/
```

For readability, Kotlin allows underscores within numerical values.

The basic mathematical operators for numbers are the ones available in most programming languages: addition (+), subtraction (-), division (/), multiplication (*) and modulus (%), which produces the remainder from integer division:

```
// NumberTypes/Modulus.kt

fun main() {
  val numerator: Int = 19
  val denominator: Int = 10
  println(numerator % denominator)
}
/* Output:
9
*/
```

Integer division truncates its result:

```
// NumberTypes/IntDivisionTruncates.kt

fun main() {
  val numerator: Int = 19
  val denominator: Int = 10
  println(numerator / denominator)
}
/* Output:
1
*/
```

If the operation had rounded the result, the output would be 2.

The order of operations follows basic arithmetic:

```
// NumberTypes/OpOrder.kt

fun main() {
  println(45 + 5 * 6)
}
/* Output:
75
*/
```

The multiplication operation 5 * 6 is performed first, followed by the addition 45 + 30.

If you want 45 + 5 to happen first, use parentheses:

```
// NumberTypes/OpOrderParens.kt

fun main() {
  println((45 + 5) * 6)
}
/* Output:
300
*/
```

Now let's calculate *body mass index* (BMI), which is weight in kilograms divided by the square of the height in meters. If you have a BMI of less than 18.5, you are underweight. Between 18.5 and 24.9 is normal weight. BMI of 25 and higher is overweight. This example also shows the preferred formatting style when you can't fit the function's parameters on a single line:

```
// NumberTypes/BMIMetric.kt

fun bmiMetric(
  weight: Double,
  height: Double
): String {
  val bmi = weight / (height * height)  // [1]
  return if (bmi < 18.5) "Underweight"
    else if (bmi < 25) "Normal weight"
    else "Overweight"
}

fun main() {
  val weight = 72.57 // 160 lbs
  val height = 1.727 // 68 inches
  val status = bmiMetric(weight, height)
  println(status)
}
/* Output:
Normal weight
*/
```

- **[1]** If you remove the parentheses, you divide `weight` by `height` then multiply that result by `height`. That's a much larger number, and the wrong answer.

`bmiMetric()` uses `Double`s for the weight and height. A `Double` holds very large and very small floating-point numbers.

Here's a version using English units, represented by `Int` parameters:

```
// NumberTypes/BMIEnglish.kt

fun bmiEnglish(
  weight: Int,
  height: Int
): String {
  val bmi =
    weight / (height * height) * 703.07 // [1]
  return if (bmi < 18.5) "Underweight"
    else if (bmi < 25) "Normal weight"
    else "Overweight"
}
```

```
fun main() {
  val weight = 160
  val height = 68
  val status = bmiEnglish(weight, height)
  println(status)
}
/* Output:
Underweight
*/
```

Why does the result differ from bmiMetric(), which uses Doubles? When you divide an integer by another integer, Kotlin produces an integer result. The standard way to deal with the remainder during integer division is *truncation*, meaning "chop it off and throw it away" (there's no rounding). So if you divide 5 by 2 you get 2, and 7/10 is zero. When Kotlin calculates bmi in expression [1], it divides 160 by 68 * 68 and gets zero. It then multiplies zero by 703.07 to get zero.

To avoid this problem, move 703.07 to the front of the calculation. The calculations are then forced to be Double:

```
val bmi = 703.07 * weight / (height * height)
```

The Double parameters in bmiMetric() prevent this problem. Convert computations to the desired type as early as possible to preserve accuracy.

All programming languages have limits to what they can store within an integer. Kotlin's Int type can take values between -2^{31} and $+2^{31}-1$, a constraint of the Int 32-bit representation. If you sum or multiply two Ints that are big enough, you'll overflow the result:

```
// NumberTypes/IntegerOverflow.kt

fun main() {
  val i: Int = Int.MAX_VALUE
  println(i + i)
}
/* Output:
-2
*/
```

`Int.MAX_VALUE` is a predefined value which is the largest number an `Int` can hold.

The overflow produces a result that is clearly incorrect, as it is both negative and much smaller than we expect. Kotlin issues a warning whenever it detects a potential overflow.

Preventing overflow is your responsibility as a developer. Kotlin can't always detect overflow during compilation, and it doesn't prevent overflow because that would produce an unacceptable performance impact.

If your program contains large numbers, you can use `Long`s, which accommodate values from -2^{63} to $+2^{63}-1$. To define a `val` of type `Long`, you can specify the type explicitly or put `L` at the end of a numeric literal, which tells Kotlin to treat that value as a `Long`:

```
// NumberTypes/LongConstants.kt

fun main() {
  val i = 0            // Infers Int
  val l1 = 0L          // L creates Long
  val l2: Long = 0     // Explicit type
  println("$l1 $l2")
}
/* Output:
0 0
*/
```

By changing to `Long`s we prevent the overflow in `IntegerOverflow.kt`:

```
// NumberTypes/UsingLongs.kt

fun main() {
  val i = Int.MAX_VALUE
  println(0L + i + i)               // [1]
  println(1_000_000 * 1_000_000L)   // [2]
}
/* Output:
4294967294
1000000000000
*/
```

Using a numeric literal in both **[1]** and **[2]** forces Long calculations, and also produces a result of type Long. The location where the L appears is unimportant. If one of the values is Long, the resulting expression is Long.

Although they can hold much larger values than Ints, Longs still have size limitations:

```
// NumberTypes/BiggestLong.kt

fun main() {
  println(Long.MAX_VALUE)
}
/* Output:
9223372036854775807
*/
```

Long.MAX_VALUE is the largest value a Long can hold.

Exercises and solutions can be found at www.AtomicKotlin.com.

Booleans

if Expressions demonstrated the "not" operator !, which negates a Boolean value. This atom introduces more *Boolean Algebra*.

We start with the operators "and" and "or":

- && (and): Produces true only if the Boolean expression on the left of the operator and the one on the right are both true.
- || (or): Produces true if either the expression on the left or right of the operator is true, or if both are true.

In this example, we determine whether a business is open or closed, based on the hour:

```
// Booleans/Open1.kt

fun isOpen1(hour: Int) {
  val open = 9
  val closed = 20
  println("Operating hours: $open - $closed")
  val status =
    if (hour >= open && hour < closed) // [1]
      true
    else
      false
  println("Open: $status")
}

fun main() = isOpen1(6)
/* Output:
Operating hours: 9 - 20
Open: false
*/
```

main() is a single function call, so we can use an expression body as described in *Functions*.

The if expression in [1] Checks whether hour is between the opening time and closing time, so we combine the expressions with the Boolean && (and).

The if expression can be simplified. The result of the expression if(cond) true else false is just cond:

```
// Booleans/Open2.kt

fun isOpen2(hour: Int) {
  val open = 9
  val closed = 20
  println("Operating hours: $open - $closed")
  val status = hour >= open && hour < closed
  println("Open: $status")
}

fun main() = isOpen2(6)
/* Output:
Operating hours: 9 - 20
Open: false
*/
```

Let's reverse the logic and check whether the business is currently closed. The "or" operator || produces true if at least one of the conditions is satisfied:

```
// Booleans/Closed.kt

fun isClosed(hour: Int) {
  val open = 9
  val closed = 20
  println("Operating hours: $open - $closed")
  val status = hour < open || hour >= closed
  println("Closed: $status")
}

fun main() = isClosed(6)
/* Output:
Operating hours: 9 - 20
Closed: true
*/
```

Boolean operators enable complicated logic in compact expressions. However, things can easily become confusing. Strive for readability and specify your intentions explicitly.

Here's an example of a complicated `Boolean` expression where different evaluation order produces different results:

```
// Booleans/EvaluationOrder.kt

fun main() {
  val sunny = true
  val hoursSleep = 6
  val exercise = false
  val temp = 55

  // [1]:
  val happy1 = sunny && temp > 50 ||
    exercise && hoursSleep > 7
  println(happy1)

  // [2]:
  val sameHappy1 = (sunny && temp > 50) ||
    (exercise && hoursSleep > 7)
  println(sameHappy1)

  // [3]:
  val notSame =
    (sunny && temp > 50 || exercise) &&
      hoursSleep > 7
  println(notSame)
}
/* Output:
true
true
false
*/
```

The `Boolean` expressions are `sunny`, `temp > 50`, `exercise`, and `hoursSleep > 7`. We read `happy1` as "It's sunny *and* the temperature is greater than 50 *or* I've exercised *and* had more than 7 hours of sleep." But does `&&` have precedence over `||`, or the opposite?

The expression in **[1]** uses Kotlin's default evaluation order. This produces the same result as the expression in **[2]** because, without parentheses, the "ands" are evaluated first, then the "or". The expression in **[3]** uses parentheses to produce a different result. In **[3]**, we're only happy if we get at least 7 hours of sleep.

Exercises and solutions can be found at www.AtomicKotlin.com.

Repetition with `while`

Computers are ideal for repetitive tasks.

The most basic form of repetition uses the `while` keyword. This repeats a block as long as the controlling *Boolean expression* is `true`:

```
while (Boolean-expression) {
  // Code to be repeated
}
```

The Boolean expression is evaluated once at the beginning of the loop and again before each further iteration through the block.

```
// RepetitionWithWhile/WhileLoop.kt

fun condition(i: Int) = i < 100   // [1]

fun main() {
  var i = 0
  while (condition(i)) {          // [2]
    print(".")
    i += 10                       // [3]
  }
}
/* Output:
..........
*/
```

- [1] The comparison operator `<` produces a `Boolean` result, so Kotlin infers `Boolean` as the result type for `condition()`.
- [2] The conditional expression for the `while` says: "repeat the statements in the body as long as `condition()` returns `true`."
- [3] The `+=` operator adds `10` to `i` and assigns the result to `i` in a single operation (`i` must be a `var` for this to work). This is equivalent to:

```
i = i + 10
```

There's a second way to use `while`, in conjunction with the `do` keyword:

```
do {
  // Code to be repeated
} while (Boolean-expression)
```

Rewriting `WhileLoop.kt` to use a do-while produces:

```
// RepetitionWithWhile/DoWhileLoop.kt

fun main() {
  var i = 0
  do {
    print(".")
    i += 10
  } while (condition(i))
}
/* Output:
. . . . . . . . . .
*/
```

The sole difference between `while` and `do-while` is that the body of the `do-while` always executes at least once, even if the Boolean expression initially produces `false`. In a `while`, if the conditional is `false` the first time, then the body never executes. In practice, `do-while` is less common than `while`.

The short versions of assignment operators are available for all the arithmetic operations: +=, -=, *=, /=, and %=. This uses -= and %=:

```
// RepetitionWithWhile/AssignmentOperators.kt

fun main() {
  var n = 10
  val d = 3
  print(n)
  while (n > d) {
    n -= d
    print(" - $d")
  }
  println(" = $n")

  var m = 10
  print(m)
  m %= d
  println(" % $d = $m")
}
/* Output:
10 - 3 - 3 - 3 = 1
10 % 3 = 1
*/
```

To calculate the remainder of the integer division of two natural numbers, we start with a `while` loop, then use the remainder operator.

Adding 1 and subtracting 1 from a number are so common that they have their own increment and decrement operators: `++` and `--`. You can replace `i += 1` with `i++`:

```
// RepetitionWithWhile/IncrementOperator.kt

fun main() {
  var i = 0
  while (i < 4) {
    print(".")
    i++
  }
}
/* Output:
....
*/
```

In practice, `while` loops are not used for iterating over a range of numbers. The `for` loop is used instead. This is covered in the next atom.

Exercises and solutions can be found at www.AtomicKotlin.com.

Looping & Ranges

The `for` keyword executes a block of code for each value in a sequence.

The set of values can be a range of integers, a `String`, or, as you'll see later in the book, a collection of items. The `in` keyword indicates that you are stepping through values:

```
for (v in values) {
  // Do something with v
}
```

Each time through the loop, `v` is given the next element in `values`.

Here's a `for` loop repeating an action a fixed number of times:

```
// LoopingAndRanges/RepeatThreeTimes.kt

fun main() {
  for (i in 1..3) {
    println("Hey $i!")
  }
}
/* Output:
Hey 1!
Hey 2!
Hey 3!
*/
```

The output shows the index `i` receiving each value in the range from 1 to 3.

A *range* is an interval of values defined by a pair of endpoints. There are two basic ways to define ranges:

```
// LoopingAndRanges/DefiningRanges.kt

fun main() {
  val range1 = 1..10         // [1]
  val range2 = 0 until 10    // [2]
  println(range1)
  println(range2)
}
/* Output:
1..10
0..9
*/
```

- **[1]** Using `..` syntax includes both bounds in the resulting range.
- **[2]** `until` excludes the end. The output shows that 10 is not part of the range.

Displaying a range produces a readable format.

This sums the numbers from 10 to 100:

```
// LoopingAndRanges/SumUsingRange.kt

fun main() {
  var sum = 0
  for (n in 10..100) {
    sum += n
  }
  println("sum = $sum")
}
/* Output:
sum = 5005
*/
```

You can iterate over a range in reverse order. You can also use a `step` value to change the interval from the default of 1:

```
// LoopingAndRanges/ForWithRanges.kt

fun showRange(r: IntProgression) {
  for (i in r) {
    print("$i ")
  }
  print("    // $r")
  println()
}

fun main() {
  showRange(1..5)
  showRange(0 until 5)
  showRange(5 downTo 1)            // [1]
  showRange(0..9 step 2)           // [2]
  showRange(0 until 10 step 3)     // [3]
  showRange(9 downTo 2 step 3)
}
/* Output:
1 2 3 4 5     // 1..5
0 1 2 3 4     // 0..4
5 4 3 2 1     // 5 downTo 1 step 1
0 2 4 6 8     // 0..8 step 2
0 3 6 9       // 0..9 step 3
9 6 3         // 9 downTo 3 step 3
*/
```

- [1] downTo produces a decreasing range.
- [2] step changes the interval. Here, the range steps by a value of two instead of one.
- [3] until can also be used with step. Notice how this affects the output.

In each case the sequence of numbers form an arithmetic progression. showRange() accepts an IntProgression parameter, which is a built-in type that includes Int ranges. Notice that the String representation of each IntProgression as it appears in output comment for each line is often different from the range passed into showRange()—the IntProgression is translating the input into an equivalent common form.

You can also produce a range of characters. This for iterates from a to z:

```
// LoopingAndRanges/ForWithCharRange.kt

fun main() {
  for (c in 'a'..'z') {
    print(c)
  }
}
/* Output:
abcdefghijklmnopqrstuvwxyz
*/
```

You can iterate over a range of elements that are whole quantities, like integers and characters, but not floating-point values.

Square brackets access characters by index. Because we start counting characters in a String at zero, s[0] selects the first character of the String s. Selecting s.lastIndex produces the final index number:

```
// LoopingAndRanges/IndexIntoString.kt

fun main() {
  val s = "abc"
  for (i in 0..s.lastIndex) {
    print(s[i] + 1)
  }
}
/* Output:
bcd
*/
```

Sometimes people describe s[0] as "the zeroth character."

Characters are stored as numbers corresponding to their Unicode[17] values, so adding an integer to a character produces a new character corresponding to the new code value:

---

[17] https://en.wikipedia.org/wiki/Unicode

```
// LoopingAndRanges/AddingIntToChar.kt

fun main() {
  val ch: Char = 'a'
  println(ch + 25)
  println(ch < 'z')
}
/* Output:
z
true
*/
```

The second `println()` shows that you can compare character codes.

A `for` loop can iterate over `String`s directly:

```
// LoopingAndRanges/IterateOverString.kt

fun main() {
  for (ch in "Jnskhm ") {
    print(ch + 1)
  }
}
/* Output:
Kotlin!
*/
```

`ch` receives each character in turn.

In the following example, the function `hasChar()` iterates over the `String` `s` and tests whether it contains a given character `ch`. The `return` in the middle of the function stops the function when the answer is found:

```
// LoopingAndRanges/HasChar.kt

fun hasChar(s: String, ch: Char): Boolean {
  for (c in s) {
    if (c == ch) return true
  }
  return false
}

fun main() {
  println(hasChar("kotlin", 't'))
  println(hasChar("kotlin", 'a'))
}
/* Output:
true
false
*/
```

The next atom shows that hasChar() is unnecessary—you can use built-in syntax instead.

If you simply want to repeat an action a fixed number of times, you may use repeat() instead of a for loop:

```
// LoopingAndRanges/RepeatHi.kt

fun main() {
  repeat(2) {
    println("hi!")
  }
}
/* Output:
hi!
hi!
*/
```

repeat() is a standard library function, not a keyword. You'll see how it was created much later in the book.

Exercises and solutions can be found at www.AtomicKotlin.com.

The `in` Keyword

The `in` keyword tests whether a value is within a range.

```
// InKeyword/MembershipInRange.kt

fun main() {
  val percent = 35
  println(percent in 1..100)
}
/* Output:
true
*/
```

In **Booleans**, you learned to check bounds explicitly:

```
// InKeyword/MembershipUsingBounds.kt

fun main() {
  val percent = 35
  println(0 <= percent && percent <= 100)
}
/* Output:
true
*/
```

`0 <= x && x <= 100` is logically equivalent to `x in 0..100`. IntelliJ IDEA suggests automatically replacing the first form with the second, which is easier to read and understand.

The `in` keyword is used for both iteration and membership. An `in` inside the control expression of a `for` loop means iteration, otherwise `in` checks membership:

```
// InKeyword/IterationVsMembership.kt

fun main() {
  val values = 1..3
  for (v in values) {
    println("iteration $v")
  }
  val v = 2
  if (v in values)
    println("$v is a member of $values")
}
/* Output:
iteration 1
iteration 2
iteration 3
2 is a member of 1..3
*/
```

The in keyword is not limited to ranges. You can also check whether a character is a part of a String. The following example uses in instead of hasChar() from the previous atom:

```
// InKeyword/InString.kt

fun main() {
  println('t' in "kotlin")
  println('a' in "kotlin")
}
/* Output:
true
false
*/
```

Later in the book you'll see that in works with other types, as well.

Here, in tests whether a character belongs to a range of characters:

```
// InKeyword/CharRange.kt

fun isDigit(ch: Char) = ch in '0'..'9'

fun notDigit(ch: Char) =
  ch !in '0'..'9'                  // [1]

fun main() {
  println(isDigit('a'))
  println(isDigit('5'))
  println(notDigit('z'))
}
/* Output:
false
true
true
*/
```

- **[1]** !in checks that a value doesn't belong to a range.

You can create a Double range, but you can only use it to check for membership:

```
// InKeyword/FloatingPointRange.kt

fun inFloatRange(n: Double) {
  val r = 1.0..10.0
  println("$n in $r? ${n in r}")
}

fun main() {
  inFloatRange(0.999999)
  inFloatRange(5.0)
  inFloatRange(10.0)
  inFloatRange(10.0000001)
}
/* Output:
0.999999 in 1.0..10.0? false
5.0 in 1.0..10.0? true
10.0 in 1.0..10.0? true
10.0000001 in 1.0..10.0? false
*/
```

You can only use .. to define a floating-point range in Kotlin.

You can check whether a String is a member of a range of Strings:

```
// InKeyword/StringRange.kt

fun main() {
  println("ab" in "aa".."az")
  println("ba" in "aa".."az")
}
/* Output:
true
false
*/
```

Here Kotlin uses alphabetic comparison.

Exercises and solutions can be found at www.AtomicKotlin.com.

Expressions & Statements

Statements and *expressions* are the smallest useful fragments of code in most programming languages.

There's a basic difference: a statement has an effect, but produces no result. An expression always produces a result.

Because it doesn't produce a result, a statement must change the state of its surroundings to be useful. Another way to say this is "a statement is called for its *side effects*" (that is, what it does *other* than producing a result). As a memory aid:

> *A statement changes state.*

One definition of "express" is "to force or squeeze out," as in "to express the juice from an orange." So

> *An expression expresses.*

That is, it produces a result.

The for loop is a statement in Kotlin. You cannot assign it because there's no result:

```
// ExpressionsStatements/ForIsAStatement.kt

fun main() {
  // Can't do this:
  // val f = for(i in 1..10) {}
  // Compiler error message:
  // for is not an expression, and
  // only expressions are allowed here
}
```

A for loop is used for its side effects.

An expression produces a value, which can be assigned or used as part of another expression, whereas a statement is always a top-level element.

Every function call is an expression. Even if the function returns Unit and is called only for its side effects, the result can still be assigned:

```
// ExpressionsStatements/UnitReturnType.kt

fun unitFun() = Unit

fun main() {
  println(unitFun())
  val u1: Unit = println(42)
  println(u1)
  val u2 = println(0) // Type inference
  println(u2)
}
/* Output:
kotlin.Unit
42
kotlin.Unit
0
kotlin.Unit
*/
```

The Unit type contains a single value called Unit, which you can return directly, as seen in unitFun(). Calling println() also returns Unit. The val u1 captures the return value of println() and is explicitly declared as Unit while u2 uses type inference.

if creates an expression, so you can assign its result:

```
// ExpressionsStatements/AssigningAnIf.kt

fun main() {
  val result1 = if (11 > 42) 9 else 5

  val result2 = if (1 < 2) {
    val a = 11
    a + 42
  } else 42

  val result3 =
    if ('x' < 'y')
      println("x < y")
    else
      println("x > y")

  println(result1)
  println(result2)
  println(result3)
}
/* Output:
x < y
5
53
kotlin.Unit
*/
```

The first output line is x < y, even though result3 isn't displayed until the end of main(). This happens because evaluating result3 calls println(), and the evaluation occurs when result3 is defined.

Notice that a is defined inside the block of code for result2. The result of the last expression becomes the result of the if expression; here, it's the sum of 11 and 42. But what about a? Once you leave the code block (move outside the curly braces), you can't access a. It is *temporary* and is discarded once you exit the *scope* of that block.

The increment operator i++ is also an expression, even if it looks like a statement. Kotlin follows the approach used by C-like languages and provides two versions of increment and decrement operators with slightly different semantics. The prefix operator appears before the operand, as in ++i, and returns the value after the increment happens. You can read it as "first do the increment, then return the resulting value." The postfix operator is placed after the operand, as in i++, and returns the value of i before the increment occurs. You can read it as "first produce the result, then do the increment."

```
// ExpressionsStatements/PostfixVsPrefix.kt

fun main() {
  var i = 10
  println(i++)
  println(i)
  var j = 20
  println(++j)
  println(j)
}
/* Output:
10
11
21
21
*/
```

The decrement operator also has two versions: --i and i--. Using increment and decrement operators within other expressions is discouraged because it can produce confusing code:

```
// ExpressionsStatements/Confusing.kt

fun main() {
  var i = 1
  println(i++ + ++i)
}
```

Try to guess what the output will be, then check it.

Exercises and solutions can be found at www.AtomicKotlin.com.

Summary 1

This atom summarizes and reviews the atoms in Section I, starting at *Hello, World!* and ending with *Expressions & Statements*.

If you're an experienced programmer, this should be your first atom. New programmers should read this atom and perform the exercises as a review of Section I.

If anything isn't clear to you, study the associated atom for that topic (the subheadings correspond to atom titles).

Hello, World

Kotlin supports both // single-line comments, and /*-to-*/ multiline comments. A program's entry point is the function `main()`:

```
// Summary1/Hello.kt

fun main() {
  println("Hello, world!")
}
/* Output:
Hello, world!
*/
```

The first line of each example in this book is a comment containing the name of the atom's subdirectory, followed by a / and the name of the file. You can find all the extracted code examples through AtomicKotlin.com[18].

`println()` is a standard library function which takes a single `String` parameter (or a parameter that can be converted to a `String`). `println()` moves the cursor to a new line after displaying its parameter, while `print()` leaves the cursor on the same line.

---
[18] http://AtomicKotlin.com

Kotlin does not require a semicolon at the end of an expression or statement. Semicolons are only necessary to separate multiple expressions or statements on a single line.

`var` & `val`, Data Types

To create an unchanging identifier, use the `val` keyword followed by the identifier name, a colon, and the type for that value. Then add an equals sign and the value to assign to that `val`:

```
val identifier: Type = initialization
```

Once a `val` is assigned, it cannot be reassigned.

Kotlin's *type inference* can usually determine the type automatically, based on the initialization value. This produces a simpler definition:

```
val identifier = initialization
```

Both of the following are valid:

```
val daysInFebruary = 28
val daysInMarch: Int = 31
```

A var (variable) definition looks the same, using `var` instead of `val`:

```
var identifier1 = initialization
var identifier2: Type = initialization
```

Unlike a `val`, you can modify a `var`, so the following is legal:

```
var hoursSpent = 20
hoursSpent = 25
```

However, the *type* can't be changed, so you get an error if you say:

```
hoursSpent = 30.5
```

Kotlin infers the `Int` type when `hoursSpent` is defined, so it won't accept the change to a floating-point value.

Functions

Functions are *named subroutines*:

```
fun functionName(arg1: Type1, arg2: Type2, ...): ReturnType {
  // Lines of code ...
  return result
}
```

The `fun` keyword is followed by the function name and the parameter list in parentheses. Each parameter must have an explicit type because Kotlin cannot infer parameter types. The function itself has a type, defined in the same way as for a `var` or `val` (a colon followed by the type). A function's type is the type of the returned result.

The function signature is followed by the function body contained within curly braces. The `return` statement provides the function's return value.

You can use an abbreviated syntax when the function consists of a single expression:

```
fun functionName(arg1: Type1, arg2: Type2, ...): ReturnType = result
```

This form is called an *expression body*. Instead of an opening curly brace, use an equals sign followed by the expression. You can omit the return type because Kotlin infers it.

Here's a function that produces the cube of its parameter, and another that adds an exclamation point to a `String`:

```
// Summary1/BasicFunctions.kt

fun cube(x: Int): Int {
  return x * x * x
}

fun bang(s: String) = s + "!"

fun main() {
  println(cube(3))
  println(bang("pop"))
}
/* Output:
27
pop!
*/
```

cube() has a block body with an explicit return statement. bang() is an expression body producing the function's return value. Kotlin infers bang()'s return type to be String.

Booleans

For Boolean algebra, Kotlin provides operators such as:
- ! (not) logically negates the value (turns true to false and vice-versa).
- && (and) returns true only if *both* conditions are true.
- || (or) returns true if at least one of the conditions is true.

```
// Summary1/Booleans.kt

fun main() {
  val opens = 9
  val closes = 20
  println("Operating hours: $opens - $closes")
  val hour = 6
  println("Current time: " + hour)

  val isOpen = hour >= opens && hour < closes
  println("Open: " + isOpen)
  println("Not open: " + !isOpen)

  val isClosed = hour < opens || hour >= closes
  println("Closed: " + isClosed)
}
/* Output:
Operating hours: 9 - 20
Current time: 6
Open: false
Not open: true
Closed: true
*/
```

isOpen's initializer uses && to test whether both conditions are true. The first condition hour >= opens is false, so the result of the entire expression becomes false. The initializer for isClosed uses ||, producing true if at least one of the conditions is true. The expression hour < opens is true, so the whole expression is true.

`if` Expressions

Because `if` is an expression, it produces a result. This result can be assigned to a `var` or `val`. Here, you also see the use of the `else` keyword:

```
// Summary1/IfResult.kt

fun main() {
  val result = if (99 < 100) 4 else 42
  println(result)
}
/* Output:
4
*/
```

Either branch of an `if` expression can be a multiline block of code surrounded by curly braces:

```
// Summary1/IfExpression.kt

fun main() {
  val activity = "swimming"
  val hour = 10

  val isOpen = if (
    activity == "swimming" ||
    activity == "ice skating") {
    val opens = 9
    val closes = 20
    println("Operating hours: " +
      opens + " - " + closes)
    hour >= opens && hour < closes
  } else {
    false
  }
  println(isOpen)
}
/* Output:
Operating hours: 9 - 20
true
*/
```

A value defined inside a block of code, such as `opens`, is not accessible outside the scope of that block. Because they are defined *globally* to the `if` expression, `activity` and `hour` are accessible inside the `if` expression.

The result of an `if` expression is the result of the last expression of the chosen branch. Here, it's `hour >= opens && hour <= closes` which is `true`.

String Templates

You can insert a value within a `String` using `String` templates. Use a `$` before the identifier name:

```
// Summary1/StrTemplates.kt

fun main() {
  val answer = 42
  println("Found $answer!")             // [1]
  val condition = true
  println(
    "${if (condition) 'a' else 'b'}")   // [2]
  println("printing a $1")              // [3]
}
/* Output:
Found 42!
a
printing a $1
*/
```

- **[1]** `$answer` substitutes the value contained in `answer`.
- **[2]** `${if(condition) 'a' else 'b'}` evaluates and substitutes the result of the expression inside `${}`.
- **[3]** If the `$` is followed by anything unrecognizable as a program identifier, nothing special happens.

Use triple-quoted `Strings` to store multiline text or text with special characters:

```
// Summary1/ThreeQuotes.kt

fun json(q: String, a: Int) = """{
  "question" : "$q",
  "answer" : $a
}"""

fun main() {
  println(json("The Ultimate", 42))
}
/* Output:
{
  "question" : "The Ultimate",
  "answer" : 42
}
*/
```

You don't need to escape special characters like " within a triple-quoted String. (In a regular String you write \" to insert a double quote). As with normal Strings, you can insert an identifier or an expression using $ inside a triple-quoted String.

Number Types

Kotlin provides integer types (Int, Long) and floating point types (Double). A whole number constant is Int by default and Long if you append an L. A constant is Double if it contains a decimal point:

```
// Summary1/NumberTypes.kt

fun main() {
  val n = 1000      // Int
  val l = 1000L     // Long
  val d = 1000.0    // Double
  println("$n $l $d")
}
/* Output:
1000 1000 1000.0
*/
```

An Int holds values between -2^{31} and $+2^{31}-1$. Integral values can overflow; for example, adding anything to Int.MAX_VALUE produces an overflow:

```
// Summary1/Overflow.kt

fun main() {
  println(Int.MAX_VALUE + 1)
  println(Int.MAX_VALUE + 1L)
}
/* Output:
-2147483648
2147483648
*/
```

In the second `println()` statement we append `L` to `1`, forcing the whole expression to be of type `Long`, which avoids the overflow. (A `Long` can hold values between -2^{63} and $+2^{63}-1$).

When you divide an `Int` with another `Int`, Kotlin produces an `Int` result, and any remainder is truncated. So `1/2` produces `0`. If a `Double` is involved, the `Int` is *promoted* to `Double` before the operation, so `1.0/2` produces `0.5`.

You might expect d1 in the following to produce `3.4`:

```
// Summary1/Truncation.kt

fun main() {
  val d1: Double = 3.0 + 2 / 5
  println(d1)
  val d2: Double = 3 + 2.0 / 5
  println(d2)
}
/* Output:
3.0
3.4
*/
```

Because of evaluation order, it doesn't. Kotlin first divides `2` by `5`, and integer math produces `0`, yielding an answer of `3.0`. The same evaluation order *does* produce the expected result for d2. Dividing `2.0` by `5` produces `0.4`. The `3` is promoted to a `Double` because we add it to a `Double` (`0.4`), which produces `3.4`.

Understanding evaluation order helps you to decipher what a program does, both with logical operations (Boolean expressions) and with mathematical operations. If you're unsure about evaluation order, use parentheses to force your intention. This also makes it clear to those reading your code.

Repetition with `while`

A `while` loop continues as long as the controlling *Boolean-expression* produces `true`:

```
while (Boolean-expression) {
  // Code to be repeated
}
```

The *Boolean expression* is evaluated once at the beginning of the loop and again before each further iteration.

```
// Summary1/While.kt

fun testCondition(i: Int) = i < 100

fun main() {
  var i = 0
  while (testCondition(i)) {
    print(".")
    i += 10
  }
}
/* Output:
..........
*/
```

Kotlin infers `Boolean` as the result type for `testCondition()`.

The short versions of assignment operators are available for all mathematical operations (+=, -=, *=, /=, %=). Kotlin also supports the increment and decrement operators ++ and --, in both prefix and postfix form.

`while` can be used with the `do` keyword:

```
do {
  // Code to be repeated
} while (Boolean-expression)
```

Rewriting `While.kt`:

```
// Summary1/DoWhile.kt

fun main() {
  var i = 0
  do {
    print(".")
    i += 10
  } while (testCondition(i))
}
/* Output:
..........
*/
```

The sole difference between `while` and `do-while` is that the body of the `do-while` always executes at least once, even if the Boolean expression produces `false` the first time.

Looping & Ranges

Many programming languages index into an iterable object by stepping through integers. Kotlin's `for` allows you to take elements directly from iterable objects like ranges and `String`s. For example, this `for` selects each character in the `String` `"Kotlin"`:

```
// Summary1/StringIteration.kt

fun main() {
  for (c in "Kotlin") {
    print("$c ")
    // c += 1 // error:
    // val cannot be reassigned
  }
}
/* Output:
K o t l i n
*/
```

`c` can't be explicitly defined as either a `var` or `val`—Kotlin automatically makes it a `val` and infers its type as `Char` (you can provide the type explicitly, but in practice this is rarely done).

You can step through integral values using *ranges*:

```
// Summary1/RangeOfInt.kt

fun main() {
  for (i in 1..10) {
    print("$i ")
  }
}
/* Output:
1 2 3 4 5 6 7 8 9 10
*/
```

Creating a range with `..` includes both bounds, but `until` excludes the top endpoint: `1 until 10` is the same as `1..9`. You can specify an increment value using `step`: `1..21 step 3`.

The `in` Keyword

The same `in` that provides `for` loop iteration also allows you to check membership in a range. `!in` returns `true` if the tested value *isn't* in the range:

```
// Summary1/Membership.kt

fun inNumRange(n: Int) = n in 50..100

fun notLowerCase(ch: Char) = ch !in 'a'..'z'

fun main() {
  val i1 = 11
  val i2 = 100
  val c1 = 'K'
  val c2 = 'k'
  println("$i1 ${inNumRange(i1)}")
  println("$i2 ${inNumRange(i2)}")
  println("$c1 ${notLowerCase(c1)}")
  println("$c2 ${notLowerCase(c2)}")
}
/* Output:
11 false
```

```
100 true
K true
k false
*/
```

`in` can also be used to test membership in floating-point ranges, although such ranges can only be defined using `..` and not `until`.

Expressions & Statements

The smallest useful fragment of code in most programming languages is either a *statement* or an *expression*. These have one basic difference:

- *A statement changes state.*
- *An expression expresses.*

That is, an expression produces a result, while a statement does not. Because it doesn't return anything, a statement must change the state of its surroundings (that is, create a *side effect*) to do anything useful.

Almost everything in Kotlin is an expression:

```
val hours = 10
val minutesPerHour = 60
val minutes = hours * minutesPerHour
```

In each case, everything to the right of the = is an expression, which produces a result that is assigned to the identifier on the left.

Functions like `println()` don't seem to produce a result, but because they are still expressions, they must return *something*. Kotlin has a special `Unit` type for these:

```
// Summary1/UnitReturn.kt

fun main() {
  val result = println("returns Unit")
  println(result)
}
/* Output:
returns Unit
kotlin.Unit
*/
```

Experienced programmers should go to *Summary 2* after working the exercises for this atom.

Exercises and solutions can be found at www.AtomicKotlin.com.

Section II: Introduction to Objects

Objects are the foundation for numerous modern languages, including Kotlin.

In an *object-oriented* (OO) programming language, you discover "nouns" in the problem you're solving, and translate those nouns to objects. Objects hold data and perform actions. An object-oriented language creates and uses objects.

Kotlin isn't just object-oriented; it's also *functional*. Functional languages focus on the actions you perform ("verbs"). Kotlin is a hybrid object-functional language.

- This section explains the basics of object-oriented programming.
- **Section IV: Functional Programming** introduces functional programming.
- **Section V: Object-Oriented Programming** covers object-oriented programming in detail.

Objects Everywhere

> Objects store data using *properties* (`val`s and `var`s) and perform operations with this data using functions.

Some definitions:

- *Class*: Defines properties and functions for what is essentially a new data type. Classes are also called *user-defined types*.
- *Member*: Either a property or a function of a class.
- *Member function*: A function that works only with a specific class of object.
- *Creating an object*: Making a `val` or `var` of a class. Also called *creating an instance* of that class.

Because classes define *state* and *behavior*, we can even refer to instances of built-in types like `Double` or `Boolean` as objects.

Consider Kotlin's `IntRange` class:

```
// ObjectsEverywhere/IntRanges.kt

fun main() {
  val r1 = IntRange(0, 10)
  val r2 = IntRange(5, 7)
  println(r1)
  println(r2)
}
/* Output:
0..10
5..7
*/
```

We create two objects (instances) of the `IntRange` *class*. Each object has its own piece of storage in memory. `IntRange` is a class, but a particular range `r1` from 0 to 10 is an object that is distinct from range `r2`.

Numerous operations are available for an IntRange object. Some are straightforward, like sum( ), and others require more understanding before you can use them. If you try calling one that needs arguments, the IDE will ask for those arguments.

To learn about a particular member function, look it up in the Kotlin documentation[19]. Notice the magnifying glass icon in the top right area of the page. Click on that and type IntRange into the search box. Click on kotlin.ranges > IntRange from the resulting search. You'll see the documentation for the IntRange class. You can study all the member functions—the *Application Programming Interface* (API)—of the class. Although you won't understand most of it at this time, it's helpful to become comfortable looking things up in the Kotlin documentation.

An IntRange is a kind of object, and a defining characteristic of an object is that you perform operations on it. Instead of "performing an operation," we say *calling a member function*. To call a member function for an object, start with the object identifier, then a dot, then the name of the operation:

```
// ObjectsEverywhere/RangeSum.kt

fun main() {
  val r = IntRange(0, 10)
  println(r.sum())
}
/* Output:
55
*/
```

Because sum( ) is a member function defined for IntRange, you call it by saying r.sum( ). This adds up all the numbers in that IntRange.

Earlier object-oriented languages used the phrase "sending a message" to describe calling a member function for an object. Sometimes you'll still see that terminology.

Classes can have many operations (member functions). It's easy to explore classes using an IDE (integrated development environment) that includes a feature called *code completion*. For example, if you type .s after an object identifier within IntelliJ IDEA, it shows all the members of that object that begin with s:

---

[19]https://kotlinlang.org/api/latest/jvm/stdlib/index.html

```
val r = IntRange(0, 10)
r.s
```

v start		Int
v step		Int
m spliterator()		Spliterator<Int>
λ sum() for Iterable<Int> in kotlin.collections		Int
λ single() for Iterable<T> in kotlin.collections		Int
λ single {...} (predicate: (Int) -> Boolean) for Iterable<T>...		Int
λ singleOrNull() for Iterable<T> in kotlin.collections		Int?
λ singleOrNull {...} (predicate: (Int) -> Boolean) for Iter...		Int?
λ sortedBy {...} (crossinline selector: (Int) -> R?) f...		List<Int>
λ sorted() for Iterable<T> in kotlin.collections		List<Int>
λ sortedByDescending {...} (crossinline selector: (Int)...		List<Int>

Did you know that Quick Definition View (⌥Space) works in completion lookups as well? >>

Code Completion

Try using code completion on other objects. For example, you can reverse a `String` or convert all the characters to lower case:

```
// ObjectsEverywhere/Strings.kt

fun main() {
  val s = "AbcD"
  println(s.reversed())
  println(s.lowercase())
}
/* Output:
DcbA
abcd
*/
```

You can easily convert a `String` to an integer and back:

```
// ObjectsEverywhere/Conversion.kt

fun main() {
  val s = "123"
  println(s.toInt())
  val i = 123
  println(i.toString())
}
/* Output:
123
123
*/
```

Later in the book we discuss strategies to handle situations when the String you want to convert doesn't represent a correct integer value.

You can also convert from one numerical type to another. To avoid confusion, conversions between number types are explicit. For example, you convert an Int i to a Long by calling i.toLong(), or to a Double with i.toDouble():

```
// ObjectsEverywhere/NumberConversions.kt

fun fraction(numerator: Long, denom: Long) =
  numerator.toDouble() / denom

fun main() {
  val num = 1
  val den = 2
  val f = fraction(num.toLong(), den.toLong())
  println(f)
}
/* Output:
0.5
*/
```

Well-defined classes are easy for a programmer to understand, and produce code that's easy to read.

Exercises and solutions can be found at www.AtomicKotlin.com.

Creating Classes

Not only can you use predefined types like `IntRange` and `String`, you can also create your own types of objects.

Indeed, creating new types comprises much of the activity in object-oriented programming. You create new types by defining *classes*.

An object is a piece of the solution for a problem you're trying to solve. Start by thinking of objects as expressing concepts. As a first approximation, if you discover a "thing" in your problem, represent that thing as an object in your solution.

Suppose you want to create a program to manage animals in a zoo. It makes sense to categorize the different types of animals based on how they behave, their needs, animals they get along with and those they fight with. Everything different about a species of animal is captured in the classification of that animal's object. Kotlin uses the `class` keyword to create a new type of object:

```kotlin
// CreatingClasses/Animals.kt

// Create some classes:
class Giraffe
class Bear
class Hippo

fun main() {
  // Create some objects:
  val g1 = Giraffe()
  val g2 = Giraffe()
  val b = Bear()
  val h = Hippo()

  // Each object() is unique:
  println(g1)
  println(g2)
  println(h)
```

```
  println(b)
}
/* Sample output:
Giraffe@28d93b30
Giraffe@1b6d3586
Hippo@4554617c
Bear@74a14482
*/
```

To define a class, start with the `class` keyword, followed by an identifier for your new class. The class name must begin with a letter (A-Z, upper or lower case), but can include things like numbers and underscores. Following convention, we capitalize the first letter of a class name, and lowercase the first letter of all `val`s and `var`s.

`Animals.kt` starts by defining three new classes, then creates four objects (also called *instances*) of those classes.

`Giraffe` is a class, but a particular five-year-old male giraffe that lives in Botswana is an *object*. Each object is different from all others, so we give them names like g1 and g2.

Notice the rather cryptic output of the last four lines. The part before the @ is the class name, and the number after the @ is the address where the object is located in your computer's memory. Yes, that's a number even though it includes some letters—it's called "hexadecimal notation"[20]. Every object in your program has its own unique address.

The classes defined here (`Giraffe`, `Bear`, and `Hippo`) are as simple as possible: the entire class definition is a single line. More complex classes use curly braces ({ and }) to create a *class body* containing the characteristics and behaviors for that class.

A function defined within a class belongs to that class. In Kotlin, we call these *member functions* of the class. Some object-oriented languages like Java choose to call them *methods*, a term that came from early object-oriented languages like Smalltalk. To emphasize the functional nature of Kotlin, the designers chose to drop the term *method*, as some beginners found the distinction confusing. Instead, the term *function* is used throughout the language.

If it is unambiguous, we will just say "function." If we must make the distinction:

---

[20]https://en.wikipedia.org/wiki/Hexadecimal

- *Member* functions belong to a class.
- *Top-level* functions exist by themselves and are not part of a class.

Here, `bark()` belongs to the `Dog` class:

```
// CreatingClasses/Dog.kt

class Dog {
  fun bark() = "yip!"
}

fun main() {
  val dog = Dog()
}
```

In `main()`, we create a `Dog` object and assign it to `val dog`. Kotlin emits a warning because we never use `dog`.

Member functions are called (*invoked*) with the object name, followed by a `.` (dot/period), followed by the function name and parameter list. Here we call the `meow()` function and display the result:

```
// CreatingClasses/Cat.kt

class Cat {
  fun meow() = "mrrrow!"
}

fun main() {
  val cat = Cat()
  // Call 'meow()' for 'cat':
  val m1 = cat.meow()
  println(m1)
}
/* Output:
mrrrow!
*/
```

A member function acts on a particular instance of a class. When you call `meow()`, you must call it with an object. During the call, `meow()` can access other members of that object.

When calling a member function, Kotlin keeps track of the object of interest by silently passing a reference to that object. That reference is available inside the member function by using the keyword `this`.

Member functions have special access to other elements within a class, simply by naming those elements. You can also explicitly *qualify* access to those elements using `this`. Here, `exercise()` calls `speak()` with and without qualification:

```
// CreatingClasses/Hamster.kt

class Hamster {
  fun speak() = "Squeak! "
  fun exercise() =
    this.speak() +    // Qualified with 'this'
      speak() +       // Without 'this'
      "Running on wheel"
}

fun main() {
  val hamster = Hamster()
  println(hamster.exercise())
}
/* Output:
Squeak! Squeak! Running on wheel
*/
```

In `exercise()`, we call `speak()` first with an explicit `this` and then omit the qualification.

Sometimes you'll see code containing an unnecessary explicit `this`. That kind of code often comes from programmers who know a different language where `this` is either required, or part of its style. Using a feature unnecessarily is confusing for the reader, who spends time trying to figure out why you're doing it. We recommend avoiding the unnecessary use of `this`.

Outside the class, you must say `hamster.exercise()` and `hamster.speak()`.

Exercises and solutions can be found at www.AtomicKotlin.com.

Properties

A *property* is a var or val that's part of a class.

Defining a property *maintains state* within a class. Maintaining state is the primary motivating reason for creating a class rather than just writing one or more standalone functions.

A var property can be reassigned, while a val property can't. Each object gets its own storage for properties:

```
// Properties/Cup.kt

class Cup {
  var percentFull = 0
}

fun main() {
  val c1 = Cup()
  c1.percentFull = 50
  val c2 = Cup()
  c2.percentFull = 100

  println(c1.percentFull)
  println(c2.percentFull)
}
/* Output:
50
100
*/
```

Defining a var or val inside a class looks just like defining it within a function. However, the var or val becomes *part* of that class, and you must refer to it by specifying its object using *dot notation*, placing a dot between the object and the name of the property. You can see dot notation used for each reference to percentFull.

The percentFull property represents the state of the corresponding Cup object. c1.percentFull and c2.percentFull contain different values, showing that each object has its own storage.

A member function can refer to a property within its object without using dot notation (that is, without *qualifying* it):

```
// Properties/Cup2.kt

class Cup2 {
  var percentFull = 0
  val max = 100
  fun add(increase: Int): Int {
    percentFull += increase
    if (percentFull > max)
      percentFull = max
    return percentFull
  }
}

fun main() {
  val cup = Cup2()
  cup.add(50)
  println(cup.percentFull)
  cup.add(70)
  println(cup.percentFull)
}
/* Output:
50
100
*/
```

The add() member function tries to add increase to percentFull but ensures that it doesn't go past 100%.

You must qualify both properties and member functions from outside a class.

You can define top-level properties:

```
// Properties/TopLevelProperty.kt

val constant = 42

var counter = 0

fun inc() {
  counter++
}
```

Defining a top-level val is safe because it cannot be modified. However, defining a mutable (var) top-level property is considered an *anti-pattern*. As your program becomes more complicated, it becomes harder to reason correctly about *shared mutable state*. If everyone in your code base can access the var counter, you can't guarantee it will change correctly: while inc() increases counter by one, some other part of the program might decrease counter by ten, producing obscure bugs. It's best to guard mutable state within a class. In **Constraining Visibility** you'll see how to make it truly hidden.

To say that vars can be changed while vals cannot is an oversimplification. As an analogy, consider a house as a val, and a sofa inside the house as a var. You can modify sofa because it's a var. You can't reassign house, though, because it's a val:

```
// Properties/ChangingAVal.kt

class House {
  var sofa: String = ""
}

fun main() {
  val house = House()
  house.sofa = "Simple sleeper sofa: $89.00"
  println(house.sofa)
  house.sofa = "New leather sofa: $3,099.00"
  println(house.sofa)
  // Cannot reassign the val to a new House:
  // house = House()
}
/* Output:
Simple sleeper sofa: $89.00
New leather sofa: $3,099.00
*/
```

Although house is a val, its object can be modified because sofa in class House is a var. Defining house as a val only prevents it from being reassigned to a new object.

If we make a property a val, it cannot be reassigned:

```
// Properties/AnUnchangingVar.kt

class Sofa {
  val cover: String = "Loveseat cover"
}

fun main() {
  var sofa = Sofa()
  // Not allowed:
  // sofa.cover = "New cover"
  // Reassigning a var:
  sofa = Sofa()
}
```

Even though sofa is a var, its object cannot be modified because cover in class Sofa is a val. However, sofa can be reassigned to a new object.

We've talked about identifiers like house and sofa as if they were objects. They are actually *references* to objects. One way to see this is to observe that two identifiers can refer to the same object:

```
// Properties/References.kt

class Kitchen {
  var table: String = "Round table"
}

fun main() {
  val kitchen1 = Kitchen()
  val kitchen2 = kitchen1
  println("kitchen1: ${kitchen1.table}")
  println("kitchen2: ${kitchen2.table}")
  kitchen1.table = "Square table"
  println("kitchen1: ${kitchen1.table}")
  println("kitchen2: ${kitchen2.table}")
}
```

```
/* Output:
kitchen1: Round table
kitchen2: Round table
kitchen1: Square table
kitchen2: Square table
*/
```

When `kitchen1` modifies `table`, `kitchen2` sees the modification. `kitchen1.table` and `kitchen2.table` display the same output.

Remember that `var` and `val` control references rather than objects. A `var` allows you to rebind a reference to a different object, and a `val` prevents you from doing so.

Mutability means an object can change its state. In the examples above, `class House` and `class Kitchen` define mutable objects while `class Sofa` defines immutable objects.

Exercises and solutions can be found at www.AtomicKotlin.com.

Constructors

> You initialize a new object by passing information to a *constructor*.

Each object is an isolated world. A program is a collection of objects, so correct initialization of each individual object solves a large part of the initialization problem. Kotlin includes mechanisms to guarantee proper object initialization.

A constructor is like a special member function that initializes a new object. The simplest form of a constructor is a single-line class definition:

```
// Constructors/Wombat.kt

class Wombat

fun main() {
  val wombat = Wombat()
}
```

In `main()`, calling `Wombat()` creates a `Wombat` object. If you are coming from another object-oriented language you might expect to see a `new` keyword used here, but `new` would be redundant in Kotlin so it was omitted.

You pass information to a constructor using a parameter list, just like a function. Here, the `Alien` constructor takes a single argument:

```
// Constructors/Arg.kt

class Alien(name: String) {
  val greeting = "Poor $name!"
}

fun main() {
  val alien = Alien("Mr. Meeseeks")
  println(alien.greeting)
  // alien.name // Error      // [1]
}
/* Output:
Poor Mr. Meeseeks!
*/
```

Creating an `Alien` object requires the argument (try it without one). `name` initializes the `greeting` property within the constructor, but it is not accessible outside the constructor—try uncommenting line **[1]**.

If you want the constructor parameter to be accessible outside the class body, define it as a `var` or `val` in the parameter list:

```
// Constructors/VisibleArgs.kt

class MutableNameAlien(var name: String)

class FixedNameAlien(val name: String)

fun main() {
  val alien1 =
    MutableNameAlien("Reverse Giraffe")
  val alien2 =
    FixedNameAlien("Krombopulos Michael")

  alien1.name = "Parasite"
  // Can't do this:
  // alien2.name = "Parasite"
}
```

These class definitions have no explicit class bodies—the bodies are implied.

When `name` is defined as a `var` or `val`, it becomes a property and is thus accessible outside the constructor. `val` constructor parameters cannot be changed, while `var` constructor parameters are mutable.

Your class can have numerous constructor parameters:

```
// Constructors/MultipleArgs.kt

class AlienSpecies(
  val name: String,
  val eyes: Int,
  val hands: Int,
  val legs: Int
) {
  fun describe() =
    "$name with $eyes eyes, " +
      "$hands hands and $legs legs"
}

fun main() {
  val kevin =
    AlienSpecies("Zigerion", 2, 2, 2)
  val mortyJr =
    AlienSpecies("Gazorpian", 2, 6, 2)
  println(kevin.describe())
  println(mortyJr.describe())
}
/* Output:
Zigerion with 2 eyes, 2 hands and 2 legs
Gazorpian with 2 eyes, 6 hands and 2 legs
*/
```

In *Complex Constructors*, you'll see that constructors can also contain complex initialization logic.

If an object is used when a `String` is expected, Kotlin calls the object's `toString()` member function. If you don't write one, you still get a default `toString()`:

```
// Constructors/DisplayAlienSpecies.kt

fun main() {
  val krombopulosMichael =
    AlienSpecies("Gromflomite", 2, 2, 2)
  println(krombopulosMichael)
}
/* Sample output:
AlienSpecies@4d7e1886
*/
```

The default `toString()` isn't very useful—it produces the class name and the physical address of the object (this varies from one program execution to the next). You can define your own `toString()`:

```
// Constructors/Scientist.kt

class Scientist(val name: String) {
  override fun toString() =
    "Scientist('$name')"
}

fun main() {
  val zeep = Scientist("Zeep Xanflorp")
  println(zeep)
}
/* Output:
Scientist('Zeep Xanflorp')
*/
```

`override` is a new keyword for us. It is required here because `toString()` already has a definition, the one producing the primitive result. `override` tells Kotlin that yes, we do actually want to replace the default `toString()` with our own definition. The explicitness of `override` clarifies the code and prevents mistakes.

A `toString()` that displays the contents of an object in a convenient form is useful for finding and fixing programming errors. To simplify the process of *debugging*, IDEs provide *debuggers*[21] that allow you to observe each step in the execution of a program and to see inside your objects.

Exercises and solutions can be found at www.AtomicKotlin.com.

---
[21] https://www.jetbrains.com/help/idea/debugging-code.html

Constraining Visibility

> If you leave a piece of code for a few days or weeks, then come back to it, you might see a much better way to write it.

This is one of the prime motivations for *refactoring*, which rewrites working code to make it more readable, understandable, and thus maintainable.

There is a tension in this desire to change and improve your code. Consumers (*client programmers*) require aspects of your code to be stable. You want to change it, and they want it to stay the same.

This is particularly important for libraries. Consumers of a library don't want to rewrite code for a new version of that library. However, the library creator must be free to make modifications and improvements, with the certainty that the client code won't be affected by those changes.

Therefore, a primary consideration in software design is:

> *Separate things that change from things that stay the same.*

To control visibility, Kotlin and some other languages provide *access modifiers*. Library creators decide what is and is not accessible by the client programmer using the modifiers `public`, `private`, `protected`, and `internal`. This atom covers `public` and `private`, with a brief introduction to `internal`. We explain `protected` later in the book.

An access modifier such as `private` appears before the definition for a class, function, or property. An access modifier only controls access for that particular definition.

A `public` definition is accessible by client programmers, so changes to that definition impact client code directly. If you don't provide a modifier, your definition is automatically `public`, so `public` is technically redundant. You will sometimes still specify `public` for the sake of clarity.

A `private` definition is hidden and only accessible from other members of the same class. Changing, or even removing, a `private` definition doesn't directly impact client programmers.

`private` classes, top-level functions, and top-level properties are accessible only inside that file:

```
// Visibility/RecordAnimals.kt

private var index = 0                     // [1]

private class Animal(val name: String)    // [2]

private fun recordAnimal(                 // [3]
  animal: Animal
) {
  println("Animal #$index: ${animal.name}")
  index++
}

fun recordAnimals() {
  recordAnimal(Animal("Tiger"))
  recordAnimal(Animal("Antelope"))
}

fun recordAnimalsCount() {
  println("$index animals are here!")
}
```

You can access `private` top-level properties (**[1]**), classes (**[2]**), and functions (**[3]**) from other functions and classes within `RecordAnimals.kt`. Kotlin prevents you from accessing a `private` top-level element from within another file, telling you it's `private` in the file:

```
// Visibility/ObserveAnimals.kt

fun main() {
  // Can't access private members
  // declared in another file.
  // Class is private:
  // val rabbit = Animal("Rabbit")
  // Function is private:
  // recordAnimal(rabbit)
  // Property is private:
  // index++

  recordAnimals()
  recordAnimalsCount()
}
/* Output:
Animal #0: Tiger
Animal #1: Antelope
2 animals are here!
*/
```

Privacy is most commonly used for members of a class:

```
// Visibility/Cookie.kt

class Cookie(
  private var isReady: Boolean    // [1]
) {
  private fun crumble() =         // [2]
    println("crumble")

  public fun bite() =             // [3]
    println("bite")

  fun eat() {                     // [4]
    isReady = true                // [5]
    crumble()
    bite()
  }
}

fun main() {
```

```
  val x = Cookie(false)
  x.bite()
  // Can't access private members:
  // x.isReady
  // x.crumble()
  x.eat()
}
/* Output:
bite
crumble
bite
*/
```

- [1] A `private` property, not accessible outside the containing class.
- [2] A `private` member function.
- [3] A `public` member function, accessible to anyone.
- [4] No access modifier means `public`.
- [5] Only members of the same class can access `private` members.

The `private` keyword means no one can access that member except other members of that class. Other classes cannot access `private` members, so it's as if you're also insulating the class against yourself and your collaborators. With `private`, you can freely change that member without worrying whether it affects another class in the same package. As a library designer you'll typically keep things as `private` as possible, and expose only functions and classes to client programmers.

Any member function that is a *helper function* for a class can be made `private` to ensure you don't accidentally use it elsewhere in the package and thus prohibit yourself from changing or removing that function.

The same is true for a `private` property inside a class. Unless you must expose the underlying implementation (which is less likely than you might think), make properties `private`. However, just because a reference to an object is `private` inside a class doesn't mean some other object can't have a `public` reference to the same object:

```
// Visibility/MultipleRef.kt

class Counter(var start: Int) {
  fun increment() {
    start += 1
  }
  override fun toString() = start.toString()
}

class CounterHolder(counter: Counter) {
  private val ctr = counter
  override fun toString() =
    "CounterHolder: " + ctr
}

fun main() {
  val c = Counter(11)                     // [1]
  val ch = CounterHolder(c)               // [2]
  println(ch)
  c.increment()                           // [3]
  println(ch)
  val ch2 = CounterHolder(Counter(9))     // [4]
  println(ch2)
}
/* Output:
CounterHolder: 11
CounterHolder: 12
CounterHolder: 9
*/
```

- [1] c is now defined in the scope *surrounding* the creation of the CounterHolder object on the following line.
- [2] Passing c as the argument to the CounterHolder constructor means that the new CounterHolder now refers to the same Counter object that c refers to.
- [3] The Counter that is supposedly private inside ch can still be manipulated via c.
- [4] Counter(9) has no other references except within CounterHolder, so it cannot be accessed or modified by anything except ch2.

Maintaining multiple references to a single object is called *aliasing* and can produce surprising behavior.

Modules

Unlike the small examples in this book, real programs are often large. It can be helpful to divide such programs into one or more *modules*. A module is a logically independent part of a codebase. The way you divide a project into modules depends on the build system (such as Gradle[22] or Maven[23]) and is beyond the scope of this book.

An `internal` definition is accessible only inside the module where it is defined. `internal` lands somewhere between `private` and `public`—use it when `private` is too restrictive but you don't want an element to be a part of the `public` API. We do not use `internal` in the book's examples or exercises.

Modules are a higher-level concept. The following atom introduces *packages*, which enable finer-grained structuring. A library is often a single module consisting of multiple packages, so `internal` elements are available within the library but are not accessible by consumers of that library.

Exercises and solutions can be found at www.AtomicKotlin.com.

---

[22] https://gradle.org/
[23] https://maven.apache.org/

Packages

A fundamental principle in programming is the acronym DRY: *Don't Repeat Yourself.*

Multiple identical pieces of code require maintenance whenever you make fixes or improvements. So duplicating code is not just extra work—every duplication creates opportunities for mistakes.

The `import` keyword reuses code from other files. One way to use `import` is to specify a class, function or property name:

```
import packagename.ClassName
import packagename.functionName
import packagename.propertyName
```

A *package* is an associated collection of code. Each package is usually designed to solve a particular problem, and often contains multiple functions and classes. For example, we can import mathematical constants and functions from the `kotlin.math` library:

```
// Packages/ImportClass.kt
import kotlin.math.PI
import kotlin.math.cos   // Cosine

fun main() {
  println(PI)
  println(cos(PI))
  println(cos(2 * PI))
}
/* Output:
3.141592653589793
-1.0
1.0
*/
```

Sometimes you want to use multiple third-party libraries containing classes or functions with the same name. The as keyword allows you to change names while importing:

```
// Packages/ImportNameChange.kt
import kotlin.math.PI as circleRatio
import kotlin.math.cos as cosine

fun main() {
  println(circleRatio)
  println(cosine(circleRatio))
  println(cosine(2 * circleRatio))
}
/* Output:
3.141592653589793
-1.0
1.0
*/
```

`as` is useful if a library name is poorly chosen or excessively long.

You can fully qualify an import in the body of your code. In the following example, the code might be less readable due to the explicit package names, but the origin of each element is absolutely clear:

```
// Packages/FullyQualify.kt

fun main() {
  println(kotlin.math.PI)
  println(kotlin.math.cos(kotlin.math.PI))
  println(kotlin.math.cos(2 * kotlin.math.PI))
}
/* Output:
3.141592653589793
-1.0
1.0
*/
```

To import everything from a package, use a star:

```
// Packages/ImportEverything.kt
import kotlin.math.*

fun main() {
  println(E)
  println(E.roundToInt())
  println(E.toInt())
}
/* Output:
2.718281828459045
3
2
*/
```

The `kotlin.math` package contains a convenient `roundToInt()` that rounds the `Double` value to the nearest integer, unlike `toInt()` which simply truncates anything after a decimal point.

To reuse your code, create a package using the `package` keyword. The `package` statement must be the first non-comment statement in the file. `package` is followed by the name of your package, which by convention is all lowercase:

```
// Packages/PythagoreanTheorem.kt
package pythagorean
import kotlin.math.sqrt

class RightTriangle(
  val a: Double,
  val b: Double
) {
  fun hypotenuse() = sqrt(a * a + b * b)
  fun area() = a * b / 2
}
```

You can name the source-code file anything you like, unlike Java which requires the file name to be the same as the class name.

Kotlin allows you to choose any name for your package, but it's considered good style for the package name to be identical to the directory name where the package files are located (this will not always be the case for the examples in this book).

The elements in the `pythagorean` package are now available using `import`:

```
// Packages/ImportPythagorean.kt
import pythagorean.RightTriangle

fun main() {
  val rt = RightTriangle(3.0, 4.0)
  println(rt.hypotenuse())
  println(rt.area())
}
/* Output:
5.0
6.0
*/
```

In the remainder of this book we use `package` statements for any file that defines functions, classes, etc., outside of `main()`, to prevent name clashes with other files in the book, but we usually won't put a `package` statement in a file that *only* contains a `main()`.

Exercises and solutions can be found at www.AtomicKotlin.com.

Testing

> Constant testing is essential for rapid program development.

If changing one part of your code breaks other code, your tests reveal the problem right away. If you don't find out immediately, changes accumulate and you can no longer tell which change caused the problem. You'll spend a *lot* longer tracking it down.

Testing is a crucial practice, so we introduce it early and use it throughout the rest of the book. This way, you become accustomed to testing as a standard part of the programming process.

Using `println()` to verify code correctness is a weak approach—you must scrutinize the output every time and consciously ensure that it's correct.

To simplify your experience while using this book, we created our own tiny testing system. The goal is a minimal approach that:

1. Shows the expected result of expressions.
2. Provides output so you know the program is running, even when all tests succeed.
3. Ingrains the concept of testing early in your practice.

Although useful for this book, ours is *not* a testing system for the workplace. Others have toiled long and hard to create such test systems. For example:

- JUnit[24] is one of the most popular Java test frameworks, and is easily used from within Kotlin.
- Kotest[25] is designed specifically for Kotlin, and takes advantage of Kotlin language features.
- The Spek Framework[26] produces a different form of testing, called *Specification Testing*.

To use our testing framework, we must first `import` it. The basic elements of the framework are `eq` (*equals*) and `neq` (*not equals*):

---

[24] https://junit.org
[25] https://github.com/kotest/kotest
[26] https://spekframework.org/

```
// Testing/TestingExample.kt
import atomictest.*

fun main() {
  val v1 = 11
  val v2 = "Ontology"

  // 'eq' means "equals":
  v1 eq 11
  v2 eq "Ontology"

  // 'neq' means "not equal"
  v2 neq "Epistemology"

  // [Error] Epistemology != Ontology
  // v2 eq "Epistemology"
}
/* Output:
11
Ontology
Ontology
*/
```

The code for the atomictest package is in **Appendix A: AtomicTest**. We don't intend that you understand everything in AtomicTest.kt right now, because it uses some features that won't appear until later in the book.

To produce a clean, comfortable appearance, AtomicTest uses a Kotlin feature you haven't seen yet: the ability to write a function call a.function(b) in the text-like form a function b. This is called *infix notation*. Only functions defined using the infix keyword can be called this way. AtomicTest.kt defines the infix eq and neq used in TestingExample.kt:

```
expression eq expected
expression neq expected
```

eq and neq are flexible—almost anything works as a test expression. If *expected* is a String, then *expression* is converted to a String and the two Strings are compared. Otherwise, *expression* and *expected* are compared directly (without converting them first). In either case, the result of *expression* appears on the console so you see something when the program runs. Even when the tests succeed, you still see the result on the left of eq or neq. If *expression* and *expected* are not equivalent, AtomicTest shows an error when the program runs.

The last test in TestingExample.kt intentionally fails so you see an example of failure output. If the two values are not equal, Kotlin displays the corresponding message starting with [Error]. If you uncomment the last line and run the example above, you will see, after all the successful tests:

```
[Error] Epistemology != Ontology
```

The actual value stored in v2 is not what it is claimed to be in the "expected" expression. AtomicTest displays the String representations for both expected and actual values.

eq and neq are the basic (infix) functions defined for AtomicTest—it truly is a minimal testing system. When you put eq and neq expressions in your examples, you'll create both a test and some console output. You verify the correctness of the program by running it.

There's a second tool in AtomicTest. The trace object captures output for later comparison:

```
// Testing/Trace1.kt
import atomictest.*

fun main() {
  trace("line 1")
  trace(47)
  trace("line 2")
  trace eq """
    line 1
    47
    line 2
  """
}
```

Adding results to trace looks like a function call, so you can effectively replace println() with trace().

In previous atoms, we displayed output and relied on human visual inspection to catch any discrepancies. That's unreliable; even in a book where we scrutinize the code over and over, we've learned that visual inspection can't be trusted to find errors. From now on we rarely use commented output blocks because `AtomicTest` will do everything for us. However, sometimes we still include commented output blocks when that produces a more useful effect.

Seeing the benefits of using testing throughout the rest of the book should help you incorporate testing into your programming process. You'll probably start feeling uncomfortable when you see code that doesn't have tests. You might even decide that code without tests is broken by definition.

Testing as Part of Programming

Testing is most effective when it's built into your software development process. Writing tests ensures you get the results you expect. Many people advocate writing tests *before* writing the implementation code—you first make the test fail before you write the code to make it pass. This technique, called *Test Driven Development* (TDD), is a way to ensure that you're really testing what you think you are. You'll find a more complete description of TDD on Wikipedia (search for "Test Driven Development").

There's another benefit to writing testably—it changes the way you craft your code. You could just display the results on the console. But in the test mindset you wonder, "How will I test this?" When you create a function, you decide you should return something from the function, if for no other reason than to test that result. Functions that do nothing but take input and produce output tend to generate better designs, as well.

Here's a simplified example using TDD to implement the BMI calculation from ***Number Types***. First, we write the tests, along with an initial implementation that fails (because we haven't yet implemented the functionality):

```
// Testing/TDDFail.kt
package testing1
import atomictest.eq

fun main() {
  calculateBMI(160, 68) eq "Normal weight"
//  calculateBMI(100, 68) eq "Underweight"
//  calculateBMI(200, 68) eq "Overweight"
}

fun calculateBMI(lbs: Int, height: Int) =
  "Normal weight"
```

Only the first test passes. The other tests fail and are commented. Next, we add code to determine which weights are in which categories. Now *all* the tests fail:

```
// Testing/TDDStillFails.kt
package testing2
import atomictest.eq

fun main() {
  // Everything fails:
  // calculateBMI(160, 68) eq "Normal weight"
  // calculateBMI(100, 68) eq "Underweight"
  // calculateBMI(200, 68) eq "Overweight"
}

fun calculateBMI(
  lbs: Int,
  height: Int
): String {
  val bmi = lbs / (height * height) * 703.07
  return if (bmi < 18.5) "Underweight"
  else if (bmi < 25) "Normal weight"
  else "Overweight"
}
```

We're using `Int`s instead of `Double`s, producing a zero result. The tests guide us to the fix:

```
// Testing/TDDWorks.kt
package testing3
import atomictest.eq

fun main() {
  calculateBMI(160.0, 68.0) eq "Normal weight"
  calculateBMI(100.0, 68.0) eq "Underweight"
  calculateBMI(200.0, 68.0) eq "Overweight"
}

fun calculateBMI(
  lbs: Double,
  height: Double
): String {
  val bmi = lbs / (height * height) * 703.07
  return if (bmi < 18.5) "Underweight"
  else if (bmi < 25) "Normal weight"
  else "Overweight"
}
```

You may choose to add additional tests for the boundary conditions.

In the exercises for this book, we include tests that your code must pass.

Exercises and solutions can be found at www.AtomicKotlin.com.

Exceptions

> The word "exception" is used in the same sense as the phrase "I take exception to that."

An exceptional condition prevents the continuation of the current function or scope. At the point the problem occurs, you might not know what to do with it, but you cannot continue within the current context. You don't have enough information to fix the problem. So you must stop and hand the problem to another context that's able to take appropriate action.

This atom covers the basics of *exceptions* as an error-reporting mechanism. In **Section VI: Preventing Failure**, we look at other ways to deal with problems.

It's important to distinguish an exceptional condition from a normal problem. A normal problem has enough information in the current context to cope with the issue. With an exceptional condition, you cannot continue processing. All you can do is leave, relegating the problem to an external context. This is what happens when you *throw an exception*. The exception is the object that is "thrown" from the site of the error.

Consider `toInt()`, which converts a `String` to an `Int`. What happens if you call this function for a `String` that doesn't contain an integer value?

```
// Exceptions/ToIntException.kt
package exceptions

fun erroneousCode() {
  // Uncomment this line to get an exception:
  // val i = "1$".toInt()        // [1]
}

fun main() {
  erroneousCode()
}
```

Uncommenting line **[1]** produces an exception. Here, the failing line is commented so we don't stop the book's build, which checks whether each example compiles and runs as expected.

When an exception is thrown, the path of execution—the one that can't be continued—stops, and the exception object ejects from the current context. Here, it exits the context of erroneousCode() and goes out to the context of main(). In this case, Kotlin only reports the error; the programmer has presumably made a mistake and must fix the code.

When an exception isn't caught, the program aborts and displays a *stack trace* containing detailed information. Uncommenting line **[1]** in ToIntException.kt, produces the following output:

```
Exception in thread "main" java.lang.NumberFormatException: For input s\
tring: "1$"
  at java.lang.NumberFormatException.forInputString(NumberFormatExcepti\
on.java:65)
  at java.lang.Integer.parseInt(Integer.java:580)
  at java.lang.Integer.parseInt(Integer.java:615)
  at ToIntExceptionKt.erroneousCode(at ToIntException.kt:6)
  at ToIntExceptionKt.main(at ToIntException.kt:10)
```

The stack trace gives details such as the file and line where the exception occurred, so you can quickly discover the issue. The last two lines show the problem: in line 10 of main() we call erroneousCode(). Then, more precisely, in line 6 of erroneousCode() we call toInt().

To avoid commenting and uncommenting code to display exceptions, we use the capture() function from the AtomicTest package:

```
// Exceptions/IntroducingCapture.kt
import atomictest.*

fun main() {
  capture {
    "1$".toInt()
  } eq "NumberFormatException: " +
    """For input string: "1$""""
}
```

Using capture(), we compare the generated exception to the expected error message. capture() isn't very helpful for normal programming—it's designed specifically for this book, so you can see the exception and know that the output has been checked by the book's build system.

Another strategy when you can't successfully produce the expected result is to return null, which is a special constant denoting "no value." You can return null instead of a value of any type. Later in **Nullable Types** we discuss the way null affects the type of the resulting expression.

The Kotlin standard library contains String.toIntOrNull() which performs the conversion if the String contains an integer number, or produces null if the conversion is impossible—null is a simple way to indicate failure:

```
// Exceptions/IntroducingNull.kt
import atomictest.eq

fun main() {
  "1$".toIntOrNull() eq null
}
```

Suppose we calculate average income over a period of months:

```
// Exceptions/AverageIncome.kt
package firstversion
import atomictest.*

fun averageIncome(income: Int, months: Int) =
  income / months

fun main() {
  averageIncome(3300, 3) eq 1100
  capture {
    averageIncome(5000, 0)
  } eq "ArithmeticException: / by zero"
}
```

If months is zero, the division in averageIncome() throws an ArithmeticException. Unfortunately, this doesn't tell us anything about why the error occurred, what the denominator means and whether it can legally be zero in the first place. This is clearly a bug in the code—averageIncome() should cope with a months of 0 in a way that prevents a divide-by-zero error.

Let's modify averageIncome() to produce more information about the source of the problem. If months is zero, we can't return a regular integer value as a result. One strategy is to return null:

```
// Exceptions/AverageIncomeWithNull.kt
package withnull
import atomictest.eq

fun averageIncome(income: Int, months: Int) =
  if (months == 0)
    null
  else
    income / months

fun main() {
  averageIncome(3300, 3) eq 1100
  averageIncome(5000, 0) eq null
}
```

If a function can return null, Kotlin requires that you check the result before using it (this is covered in **Nullable Types**). Even if you only want to display output to the user, it's better to say "No full month periods have passed," rather than "Your average income for the period is: null."

Instead of executing averageIncome() with the wrong arguments, you can throw an exception—escape and force some other part of the program to manage the issue. You *could* just allow the default ArithmeticException, but it's often more useful to throw a specific exception with a detailed error message. When, after a couple of years in production, your application suddenly throws an exception because a new feature calls averageIncome() without properly checking the arguments, you'll be grateful for that message:

```
// Exceptions/AverageIncomeWithException.kt
package properexception
import atomictest.*

fun averageIncome(income: Int, months: Int) =
  if (months == 0)
    throw IllegalArgumentException(    // [1]
      "Months can't be zero")
  else
    income / months

fun main() {
  averageIncome(3300, 3) eq 1100
  capture {
    averageIncome(5000, 0)
  } eq "IllegalArgumentException: " +
    "Months can't be zero"
}
```

- [1] When throwing an exception, the throw keyword is followed by the exception to be thrown, along with any arguments it might need. Here we use the standard exception class IllegalArgumentException.

Your goal is to generate the most useful messages possible to simplify the support of your application in the future. Later you'll learn to define your own exception types and make them specific to your circumstances.

Exercises and solutions can be found at www.AtomicKotlin.com.

Lists

A List is a *container*, which is an object that holds other objects.

Containers are also called *collections*. When we need a basic container for the examples in this book, we normally use a List.

Lists are part of the standard Kotlin package so they don't require an import.

The following example creates a List populated with Ints by calling the standard library function listOf() with initialization values:

```
// Lists/Lists.kt
import atomictest.eq

fun main() {
  val ints = listOf(99, 3, 5, 7, 11, 13)
  ints eq "[99, 3, 5, 7, 11, 13]"    // [1]

  // Select each element in the List:
  var result = ""
  for (i in ints) {                  // [2]
    result += "$i "
  }
  result eq "99 3 5 7 11 13"

  // "Indexing" into the List:
  ints[4] eq 11                      // [3]
}
```

- **[1]** A List uses square brackets when displaying itself.
- **[2]** for loops work well with Lists: for(i in ints) means i receives each value in ints. You don't declare val i or give its type; Kotlin knows from the context that i is a for loop identifier.

- **[3]** Square brackets *index* into a List. A List keeps its elements in initialization order, and you select them individually by number. Like most programming languages, Kotlin starts indexing at element zero, which in this case produces the value 99. Thus an index of 4 produces the value 11.

Forgetting that indexing starts at zero produces the so-called *off-by-one* error. In a language like Kotlin we often don't select elements one at a time, but instead *iterate* through an entire container using in. This eliminates off-by-one errors.

If you use an index beyond the last element in a List, Kotlin throws an ArrayIndexOutOfBoundsException:

```
// Lists/OutOfBounds.kt
import atomictest.*

fun main() {
  val ints = listOf(1, 2, 3)
  capture {
    ints[3]
  } contains
    listOf("ArrayIndexOutOfBoundsException")
}
```

A List can hold all different types. Here's a List of Doubles and a List of Strings:

```
// Lists/ListUsefulFunction.kt
import atomictest.eq

fun main() {
  val doubles =
    listOf(1.1, 2.2, 3.3, 4.4)
  doubles.sum() eq 11.0

  val strings = listOf("Twas", "Brillig",
    "And", "Slithy", "Toves")
  strings eq listOf("Twas", "Brillig",
    "And", "Slithy", "Toves")
  strings.sorted() eq listOf("And",
    "Brillig", "Slithy", "Toves", "Twas")
  strings.reversed() eq listOf("Toves",
    "Slithy", "And", "Brillig", "Twas")
  strings.first() eq "Twas"
```

```
  strings.takeLast(2) eq
    listOf("Slithy", "Toves")
}
```

This shows some of `List`'s operations. Note the name "sorted" instead of "sort." When you call `sorted()` it *produces* a new `List` containing the same elements as the old, in sorted order—but it leaves the original `List` alone. Calling it "sort" implies that the original `List` is changed directly (a.k.a. *sorted in place*). Throughout Kotlin, you see this tendency of "leaving the original object alone and producing a new object." `reversed()` also produces a new `List`.

Parameterized Types

We consider it good practice to use type inference—it tends to make the code cleaner and easier to read. Sometimes, however, Kotlin complains that it can't figure out what type to use, and in other cases explicitness makes the code more understandable. Here's how we tell Kotlin the type contained by a `List`:

```
// Lists/ParameterizedTypes.kt
import atomictest.eq

fun main() {
  // Type is inferred:
  val numbers = listOf(1, 2, 3)
  val strings =
    listOf("one", "two", "three")
  // Exactly the same, but explicitly typed:
  val numbers2: List<Int> = listOf(1, 2, 3)
  val strings2: List<String> =
    listOf("one", "two", "three")
  numbers eq numbers2
  strings eq strings2
}
```

Kotlin uses the initialization values to infer that `numbers` contains a `List` of `Int`s, while `strings` contains a `List` of `String`s.

`numbers2` and `strings2` are explicitly-typed versions of `numbers` and `strings`, created by adding the type declarations `List<Int>` and `List<String>`. You haven't seen angle brackets before—they denote a *type parameter*, allowing you to say, "this container holds 'parameter' objects." We pronounce `List<Int>` as "List of Int."

Type parameters are useful for components other than containers, but you often see them with container-like objects.

Return values can also have type parameters:

```
// Lists/ParameterizedReturn.kt
package lists
import atomictest.eq

// Return type is inferred:
fun inferred(p: Char, q: Char) =
  listOf(p, q)

// Explicit return type:
fun explicit(p: Char, q: Char): List<Char> =
  listOf(p, q)

fun main() {
  inferred('a', 'b') eq "[a, b]"
  explicit('y', 'z') eq "[y, z]"
}
```

Kotlin infers the return type for `inferred()`, while `explicit()` specifies the function return type. You can't just say it returns a `List`; Kotlin will complain, so you must give the type parameter as well. When you specify the return type of a function, Kotlin enforces your intention.

Read-Only and Mutable Lists

If you don't explicitly say you want a mutable `List`, you won't get one. `listOf()` produces a read-only `List` that has no mutating functions.

If you're creating a `List` gradually (that is, you don't have all the elements at creation time), use `mutableListOf()`. This produces a `MutableList` that can be modified:

```
// Lists/MutableList.kt
import atomictest.eq

fun main() {
  val list = mutableListOf<Int>()

  list.add(1)
  list.addAll(listOf(2, 3))

  list += 4
  list += listOf(5, 6)

  list eq listOf(1, 2, 3, 4, 5, 6)
}
```

Because `list` has no initial elements, we must tell Kotlin what type it is by providing the `<Int>` specification in the call to `mutableListOf()`. You can add elements to a `MutableList` using `add()` and `addAll()`, or the operator `+=` which adds either a single element or another collection.

A `MutableList` can be treated as a `List`, in which case it cannot be changed. You can't, however, treat a read-only `List` as a `MutableList`:

```
// Lists/MutListIsList.kt
package lists
import atomictest.eq

fun makeList(): List<Int> =
  mutableListOf(1, 2, 3)

fun main() {
  // makeList() produces a read-only List:
  val list = makeList()
  // list.add(3) // Unresolved reference: add
  list eq listOf(1, 2, 3)
}
```

`list` lacks mutation functions despite being originally created using `mutableListOf()` inside `makeList()`. Notice that the result type of `makeList()` is `List<Int>`. The original object is still a `MutableList`, but it is viewed through the lens of a `List`.

A List is *read-only*—you can read its contents but not write to it. If the underlying implementation is a MutableList and you retain a mutable reference to that implementation, you can still modify it via that mutable reference, and any read-only references will see those changes. This is another example of *aliasing*, introduced in *Constraining Visibility*:

```
// Lists/MultipleListRefs.kt
import atomictest.eq

fun main() {
  val first = mutableListOf(1)
  val second: List<Int> = first
  second eq listOf(1)
  first.add(2)
  // second sees the change:
  second eq listOf(1, 2)
}
```

first is an immutable reference (val) to the mutable object produced by mutableListOf(1). When second is aliased to first it becomes a view of that same object. second is read-only because List<Int> does not include modification functions. Without the explicit List<Int> type declaration, Kotlin would infer that second was also a reference to a mutable object.

We're able to add an element (2) to the object because first is a reference to a mutable List. Note that second observes these changes—it cannot change the List although the List changes via first.

The += Puzzle

The += operator can give the appearance that an immutable List is actually mutable:

```
// Lists/ApparentlyMutableList.kt
import atomictest.eq

fun main() {
  var list = listOf('X') // Immutable
  list += 'Y' // Appears to be mutable
  list eq "[X, Y]"
}
```

`listOf()` produces an immutable `List`, but `list += 'Y'` seems to be modifying that `List`. Does `+=` somehow violate immutability?

This only happens because `list` is a `var`. Here's a more detailed example that shows the different combinations of mutable/immutable `List`s with `val`/`var`:

```
// Lists/PlusAssignPuzzle.kt
import atomictest.eq

fun main() {
    // Mutable List assigned to a 'val'/'var':
    val list1 = mutableListOf('A') // or 'var'
    list1 += 'A' // Is the same as:
    list1.plusAssign('A')                // [1]

    // Immutable List assigned to a 'val':
    val list2 = listOf('B')
    // list2 += 'B' // Is the same as:
    // list2 = list2 + 'B'                // [2]

    // Immutable List assigned to a 'var':
    var list3 = listOf('C')
    list3 += 'C' // Is the same as:
    val newList = list3 + 'C'            // [3]
    list3 = newList                      // [4]

    list1 eq "[A, A, A]"
    list2 eq "[B]"
    list3 eq "[C, C, C]"
}
```

- **[1]** `list1` refers to a mutable object, which can therefore be modified in place. The compiler translates `+=` to the `plusAssign()` call. It doesn't matter if `list1` is a `val` or a `var` because nothing is ever *reassigned* to `list1` after creation—it always refers to the same mutable list. Make it a `var` and IntelliJ points out that it never changes and suggests that it be a `val`.

- **[2]** This tries to create a new `List` by combining `list2` and `'B'`, but it can't reassign that new `List` to `list2` because `list2` is a `val`. Without the ability to perform that reassignment, the `+=` cannot compile.
- **[3]** Creates `newList` without modifying the existing immutable `List` referred to by `list3`.
- **[4]** Because `list3` is a `var`, the compiler assigns `newList` back into `list3`. The previous contents of `list3` are then forgotten, and it appears that `list3` has been mutated. Actually, the old `list3` has been discarded and replaced by the newly-created `newList`, giving the illusion that `list3` is mutable.

This behavior of `+=` happens with other collections, as well. The resulting confusion is another reason to choose `val` over `var` for your identifiers.

Exercises and solutions can be found at www.AtomicKotlin.com.

Variable Argument Lists

The vararg keyword produces a flexibly-sized argument list.

In *Lists* we introduced listOf( ), which takes any number of parameters and produces a List:

```
// Varargs/ListOf.kt
import atomictest.eq

fun main() {
  listOf(1) eq "[1]"
  listOf("a", "b") eq "[a, b]"
}
```

Using the vararg keyword, you can define a function that takes any number of arguments, just like listOf( ) does. vararg is short for *variable argument list*:

```
// Varargs/VariableArgList.kt
package varargs

fun v(s: String, vararg d: Double) {}

fun main() {
  v("abc", 1.0, 2.0)
  v("def", 1.0, 2.0, 3.0, 4.0)
  v("ghi", 1.0, 2.0, 3.0, 4.0, 5.0, 6.0)
}
```

A function definition may specify only one parameter as vararg. Although it's possible to specify any item in the parameter list as vararg, it's usually simplest to do it for the last one.

vararg allows you to pass any number (including zero) of arguments. All arguments must be of the specified type. vararg arguments are accessed using the parameter name, which becomes an Array:

```
// Varargs/VarargSum.kt
package varargs
import atomictest.eq

fun sum(vararg numbers: Int): Int {
  var total = 0
  for (n in numbers) {
    total += n
  }
  return total
}

fun main() {
  sum(13, 27, 44) eq 84
  sum(1, 3, 5, 7, 9, 11) eq 36
  sum() eq 0
}
```

Although `Array`s and `List`s look similar, they are implemented differently—`List` is a regular library class while `Array` has special low-level support. `Array` comes from Kotlin's requirement for compatibility with other languages, especially Java.

In day-to-day programming, use a `List` when you need a simple sequence. Use `Array`s only when a third-party API requires an `Array`, or when you're dealing with varargs.

In most cases you can just ignore the fact that `vararg` produces an `Array` and treat it as if it were a `List`:

```
// Varargs/VarargLikeList.kt
package varargs
import atomictest.eq

fun evaluate(vararg ints: Int) =
  "Size: ${ints.size}\n" +
  "Sum: ${ints.sum()}\n" +
  "Average: ${ints.average()}"

fun main() {
  evaluate(10, -3, 8, 1, 9) eq """
    Size: 5
    Sum: 25
```

```
    Average: 5.0
    """
}
```

You can pass an Array of elements wherever a vararg is accepted. To create an Array, use arrayOf() in the same way you use listOf(). An Array is always mutable. To convert an Array into a sequence of arguments (not just a single element of type Array), use the *spread operator*, `*`:

```
// Varargs/SpreadOperator.kt
import varargs.sum
import atomictest.eq

fun main() {
  val array = intArrayOf(4, 5)
  sum(1, 2, 3, *array, 6) eq 21   // [1]
  // Doesn't compile:
  // sum(1, 2, 3, array, 6)

  val list = listOf(9, 10, 11)
  sum(*list.toIntArray()) eq 30   // [2]
}
```

If you pass an Array of primitive types (like Int, Double or Boolean) as in the example above, the Array creation function must be specifically typed. If you use arrayOf(4, 5) instead of intArrayOf(4, 5), line [1] will produce an error complaining that *inferred type is Array<Int> but IntArray was expected.*

The spread operator only works with arrays. If you have a List that you want to pass as a sequence of arguments, first convert it to an Array and then apply the spread operator, as in [2]. Because the result is an Array of a primitive type, we must again use the specific conversion function toIntArray().

The spread operator is especially helpful when you must pass vararg arguments to another function that also expects varargs:

```
// Varargs/TwoFunctionsWithVarargs.kt
package varargs
import atomictest.eq

fun first(vararg numbers: Int): String {
  var result = ""
  for (i in numbers) {
    result += "[$i]"
  }
  return result
}

fun second(vararg numbers: Int) =
  first(*numbers)

fun main() {
  second(7, 9, 32) eq "[7][9][32]"
}
```

Command-Line Arguments

When invoking a program on the command line, you can pass it a variable number of arguments. To capture command-line arguments, you must provide a particular parameter to main():

```
// Varargs/MainArgs.kt

fun main(args: Array<String>) {
  for (a in args) {
    println(a)
  }
}
```

The parameter is traditionally called args (although you can call it anything), and the type for args can only be Array<String> (Array of String).

If you are using IntelliJ IDEA, you can pass program arguments by editing the corresponding "Run configuration," as shown in the last exercise for this atom.

You can also use the `kotlinc` compiler to produce a command-line program. If `kotlinc` isn't on your computer, follow the instructions on the Kotlin main site[27]. Once you've entered and saved the code for `MainArgs.kt`, type the following at a command prompt:

```
kotlinc MainArgs.kt
```

You provide the command-line arguments following the program invocation, like this:

```
kotlin MainArgsKt hamster 42 3.14159
```

You'll see this output:

```
hamster
42
3.14159
```

If you want to turn a `String` parameter into a specific type, Kotlin provides conversion functions, such as a `toInt()` for converting to an `Int`, and `toFloat()` for converting to a `Float`. Using these assumes that the command-line arguments appear in a particular order. Here, the program expects a `String`, followed by something convertible to an `Int`, followed by something convertible to a `Float`:

```
// Varargs/MainArgConversion.kt

fun main(args: Array<String>) {
  if (args.size < 3) return
  val first = args[0]
  val second = args[1].toInt()
  val third = args[2].toFloat()
  println("$first  $second  $third")
}
```

The first line in `main()` quits the program if there aren't enough arguments. If you don't provide something convertible to an `Int` and a `Float` as the second and third command-line arguments, you will see runtime errors (try it to see the errors).

Compile and run `MainArgConversion.kt` with the same command-line arguments we used before, and you'll see:

```
hamster 42 3.14159
```

Exercises and solutions can be found at www.AtomicKotlin.com.

---
[27] https://kotlinlang.org/

Sets

A Set is a collection that allows only one element of each value.

The most common Set activity is to test for membership using in or contains():

```
// Sets/Sets.kt
import atomictest.eq

fun main() {
  val intSet = setOf(1, 1, 2, 3, 9, 9, 4)
  // No duplicates:
  intSet eq setOf(1, 2, 3, 4, 9)

  // Element order is unimportant:
  setOf(1, 2) eq setOf(2, 1)

  // Set membership:
  (9 in intSet) eq true
  (99 in intSet) eq false

  intSet.contains(9) eq true
  intSet.contains(99) eq false

  // Does this set contain another set?
  intSet.containsAll(setOf(1, 9, 2)) eq true

  // Set union:
  intSet.union(setOf(3, 4, 5, 6)) eq
    setOf(1, 2, 3, 4, 5, 6, 9)

  // Set intersection:
  intSet intersect setOf(0, 1, 2, 7, 8) eq
    setOf(1, 2)

  // Set difference:
  intSet subtract setOf(0, 1, 9, 10) eq
```

```
    setOf(2, 3, 4)
  intSet - setOf(0, 1, 9, 10) eq
    setOf(2, 3, 4)
}
```

This example shows:

1. Placing duplicate items into a Set automatically removes those duplicates.
2. Element order is not important for sets. Two sets are equal if they contain the same elements.
3. Both in and contains() test for membership.
4. You can perform the usual Venn-diagram operations like checking for subset, union, intersection and difference, using either dot notation (set.union(other)) or infix notation (set intersect other). The functions union, intersect and subtract can be used with infix notation.
5. Set difference can be expressed with either subtract() or the minus operator.

To remove duplicates from a List, convert it to a Set:

```
// Sets/RemoveDuplicates.kt
import atomictest.eq

fun main() {
  val list = listOf(3, 3, 2, 1, 2)
  list.toSet() eq setOf(1, 2, 3)
  list.distinct() eq listOf(3, 2, 1)
  "abbcc".toSet() eq setOf('a', 'b', 'c')
}
```

You can also use distinct(), which returns a List. You may call toSet() on a String to convert it into a set of unique characters.

As with List, Kotlin provides two creation functions for Set. The result of setOf() is read-only. To create a mutable Set, use mutableSetOf():

```
// Sets/MutableSet.kt
import atomictest.eq

fun main() {
  val mutableSet = mutableSetOf<Int>()
  mutableSet += 42
  mutableSet += 42
  mutableSet eq setOf(42)
  mutableSet -= 42
  mutableSet eq setOf<Int>()
}
```

The operators += and -= add and remove elements to Sets, just as with Lists.

Exercises and solutions can be found at www.AtomicKotlin.com.

Maps

A Map connects *keys* to *values* and looks up a value when given a key.

You create a Map by providing key-value pairs to mapOf( ). Using to, we separate each key from its associated value:

```
// Maps/Maps.kt
import atomictest.eq

fun main() {
  val constants = mapOf(
    "Pi" to 3.141,
    "e" to 2.718,
    "phi" to 1.618
  )
  constants eq
    "{Pi=3.141, e=2.718, phi=1.618}"

  // Look up a value from a key:
  constants["e"] eq 2.718              // [1]
  constants.keys eq setOf("Pi", "e", "phi")
  constants.values eq "[3.141, 2.718, 1.618]"

  var s = ""
  // Iterate through key-value pairs:
  for (entry in constants) {           // [2]
    s += "${entry.key}=${entry.value}, "
  }
  s eq "Pi=3.141, e=2.718, phi=1.618,"

  s = ""
  // Unpack during iteration:
  for ((key, value) in constants)      // [3]
    s += "$key=$value, "
  s eq "Pi=3.141, e=2.718, phi=1.618,"
}
```

- **[1]** The `[ ]` operator looks up a value using a key. You can produce all the keys using `keys` and all the values using `values`. Calling `keys` produces a `Set` because all keys in a `Map` must be unique, otherwise you'd have ambiguity during a lookup.
- **[2]** Iterating through a `Map` produces key-value pairs as map entries.
- **[3]** You can unpack keys and values as you iterate.

A plain `Map` is read-only. Here's a `MutableMap`:

```
// Maps/MutableMaps.kt
import atomictest.eq

fun main() {
  val m =
    mutableMapOf(5 to "five", 6 to "six")
  m[5] eq "five"
  m[5] = "5ive"
  m[5] eq "5ive"
  m += 4 to "four"
  m eq mapOf(5 to "5ive",
    4 to "four", 6 to "six")
}
```

`map[key] = value` adds or changes the `value` associated with `key`. You can also explicitly add a pair by saying `map += key to value`.

`mapOf()` and `mutableMapOf()` preserve the order in which the elements are put into the `Map`. This is not guaranteed for other types of `Map`.

A read-only `Map` doesn't allow mutations:

```
// Maps/ReadOnlyMaps.kt
import atomictest.eq

fun main() {
  val m = mapOf(5 to "five", 6 to "six")
  m[5] eq "five"
  // m[5] = "5ive" // Fails
  // m += (4 to "four") // Fails
  m + (4 to "four") // Doesn't change m
  m eq mapOf(5 to "five", 6 to "six")
  val m2 = m + (4 to "four")
  m2 eq mapOf(
    5 to "five", 6 to "six", 4 to "four")
}
```

The definition of m creates a Map associating Ints with Strings. If we try to replace a String, Kotlin emits an error.

An expression with + creates a new Map that includes both the old elements and the new one, but doesn't affect the original Map. The only way to "add" an element to a read-only Map is by creating a new Map.

A Map returns null if it doesn't contain an entry for a given key. If you need a result that can't be null, use getValue() and catch NoSuchElementException if the key is missing:

```
// Maps/GetValue.kt
import atomictest.*

fun main() {
  val map = mapOf('a' to "attempt")
  map['b'] eq null
  capture {
    map.getValue('b')
  } eq "NoSuchElementException: " +
    "Key b is missing in the map."
  map.getOrDefault('a', "??") eq "attempt"
  map.getOrDefault('b', "??") eq "??"
}
```

getOrDefault() is usually a nicer alternative to null or an exception.

You can store class instances as values in a Map. Here's a map that retrieves a Contact using a number String:

```
// Maps/ContactMap.kt
package maps
import atomictest.eq

class Contact(
  val name: String,
  val phone: String
) {
  override fun toString() =
    "Contact('$name', '$phone')"
}

fun main() {
  val miffy = Contact("Miffy", "1-234-567890")
  val cleo = Contact("Cleo", "098-765-4321")
  val contacts = mapOf(
    miffy.phone to miffy,
    cleo.phone to cleo)
  contacts["1-234-567890"] eq miffy
  contacts["1-111-111111"] eq null
}
```

It's possible to use class instances as keys in a Map, but that's trickier so we discuss it later in the book.

- -

Maps look like simple little databases. They are sometimes called *associative arrays*, because they associate keys with values. Although they are quite limited compared to a full-featured database, they are nonetheless remarkably useful (and far more efficient than a database).

Exercises and solutions can be found at www.AtomicKotlin.com.

Property Accessors

To read a property, use its name. To assign a value to a mutable property, use the assignment operator =.

This reads and writes the property i:

```
// PropertyAccessors/Data.kt
package propertyaccessors
import atomictest.eq

class Data(var i: Int)

fun main() {
  val data = Data(10)
  data.i eq 10  // Read the 'i' property
  data.i = 20   // Write to the 'i' property
}
```

This appears to be straightforward access to the piece of storage named i. However, Kotlin calls functions to perform the read and write operations. As you expect, the default behavior of those functions reads and writes the data stored in i. In this atom you'll learn to write your own *property accessors* to customize the reading and writing actions.

The accessor used to get the value of a property is called a *getter*. You create a getter by defining get() immediately after the property definition. The accessor used to modify a mutable property is called a *setter*. You create a setter by defining set() immediately after the property definition.

The property accessors defined in the following example imitate the default implementations generated by Kotlin. We display additional information so you can see that the property accessors are indeed called during reads and writes. We indent get() and set() to visually associate them with the property, but the actual association happens because get() and set() are defined immediately after that property (Kotlin doesn't care about the indentation):

```
// PropertyAccessors/Default.kt
package propertyaccessors
import atomictest.*

class Default {
  var i: Int = 0
    get() {
      trace("get()")
      return field         // [1]
    }
    set(value) {
      trace("set($value)")
      field = value        // [2]
    }
}

fun main() {
  val d = Default()
  d.i = 2
  trace(d.i)
  trace eq """
    set(2)
    get()
    2
  """
}
```

The definition order for get() and set() is unimportant. You can define get() without defining set(), and vice-versa.

The default behavior for a property returns its stored value from a getter and modifies it with a setter—the actions of **[1]** and **[2]**. Inside the getter and setter, the stored value is manipulated indirectly using the field keyword, which is only accessible within these two functions.

This next example uses the default implementation of the getter and adds a setter to trace changes to the property n:

```
// PropertyAccessors/LogChanges.kt
package propertyaccessors
import atomictest.*

class LogChanges {
  var n: Int = 0
    set(value) {
      trace("$field becomes $value")
      field = value
    }
}

fun main() {
  val lc = LogChanges()
  lc.n eq 0
  lc.n = 2
  lc.n eq 2
  trace eq "0 becomes 2"
}
```

If you define a property as `private`, both accessors become `private`. You can also make the setter `private` and the getter `public`. Then you can read the property outside the class, but only change its value inside the class:

```
// PropertyAccessors/Counter.kt
package propertyaccessors
import atomictest.eq

class Counter {
  var value: Int = 0
    private set
  fun inc() = value++
}

fun main() {
  val counter = Counter()
  repeat(10) {
    counter.inc()
  }
  counter.value eq 10
}
```

Using `private set`, we control the `value` property so it can only be incremented by one.

Normal properties store their data in a field. You can also create a property that doesn't have a field:

```
// PropertyAccessors/Hamsters.kt
package propertyaccessors
import atomictest.eq

class Hamster(val name: String)

class Cage(private val maxCapacity: Int) {
  private val hamsters =
    mutableListOf<Hamster>()
  val capacity: Int
    get() = maxCapacity - hamsters.size
  val full: Boolean
    get() = hamsters.size == maxCapacity
  fun put(hamster: Hamster): Boolean =
    if (full)
      false
    else {
      hamsters += hamster
      true
    }
  fun take(): Hamster =
    hamsters.removeAt(0)
}

fun main() {
  val cage = Cage(2)
  cage.full eq false
  cage.capacity eq 2
  cage.put(Hamster("Alice")) eq true
  cage.put(Hamster("Bob")) eq true
  cage.full eq true
  cage.capacity eq 0
  cage.put(Hamster("Charlie")) eq false
  cage.take()
  cage.capacity eq 1
}
```

The properties `capacity` and `full` contain no underlying state—they are computed at the time of each access. Both `capacity` and `full` are similar to functions, and you can define them as such:

```
// PropertyAccessors/Hamsters2.kt
package propertyaccessors

class Cage2(private val maxCapacity: Int) {
  private val hamsters =
    mutableListOf<Hamster>()
  fun capacity(): Int =
    maxCapacity - hamsters.size
  fun isFull(): Boolean =
    hamsters.size == maxCapacity
}
```

In this case, using properties improves readability because capacity and fullness are properties of the cage. However, don't just convert all your functions to properties—first, see how they read.

- -

The Kotlin style guide prefers properties over functions when the value is cheap to calculate and the property returns the same result for each invocation as long as the object state hasn't changed.

Property accessors provide a kind of protection for properties. Many object-oriented languages rely on making a physical field `private` to control access to that property. With property accessors you can add code to control or modify that access, while allowing anyone to use a property.

Exercises and solutions can be found at www.AtomicKotlin.com.

Summary 2

This atom summarizes and reviews the atoms in Section II, from *Objects Everywhere* through *Property Accessors*.

If you're an experienced programmer, this is your next atom after *Summary 1*, and you will go through the atoms sequentially after this.

New programmers should read this atom and perform the exercises as review. If any information here isn't clear to you, go back and study the atom for that topic.

The topics appear in appropriate order for experienced programmers, which is not the same as the order of the atoms in the book. For example, we start by introducing packages and imports so we can use our minimal test framework for the rest of the atom.

Packages & Testing

Any number of reusable library components can be bundled under a single library name using the `package` keyword:

```
// Summary2/ALibrary.kt
package com.yoururl.libraryname

// Components to reuse ...
fun f() = "result"
```

You can put multiple components in a single file, or spread components out among multiple files under the same package name. Here we've defined `f()` as the sole component.

To make it unique, the package name conventionally begins with your reversed domain name. In this example, the domain name is `yoururl.com`.

In Kotlin, the package name can be independent from the directory where its contents are located. Java requires that the directory structure correspond to the fully-qualified package name, so the package com.yoururl.libraryname should be located under the com/yoururl/libraryname directory. For mixed Kotlin and Java projects, Kotlin's style guide recommends the same practice. For pure Kotlin projects, put the directory libraryname at the top level of your project's directory structure.

An import statement brings one or more names into the current namespace:

```
// Summary2/UseALibrary.kt
import com.yoururl.libraryname.*

fun main() {
  val x = f()
}
```

The star after libraryname tells Kotlin to import all the components of a library. You can also select components individually; details are in *Packages*.

In the remainder of this book we use package statements for any file that defines functions, classes, etc., outside of main(). This prevents name clashes with other files in the book. We usually won't put a package statement in a file that *only* contains a main().

An important library for this book is atomictest, our simple testing framework. atomictest is defined in *Appendix A: AtomicTest*, although it uses language features you will not understand at this point in the book.

After importing atomictest, you use eq (equals) and neq (not equals) almost as if they were language keywords:

```
// Summary2/UsingAtomicTest.kt
import atomictest.*

fun main() {
  val pi = 3.14
  val pie = "A round dessert"
  pi eq 3.14
  pie eq "A round dessert"
  pi neq pie
}
/* Output:
3.14
A round dessert
3.14
*/
```

The ability to use eq/neq without any dots or parentheses is called *infix notation*. You can call infix functions either in the regular way: pi.eq(3.14), or using infix notation: pi eq 3.14. Both eq and neq are assertions of truth that also display the result from the left side of the eq/neq statement, and an error message if the expression on the right of the eq isn't equivalent to the left (or *is* equivalent, in the case of neq). This way you see verified results in the source code.

atomictest.trace uses function-call syntax for adding results, which can then be validated using eq:

```
// Testing/UsingTrace.kt
import atomictest.*

fun main() {
  trace("Hello,")
  trace(47)
  trace("World!")
  trace eq """
    Hello,
    47
    World!
  """
}
```

You can effectively replace println() with trace().

Objects Everywhere

Kotlin is a *hybrid object-functional* language: it supports both object-oriented and functional programming paradigms.

Objects contain vals and vars to store data (these are called *properties*) and perform operations using functions defined within a class, called *member functions* (when it's unambiguous, we just say "functions"). A *class* defines properties and member functions for what is essentially a new, user-defined data type. When you create a val or var of a class, it's called *creating an object* or *creating an instance*.

An especially useful type of object is the *container*, also called *collection*. A container is an object that holds other objects. In this book, we often use the List because it's the most general-purpose sequence. Here we perform several operations on a List that holds Doubles. listOf() creates a new List from its arguments:

```
// Summary2/ListCollection.kt
import atomictest.eq

fun main() {
  val lst = listOf(19.2, 88.3, 22.1)
  lst[1] eq 88.3  // Indexing
  lst.reversed() eq listOf(22.1, 88.3, 19.2)
  lst.sorted() eq listOf(19.2, 22.1, 88.3)
  lst.sum() eq 129.6
}
```

No import statement is required to use a List.

Kotlin uses square brackets for indexing into sequences. Indexing is zero-based.

This example also shows a few of the many standard library functions available for Lists: sorted(), reversed(), and sum(). To understand these functions, consult the online Kotlin documentation[28].

When you call sorted() or reversed(), lst is not modified. Instead, a new List is created and returned, containing the desired result. This approach of never modifying the original object is consistent throughout Kotlin libraries and you should endeavor to follow this pattern when writing your own code.

---

[28] https://kotlinlang.org/docs/reference/

Creating Classes

A class definition consists of the `class` keyword, a name for the class, and an optional body. The body contains property definitions (`val`s and `var`s) and function definitions.

This example defines a `NoBody` class without a body, and classes with `val` properties:

```
// Summary2/ClassBodies.kt
package summary2

class NoBody

class SomeBody {
  val name = "Janet Doe"
}

class EveryBody {
  val all = listOf(SomeBody(),
    SomeBody(), SomeBody())
}

fun main() {
  val nb = NoBody()
  val sb = SomeBody()
  val eb = EveryBody()
}
```

To create an instance of a class, put parentheses after its name, along with arguments if those are required.

Properties within class bodies can be any type. `SomeBody` contains a property of type `String`, and `EveryBody`'s property is a `List` holding `SomeBody` objects.

Here's a class with member functions:

```kotlin
// Summary2/Temperature.kt
package summary2
import atomictest.eq

class Temperature {
  var current = 0.0
  var scale = "f"
  fun setFahrenheit(now: Double) {
    current = now
    scale = "f"
  }
  fun setCelsius(now: Double) {
    current = now
    scale = "c"
  }
  fun getFahrenheit(): Double =
    if (scale == "f")
      current
    else
      current * 9.0 / 5.0 + 32.0
  fun getCelsius(): Double =
    if (scale == "c")
      current
    else
      (current - 32.0) * 5.0 / 9.0
}

fun main() {
  val temp = Temperature()    // [1]
  temp.setFahrenheit(98.6)
  temp.getFahrenheit() eq 98.6
  temp.getCelsius() eq 37.0
  temp.setCelsius(100.0)
  temp.getFahrenheit() eq 212.0
}
```

These member functions are just like the top-level functions we've defined *outside* of classes, except they belong to the class and have unqualified access to the other members of the class, such as `current` and `scale`. Member functions can also call other member functions in the same class without qualification.

- **[1]** Although `temp` is a `val`, we later modify the `Temperature` object. The `val` definition prevents the reference `temp` from being reassigned to a new object, but it does not restrict the behavior of the object itself.

The following two classes are the foundation of a tic-tac-toe game:

```
// Summary2/TicTacToe.kt
package summary2
import atomictest.eq

class Cell {
  var entry = ' '                        // [1]
  fun setValue(e: Char): String =        // [2]
    if (entry == ' ' &&
      (e == 'X' || e == 'O')) {
      entry = e
      "Successful move"
    } else
      "Invalid move"
}

class Grid {
  val cells = listOf(
    listOf(Cell(), Cell(), Cell()),
    listOf(Cell(), Cell(), Cell()),
    listOf(Cell(), Cell(), Cell())
  )
  fun play(e: Char, x: Int, y: Int): String =
    if (x !in 0..2 || y !in 0..2)
      "Invalid move"
    else
      cells[x][y].setValue(e)            // [3]
}

fun main() {
  val grid = Grid()
  grid.play('X', 1, 1) eq "Successful move"
  grid.play('X', 1, 1) eq "Invalid move"
  grid.play('O', 1, 3) eq "Invalid move"
}
```

The `Grid` class holds a `List` containing three `List`s, each containing three `Cell`s—a matrix.

- [1] The `entry` property in `Cell` is a `var` so it can be modified. The single quotes in the initialization produce a `Char` type, so all assignments to `entry` must also be `Char`s.
- [2] `setValue()` tests that the `Cell` is available and that you've passed the correct character. It returns a `String` result to indicate success or failure.
- [3] `play()` checks to see if the `x` and `y` arguments are within range, then indexes into the matrix, relying on the tests performed by `setValue()`.

Constructors

Constructors create new objects. You pass information to a constructor using its parameter list, placed in parentheses directly after the class name. A constructor call thus looks like a function call, except that the initial letter of the name is capitalized (following the Kotlin style guide). The constructor returns an object of the class:

```
// Summary2/WildAnimals.kt
package summary2
import atomictest.eq

class Badger(id: String, years: Int) {
  val name = id
  val age = years
  override fun toString() =
    "Badger: $name, age: $age"
}

class Snake(
  var type: String,
  var length: Double
) {
  override fun toString() =
    "Snake: $type, length: $length"
}

class Moose(
  val age: Int,
  val height: Double
) {
```

```
  override fun toString() =
    "Moose, age: $age, height: $height"
}

fun main() {
  Badger("Bob", 11) eq "Badger: Bob, age: 11"
  Snake("Garden", 2.4) eq
    "Snake: Garden, length: 2.4"
  Moose(16, 7.2) eq
    "Moose, age: 16, height: 7.2"
}
```

The parameters id and years in Badger are only available in the *constructor body*. The constructor body consists of the lines of code other than function definitions; in this case, the definitions for name and age.

Often you want the constructor parameters to be available in parts of the class other than the constructor body, but without the trouble of explicitly defining new identifiers as we did with name and age. If you define your parameters as vars or vals, they becomes properties and are accessible everywhere in the class. Both Snake and Moose use this approach, and you can see that the constructor parameters are now available inside their respective toString() functions.

Constructor parameters declared with val cannot be changed, but those declared with var can.

Whenever you use an object in a situation that expects a String, Kotlin produces a String representation of that object by calling its toString() member function. To define a toString(), you must understand a new keyword: override. This is necessary (Kotlin insists on it) because toString() is already defined. override tells Kotlin that we do actually want to replace the default toString() with our own definition. The explicitness of override makes this clear to the reader and helps prevent mistakes.

Notice the formatting of the multiline parameter list for Snake and Moose—this is the recommended standard when you have too many parameters to fit on one line, for both constructors and functions.

Constraining Visibility

Kotlin provides *access modifiers* similar to those available in other languages like C++ or Java. These allow component creators to decide what is available to the client programmer. Kotlin's access modifiers include the `public`, `private`, `protected`, and `internal` keywords. `protected` is explained later.

An access modifier like `public` or `private` appears before the definition for a class, function or property. Each access modifier only controls the access for that particular definition.

A `public` definition is available to everyone, in particular to the client programmer who uses that component. Thus, any changes to a `public` definition will impact client code.

If you don't provide a modifier, your definition is automatically `public`. For clarity in certain cases, programmers still sometimes redundantly specify `public`.

If you define a class, top-level function, or property as `private`, it is available only within that file:

```
// Summary2/Boxes.kt
package summary2
import atomictest.*

private var count = 0                      // [1]

private class Box(val dimension: Int) {    // [2]
  fun volume() =
    dimension * dimension * dimension
  override fun toString() =
    "Box volume: ${volume()}"
}

private fun countBox(box: Box) {           // [3]
  trace("$box")
  count++
}

fun countBoxes() {
  countBox(Box(4))
```

```
  countBox(Box(5))
}

fun main() {
  countBoxes()
  trace("$count boxes")
  trace eq """
    Box volume: 64
    Box volume: 125
    2 boxes
  """
}
```

You can access private properties (**[1]**), classes (**[2]**), and functions (**[3]**) only from other functions and classes in the Boxes.kt file. Kotlin prevents you from accessing private top-level elements from another file.

Class members can be private:

```
// Summary2/JetPack.kt
package summary2
import atomictest.eq

class JetPack(
  private var fuel: Double    // [1]
) {
  private var warning = false
  private fun burn() =         // [2]
    if (fuel - 1 <= 0) {
      fuel = 0.0
      warning = true
    } else
      fuel -= 1
  public fun fly() = burn()   // [3]
  fun check() =               // [4]
    if (warning)              // [5]
      "Warning"
    else
      "OK"
}

fun main() {
```

```
  val jetPack = JetPack(3.0)
  while (jetPack.check() != "Warning") {
    jetPack.check() eq "OK"
    jetPack.fly()
  }
  jetPack.check() eq "Warning"
}
```

- **[1]** `fuel` and `warning` are both `private` properties and can't be used by non-members of `JetPack`.
- **[2]** `burn()` is `private`, and thus only accessible inside `JetPack`.
- **[3]** `fly()` and `check()` are `public` and can be used everywhere.
- **[4]** No access modifier means `public` visibility.
- **[5]** Only members of the same class can access `private` members.

Because a `private` definition is *not* available to everyone, you can generally change it without concern for the client programmer. As a library designer, you'll typically keep everything as `private` as possible, and expose only functions and classes you want client programmers to use. To limit the size and complexity of example listings in this book, we only use `private` in special cases.

Any function you're certain is only a *helper function* can be made `private`, to ensure you don't accidentally use it elsewhere and thus prohibit yourself from changing or removing the function.

It can be useful to divide large programs into *modules*. A module is a logically independent part of a codebase. An `internal` definition is accessible only inside the module where it is defined. The way you divide a project into modules depends on the build system (such as Gradle[29] or Maven[30]) and is beyond the scope of this book.

Modules are a higher-level concept, while *packages* enable finer-grained structuring.

Exceptions

Consider `toDouble()`, which converts a `String` to a `Double`. What happens if you call it for a `String` that doesn't translate into a `Double`?

[29] https://gradle.org/
[30] https://maven.apache.org/

```
// Summary2/ToDoubleException.kt

fun main() {
  // val i = "$1.9".toDouble()
}
```

Uncommenting the line in main() produces an exception. Here, the failing line is commented so we don't stop the book's build (which checks whether each example compiles and runs as expected).

When an exception is thrown, the current path of execution stops, and the exception object ejects from the current context. When an exception isn't caught, the program aborts and displays a *stack trace* containing detailed information.

To avoid displaying exceptions by commenting and uncommenting code, atomictest.capture() stores the exception and compares it to what we expect:

```
// Summary2/AtomicTestCapture.kt
import atomictest.*

fun main() {
  capture {
    "$1.9".toDouble()
  } eq "NumberFormatException: " +
    """For input string: "$1.9""""
}
```

capture() is designed specifically for this book, so you can see the exception and know that the output has been checked by the book's build system.

Another strategy when your function can't successfully produce the expected result is to return null. Later in **Nullable Types** we discuss how null affects the type of the resulting expression.

To throw an exception, use the throw keyword followed by the exception you want to throw, along with any arguments it might need. quadraticZeroes() in the following example solves the quadratic equation[31] that defines a parabola:

$ax^2 + bx + c = 0$

The solution is the *quadratic formula*:

---
[31] https://en.wikipedia.org/wiki/Quadratic_formula

$$x = \frac{-b \pm \sqrt{b^2 - 4ac}}{2a}$$

The Quadratic Formula

The example finds the *zeroes* of the parabola, where the lines cross the x-axis. We throw exceptions for two limitations:

1. a cannot be zero.
2. For zeroes to exist, **b²** - **4ac** cannot be negative.

If zeroes exist, there are two of them, so we create the Roots class to hold the return values:

```
// Summary2/Quadratic.kt
package summary2
import kotlin.math.sqrt
import atomictest.*

class Roots(
  val root1: Double,
  val root2: Double
)

fun quadraticZeroes(
  a: Double,
  b: Double,
  c: Double
): Roots {
  if (a == 0.0)
    throw IllegalArgumentException(
      "a is zero")
  val underRadical = b * b - 4 * a * c
  if (underRadical < 0)
    throw IllegalArgumentException(
      "Negative underRadical: $underRadical")
  val squareRoot = sqrt(underRadical)
  val root1 = (-b - squareRoot) / (2 * a)
  val root2 = (-b + squareRoot) / (2 * a)
  return Roots(root1, root2)
}
```

```kotlin
fun main() {
  capture {
    quadraticZeroes(0.0, 4.0, 5.0)
  } eq "IllegalArgumentException: " +
    "a is zero"
  capture {
    quadraticZeroes(3.0, 4.0, 5.0)
  } eq "IllegalArgumentException: " +
    "Negative underRadical: -44.0"
  val roots = quadraticZeroes(1.0, 2.0, -8.0)
  roots.root1 eq -4.0
  roots.root2 eq 2.0
}
```

Here we use the standard exception class `IllegalArgumentException`. Later you'll learn to define your own exception types and to make them specific to your circumstances. Your goal is to generate the most useful messages possible, to simplify the support of your application in the future.

Lists

`Lists` are Kotlin's basic sequential container type. You create a read-only list using `listOf()` and a mutable list using `mutableListOf()`:

```kotlin
// Summary2/ReadonlyVsMutableList.kt
import atomictest.*

fun main() {
  val ints = listOf(5, 13, 9)
  // ints.add(11) // 'add()' not available
  for (i in ints) {
    if (i > 10) {
      trace(i)
    }
  }
  val chars = mutableListOf('a', 'b', 'c')
  chars.add('d') // 'add()' available
  chars += 'e'
```

```
  trace(chars)
  trace eq """
    13
    [a, b, c, d, e]
  """
}
```

A basic List is read-only, and does not include modification functions. Thus, the modification function add() doesn't work with ints.

for loops work well with Lists: for(i in ints) means i gets each value in ints.

chars is created as a MutableList; it can be modified using functions like add() or remove(). You can also use += and -= to add or remove elements.

A read-only List is not the same as an *immutable* List, which can't be modified at all. Here, we assign first, a mutable List, to second, a read-only List reference. The read-only characteristic of second doesn't prevent the List from changing via first:

```
// Summary2/MultipleListReferences.kt
import atomictest.eq

fun main() {
  val first = mutableListOf(1)
  val second: List<Int> = first
  second eq listOf(1)
  first += 2
  // second sees the change:
  second eq listOf(1, 2)
}
```

first and second refer to the same object in memory. We mutate the List via the first reference, and then observe this change in the second reference.

Here's a List of Strings created by breaking up a triple-quoted paragraph. This shows the power of some of the standard library functions. Notice how those functions can be chained:

```
// Summary2/ListOfStrings.kt
import atomictest.*

fun main() {
  val wocky = """
    Twas brillig, and the slithy toves
      Did gyre and gimble in the wabe:
    All mimsy were the borogoves,
      And the mome raths outgrabe.
  """.trim().split(Regex("\\W+"))
  trace(wocky.take(5))
  trace(wocky.slice(6..12))
  trace(wocky.slice(6..18 step 2))
  trace(wocky.sorted().takeLast(5))
  trace(wocky.sorted().distinct().takeLast(5))
  trace eq """
    [Twas, brillig, and, the, slithy]
    [Did, gyre, and, gimble, in, the, wabe]
    [Did, and, in, wabe, mimsy, the, And]
    [the, the, toves, wabe, were]
    [slithy, the, toves, wabe, were]
  """
}
```

trim() produces a new String with the leading and trailing whitespace characters (including newlines) removed. split() divides the String according to its argument. In this case we use a Regex object, which creates a *regular expression*—a pattern that matches the parts to split. \W is a special pattern that means "not a word character," and + means "one or more of the preceding." Thus split() will break at one or more non-word characters, and so divides the block of text into its component words.

In a String literal, \ precedes a special character and produces, for example, a newline character (\n), or a tab (\t). To produce an actual \ in the resulting String you need two backslashes: "\\". Thus all regular expressions require an extra \ to insert a backslash, unless you use a triple-quoted String: """\W+""".

take(n) produces a new List containing the first n elements. slice() produces a new List containing the elements selected by its Range argument, and this Range can include a step.

Note the name sorted() instead of sort(). When you call sorted() it *produces* a sorted List, leaving the original List alone. sort() only works with a MutableList, and that list is *sorted in place*—the original List is modified.

As the name implies, takeLast(n) produces a new List of the last n elements. You can see from the output that "the" is duplicated. This is eliminated by adding the distinct() function to the call chain.

Parameterized Types

Type parameters allow us to describe compound types, most commonly containers. In particular, type parameters specify what a container holds. Here, we tell Kotlin that numbers contain a List of Int, while strings contain a List of String:

```
// Summary2/ExplicitTyping.kt
package summary2
import atomictest.eq

fun main() {
  val numbers: List<Int> = listOf(1, 2, 3)
  val strings: List<String> =
    listOf("one", "two", "three")
  numbers eq "[1, 2, 3]"
  strings eq "[one, two, three]"
  toCharList("seven") eq "[s, e, v, e, n]"
}

fun toCharList(s: String): List<Char> =
  s.toList()
```

For both the numbers and strings definitions, we add colons and the type declarations List<Int> and List<String>. The angle brackets denote a *type parameter*, allowing us to say, "the container holds 'parameter' objects." You typically pronounce List<Int> as "List of Int."

A return value can also have a type parameter, as seen in toCharList(). You can't just say it returns a List—Kotlin complains, so you must give the type parameter as well.

Variable Argument Lists

The `vararg` keyword is short for *variable argument list*, and allows a function to accept any number of arguments (including zero) of the specified type. The `vararg` becomes an `Array`, which is similar to a `List`:

```
// Summary2/VarArgs.kt
package summary2
import atomictest.*

fun varargs(s: String, vararg ints: Int) {
  for (i in ints) {
    trace("$i")
  }
  trace(s)
}

fun main() {
  varargs("primes", 5, 7, 11, 13, 17, 19, 23)
  trace eq "5 7 11 13 17 19 23 primes"
}
```

A function definition may specify only one parameter as `vararg`. Any parameter in the list can be the `vararg`, but the final one is generally simplest.

You can pass an `Array` of elements wherever a `vararg` is accepted. To create an `Array`, use `arrayOf()` in the same way you use `listOf()`. An `Array` is always mutable. To convert an `Array` into a sequence of arguments (not just a single element of type `Array`), use the *spread operator* `*`:

```
// Summary2/ArraySpread.kt
import summary2.varargs
import atomictest.trace

fun main() {
  val array = intArrayOf(4, 5)        // [1]
  varargs("x", 1, 2, 3, *array, 6)    // [2]
  val list = listOf(9, 10, 11)
  varargs(
    "y", 7, 8, *list.toIntArray())    // [3]
  trace eq "1 2 3 4 5 6 x 7 8 9 10 11 y"
}
```

If you pass an Array of primitive types as in the example above, the Array creation function must be specifically typed. If **[1]** uses arrayOf(4, 5) instead of intArrayOf(4, 5), **[2]** produces an error: *inferred type is Array<Int> but IntArray was expected.*

The spread operator only works with arrays. If you have a List to pass as a sequence of arguments, first convert it to an Array and then apply the spread operator, as in **[3]**. Because the result is an Array of a primitive type, we must use the specific conversion function toIntArray().

Sets

Sets are collections that allow only one element of each value. A Set automatically prevents duplicates.

```
// Summary2/ColorSet.kt
package summary2
import atomictest.eq

val colors =
  "Yellow Green Green Blue"
    .split(Regex("""\W+""")).sorted()  // [1]

fun main() {
  colors eq
    listOf("Blue", "Green", "Green", "Yellow")
```

```
  val colorSet = colors.toSet()         // [2]
  colorSet eq
    setOf("Yellow", "Green", "Blue")
  (colorSet + colorSet) eq colorSet     // [3]
  val mSet = colorSet.toMutableSet()    // [4]
  mSet -= "Blue"
  mSet += "Red"                         // [5]
  mSet eq
    setOf("Yellow", "Green", "Red")
  // Set membership:
  ("Green" in colorSet) eq true         // [6]
  colorSet.contains("Red") eq false
}
```

- [1] The `String` is `split()` using a regular expression as described earlier for `ListOfStrings.kt`.
- [2] When `colors` is copied into the read-only `Set` `colorSet`, one of the two `"Green"` `String`s is removed, because it is a duplicate.
- [3] Here we create and display a new `Set` using the `+` operator. Placing duplicate items into a `Set` automatically removes those duplicates.
- [4] `toMutableSet()` produces a new `MutableSet` from a read-only `Set`.
- [5] For a `MutableSet`, the operators `+=` and `-=` add and remove elements, as they do with `MutableList`s.
- [6] Test for `Set` membership using `in` or `contains()`

The normal mathematical set operations such as union, intersection, difference, etc., are all available.

Maps

A `Map` connects *keys* to *values* and looks up a value when given a key. You create a `Map` by providing key-value pairs to `mapOf()`. Using `to`, we separate each key from its associated value:

```kotlin
// Summary2/ASCIIMap.kt
import atomictest.eq

fun main() {
  val ascii = mapOf(
    "A" to 65,
    "B" to 66,
    "C" to 67,
    "I" to 73,
    "J" to 74,
    "K" to 75
  )
  ascii eq
    "{A=65, B=66, C=67, I=73, J=74, K=75}"
  ascii["B"] eq 66                    // [1]
  ascii.keys eq "[A, B, C, I, J, K]"
  ascii.values eq
    "[65, 66, 67, 73, 74, 75]"
  var kv = ""
  for (entry in ascii) {              // [2]
    kv += "${entry.key}:${entry.value},"
  }
  kv eq "A:65,B:66,C:67,I:73,J:74,K:75,"
  kv = ""
  for ((key, value) in ascii)         // [3]
    kv += "$key:$value,"
  kv eq "A:65,B:66,C:67,I:73,J:74,K:75,"
  val mutable = ascii.toMutableMap() // [4]
  mutable.remove("I")
  mutable eq
    "{A=65, B=66, C=67, J=74, K=75}"
  mutable.put("Z", 90)
  mutable eq
    "{A=65, B=66, C=67, J=74, K=75, Z=90}"
  mutable.clear()
  mutable["A"] = 100
  mutable eq "{A=100}"
}
```

- [1] A key ("B") is used to look up a value with the [] operator. You can produce all the keys using keys and all the values using values. Accessing keys

produces a Set because all keys in a Map must already be unique (otherwise you'd have ambiguity during a lookup).
- [2] Iterating through a Map produces key-value pairs as map entries.
- [3] You can unpack key-value pairs as you iterate.
- [4] You can create a MutableMap from a read-only Map using toMutableMap(). Now we can perform operations that modify mutable, such as remove(), put(), and clear(). Square brackets can assign a new key-value pair into mutable. You can also add a pair by saying map += key to value.

Property Accessors

Accessing the property i appears straightforward:

```
// Summary2/PropertyReadWrite.kt
package summary2
import atomictest.eq

class Holder(var i: Int)

fun main() {
  val holder = Holder(10)
  holder.i eq 10 // Read the 'i' property
  holder.i = 20  // Write to the 'i' property
}
```

However, Kotlin calls functions to perform the read and write operations. The default behavior of those functions is to read and write the data stored in i. By creating *property accessors*, you change the actions that occur during reading and writing.

The accessor used to fetch the value of a property is called a *getter*. To create your own getter, define get() immediately after the property declaration. The accessor used to modify a mutable property is called a *setter*. To create your own setter, define set() immediately after the property declaration. The order of definition of getters and setters is unimportant, and you can define one without the other.

The property accessors in the following example imitate the default implementations while displaying additional information so you can see that the property accessors are indeed called during reads and writes. We indent the get() and set() functions to visually associate them with the property, but the actual association happens because they are defined immediately after that property:

```kotlin
// Summary2/GetterAndSetter.kt
package summary2
import atomictest.*

class GetterAndSetter {
  var i: Int = 0
    get() {
      trace("get()")
      return field
    }
    set(value) {
      trace("set($value)")
      field = value
    }
}

fun main() {
  val gs = GetterAndSetter()
  gs.i = 2
  trace(gs.i)
  trace eq """
    set(2)
    get()
    2
  """
}
```

Inside the getter and setter, the stored value is manipulated indirectly using the `field` keyword, which is only accessible within these two functions. You can also create a property that doesn't have a `field`, but simply calls the getter to produce a result.

If you declare a `private` property, both accessors become `private`. You can make the setter `private` and the getter `public`. This means you can read the property outside the class, but only change its value inside the class.

Exercises and solutions can be found at www.AtomicKotlin.com.

Section III: Usability

Computer languages differ not so much in what they make possible, but in what they make easy—**Larry Wall**, inventor of the Perl language

Extension Functions

Suppose you discover a library that does everything you need ... almost. If it only had one or two additional member functions, it would solve your problem perfectly.

But it's not your code—either you don't have access to the source code or you don't control it. You'd have to repeat your modifications every time a new version came out.

Kotlin's *extension functions* effectively add member functions to existing classes. The type you extend is called the *receiver*. To define an extension function, you precede the function name with the receiver type:

```
fun ReceiverType.extensionFunction() { ... }
```

This adds two extension functions to the String class:

```
// ExtensionFunctions/Quoting.kt
package extensionfunctions
import atomictest.eq

fun String.singleQuote() = "'$this'"
fun String.doubleQuote() = "\"$this\""

fun main() {
  "Hi".singleQuote() eq "'Hi'"
  "Hi".doubleQuote() eq "\"Hi\""
}
```

You call extension functions as if they were members of the class.

To use extensions from another package, you must import them:

```
// ExtensionFunctions/Quote.kt
package other
import atomictest.eq
import extensionfunctions.doubleQuote
import extensionfunctions.singleQuote

fun main() {
  "Single".singleQuote() eq "'Single'"
  "Double".doubleQuote() eq "\"Double\""
}
```

You can access member functions or other extensions using the `this` keyword. `this` can also be omitted in the same way it can be omitted inside a class, so you don't need explicit qualification:

```
// ExtensionFunctions/StrangeQuote.kt
package extensionfunctions
import atomictest.eq

// Apply two sets of single quotes:
fun String.strangeQuote() =
  this.singleQuote().singleQuote()   // [1]

fun String.tooManyQuotes() =
  doubleQuote().doubleQuote()        // [2]

fun main() {
  "Hi".strangeQuote() eq "''Hi''"
  "Hi".tooManyQuotes() eq "\"\"Hi\"\""
}
```

- [1] `this` refers to the `String` receiver.
- [2] We omit the receiver object (`this`) of the first `doubleQuote()` function call.

Creating extensions to your own classes can sometimes produce simpler code:

```
// ExtensionFunctions/BookExtensions.kt
package extensionfunctions
import atomictest.eq

class Book(val title: String)

fun Book.categorize(category: String) =
  """title: "$title", category: $category"""

fun main() {
  Book("Dracula").categorize("Vampire") eq
    """title: "Dracula", category: Vampire"""
}
```

Inside `categorize()`, we access the `title` property without explicit qualification.

- -

Extension functions can only access `public` elements of the type being extended. Thus, extensions can only perform the same actions as regular functions. You can rewrite `Book.categorize(String)` as `categorize(Book, String)`. The only reason for using an extension function is the syntax, but this syntax sugar is powerful. To the calling code, extensions look the same as member functions, and IDEs show extensions when listing the functions that you can call for an object.

Exercises and solutions can be found at www.AtomicKotlin.com.

Named & Default Arguments

> You can provide argument names during a function call.

Named arguments improve code readability. This is especially true for long and complex argument lists—named arguments can be clear enough that the reader can understand a function call without looking at the documentation.

In this example, all parameters are `Int`. Named arguments clarify their meaning:

```
// NamedAndDefaultArgs/NamedArguments.kt
package color1
import atomictest.eq

fun color(red: Int, green: Int, blue: Int) =
  "($red, $green, $blue)"

fun main() {
  color(1, 2, 3) eq "(1, 2, 3)"   // [1]
  color(
    red = 76,                      // [2]
    green = 89,
    blue = 0
  ) eq "(76, 89, 0)"
  color(52, 34, blue = 0) eq       // [3]
    "(52, 34, 0)"
}
```

- **[1]** This doesn't tell you much. You'll have to look at the documentation to know what the arguments mean.
- **[2]** The meaning of every argument is clear.
- **[3]** You aren't required to name all arguments.

Named arguments allow you to change the order of the colors. Here, we specify `blue` first:

```
// NamedAndDefaultArgs/ArgumentOrder.kt
import color1.color
import atomictest.eq

fun main() {
  color(blue = 0, red = 99, green = 52) eq
    "(99, 52, 0)"
  color(red = 255, 255, 0) eq
    "(255, 255, 0)"
}
```

You can mix named and regular (positional) arguments. If you change argument order, you should use named arguments throughout the call—not only for readability, but the compiler often needs to be told where the arguments are.

Named arguments are even more useful when combined with *default arguments*, which are default values for arguments, specified in the function definition:

```
// NamedAndDefaultArgs/Color2.kt
package color2
import atomictest.eq

fun color(
  red: Int = 0,
  green: Int = 0,
  blue: Int = 0,
) = "($red, $green, $blue)"

fun main() {
  color(139) eq "(139, 0, 0)"
  color(blue = 139) eq "(0, 0, 139)"
  color(255, 165) eq "(255, 165, 0)"
  color(red = 128, blue = 128) eq
    "(128, 0, 128)"
}
```

Any argument you don't provide gets its default value, so you only need to provide arguments that differ from the defaults. If you have a long argument list, this simplifies the resulting code, making it easier to write and—more importantly—to read.

This example also uses a *trailing comma* in the definition for color(). The trailing comma is the extra comma after the last parameter (blue). This is useful when your parameters or values are written on multiple lines. With a trailing comma, you can add new items and change their order without adding or removing commas.

Named and default arguments (as well as trailing commas) also work for constructors:

```
// NamedAndDefaultArgs/Color3.kt
package color3
import atomictest.eq

class Color(
  val red: Int = 0,
  val green: Int = 0,
  val blue: Int = 0,
) {
  override fun toString() =
    "($red, $green, $blue)"
}

fun main() {
  Color(red = 77).toString() eq "(77, 0, 0)"
}
```

joinToString() is a standard library function that uses default arguments. It combines the contents of an iterable (a list, set or range) into a String. You can specify a separator, a prefix element and a postfix element:

```
// NamedAndDefaultArgs/CreateString.kt
import atomictest.eq

fun main() {
  val list = listOf(1, 2, 3,)
  list.toString() eq "[1, 2, 3]"
  list.joinToString() eq "1, 2, 3"
  list.joinToString(prefix = "(",
    postfix = ")") eq "(1, 2, 3)"
  list.joinToString(separator = ":") eq
    "1:2:3"
}
```

The default `toString()` for a `List` returns the contents in square brackets, which might not be what you want. The default values for `joinToString()`s parameters are a comma for `separator` and empty `String`s for `prefix` and `postfix`. In the above example, we use named and default arguments to specify only the arguments we want to change.

The initializer for `list` includes a trailing comma. Normally you'll only use a trailing comma when each element is on its own line.

If you use an object as a default argument, a new instance of that object is created for each invocation:

If you pass an object instance as a default argument (`da` within `g()` in the following example), that same instance is used for each call to `g()`. If you pass the syntax for a constructor call (`DefaultArg()` within `h()`), that constructor is called every time you call `h()`:

```
// NamedAndDefaultArgs/Evaluation.kt
package namedanddefault

class DefaultArg
val da = DefaultArg()

fun g(d: DefaultArg = da) = println(d)

fun h(d: DefaultArg = DefaultArg()) =
  println(d)

fun main() {
  g()
  g()
  h()
  h()
}
/* Sample output:
namedanddefault.DefaultArg@7440e464
namedanddefault.DefaultArg@7440e464
namedanddefault.DefaultArg@49476842
namedanddefault.DefaultArg@78308db1
*/
```

The output of the two `g()` calls shows identical object addresses. For the two calls to h(), the addresses of the `DefaultArg` objects are different, showing that there are two distinct objects.

Specify argument names when they improve readability. Compare the following two calls to `joinToString()`:

```
// NamedAndDefaultArgs/CreateString2.kt
import atomictest.eq

fun main() {
  val list = listOf(1, 2, 3)
  list.joinToString(". ", "", "!") eq
    "1. 2. 3!"
  list.joinToString(separator = ". ",
    postfix = "!") eq "1. 2. 3!"
}
```

It's hard to guess whether ". " or "" is a separator unless you memorize the parameter order, which is impractical.

As another example of default arguments, `trimMargin()` is a standard library function that formats multi-line `String`s. It uses a margin prefix `String` to establish the beginning of each line. `trimMargin()` trims leading whitespace characters followed by the margin prefix from every line of the source `String`. It removes the first and last lines if they are blank:

```
// NamedAndDefaultArgs/TrimMargin.kt
import atomictest.eq

fun main() {
  val poem = """
    |->Last night I saw upon the stair
        |->A little man who wasn't there
          |->He wasn't there again today
|->Oh, how I wish he'd go away."""
  poem.trimMargin() eq
"""->Last night I saw upon the stair
->A little man who wasn't there
->He wasn't there again today
->Oh, how I wish he'd go away."""
  poem.trimMargin(marginPrefix = "|->") eq
"""Last night I saw upon the stair
```

```
A little man who wasn't there
He wasn't there again today
Oh, how I wish he'd go away."""
}
```

The | ("pipe") is the default argument for the margin prefix, and you can replace it with a `String` of your choosing.

Exercises and solutions can be found at www.AtomicKotlin.com.

Overloading

> Languages without support for default arguments often use overloading to imitate that feature.

The term *overload* refers to the name of a function: You use the same name ("overload" that name) for different functions as long as the parameter lists differ. Here, we overload the member function `f()`:

```
// Overloading/Overloading.kt
package overloading
import atomictest.eq

class Overloading {
  fun f() = 0
  fun f(n: Int) = n + 2
}

fun main() {
  val o = Overloading()
  o.f() eq 0
  o.f(11) eq 13
}
```

In `Overloading`, you see two functions with the same name, `f()`. The function's *signature* consists of the name, parameter list and return type. Kotlin distinguishes one function from another by comparing signatures. When overloading functions, the parameter lists must be unique—you cannot overload on return types.

The calls show that they are indeed different functions. A function signature also includes information about the enclosing class (or the receiver type, if it's an extension function).

If a class already has a member function with the same signature as an extension function, Kotlin prefers the member function. However, you can overload the member function with an extension function:

```
// Overloading/MemberVsExtension.kt
package overloading
import atomictest.eq

class My {
  fun foo() = 0
}

fun My.foo() = 1             // [1]

fun My.foo(i: Int) = i + 2   // [2]

fun main() {
  My().foo() eq 0
  My().foo(1) eq 3
}
```

- **[1]** It's senseless to declare an extension that duplicates a member, because it can never be called.
- **[2]** You can overload a member function using an extension function by providing a different parameter list.

Don't use overloading to imitate default arguments. That is, don't do this:

```
// Overloading/WithoutDefaultArguments.kt
package withoutdefaultarguments
import atomictest.eq

fun f(n: Int) = n + 373
fun f() = f(0)

fun main() {
  f() eq 373
}
```

The function without parameters just calls the first function. The two functions can be replaced with a single function by using a default argument:

```
// Overloading/WithDefaultArguments.kt
package withdefaultarguments
import atomictest.eq

fun f(n: Int = 0) = n + 373

fun main() {
  f() eq 373
}
```

In both examples you can call the function either without an argument or by passing an integer value. Prefer the form in `WithDefaultArguments.kt`.

When using overloaded functions together with default arguments, calling the overloaded function searches for the "closest" match. In the following example, the `foo()` call in `main()` does *not* call the first version of the function using its default argument of 99, but instead calls the second version, the one without parameters:

```
// Overloading/OverloadedVsDefaultArg.kt
package overloadingvsdefaultargs
import atomictest.*

fun foo(n: Int = 99) = trace("foo-1-$n")

fun foo() {
  trace("foo-2")
  foo(14)
}

fun main() {
  foo()
  trace eq """
    foo-2
    foo-1-14
  """
}
```

You can never utilize the default argument of 99, because `foo()` always calls the second version of `f()`.

Why is overloading useful? It allows you to express "variations on a theme" more clearly than if you were forced to use different function names. Suppose you want addition functions:

```
// Overloading/OverloadingAdd.kt
package overloading
import atomictest.eq

fun addInt(i: Int, j: Int) = i + j
fun addDouble(i: Double, j: Double) = i + j

fun add(i: Int, j: Int) = i + j
fun add(i: Double, j: Double) = i + j

fun main() {
  addInt(5, 6) eq add(5, 6)
  addDouble(56.23, 44.77) eq
    add(56.23, 44.77)
}
```

addInt() takes two Ints and returns an Int, while addDouble() takes two Doubles and returns a Double. Without overloading, you can't just name the operation add(), so programmers typically conflate *what* with *how* to produce unique names (you can also create unique names using random characters but the typical pattern is to use meaningful information like parameter types). In contrast, the overloaded add() is much clearer.

- -

The lack of overloading in a language is not a terrible hardship, but the feature provides valuable simplification, producing more readable code. With overloading, you just say *what*, which raises the level of abstraction and puts less mental load on the reader. If you want to know *how*, look at the parameters. Notice also that overloading reduces redundancy: If we must say addInt() and addDouble(), then we essentially repeat the parameter information in the function name.

Exercises and solutions can be found at www.AtomicKotlin.com.

when Expressions

> A large part of computer programming is performing an action when a pattern matches.

Anything that simplifies this task is a boon for programmers. If you have more than two or three choices to make, *when expressions* are much nicer than *if expressions*.

A when expression compares a value against a selection of possibilities. It begins with the keyword when and the parenthesized value to compare. This is followed by a body containing a set of possible matches and their associated actions. Each match is an expression followed by a right arrow ->. The arrow is the two separate characters - and > with no white space between them. The expression is evaluated and compared to the target value. If it matches, the expression to the right of the -> produces the result of the when expression.

ordinal() in the following example builds the German word for an ordinal number based on a word for the cardinal number. It matches an integer to a fixed set of numbers to check whether it applies to a general rule or is an exception (which happens painfully often in German):

```
// WhenExpressions/GermanOrdinals.kt
package whenexpressions
import atomictest.eq

val numbers = mapOf(
  1 to "eins", 2 to "zwei", 3 to "drei",
  4 to "vier", 5 to "fuenf", 6 to "sechs",
  7 to "sieben", 8 to "acht", 9 to "neun",
  10 to "zehn", 11 to "elf", 12 to "zwoelf",
  13 to "dreizehn", 14 to "vierzehn",
  15 to "fuenfzehn", 16 to "sechzehn",
  17 to "siebzehn", 18 to "achtzehn",
  19 to "neunzehn", 20 to "zwanzig"
)
```

```
fun ordinal(i: Int): String =
  when (i) {                              // [1]
    1 -> "erste"                          // [2]
    3 -> "dritte"
    7 -> "siebte"
    8 -> "achte"
    20 -> "zwanzigste"
    else -> numbers.getValue(i) + "te"    // [3]
  }

fun main() {
  ordinal(2) eq "zweite"
  ordinal(3) eq "dritte"
  ordinal(11) eq "elfte"
}
```

- [1] The when expression compares i to the match expressions in the body.
- [2] The first successful match completes execution of the when expression—here, a String is produced which becomes the return value of ordinal().
- [3] The else keyword provides a "fall through" when there are no matches. The else case always appears last in the match list. When we test against 2, it doesn't match 1, 3, 7, 8 or 20, and so falls through to the else case.

If you forget the else branch in the example above, the compile-time error is: *'when' expression must be exhaustive, add necessary 'else' branch*. If you treat a when expression as a statement—that is, you don't use the result of the when—you can omit the else branch. Unmatched values are then just ignored.

In the following example, Coordinates reports changes to its properties using *Property Accessors*. The when expression processes each item from inputs:

```kotlin
// WhenExpressions/AnalyzeInput.kt
package whenexpressions
import atomictest.*

class Coordinates {
  var x: Int = 0
    set(value) {
      trace("x gets $value")
      field = value
    }
  var y: Int = 0
    set(value) {
      trace("y gets $value")
      field = value
    }
  override fun toString() = "($x, $y)"
}

fun processInputs(inputs: List<String>) {
  val coordinates = Coordinates()
  for (input in inputs) {
    when (input) {                      // [1]
      "up", "u" -> coordinates.y--      // [2]
      "down", "d" -> coordinates.y++
      "left", "l" -> coordinates.x--
      "right", "r" -> {                 // [3]
        trace("Moving right")
        coordinates.x++
      }
      "nowhere" -> {}                   // [4]
      "exit" -> return                  // [5]
      else -> trace("bad input: $input")
    }
  }
}

fun main() {
  processInputs(listOf("up", "d", "nowhere",
    "left", "right", "exit", "r"))
  trace eq """
    y gets -1
    y gets 0
```

```
    x gets -1
    Moving right
    x gets 0
  """
}
```

- **[1]** `input` is matched against the different options.
- **[2]** You can list several values in one branch using commas. Here, if the user enters either "up" or "u" we interpret it as a move up.
- **[3]** Multiple actions within a branch must be in a block body.
- **[4]** "Doing nothing" is expressed with an empty block.
- **[5]** Returning from the outer function is a valid action within a branch. In this case, the `return` terminates the call to `processInputs()`.

Any expression can be an argument for `when`, and the matches can be any values (not just constants):

```
// WhenExpressions/MatchingAgainstVals.kt
import atomictest.*

fun main() {
  val yes = "A"
  val no = "B"
  for (choice in listOf(yes, no, yes)) {
    when (choice) {
      yes -> trace("Hooray!")
      no -> trace("Too bad!")
    }
    // The same logic using 'if':
    if (choice == yes) trace("Hooray!")
    else if (choice == no) trace("Too bad!")
  }
  trace eq """
    Hooray!
    Hooray!
    Too bad!
    Too bad!
    Hooray!
    Hooray!
  """
}
```

when expressions can overlap the functionality of if expressions. when is more flexible, so prefer it over if when there's a choice.

We can match a Set of values against another Set of values:

```
// WhenExpressions/MixColors.kt
package whenexpressions
import atomictest.eq

fun mixColors(first: String, second: String) =
  when (setOf(first, second)) {
    setOf("red", "blue") -> "purple"
    setOf("red", "yellow") -> "orange"
    setOf("blue", "yellow") -> "green"
    else -> "unknown"
  }

fun main() {
  mixColors("red", "blue") eq "purple"
  mixColors("blue", "red") eq "purple"
  mixColors("blue", "purple") eq "unknown"
}
```

Inside `mixColors()` we use a Set as a when argument and compare it with different Sets. We use a Set because the order of elements is unimportant—we need the same result when we mix "red" and "blue" as when we mix "blue" and "red."

when has a special form that takes no argument. Omitting the argument means the branches can check different Boolean conditions. You can use any Boolean expression as a branch condition. As an example, we rewrite `bmiMetric()` introduced in *Number Types*, first showing the original solution, then using when instead of if:

```
// WhenExpressions/BmiWhen.kt
package whenexpressions
import atomictest.eq

fun bmiMetricOld(
  kg: Double,
  heightM: Double
): String {
  val bmi = kg / (heightM * heightM)
  return if (bmi < 18.5) "Underweight"
    else if (bmi < 25) "Normal weight"
    else "Overweight"
}

fun bmiMetricWithWhen(
  kg: Double,
  heightM: Double
): String {
  val bmi = kg / (heightM * heightM)
  return when {
    bmi < 18.5 -> "Underweight"
    bmi < 25 -> "Normal weight"
    else -> "Overweight"
  }
}

fun main() {
  bmiMetricOld(72.57, 1.727) eq
    bmiMetricWithWhen(72.57, 1.727)
}
```

The solution using when is a more elegant way to choose between several options. The simpler syntax makes it easier to distinguish between those options.

Exercises and solutions can be found at www.AtomicKotlin.com.

Enumerations

An *enumeration* is a collection of names.

Kotlin's `enum class` is a convenient way to manage these names:

```
// Enumerations/Level.kt
package enumerations
import atomictest.eq

enum class Level {
  Overflow, High, Medium, Low, Empty
}

fun main() {
  Level.Medium eq "Medium"
}
```

Creating an enum generates `toString()`s for the enum names.

You must qualify each reference to an enumeration name, as with `Level.Medium` in `main()`. You can eliminate this qualification using an `import` to bring all names from the enumeration into the current *namespace* (namespaces keep names from colliding with each other):

```
// Enumerations/EnumImport.kt
import atomictest.eq
import enumerations.Level.*   // [1]

fun main() {
  Overflow eq "Overflow"
  High eq "High"
}
```

- **[1]** The `*` imports all the names inside the `Level` enumeration, but does *not* import the name `Level`.

You can import enum values into the same file where the enum class is defined:

```
// Enumerations/RecursiveEnumImport.kt
package enumerations
import atomictest.eq
import enumerations.Size.*          // [1]

enum class Size {
  Tiny, Small, Medium, Large, Huge, Gigantic
}

fun main() {
  Gigantic eq "Gigantic"             // [2]
  Size.values().toList() eq          // [3]
    listOf(Tiny, Small, Medium,
      Large, Huge, Gigantic)
  Tiny.ordinal eq 0                  // [4]
  Huge.ordinal eq 4
}
```

- **[1]** We import the values of Size before the Size definition appears in the file.
- **[2]** After the import, we no longer need to qualify access to the enumeration names.
- **[3]** You can iterate through the enumeration names using values(). values() returns an Array, so we call toList() to convert it to a List.
- **[4]** The first declared constant of an enum has an ordinal value of zero. Each subsequent constant receives the next integer value.

You can perform different actions for different enum entries using a when expression. Here we import the name Level, as well as all its entries:

```
// Enumerations/CheckingOptions.kt
package checkingoptions
import atomictest.*
import enumerations.Level
import enumerations.Level.*

fun checkLevel(level: Level) {
  when (level) {
    Overflow -> trace(">>> Overflow!")
    Empty -> trace("Alert: Empty")
    else -> trace("Level $level OK")
  }
}
```

```
}

fun main() {
  checkLevel(Empty)
  checkLevel(Low)
  checkLevel(Overflow)
  trace eq """
    Alert: Empty
    Level Low OK
    >>> Overflow!
  """
}
```

`checkLevel()` performs specific actions for only two of the constants, while behaving ordinarily (the `else` case) for all other options.

An enumeration is a special kind of class with a fixed number of instances, all listed within the class body. In other ways, an `enum` class behaves like a regular class, so you can define member properties and functions. If you include additional elements, you must add a semicolon after the last enumeration value:

```
// Enumerations/Direction.kt
package enumerations
import atomictest.eq
import enumerations.Direction.*

enum class Direction(val notation: String) {
  North("N"), South("S"),
  East("E"), West("W");  // Semicolon required
  val opposite: Direction
    get() = when (this) {
      North -> South
      South -> North
      West -> East
      East -> West
    }
}

fun main() {
  North.notation eq "N"
  North.opposite eq South
  West.opposite.opposite eq West
```

```
  North.opposite.notation eq "S"
}
```

The Direction class contains a notation property holding a different value for each instance. You pass values for the notation constructor parameter in parentheses (North("N")), just like you construct an instance of a regular class.

The getter for the opposite property dynamically computes the result when it is accessed.

Notice that when doesn't require an else branch in this example, because all possible enum entries are covered.

-

Enumerations can make your code more readable, which is always desirable.

Exercises and solutions can be found at www.AtomicKotlin.com.

Data Classes

> Kotlin reduces repetitive coding.

The `class` mechanism performs a fair amount of work for you. However, creating classes that primarily hold data still requires a significant amount of repetitive code. When you need a class that's essentially a data holder, `data` classes simplify your code and perform common tasks.

You define a `data` class using the `data` keyword, which tells Kotlin to generate additional functionality. Each constructor parameter must be preceded by `var` or `val`:

```
// DataClasses/Simple.kt
package dataclasses
import atomictest.eq

data class Simple(
  val arg1: String,
  var arg2: Int
)

fun main() {
  val s1 = Simple("Hi", 29)
  val s2 = Simple("Hi", 29)
  s1 eq "Simple(arg1=Hi, arg2=29)"
  s1 eq s2
}
```

This example reveals two features of `data` classes:

1. The `String` produced by `s1` is different than what we usually see; it includes the parameter names and values of the data held by the object. `data` classes display objects in a nice, readable format without requiring any additional code.

2. If you create two instances of the same data class containing identical data (equal values for properties), you probably also want those two instances to be equal. To achieve that behavior for a regular class, you must define a special function equals() to compare instances. In data classes, this function is automatically generated; it compares the values of all properties specified as constructor parameters.

Here's an ordinary class Person and a data class Contact:

```kotlin
// DataClasses/DataClasses.kt
package dataclasses
import atomictest.*

class Person(val name: String)

data class Contact(
  val name: String,
  val number: String
)

fun main() {
  // These seem the same, but they're not:
  Person("Cleo") neq Person("Cleo")
  // A data class defines equality sensibly:
  Contact("Miffy", "1-234-567890") eq
    Contact("Miffy", "1-234-567890")
}
/* Sample output:
dataclasses.Person@54bedef2
Contact(name=Miffy, number=1-234-567890)
*/
```

Because the Person class is defined without the data keyword, two instances containing the same name are not equal. Fortunately, creating Contact as a data class produces a reasonable result.

Notice the difference between the display format of the data class, and Person, which just shows default object information.

Another useful function generated for every data class is copy(), which creates a new object containing the data from the current object. However, it also allows you to change selected values in the process:

```
// DataClasses/CopyDataClass.kt
package dataclasses
import atomictest.eq

data class DetailedContact(
  val name: String,
  val surname: String,
  val number: String,
  val address: String
)

fun main() {
  val contact = DetailedContact(
    "Miffy",
    "Miller",
    "1-234-567890",
    "1600 Amphitheater Parkway")
  val newContact = contact.copy(
    number = "098-765-4321",
    address = "Brandschenkestrasse 110")
  newContact eq DetailedContact(
    "Miffy",
    "Miller",
    "098-765-4321",
    "Brandschenkestrasse 110")
}
```

The parameter names for copy() are identical to the constructor parameters. All arguments have default values that are equal to the current values, so you provide only the ones you want to replace.

HashMap and HashSet

Creating a data class also generates an appropriate *hash function* so that objects can be used as keys in HashMaps and HashSets:

```
// DataClasses/HashCode.kt
package dataclasses
import atomictest.eq

data class Key(val name: String, val id: Int)

fun main() {
  val korvo: Key = Key("Korvo", 19)
  korvo.hashCode() eq -2041757108
  val map = HashMap<Key, String>()
  map[korvo] = "Alien"
  map[korvo] eq "Alien"
  val set = HashSet<Key>()
  set.add(korvo)
  set.contains(korvo) eq true
}
```

hashCode() is used in conjunction with equals() to rapidly look up a Key in a HashMap or a HashSet. Creating a correct hashCode() by hand is tricky and error-prone, so it is quite beneficial to have the data class do it for you. *Operator Overloading* covers equals() and hashCode() in more detail.

Exercises and solutions can be found at www.AtomicKotlin.com.

Destructuring Declarations

Suppose you want to return more than one item from a function, such as a result along with some information about that result.

The `Pair` class, which is part of the standard library, allows you to return two values:

```
// Destructuring/Pairs.kt
package destructuring
import atomictest.eq

fun compute(input: Int): Pair<Int, String> =
  if (input > 5)
    Pair(input * 2, "High")
  else
    Pair(input * 2, "Low")

fun main() {
  compute(7) eq Pair(14, "High")
  compute(4) eq Pair(8, "Low")
  val result = compute(5)
  result.first eq 10
  result.second eq "Low"
}
```

We specify the return type of `compute()` as `Pair<Int, String>`. A `Pair` is a parameterized type, like `List` or `Set`.

Returning multiple values is helpful, but we'd also like a convenient way to unpack the results. As shown above, you can access the components of a `Pair` using its `first` and `second` properties, but you can also declare and initialize several identifiers simultaneously using a *destructuring declaration*:

```
val (a, b, c) = composedValue
```

This destructures a composed value and positionally assigns its components. The syntax differs from defining a single identifier—for destructuring, you put the names of the identifiers inside parentheses.

Here's a destructuring declaration for the `Pair` returned from `compute()`:

```
// Destructuring/PairDestructuring.kt
import destructuring.compute
import atomictest.eq

fun main() {
  val (value, description) = compute(7)
  value eq 14
  description eq "High"
}
```

The `Triple` class combines three values, but that's as far as it goes. This is intentional: if you need to store more values, or if you find yourself using many `Pair`s or `Triple`s, consider creating special classes instead.

data Classes automatically allow destructuring declarations:

```
// Destructuring/Computation.kt
package destructuring
import atomictest.eq

data class Computation(
  val data: Int,
  val info: String
)

fun evaluate(input: Int) =
  if (input > 5)
    Computation(input * 2, "High")
  else
    Computation(input * 2, "Low")

fun main() {
  val (value, description) = evaluate(7)
  value eq 14
  description eq "High"
}
```

It's clearer to return a Computation instead of a Pair<Int, String>. Choosing a good name for the result is almost as important as choosing a good self-explanatory name for the function itself. Adding or removing Computation information is simpler if it's a separate class rather than a Pair.

When you unpack an instance of a data class, you must assign values to the new identifiers in the same order you define the properties in the class:

```
// Destructuring/Tuple.kt
package destructuring
import atomictest.eq

data class Tuple(
  val i: Int,
  val d: Double,
  val s: String,
  val b: Boolean,
  val l: List<Int>
)

fun main() {
  val tuple = Tuple(
    1, 3.14, "Mouse", false, listOf())
  val (i, d, s, b, l) = tuple
  i eq 1
  d eq 3.14
  s eq "Mouse"
  b eq false
  l eq listOf()

  val (_, _, animal) = tuple    // [1]
  animal eq "Mouse"
}
```

- **[1]** If you don't need some of the identifiers, you may use underscores instead of their names, or omit them completely if they appear at the end. Here, the unpacked values 1 and 3.14 are discarded using underscores, "Mouse" is captured into animal, and false and the empty List are discarded because they are at the end of the list.

The properties of a data class are assigned by order, not by name. If you destructure an object and later add a property anywhere except the end of its data class, that new property will be destructured on top of your previous identifier, producing unexpected results (see Exercise 3). If your custom `data` class has properties with identical types, the compiler can't detect misuse so you may want to avoid destructuring it. Destructuring library `data` classes like `Pair` or `Triple` is safe, because they don't change.

Using a `for` loop, you can iterate over a `Map` or a `List` of pairs (or other `data` classes) and destructure each element:

```
// Destructuring/ForLoop.kt
import atomictest.eq

fun main() {
  var result = ""
  val map = mapOf(1 to "one", 2 to "two")
  for ((key, value) in map) {
    result += "$key = $value, "
  }
  result eq "1 = one, 2 = two,"

  result = ""
  val listOfPairs =
    listOf(Pair(1, "one"), Pair(2, "two"))
  for ((i, s) in listOfPairs) {
    result += "($i, $s), "
  }
  result eq "(1, one), (2, two),"
}
```

`withIndex()` is a standard library extension function for `List`. It returns a collection of `IndexedValues`, which can be destructured:

```
// Destructuring/LoopWithIndex.kt
import atomictest.trace

fun main() {
  val list = listOf('a', 'b', 'c')
  for ((index, value) in list.withIndex()) {
    trace("$index:$value")
  }
  trace eq "0:a 1:b 2:c"
}
```

Destructuring declarations are only allowed for local vars and vals, and cannot be used to create class properties.

Exercises and solutions can be found at www.AtomicKotlin.com.

Nullable Types

Consider a function that sometimes produces "no result." When this happens, the function doesn't produce an error per se. Nothing went wrong, there's just "no answer."

A good example is retrieving a value from a Map. If the Map doesn't contain a value for a given key, it can't give you an answer and returns a null reference to indicate "no value":

```
// NullableTypes/NullInMaps.kt
import atomictest.eq

fun main() {
  val map = mapOf(0 to "yes", 1 to "no")
  map[2] eq null
}
```

Languages like Java allow a result to be either null or a meaningful value. Unfortunately, if you treat null the same way you treat a meaningful value, you get a dramatic failure (In Java, this produces a NullPointerException; in a more primitive language like C, a null pointer can crash the process or even the operating system or machine). The creator of the null reference, Tony Hoare[32], refers to it as "my billion-dollar mistake" (although it has arguably cost much more than that).

One possible solution to this problem is for a language to never allow nulls in the first place, and instead introduce a special "no value" indicator. Kotlin might have done this, except that it must interact with Java, and Java uses nulls.

Kotlin's solution is arguably the best compromise: types default to non-nullable. If something *can* produce a null result, you must append a question mark to the type name to explicitly tag that result as nullable:

---

[32] https://en.wikipedia.org/wiki/Tony_Hoare

```
// NullableTypes/NullableTypes.kt
import atomictest.eq

fun main() {
  val s1 = "abc"              // [1]

  // Compile-time error:
  // val s2: String = null    // [2]

  // Nullable definitions:
  val s3: String? = null      // [3]
  val s4: String? = s1        // [4]

  // Compile-time error:
  // val s5: String = s4      // [5]
  val s6 = s4                 // [6]

  s1 eq "abc"
  s3 eq null
  s4 eq "abc"
  s6 eq "abc"
}
```

- **[1]** s1 can't contain a null reference. All the vars and vals we've created in the book so far are automatically non-nullable.
- **[2]** The error message is: *null can not be a value of a non-null type String*.
- **[3]** To define an identifier that can contain a null reference, you put a ? at the end of the type name. Such an identifier can contain either null or a regular value.
- **[4]** Both nulls and regular non-nullable values can be stored in a nullable type.
- **[5]** You can't assign an identifier of a nullable type to an identifier of a non-null type. Kotlin emits: *Type mismatch: inferred type is String? but String was expected*. Even if the actual value is non-null as in this case (we know it's "abc"), Kotlin won't allow it because they are two different types.
- **[6]** If you use type inference, Kotlin produces the appropriate type. Here, s6 is nullable because s4 is nullable.

Even though it looks like we just modify an existing type by adding a ? at the end, we're actually specifying a *different type*. For example, String and String? are two different types. The `String` type forbids the operations in lines **[2]** and **[5]**, thus guaranteeing that a value of a non-nullable type is never `null`.

Retrieving a value from a `Map` using square brackets produces a nullable result, because the underlying `Map` implementation comes from Java:

```
// NullableTypes/NullableInMap.kt
import atomictest.eq

fun main() {
  val map = mapOf(0 to "yes", 1 to "no")
  val first: String? = map[0]
  val second: String? = map[2]
  first eq "yes"
  second eq null
}
```

Why is it important to know that a value can't be `null`? Many operations implicitly assume a non-nullable result. For example, calling a member function will fail with an exception if the receiver value is `null`. In Java such a call will fail with a `NullPointerException` (often abbreviated *NPE*). Because almost any value can be `null` in Java, any function invocation can fail this way. In these cases you must write code to check for `null` results, or rely on other parts of the code to guard against `null`s.

In Kotlin you can't simply *dereference* (call a member function or access a member property) a nullable identifier:

```
// NullableTypes/Dereference.kt
import atomictest.eq

fun main() {
  val s1: String = "abc"
  val s2: String? = s1

  s1.length eq 3           // [1]
  // Doesn't compile:
  // s2.length             // [2]
}
```

You can access members of a non-nullable type as in **[1]**. If you reference members of a nullable type, as in **[2]**, Kotlin emits an error.

Values of most types are stored as references to the objects in memory. That's the meaning of the term *dereference*—to access an object, you retrieve its value from memory.

The most straightforward way to ensure that dereferencing a nullable type won't throw a `NullPointerException` is to explicitly check that the reference is not `null`:

```
// NullableTypes/ExplicitCheck.kt
import atomictest.eq

fun main() {
  val s: String? = "abc"
  if (s != null)
    s.length eq 3
}
```

After the explicit `if`-check, Kotlin allows you to dereference a nullable. But writing this `if` whenever you work with nullable types is too noisy for such a common operation. Kotlin has concise syntax to alleviate this problem, which you'll learn about in subsequent atoms.

Whenever you create a new class, Kotlin automatically includes nullable and non-nullable types:

```
// NullableTypes/Amphibian.kt
package nullabletypes

class Amphibian

enum class Species {
  Frog, Toad, Salamander, Caecilian
}

fun main() {
  val a1: Amphibian = Amphibian()
  val a2: Amphibian? = null
  val at1: Species = Species.Toad
  val at2: Species? = null
}
```

As you can see, we didn't do anything special to produce the complementary nullable types—they're available by default.

Exercises and solutions can be found at www.AtomicKotlin.com.

Safe Calls & the Elvis Operator

> Kotlin provides convenient operations for handling nullability.

Nullable types come with numerous restrictions. You can't simply dereference a nullable identifier:

```
// SafeCallsAndElvis/DereferenceNull.kt

fun main() {
  val s: String? = null
  // Doesn't compile:
  // s.length         // [1]
}
```

Uncommenting **[1]** produces a compile-time error: *Only safe (`?.`) or non-null asserted (`!!.`) calls are allowed on a nullable receiver of type* `String?`.

A *safe call* replaces the dot (`.`) in a regular call with a question mark and a dot (`?.`), without intervening space. Safe calls access members of a nullable in a way that ensures no exceptions are thrown. They only perform an operation when the receiver is not `null`:

```
// SafeCallsAndElvis/SafeOperation.kt
package safecalls
import atomictest.*

fun String.echo() {
  trace(uppercase())
  trace(this)
  trace(lowercase())
}

fun main() {
  val s1: String? = "Howdy!"
  s1?.echo()                    // [1]
```

```
  val s2: String? = null
  s2?.echo()                    // [2]
  trace eq """
    HOWDY!
    Howdy!
    howdy!
  """
}
```

Line **[1]** calls `echo()` and produces results in the `trace`, while line **[2]** does nothing because the receiver `s2` is `null`.

Safe calls are a clean way to capture results:

```
// SafeCallsAndElvis/SafeCall.kt
package safecalls
import atomictest.eq

fun checkLength(s: String?, expected: Int?) {
  val length1 =
    if (s != null) s.length else null  // [1]
  val length2 = s?.length              // [2]
  length1 eq expected
  length2 eq expected
}

fun main() {
  checkLength("abc", 3)
  checkLength(null, null)
}
```

Line **[2]** achieves the same effect as line **[1]**. If the receiver is not `null` it performs a normal access (`s.length`). If the receiver is `null` it doesn't perform the `s.length` call (which would cause an exception), but produces `null` for the expression.

What if you need something more than the `null` produced by `?.`? The *Elvis operator* provides an alternative. This operator is a question mark followed by a colon (`?:`), with no intervening space. It is named for an emoticon of the musician Elvis Presley, and is also a play on the words "else-if" (which sounds vaguely like "Elvis").

A number of programming languages provide a *null coalescing operator* that performs the same action as Kotlin's Elvis operator.

If the expression on the left of ?: is not null, that expression becomes the result. If the left-hand expression *is* null, then the expression on the right of the ?: becomes the result:

```
// SafeCallsAndElvis/ElvisOperator.kt
import atomictest.eq

fun main() {
  val s1: String? = "abc"
  (s1 ?: "---") eq "abc"

  val s2: String? = null
  (s2 ?: "---") eq "---"
}
```

s1 is not null, so the Elvis operator produces "abc" as the result. Because s2 is null, the Elvis operator produces the alternate result of "---".

The Elvis operator is typically used after a safe call, to produce a meaningful value instead of the default null, as you see in **[2]**:

```
// SafeCallsAndElvis/ElvisCall.kt
package safecalls
import atomictest.eq

fun checkLength(s: String?, expected: Int) {
  val length1 =
    if (s != null) s.length else 0      // [1]
  val length2 = s?.length ?: 0          // [2]
  length1 eq expected
  length2 eq expected
}

fun main() {
  checkLength("abc", 3)
  checkLength(null, 0)
}
```

This checkLength() function is quite similar to the one in SafeCall.kt above. The expected parameter type is now non-nullable. **[1]** and **[2]** produce zero instead of null.

Safe calls allow you to write chained calls concisely, when some elements in the chain might be null and you're only interested in the final result:

```
// SafeCallsAndElvis/ChainedCalls.kt
package safecalls
import atomictest.eq

class Person(
  val name: String,
  var friend: Person? = null
)

fun main() {
  val alice = Person("Alice")
  alice.friend?.friend?.name eq null    // [1]

  val bob = Person("Bob")
  val charlie = Person("Charlie", bob)
  bob.friend = charlie
  bob.friend?.friend?.name eq "Bob"     // [2]

  (alice.friend?.friend?.name
    ?: "Unknown") eq "Unknown"          // [3]
}
```

When you chain access to several members using safe calls, the result is null if any intermediate expressions are null.

- **[1]** The property alice.friend is null, so the rest of the calls return null.
- **[2]** All intermediate calls produce meaningful values.
- **[3]** An Elvis operator after the chain of safe calls provides an alternate value if any intermediate element is null.

Exercises and solutions can be found at www.AtomicKotlin.com.

Non-Null Assertions

A second approach to the problem of nullable types is to have special knowledge that the reference in question isn't null.

To make this claim, use the double exclamation point, !!, called the *non-null assertion*. If this looks alarming, it should: believing that something can't be null is the source of most null-related program failures (the rest come from not *realizing* that a null can happen).

x!! means "forget the fact that x might be null—I guarantee that it's *not* null." x!! produces x if x isn't null, otherwise it throws an exception:

```
// NonNullAssertions/NonNullAssert.kt
import atomictest.*

fun main() {
  var x: String? = "abc"
  x!! eq "abc"
  x = null
  capture {
    val s: String = x!!
  } eq "NullPointerException"
}
```

The definition val s: String = x!! tells Kotlin to ignore what it thinks it knows about x and just assign it to s, which is a non-nullable reference. Fortunately, there's run-time support that throws a NullPointerException when x is null.

Ordinarily you won't use the !! by itself, but instead in conjunction with a . dereference:

```
// NonNullAssertions/NonNullAssertCall.kt
import atomictest.eq

fun main() {
  val s: String? = "abc"
  s!!.length eq 3
}
```

If you limit yourself to a single non-null asserted call per line, it's easier to locate a failure when the exception gives you a line number.

The safe call `?.` is a single operator, but a non-null asserted call consists of two operators: the non-null assertion (`!!`) and a dereference (`.`). As you saw in `NonNullAssert.kt`, you can use a non-null assertion by itself.

Avoid non-null assertions and prefer safe calls or explicit checks. Non-null assertions were introduced to enable interaction between Kotlin and Java, and for the rare cases when Kotlin isn't smart enough to ensure the necessary checks are performed.

If you frequently use non-null assertions in your code for the same operation, it's better to use a separate function with a specific assertion describing the problem. As an example, suppose your program logic requires a particular key to be present in a `Map`, and you prefer getting an exception instead of silently doing nothing if the key is absent. Instead of extracting the value with the usual approach (square brackets), `getValue()` throws `NoSuchElementException` if a key is missing:

```
// NonNullAssertions/ValueFromMap.kt
import atomictest.*

fun main() {
  val map = mapOf(1 to "one")
  map[1]!!.uppercase() eq "ONE"
  map.getValue(1).uppercase() eq "ONE"
  capture {
    map[2]!!.uppercase()
  } eq "NullPointerException"
  capture {
    map.getValue(2).uppercase()
  } eq "NoSuchElementException: " +
    "Key 2 is missing in the map."
}
```

Throwing the specific `NoSuchElementException` gives you more useful details when something goes wrong.

- -

Optimal code uses only safe calls and special functions that throw detailed exceptions. Only use non-`null` asserted calls when you absolutely must. Although non-`null` assertions were included to support interaction with Java code, there are better ways to interact with Java, which you can learn about in ***Appendix B: Java Interoperability***.

Exercises and solutions can be found at www.AtomicKotlin.com.

Extensions for Nullable Types

> Sometimes it's not what it looks like.

`s?.f()` implies that `s` is nullable—otherwise you could simply call `s.f()`. Similarly, `t.f()` seems to imply that `t` is non-nullable because Kotlin doesn't require a safe call or programmatic check. However, `t` is not necessarily non-nullable.

The Kotlin standard library provides `String` extension functions, including:

- `isNullOrEmpty()`: Tests whether the receiver `String` is `null` or empty.
- `isNullOrBlank()`: Performs the same check as `isNullOrEmpty()` *and* allows the receiver `String` to consist solely of whitespace characters, including tabs (`\t`) and newlines (`\n`).

Here's a basic test of these functions:

```
// NullableExtensions/StringIsNullOr.kt
import atomictest.eq

fun main() {
  val s1: String? = null
  s1.isNullOrEmpty() eq true
  s1.isNullOrBlank() eq true

  val s2 = ""
  s2.isNullOrEmpty() eq true
  s2.isNullOrBlank() eq true

  val s3: String = " \t\n"
  s3.isNullOrEmpty() eq false
  s3.isNullOrBlank() eq true
}
```

The function names suggest they are for nullable types. However, even though `s1` is nullable, you can call `isNullOrEmpty()` or `isNullOrBlank()` without a safe call or explicit check. That's because these are extension functions on the nullable type `String?`.

We can rewrite `isNullOrEmpty()` as a non-extension function that takes the nullable `String` `s` as a parameter:

```
// NullableExtensions/NullableParameter.kt
package nullableextensions
import atomictest.eq

fun isNullOrEmpty(s: String?): Boolean =
  s == null || s.isEmpty()

fun main() {
  isNullOrEmpty(null) eq true
  isNullOrEmpty("") eq true
}
```

Because `s` is nullable, we explicitly check for `null` or empty. The expression `s == null || s.isEmpty()` uses *short-circuiting*: if the first part of the expression is `true`, the rest of the expression is not evaluated, thus preventing a `null` pointer exception.

Extension functions use `this` to represent the receiver (the object of the type being extended). To make the receiver nullable, add `?` to the type being extended:

```
// NullableExtensions/NullableExtension.kt
package nullableextensions
import atomictest.eq

fun String?.isNullOrEmpty(): Boolean =
  this == null || isEmpty()

fun main() {
  "".isNullOrEmpty() eq true
}
```

`isNullOrEmpty()` is more readable as an extension function.

- -

Take care when using extensions for nullable types. They are great for simple cases like `isNullOrEmpty()` and `isNullOrBlank()`, especially with self-explanatory names that imply the receiver might be `null`. In general, it's better to declare regular (non-nullable) extensions. Safe calls and explicit checks clarify the receiver's nullability, while extensions for nullable types may conceal nullability and confuse the reader of your code (probably, "future you").

Exercises and solutions can be found at www.AtomicKotlin.com.

Introduction to Generics

Generics create *parameterized types*: components that work across multiple types.

The term "generic" means "pertaining or appropriate to large groups of classes." The original intent of generics in programming languages was to provide the programmer maximum expressiveness when writing classes or functions, by loosening type constraints on those classes or functions.

One of the most compelling initial motivations for generics is to create collection classes, which you've seen in the `List`s, `Set`s and `Map`s used for the examples in this book. A collection is an object that holds other objects. Many programs require you to hold a group of objects while you use them, so collections are one of the most reusable of class libraries.

Let's look at a class that holds a single object. This class specifies the exact type of that object:

```
// IntroGenerics/RigidHolder.kt
package introgenerics
import atomictest.eq

data class Automobile(val brand: String)

class RigidHolder(private val a: Automobile) {
  fun getValue() = a
}

fun main() {
  val holder = RigidHolder(Automobile("BMW"))
  holder.getValue() eq
    "Automobile(brand=BMW)"
}
```

`RigidHolder` is not a particularly reusable tool; it can't hold anything but an `Automobile`. We would prefer not to write a new type of holder for every different type. To achieve this, we use a *type parameter* instead of `Automobile`.

To define a generic type, add angle brackets (`<>`) containing one or more generic placeholders and put this generic specification after the class name. Here, the generic placeholder `T` represents the unknown type and is used within the class as if it were a regular type:

```
// IntroGenerics/GenericHolder.kt
package introgenerics
import atomictest.eq

class GenericHolder<T>(                    // [1]
  private val value: T
) {
  fun getValue(): T = value
}

fun main() {
  val h1 = GenericHolder(Automobile("Ford"))
  val a: Automobile = h1.getValue()   // [2]
  a eq "Automobile(brand=Ford)"

  val h2 = GenericHolder(1)
  val i: Int = h2.getValue()          // [3]
  i eq 1

  val h3 = GenericHolder("Chartreuse")
  val s: String = h3.getValue()       // [4]
  s eq "Chartreuse"
}
```

- **[1]** `GenericHolder` stores a T. Its member function `getValue()` returns a T.

When you call `getValue()` as in **[2]**, **[3]** or **[4]** , the result is automatically the right type.

It seems like we might be able to solve this problem with a "universal type"—a type that is the parent of all other types. In Kotlin, this universal type is called `Any`. As the name implies, `Any` allows any type of argument. If you want to pass a variety of types to a function and they have nothing in common, `Any` solves the problem.

At a glance, it looks like we might be able to use `Any` instead of `T` in GenericHolder.kt:

```
// IntroGenerics/AnyInstead.kt
package introgenerics
import atomictest.eq

class AnyHolder(private val value: Any) {
  fun getValue(): Any = value
}

class Dog {
  fun bark() = "Ruff!"
}

fun main() {
  val holder = AnyHolder(Dog())
  val any = holder.getValue()
  // Doesn't compile:
  // any.bark()

  val genericHolder = GenericHolder(Dog())
  val dog = genericHolder.getValue()
  dog.bark() eq "Ruff!"
}
```

`Any` does in fact work for simple cases, but as soon as we need the specific type—to call `bark()` for the `Dog`—it doesn't work because we lose track of the fact that it's a `Dog` when it is assigned to the `Any`. When we pass a `Dog` as an `Any`, the result is just an `Any`, which has no `bark()`.

`GenericHolder` retains the information that, in this case, we actually have a `Dog`, which means we can perform `Dog` operations on the object returned by `getValue()`.

Generic Functions

To define a generic function, specify a generic type parameter in angle brackets *before* the function name:

```
// IntroGenerics/GenericFunction.kt
package introgenerics
import atomictest.eq

fun <T> identity(arg: T): T = arg

fun main() {
  identity("Yellow") eq "Yellow"
  identity(1) eq 1
  val d: Dog = identity(Dog())
  d.bark() eq "Ruff!"
}
```

d has type Dog because identity() is a generic function and returns a T.

The Kotlin standard library contains many generic extension functions for collections. To write a generic extension function, put the generic specification before the receiver. For example, notice how first() and firstOrNull() are defined:

```
// IntroGenerics/GenericListExtensions.kt
package introgenerics
import atomictest.eq

fun <T> List<T>.first(): T {
  if (isEmpty())
    throw NoSuchElementException("Empty List")
  return this[0]
}

fun <T> List<T>.firstOrNull(): T? =
  if (isEmpty()) null else this[0]

fun main() {
  listOf(1, 2, 3).first() eq 1

  val i: Int? =                      // [1]
    listOf(1, 2, 3).firstOrNull()
  i eq 1

  val s: String? =                   // [2]
    listOf<String>().firstOrNull()
  s eq null
}
```

`first()` and `firstOrNull()` work with any kind of `List`. To return a `T`, they must be generic functions.

Notice how `firstOrNull()` specifies a nullable return type. Line **[1]** shows that calling the function on `List<Int>` returns the nullable type `Int?`. Line **[2]** shows that calling `firstOrNull()` on `List<String>` returns `String?`. Kotlin requires the `?` on lines **[1]** and **[2]**—take them out and see the error messages.

Exercises and solutions can be found at www.AtomicKotlin.com.

Extension Properties

Just as functions can be extension functions, properties can be *extension properties*.

The receiver type specification for extension properties is similar to the syntax for extension functions—the extended type comes right before the function or property name:

```
fun ReceiverType.extensionFunction() { ... }
val ReceiverType.extensionProperty: PropType
  get() { ... }
```

An extension property requires a custom getter. The property value is computed for each access:

```
// ExtensionProperties/StringIndices.kt
package extensionproperties
import atomictest.eq

val String.indices: IntRange
  get() = 0 until length

fun main() {
  "abc".indices eq 0..2
}
```

Although you can convert any extension function without parameters into a property, we recommend thinking about it first. The reasons described in **Property Accessors** for choosing between properties and functions also apply to extension properties. Preferring a property over a function makes sense only if it's simple enough and improves readability.

You can define a generic extension property. Here, we convert `firstOrNull()` from **Introduction to Generics** to an extension property:

```
// ExtensionProperties/GenericListExt.kt
package extensionproperties
import atomictest.eq

val <T> List<T>.firstOrNull: T?
  get() = if (isEmpty()) null else this[0]

fun main() {
  listOf(1, 2, 3).firstOrNull eq 1
  listOf<String>().firstOrNull eq null
}
```

The Kotlin Style Guide[33] recommends a function over a property if the function throws an exception.

When the generic argument type isn't used, you may replace it with *. This is called a *star projection*:

```
// ExtensionProperties/ListOfStar.kt
package extensionproperties
import atomictest.eq

val List<*>.indices: IntRange
  get() = 0 until size

fun main() {
  listOf(1).indices eq 0..0
  listOf('a', 'b', 'c', 'd').indices eq 0..3
  emptyList<Int>().indices eq IntRange.EMPTY
}
```

When you use List<*>, you lose all specific information about the type contained in the List. For example, an element of a List<*> can only be assigned to Any?:

---

[33]https://kotlinlang.org/docs/reference/coding-conventions.html

```
// ExtensionProperties/AnyFromListOfStar.kt
import atomictest.eq

fun main() {
  val list: List<*> = listOf(1, 2)
  val any: Any? = list[0]
  any eq 1
}
```

We have no information whether a value stored in a List<*> is nullable or not, which is why it can be only assigned to a nullable Any? type.

Exercises and solutions can be found at www.AtomicKotlin.com.

break & continue

> `break` and `continue` abandon the remainder of the code in a loop and `break` to the end or `continue` at the beginning that loop.

Early programmers wrote directly to the processor, using either numerical *opcodes* as instructions, or *assembly language*, which translates into opcodes. This kind of programming is as low-level as you can get. For example, many coding decisions were facilitated by "jumping" directly to other places in the code. Early higher-level languages (including FORTRAN, ALGOL, Pascal, C and C++) duplicated this practice by implementing a `goto` keyword.

`goto` made assembly-language programmers more comfortable as they transitioned to higher-level languages. As we accumulated more experience, however, the programming community discovered that unconstrained jumps produce complicated and un-maintainable code that is difficult to reason about. This generated a backlash against `goto`, and most subsequent languages have avoided any kind of unconstrained jump.

We still need to be able to decide we don't want to execute the remainder of the code in a block—that is, to abandon the rest of the current action. This *could* be solved with a `goto` but the open-ended nature of the unconstrained jump brings too much negative baggage with it.

To abandon the rest of the current action, use `break` and `continue`. These are only available within the looping constructs `for`, `while` and `do-while`. Calling `continue` goes back to the beginning of a loop, while `break` goes to the end of a loop.

In practice you rarely use `break` and `continue` when writing Kotlin code. These features are artifacts from earlier languages. Although they are occasionally useful, you'll learn in this book that Kotlin provides superior alternatives.

Here's a `for` loop that contains both a `continue` and a `break`:

```
// BreakAndContinue/ForControl.kt
import atomictest.eq

fun main() {
  val nums = mutableListOf(0)
  for (i in 4 until 100 step 4) {    // [1]
    if (i == 8) continue             // [2]
    if (i == 40) break               // [3]
    nums.add(i)
  }                                  // [4]
  nums eq "[0, 4, 12, 16, 20, 24, 28, 32, 36]"
}
```

This aggregates `Ints` into a mutable `List`. The `continue` at **[2]** abandons the rest of the block and goes back to the beginning of the loop at **[1]**. It "continues" execution starting with the next iteration of the loop. The code following `continue` is abandoned: `nums.add(i)` is not called when `i == 8` so you don't see it in the resulting `nums`.

When `i == 40`, `break` is executed at **[3]**, which abandons the rest of the block and goes to the end of the scope at **[4]**. The numbers beginning at 40 are not added to the resulting `List` because the rest of the `for` loop is not executed.

Lines **[2]** and **[3]** are interchangeable because their logic doesn't overlap. Try swapping the lines and verify that the output doesn't change.

We can rewrite `ForControl.kt` using a `while` loop:

```
// BreakAndContinue/WhileControl.kt
import atomictest.eq

fun main() {
  val nums = mutableListOf(0)
  var i = 0
  while (i < 100) {
    i += 4
    if (i == 8) continue
    if (i == 40) break
    nums.add(i)
  }
  nums eq "[0, 4, 12, 16, 20, 24, 28, 32, 36]"
}
```

The `break` and `continue` behavior remains the same, as it does for a do-while loop:

```
// BreakAndContinue/DoWhileControl.kt
import atomictest.eq

fun main() {
  val nums = mutableListOf(0)
  var i = 0
  do {
    i += 4
    if (i == 8) continue
    if (i == 40) break
    nums.add(i)
  } while (i < 100)
  nums eq "[0, 4, 12, 16, 20, 24, 28, 32, 36]"
}
```

A do-while loop always executes at least once, because the `while` test is at the end of the loop.

Labels

Plain `break` and `continue` can go no further than the boundaries of their local loop. *Labels* allow `break` and `continue` to jump to the boundaries of *enclosing* loops, so you aren't limited to the scope of the current loop.

You create a label using `label@`, where `label` can be any name. Here, the label is `outer`:

```
// BreakAndContinue/ForLabeled.kt
import atomictest.eq

fun main() {
  val strings = mutableListOf<String>()
  outer@ for (c in 'a'..'e') {
    for (i in 1..9) {
      if (i == 5) continue@outer
      if ("$c$i" == "c3") break@outer
      strings.add("$c$i")
    }
```

```
  }
  strings eq listOf("a1", "a2", "a3", "a4",
    "b1", "b2", "b3", "b4", "c1", "c2")
}
```

The labeled `continue` expression `continue@outer` continues back to the label `outer@`. The labeled `break` expression `break@outer` finds the end of the block named `outer@`, and proceeds from there.

Labels also work with `while` and `do-while`:

```
// BreakAndContinue/WhileLabeled.kt
import atomictest.eq

fun main() {
  val strings = mutableListOf<String>()
  var c = 'a' - 1
  outer@ while (c < 'f') {
    c += 1
    var i = 0
    do {
      i++
      if (i == 5) continue@outer
      if ("$c$i" == "c3") break@outer
      strings.add("$c$i")
    } while (i < 10)
  }
  strings eq listOf("a1", "a2", "a3", "a4",
    "b1", "b2", "b3", "b4", "c1", "c2")
}
```

`WhileLabeled.kt` can be rewritten as:

```
// BreakAndContinue/Improved.kt
import atomictest.eq

fun main() {
  val strings = mutableListOf<String>()
  for (c in 'a'..'c') {
    for (i in 1..4) {
      val value = "$c$i"
      if (value < "c3") {      // [1]
        strings.add(value)
      }
    }
  }
  strings eq listOf("a1", "a2", "a3", "a4",
    "b1", "b2", "b3", "b4", "c1", "c2")
}
```

This is far more comprehensible. In line **[1]**, we only add `Strings` that occur (alphabetically) before `"c3"`. This produces the same behavior as using `break` when reaching `"c3"` in the previous versions of the example.

- -

`break` and `continue` tend to create complicated and un-maintainable code. Although these constructs are more civilized than "goto," they still interrupt program flow. Code without jumps is almost always easier to understand.

In some cases, you can write the conditions for iteration explicitly instead of using `break` and `continue`, as we did in `Improved.kt`. In other cases, you can restructure your code and introduce new functions. Both `break` and `continue` can be replaced with `return` if you extract the whole loop or the loop body into new functions. In the next section, **Functional Programming**, you'll learn to write clear code without using `break` and `continue`.

Consider alternative approaches, and choose the simpler and more readable solution. This typically won't include `break` and `continue`.

Exercises and solutions can be found at www.AtomicKotlin.com.

Section IV: Functional Programming

The unavoidable price of reliability is simplicity—C.A.R. Hoare

Lambdas

> Lambdas produce compact code that's easier to understand.

A *lambda* (also called a *function literal*) is a low-ceremony function: it has no name, requires a minimal amount of code to create, and you can insert it directly into other code.

As a starting point, consider map( ), which works with collections like List. The parameter for map( ) is a transformation function which is applied to each element in a collection. map( ) returns a new List containing all the transformed elements. Here, we transform each List item to a String surrounded with []:

```
// Lambdas/BasicLambda.kt
import atomictest.eq

fun main() {
  val list = listOf(1, 2, 3, 4)
  val result = list.map({ n: Int -> "[$n]" })
  result eq listOf("[1]", "[2]", "[3]", "[4]")
}
```

The lambda is the code within the curly braces used in the initialization of result. The parameter list is separated from the function body by an arrow -> (the same arrow used in when expressions).

The function body can be one or more expressions. The final expression becomes the return value of the lambda.

BasicLambda.kt shows the full lambda syntax, but this can often be simplified. We typically create and use a lambda in place, which means Kotlin can usually infer type information. Here, the type of n is inferred:

```
// Lambdas/LambdaTypeInference.kt
import atomictest.eq

fun main() {
  val list = listOf(1, 2, 3, 4)
  val result = list.map({ n -> "[$n]" })
  result eq listOf("[1]", "[2]", "[3]", "[4]")
}
```

Kotlin can tell n is an Int because the lambda is being used with a List<Int>.

If there's only a single parameter, Kotlin generates the name it for that parameter, which means we no longer need the n ->:

```
// Lambdas/LambdaIt.kt
import atomictest.eq

fun main() {
  val list = listOf(1, 2, 3, 4)
  val result = list.map({ "[$it]" })
  result eq listOf("[1]", "[2]", "[3]", "[4]")
}
```

map() works with a List of any type. Here, Kotlin infers the type of the lambda argument it to be Char:

```
// Lambdas/Mapping.kt
import atomictest.eq

fun main() {
  val list = listOf('a', 'b', 'c', 'd')
  val result =
    list.map({ "[${it.uppercaseChar()}]" })
  result eq listOf("[A]", "[B]", "[C]", "[D]")
}
```

If the lambda is the only function argument, or the last argument, you can remove the parentheses around the curly braces, producing cleaner syntax:

```
// Lambdas/OmittingParentheses.kt
import atomictest.eq

fun main() {
  val list = listOf('a', 'b', 'c', 'd')
  val result =
    list.map { "[${it.uppercaseChar()}]" }
  result eq listOf("[A]", "[B]", "[C]", "[D]")
}
```

If the function takes more than one argument, all except the last lambda argument must be in parentheses. For example, you can specify the last argument for joinToString() as a lambda. The lambda is used to transform each element to a String, then all the elements are joined:

```
// Lambdas/JoinToString.kt
import atomictest.eq

fun main() {
  val list = listOf(9, 11, 23, 32)
  list.joinToString(" ") { "[$it]" } eq
    "[9] [11] [23] [32]"
}
```

If you want to provide the lambda as a named argument, you must place the lambda inside the parentheses of the argument list:

```
// Lambdas/LambdaAndNamedArgs.kt
import atomictest.eq

fun main() {
  val list = listOf(9, 11, 23, 32)
  list.joinToString(
    separator = " ",
    transform = { "[$it]" }
  ) eq "[9] [11] [23] [32]"
}
```

Here's the syntax for a lambda with more than one parameter:

```
// Lambdas/TwoArgLambda.kt
import atomictest.eq

fun main() {
  val list = listOf('a', 'b', 'c')
  list.mapIndexed { index, element ->
    "[$index: $element]"
  } eq listOf("[0: a]", "[1: b]", "[2: c]")
}
```

This uses the `mapIndexed()` library function, which takes each element in `list` and produces the index of that element together with the element. The lambda that we apply after `mapIndexed()` requires two arguments to match the index and the element (which is a character, in the case of `List<Char>`).

If you aren't using a particular argument, you can ignore it using an underscore to eliminate compiler warnings about unused identifiers:

```
// Lambdas/Underscore.kt
import atomictest.eq

fun main() {
  val list = listOf('a', 'b', 'c')
  list.mapIndexed { index, _ ->
    "[$index]"
  } eq listOf("[0]", "[1]", "[2]")
}
```

`Underscore.kt` can be rewritten using `list.indices`:

```
// Lambdas/ListIndicesMap.kt
import atomictest.eq

fun main() {
  val list = listOf('a', 'b', 'c')
  list.indices.map {
    "[$it]"
  } eq listOf("[0]", "[1]", "[2]")
}
```

Lambdas can have zero parameters, in which case you can leave the arrow for emphasis, but the Kotlin style guide recommends omitting the arrow:

```
// Lambdas/ZeroArguments.kt
import atomictest.*

fun main() {
  run { -> trace("A Lambda") }
  run { trace("Without args") }
  trace eq """
    A Lambda
    Without args
  """
}
```

The standard library `run()` simply calls its lambda argument.

- -

You can use a lambda anywhere you use a regular function, but if the lambda becomes too complex it's often better to define a named function, for clarity, even if you're only going to use it once.

Exercises and solutions can be found at www.AtomicKotlin.com.

The Importance of Lambdas

> Lambdas may seem like syntax sugar, but they provide important power to your programming.

Code often manipulates the contents of a collection, and typically repeats these manipulations with minor modifications. Consider selecting elements from a collection, such as people under a given age, employees with a specific role, citizens of a particular city, or unfinished orders. Here's an example that selects even numbers from a list. Suppose we don't have a rich library of functions for working with collections—we'd have to implement our own `filterEven()` operation:

```
// ImportanceOfLambdas/FilterEven.kt
package importanceoflambdas
import atomictest.eq

fun filterEven(nums: List<Int>): List<Int> {
  val result = mutableListOf<Int>()
  for (i in nums) {
    if (i % 2 == 0) {    // [1]
      result += i
    }
  }
  return result
}

fun main() {
  filterEven(listOf(1, 2, 3, 4)) eq
    listOf(2, 4)
}
```

If an element has a remainder of 0 when divided by 2, it's appended to the result.

Imagine you need something similar, but for numbers that are greater than 2. You can copy `filterEven()` and modify the small part that chooses the elements included in the result:

```
// ImportanceOfLambdas/GreaterThan2.kt
package importanceoflambdas
import atomictest.eq

fun greaterThan2(nums: List<Int>): List<Int> {
  val result = mutableListOf<Int>()
  for (i in nums) {
    if (i > 2) {           // [1]
      result += i
    }
  }
  return result
}

fun main() {
  greaterThan2(listOf(1, 2, 3, 4)) eq
    listOf(3, 4)
}
```

The only notable difference between the previous two examples is the line of code ([1] in both cases) specifying the desired elements.

With lambdas, we can use the same function for both cases. The standard library function filter() takes a predicate specifying the elements you want to preserve, and this predicate can be a lambda:

```
// ImportanceOfLambdas/Filter.kt
import atomictest.eq

fun main() {
  val list = listOf(1, 2, 3, 4)
  val even = list.filter { it % 2 == 0 }
  val greaterThan2 = list.filter { it > 2 }
  even eq listOf(2, 4)
  greaterThan2 eq listOf(3, 4)
}
```

Now we have clear, concise code that avoids repetition. Both even and greaterThan2 use filter() and differ only in the predicate. filter() has been heavily tested, so you're less likely to introduce a bug.

Notice that filter() handles the iteration that would otherwise require handwritten code. Although managing the iteration yourself might not seem like much effort, it's one more error-prone detail and one more place to make a mistake. Because they're so "obvious," such mistakes are particularly hard to find.

This is one of the hallmarks of *functional programming*, of which `map()` and `filter()` are examples. Functional programming solves problems in small steps. The functions often do things that seem trivial—it's not that hard to write your own code rather than using `map()` and `filter()`. However, once you have a collection of these small, debugged solutions, you can easily combine them without debugging at every level. This allows you to create more robust code, more quickly.

You can store a lambda in a `var` or `val`. This allows reuse of that lambda's logic, by passing it as an argument to different functions:

```
// ImportanceOfLambdas/StoringLambda.kt
import atomictest.eq

fun main() {
  val list = listOf(1, 2, 3, 4)
  val isEven = { e: Int -> e % 2 == 0 }
  list.filter(isEven) eq listOf(2, 4)
  list.any(isEven) eq true
}
```

`isEven` checks whether a number is even, and this reference is passed as an argument to both `filter()` and `any()`. The library function `any()` checks whether there's at least one element in the `List` satisfying a given predicate. When we define `isEven` we must specify the parameter type because there is no context for the type inferencer.

Another important quality of lambdas is the ability to refer to elements outside their scope. When a function "closes over" or "captures" the elements in its environment, we call it a *closure*. Unfortunately, some languages conflate the term "closure" with the idea of a lambda. The two concepts are completely distinct: you can have lambdas without closures, and closures without lambdas.

When a language supports closures, it "just works" the way you expect:

```
// ImportanceOfLambdas/Closures.kt
import atomictest.eq

fun main() {
  val list = listOf(1, 5, 7, 10)
  val divider = 5
  list.filter { it % divider == 0 } eq
    listOf(5, 10)
}
```

Here, the lambda "captures" the val divider that is defined outside the lambda. The lambda not only reads captured elements, it can also modify them:

```
// ImportanceOfLambdas/Closures2.kt
import atomictest.eq

fun main() {
  val list = listOf(1, 5, 7, 10)
  var sum = 0
  val divider = 5
  list.filter { it % divider == 0 }
    .forEach { sum += it }
  sum eq 15
}
```

The forEach() library function applies the specified action to each element of the collection.

Although you can capture the mutable variable sum as in Closures2.kt, you can usually change your code and avoid modifying the state of your environment:

```
// ImportanceOfLambdas/Sum.kt
import atomictest.eq

fun main() {
  val list = listOf(1, 5, 7, 10)
  val divider = 5
  list.filter { it % divider == 0 }
    .sum() eq 15
}
```

sum() works on a list of numbers, adding all the elements in the list.

An ordinary function can also close over surrounding elements:

```
// ImportanceOfLambdas/FunctionClosure.kt
package importanceoflambdas
import atomictest.eq

var x = 100

fun useX() {
  x++
}

fun main() {
  useX()
  x eq 101
}
```

useX() captures and modifies x from its surroundings.

Exercises and solutions can be found at www.AtomicKotlin.com.

Operations on Collections

> An essential aspect of functional languages is the ability to easily perform batch operations on collections of objects.

Most functional languages provide powerful support for working with collections, and Kotlin is no exception. You've already seen `map()`, `filter()`, `any()` and `forEach()`. This atom shows additional operations available for `List`s and other collections.

We start by looking at various ways to manufacture `List`s. Here, we initialize `List`s using lambdas:

```
// OperationsOnCollections/CreatingLists.kt
import atomictest.eq

fun main() {
  // The lambda argument is the element index:
  val list1 = List(10) { it }
  list1 eq "[0, 1, 2, 3, 4, 5, 6, 7, 8, 9]"

  // A list of a single value:
  val list2 = List(10) { 0 }
  list2 eq "[0, 0, 0, 0, 0, 0, 0, 0, 0, 0]"

  // A list of letters:
  val list3 = List(10) { 'a' + it }
  list3 eq "[a, b, c, d, e, f, g, h, i, j]"

  // Cycle through a sequence:
  val list4 = List(10) { list3[it % 3] }
  list4 eq "[a, b, c, a, b, c, a, b, c, a]"
}
```

This version of the `List` constructor has two parameters: the size of the `List` and a lambda that initializes each `List` element (the element index is passed in as the `it` argument). Remember that if a lambda is the last argument, it can be separated from the argument list.

`MutableLists` can be initialized in the same way. Here we see the initialization lambda both inside the argument list (`mutableList1`) and separated from the argument list (`mutableList2`):

```
// OperationsOnCollections/ListInit.kt
import atomictest.eq

fun main() {
  val mutableList1 =
    MutableList(5, { 10 * (it + 1) })
  mutableList1 eq "[10, 20, 30, 40, 50]"
  val mutableList2 =
    MutableList(5) { 10 * (it + 1) }
  mutableList2 eq "[10, 20, 30, 40, 50]"
}
```

`List()` and `MutableList()` are not constructors, but functions. Their names intentionally begin with an upper-case letter to make them look like constructors.

Many collection functions take a predicate and test it against the elements of a collection, some of which we've already seen:

- `filter()` produces a list containing all elements matching the given predicate.
- `any()` returns `true` if at least one element matches the predicate.
- `all()` checks whether all elements match the predicate.
- `none()` checks that no elements match the predicate.
- `find()` and `firstOrNull()` both return the first element matching the predicate, or `null` if no such element was found.
- `lastOrNull()` returns the last element matching the predicate, or `null`.
- `count()` returns the number of elements matching the predicate.

Here are simple examples for each function:

```
// OperationsOnCollections/Predicates.kt
import atomictest.eq

fun main() {
  val list = listOf(-3, -1, 5, 7, 10)

  list.filter { it > 0 } eq listOf(5, 7, 10)
  list.count { it > 0 } eq 3

  list.find { it > 0 } eq 5
  list.firstOrNull { it > 0 } eq 5
  list.lastOrNull { it < 0 } eq -1

  list.any { it > 0 } eq true
  list.any { it != 0 } eq true

  list.all { it > 0 } eq false
  list.all { it != 0 } eq true

  list.none { it > 0 } eq false
  list.none { it == 0 } eq true
}
```

filter() and count() apply the predicate against each element, while any() or find() stop when the first matching result is found. For example, if the first element satisfies the predicate, any() returns true right away, while find() returns the first matching element. The only time all the elements are processed is if the list contains no elements matching the given predicate.

filter() returns a group of elements satisfying the given predicate. Sometimes you may be interested in the remaining group—the elements that don't satisfy the predicate. filterNot() produces this remaining group, but partition() can be more useful because it simultaneously produces both lists:

```
// OperationsOnCollections/Partition.kt
import atomictest.eq

fun main() {
  val list = listOf(-3, -1, 5, 7, 10)
  val isPositive = { i: Int -> i > 0 }

  list.filter(isPositive) eq "[5, 7, 10]"
  list.filterNot(isPositive) eq "[-3, -1]"

  val (pos, neg) = list.partition { it > 0 }
  pos eq "[5, 7, 10]"
  neg eq "[-3, -1]"
}
```

partition() produces a Pair object containing Lists. Using **Destructuring Declarations**, you can assign the elements of the Pair to a parenthesized group of vars or vals. *Destructuring* means defining multiple vars or vals and initializing them simultaneously, from the expression on the right side of the assignment. Here, destructuring is used with a custom function:

```
// OperationsOnCollections/PairOfLists.kt
package operationsoncollections
import atomictest.eq

fun createPair() = Pair(1, "one")

fun main() {
  val (i, s) = createPair()
  i eq 1
  s eq "one"
}
```

filterNotNull() produces a new List with the nulls removed:

```
// OperationsOnCollections/FilterNotNull.kt
import atomictest.eq

fun main() {
  val list = listOf(1, 2, null)
  list.filterNotNull() eq "[1, 2]"
}
```

In *Lists*, we saw functions such as sum() or sorted() applied to a list of comparable elements. These functions can't be called on lists of non-summable or non-comparable elements, but they have counterparts named sumOf() and sortedBy(). You pass a function (often a lambda) as an argument, which specifies the attribute to use for the operation:

```
// OperationsOnCollections/ByOperations.kt
package operationsoncollections
import atomictest.eq

data class Product(
  val description: String,
  val price: Double
)

fun main() {
  val products = listOf(
    Product("bread", 2.0),
    Product("wine", 5.0)
  )

  products.sumOf { it.price } eq 7.0

  products.sortedByDescending { it.price } eq
    "[Product(description=wine, price=5.0)," +
    " Product(description=bread, price=2.0)]"

  products.minByOrNull { it.price } eq
    Product("bread", 2.0)
}
```

sumOf() sums up the values produced by calling the lambda argument on each element. sorted() and sortedBy() sort the collection in ascending order, while `sortedDescending()` and `sortedByDescending()` sort the collection in descending order.

`minByOrNull` returns a minimum value based on a given criteria or `null` if the list is empty.

`take()` and `drop()` produce or remove (respectively) the first element, while `takeLast()` and `dropLast()` produce or remove the last element. These have counterparts that accept a predicate specifying the elements to take or drop:

```
// OperationsOnCollections/TakeOrDrop.kt
import atomictest.eq

fun main() {
  val list = listOf('a', 'b', 'c', 'X', 'Z')
  list.takeLast(3) eq "[c, X, Z]"
  list.takeLastWhile { it.isUpperCase() } eq
    "[X, Z]"
  list.drop(1) eq "[b, c, X, Z]"
  list.dropWhile { it.isLowerCase() } eq
    "[X, Z]"
}
```

Operations like those you've seen for `List`s are also available for `Set`s:

```
// OperationsOnCollections/SetOperations.kt
import atomictest.eq

fun main() {
  val set = setOf("a", "ab", "ac")
  set.maxByOrNull { it.length }?.length eq 2
  set.filter {
    it.contains('b')
  } eq listOf("ab")
  set.map { it.length } eq listOf(1, 2, 2)
}
```

`maxByOrNull()` returns `null` if a collection is empty, so its result is nullable.

When applied to a `Set`, `filter()` and `map()` return their results in a `List`.

Exercises and solutions can be found at www.AtomicKotlin.com.

Member References

You can pass a member reference as a function argument.

Member references—for functions, properties and constructors—can replace trivial lambdas that simply call the corresponding function, property or constructor.

A member reference uses a double colon to separate the class name from the function or property. Here, `Message::isRead` is a member reference:

```
// MemberReferences/PropertyReference.kt
package memberreferences1
import atomictest.eq

data class Message(
  val sender: String,
  val text: String,
  val isRead: Boolean
)

fun main() {
  val messages = listOf(
    Message("Kitty", "Hey!", true),
    Message("Kitty", "Where are you?", false))
  val unread =
    messages.filterNot(Message::isRead)
  unread.size eq 1
  unread.single().text eq "Where are you?"
}
```

To filter for unread messages, we use the library function `filterNot()`, which takes a predicate. In our case, the predicate indicates whether a message is already read. We could pass a lambda, but instead we pass the property reference `Message::isRead`.

Property references are useful when specifying a non-trivial sort order:

```
// MemberReferences/SortWith.kt
import memberreferences1.Message
import atomictest.eq

fun main() {
  val messages = listOf(
    Message("Kitty", "Hey!", true),
    Message("Kitty", "Where are you?", false),
    Message("Boss", "Meeting today", false))
  messages.sortedWith(compareBy(
    Message::isRead, Message::sender)) eq
    listOf(
      // First unread, sorted by sender:
      Message("Boss", "Meeting today", false),
      Message("Kitty",
        "Where are you?", false),
      // Then read, also sorted by sender:
      Message("Kitty", "Hey!", true))
}
```

The library function sortedWith() sorts a list using a *comparator*, which is an object used to compare two elements. The library function compareBy() builds a comparator based on its parameters, which are a list of predicates. Using compareBy() with a single argument is equivalent to calling sortedBy().

Function References

Suppose you want to check whether a List contains any important messages, not just unread messages. You might have a number of complicated criteria to decide what "important" means. You can put this logic into a lambda, but that lambda could easily become large and complex. The code is more understandable if you extract it into a separate function. In Kotlin you can't pass a function where a function type is expected, but you can pass a *reference* to that function:

```kotlin
// MemberReferences/FunctionReference.kt
package memberreferences2
import atomictest.eq

data class Message(
  val sender: String,
  val text: String,
  val isRead: Boolean,
  val attachments: List<Attachment>
)

data class Attachment(
  val type: String,
  val name: String
)

fun Message.isImportant(): Boolean =
  text.contains("Salary increase") ||
    attachments.any {
      it.type == "image" &&
        it.name.contains("cat")
    }

fun main() {
  val messages = listOf(Message(
    "Boss", "Let's discuss goals " +
    "for next year", false,
    listOf(Attachment("image", "cute cats"))))
  messages.any(Message::isImportant) eq true
}
```

This new `Message` class adds an `attachments` property, and the extension function `Message.isImportant()` uses this information. In the call to `messages.any()`, we create a reference to an extension function—references are not limited to member functions.

If you have a top-level function taking `Message` as its only parameter, you can pass it as a reference. When you create a reference to a top-level function, there's no class name, so it's written `::function`:

```
// MemberReferences/TopLevelFunctionRef.kt
package memberreferences2
import atomictest.eq

fun ignore(message: Message) =
  !message.isImportant() &&
    message.sender in setOf("Boss", "Mom")

fun main() {
  val text = "Let's discuss goals " +
    "for the next year"
  val msgs = listOf(
    Message("Boss", text, false, listOf()),
    Message("Boss", text, false, listOf(
      Attachment("image", "cute cats"))))
  msgs.filter(::ignore).size eq 1
  msgs.filterNot(::ignore).size eq 1
}
```

Constructor References

You can create a reference to a constructor using the class name.

Here, `names.mapIndexed()` takes the constructor reference `::Student`:

```
// MemberReferences/ConstructorReference.kt
package memberreferences3
import atomictest.eq

data class Student(
  val id: Int,
  val name: String
)

fun main() {
  val names = listOf("Alice", "Bob")
  val students =
    names.mapIndexed { index, name ->
      Student(index, name)
    }
```

```
    students eq listOf(Student(0, "Alice"),
      Student(1, "Bob"))
    names.mapIndexed(::Student) eq students
}
```

mapIndexed() was introduced in **Lambdas**. It turns each element in names into the index of that element along with the element. In the definition of students, these are explicitly mapped into the constructor, but the identical effect is achieved with names.mapIndexed(::Student). Thus, function and constructor references can eliminate specifying a long list of parameters that are simply passed into a lambda. Function and constructor references are often more readable than lambdas.

Extension Function References

To produce a reference to an extension function, prefix the reference with the name of the extended type:

```
// MemberReferences/ExtensionReference.kt
package memberreferences
import atomictest.eq

fun Int.times47() = times(47)

class Frog
fun Frog.speak() = "Ribbit!"

fun goInt(n: Int, g: (Int) -> Int) = g(n)

fun goFrog(frog: Frog, g: (Frog) -> String) =
  g(frog)

fun main() {
  goInt(12, Int::times47) eq 564
  goFrog(Frog(), Frog::speak) eq "Ribbit!"
}
```

In goInt(), g is a function that expects an Int argument and produces an Int. In goFrog(), g expects a Frog and produces a String.

Exercises and solutions can be found at www.AtomicKotlin.com.

Higher-Order Functions

A language supports *higher-order functions* if its functions can accept other functions as arguments and produce functions as return values.

Higher-order functions are an essential part of functional programming languages. In previous atoms, we've seen higher-order functions such as `filter()`, `map()`, and `any()`.

You can store a lambda in a reference. Let's look at the type of this storage:

```
// HigherOrderFunctions/IsPlus.kt
package higherorderfunctions
import atomictest.eq

val isPlus: (Int) -> Boolean = { it > 0 }

fun main() {
  listOf(1, 2, -3).any(isPlus) eq true
}
```

`(Int) -> Boolean` is the function type: it starts with parentheses surrounding zero or more parameter types, then an arrow (`->`), followed by the return type:

```
(Arg1Type, Arg2Type... ArgNType) -> ReturnType
```

The syntax for calling a function through a reference is identical to an ordinary function call:

```
// HigherOrderFunctions/CallingReference.kt
package higherorderfunctions
import atomictest.eq

val helloWorld: () -> String =
  { "Hello, world!" }

val sum: (Int, Int) -> Int =
  { x, y -> x + y }

fun main() {
  helloWorld() eq "Hello, world!"
  sum(1, 2) eq 3
}
```

When a function accepts a function parameter, you can either pass it a function reference or a lambda. Consider how you might define any() from the standard library:

```
// HigherOrderFunctions/Any.kt
package higherorderfunctions
import atomictest.eq

fun <T> List<T>.any(                        // [1]
  predicate: (T) -> Boolean                 // [2]
): Boolean {
  for (element in this) {
    if (predicate(element))                 // [3]
      return true
  }
  return false
}

fun main() {
  val ints = listOf(1, 2, -3)
  ints.any { it > 0 } eq true               // [4]

  val strings = listOf("abc", " ")
  strings.any { it.isBlank() } eq true      // [5]
  strings.any(String::isNotBlank) eq        // [6]
    true
}
```

- **[1]** `any()` should be usable with `List`s of different types so we define it as an extension to the generic `List<T>`.
- **[2]** The `predicate` function is callable with a parameter of type `T` so we can apply it to the `List` elements.
- **[3]** Applying `predicate()` tells whether that `element` fits our criteria.
- The type of the lambda differs: it's `Int` in **[4]** and `String` in **[5]**.
- **[6]** A member reference is another way to pass a function reference.

`repeat()` from the standard library takes a function as its second parameter. It repeats an action an `Int` number of times:

```
// HigherOrderFunctions/RepeatByInt.kt
import atomictest.*

fun main() {
  repeat(4) { trace("hi!") }
  trace eq "hi! hi! hi! hi!"
}
```

Consider how `repeat()` might be defined:

```
// HigherOrderFunctions/Repeat.kt
package higherorderfunctions
import atomictest.*

fun repeat(
  times: Int,
  action: (Int) -> Unit          // [1]
) {
  for (index in 0 until times) {
    action(index)                // [2]
  }
}

fun main() {
  repeat(3) { trace("#$it") }    // [3]
  trace eq "#0 #1 #2"
}
```

- **[1]** `repeat()` takes a parameter `action` of the function type `(Int) -> Unit`.

- **[2]** When `action()` is called, it is passed the current repetition `index`.
- **[3]** When calling `repeat()`, you access the repetition `index` using `it` inside the lambda.

A function return type can be nullable:

```
// HigherOrderFunctions/NullableReturn.kt
import atomictest.eq

fun main() {
  val transform: (String) -> Int? =
    { s: String -> s.toIntOrNull() }
  transform("112") eq 112
  transform("abc") eq null
  val x = listOf("112", "abc")
  x.mapNotNull(transform) eq "[112]"
  x.mapNotNull { it.toIntOrNull() } eq "[112]"
}
```

`toIntOrNull()` might return `null`, so `transform()` accepts a `String` and returns a nullable `Int?`. `mapNotNull()` converts each element in a `List` into a nullable value and removes all `null`s from the result. It has the same effect as first calling `map()`, then applying `filterNotNull()` to the resulting list.

Note the difference between making the return type nullable versus making the whole function type nullable:

```
// HigherOrderFunctions/NullableFunction.kt
import atomictest.eq

fun main() {
  val returnTypeNullable: (String) -> Int? =
    { null }
  val mightBeNull: ((String) -> Int)? = null
  returnTypeNullable("abc") eq null
  // Doesn't compile without a null check:
  // mightBeNull("abc")
  if (mightBeNull != null) {
    mightBeNull("abc")
  }
}
```

Before calling the function stored in `mightBeNull`, we must ensure that the function reference itself is not `null`.

Exercises and solutions can be found at www.AtomicKotlin.com.

Manipulating Lists

Zipping and *flattening* are two common operations that manipulate Lists.

Zipping

zip() combines two Lists by mimicking the behavior of the zipper on your jacket, pairing adjacent List elements:

```
// ManipulatingLists/Zipper.kt
import atomictest.eq

fun main() {
  val left = listOf("a", "b", "c", "d")
  val right = listOf("q", "r", "s", "t")

  left.zip(right) eq                  // [1]
    "[(a, q), (b, r), (c, s), (d, t)]"

  left.zip(0..4) eq                   // [2]
    "[(a, 0), (b, 1), (c, 2), (d, 3)]"

  (10..100).zip(right) eq             // [3]
    "[(10, q), (11, r), (12, s), (13, t)]"
}
```

- **[1]** Zipping `left` with `right` results in a List of Pairs, combining each element in `left` with its corresponding element in `right`.
- **[2]** You can also zip() a List with a range.
- **[3]** The range `10..100` is much larger than `right`, but the zipping process stops when one sequence runs out.

zip() can also perform an operation on each Pair it creates:

```
// ManipulatingLists/ZipAndTransform.kt
package manipulatinglists
import atomictest.eq

data class Person(
  val name: String,
  val id: Int
)

fun main() {
  val names = listOf("Bob", "Jill", "Jim")
  val ids = listOf(1731, 9274, 8378)
  names.zip(ids) { name, id ->
    Person(name, id)
  } eq "[Person(name=Bob, id=1731), " +
    "Person(name=Jill, id=9274), " +
    "Person(name=Jim, id=8378)]"
}
```

`names.zip(ids) { ... }` produces a sequence of name-id `Pair`s, and applies the lambda to each `Pair`. The result is a `List` of initialized `Person` objects.

To zip two adjacent elements from a single `List`, use `zipWithNext()`:

```
// ManipulatingLists/ZippingWithNext.kt
import atomictest.eq

fun main() {
  val list = listOf('a', 'b', 'c', 'd')

  list.zipWithNext() eq listOf(
    Pair('a', 'b'),
    Pair('b', 'c'),
    Pair('c', 'd'))

  list.zipWithNext { a, b -> "$a$b" } eq
    "[ab, bc, cd]"
}
```

The second call to `zipWithNext()` performs an additional operation after zipping.

Flattening

`flatten()` takes a `List` containing elements that are themselves `List`s—a `List` of `List`s—and flattens it into a `List` of single elements:

```
// ManipulatingLists/Flatten.kt
import atomictest.eq

fun main() {
  val list = listOf(
    listOf(1, 2),
    listOf(4, 5),
    listOf(7, 8),
  )
  list.flatten() eq "[1, 2, 4, 5, 7, 8]"
}
```

`flatten()` helps us understand another important operation on collections: `flatMap()`. Let's produce all possible `Pair`s of a range of `Int`s:

```
// ManipulatingLists/FlattenAndFlatMap.kt
import atomictest.eq

fun main() {
  val intRange = 1..3

  intRange.map { a ->           // [1]
    intRange.map { b -> a to b }
  } eq "[" +
    "[(1, 1), (1, 2), (1, 3)], " +
    "[(2, 1), (2, 2), (2, 3)], " +
    "[(3, 1), (3, 2), (3, 3)]" +
    "]"

  intRange.map { a ->           // [2]
    intRange.map { b -> a to b }
  }.flatten() eq "[" +
    "(1, 1), (1, 2), (1, 3), " +
    "(2, 1), (2, 2), (2, 3), " +
    "(3, 1), (3, 2), (3, 3)" +
    "]"
```

```kotlin
  intRange.flatMap { a ->        // [3]
    intRange.map { b -> a to b }
  } eq "[" +
    "(1, 1), (1, 2), (1, 3), " +
    "(2, 1), (2, 2), (2, 3), " +
    "(3, 1), (3, 2), (3, 3)" +
    "]"
}
```

The lambda in each case is identical: every `intRange` element is combined with every `intRange` element to produce all possible `a to b` `Pair`s. But in **[1]**, `map()` helpfully preserves the extra information that we have produced three `List`s, one for each element in `intRange`. There are situations where this extra information is essential, but here we don't want it—we just need a single flat `List` of all combinations, with no additional structure.

There are two options. **[2]** shows the application of the `flatten()` function to remove this additional structure and flatten the result into a single `List`, which is an acceptable approach. However, this is such a common task that Kotlin provides a combined operation called `flatMap()`, which performs both `map()` and `flatten()` with a single call. **[3]** shows `flatMap()` in action. You'll find `flatMap()` in most languages that support functional programming.

Here's a second example of `flatMap()`:

```kotlin
// ManipulatingLists/WhyFlatMap.kt
package manipulatinglists
import atomictest.eq

class Book(
  val title: String,
  val authors: List<String>
)

fun main() {
  val books = listOf(
    Book("1984", listOf("George Orwell")),
    Book("Ulysses", listOf("James Joyce"))
  )
  books.map { it.authors }.flatten() eq
```

```
    listOf("George Orwell", "James Joyce")
  books.flatMap { it.authors } eq
    listOf("George Orwell", "James Joyce")
}
```

We'd like a List of authors. map() produces a List of List of authors, which isn't very convenient. flatten() takes that and produces a simple List. flatMap() produces the same results in a single step.

Here, we use map() and flatMap() to combine the enums Suit and Rank, producing a deck of Cards:

```
// ManipulatingLists/PlayingCards.kt
package manipulatinglists
import kotlin.random.Random
import atomictest.*

enum class Suit {
  Spade, Club, Heart, Diamond
}

enum class Rank(val faceValue: Int) {
  Ace(1), Two(2), Three(3), Four(4), Five(5),
  Six(6), Seven(7), Eight(8), Nine(9),
  Ten(10), Jack(10), Queen(10), King(10)
}

class Card(val rank: Rank, val suit: Suit) {
  override fun toString() =
    "$rank of ${suit}s"
}

val deck: List<Card> =
  Suit.values().flatMap { suit ->
    Rank.values().map { rank ->
      Card(rank, suit)
    }
  }

fun main() {
  val rand = Random(26)
  repeat(7) {
```

```
    trace("'${deck.random(rand)}'")
  }
  trace eq """
    'Jack of Hearts' 'Four of Hearts'
    'Five of Clubs' 'Seven of Clubs'
    'Jack of Diamonds' 'Ten of Spades'
    'Seven of Spades'
  """
}
```

In the initialization of deck, the inner Rank.values().map produces four Lists, one for each Suit, so we use flatMap() on the outer loop to produce a List<Card> for deck.

Exercises and solutions can be found at www.AtomicKotlin.com.

Building Maps

Maps are extremely useful programming tools, and there are numerous ways to construct them.

To create a repeatable set of data, we use the technique shown in ***Manipulating Lists***, where two Lists are zipped and the result is used in a lambda to call a constructor, producing a List<Person>:

```
// BuildingMaps/People.kt
package buildingmaps

data class Person(
  val name: String,
  val age: Int
)

val names = listOf("Alice", "Arthricia",
  "Bob", "Bill", "Birdperson", "Charlie",
  "Crocubot", "Franz", "Revolio")

val ages = listOf(21, 15, 25, 25, 42, 21,
  42, 21, 33)

fun people(): List<Person> =
  names.zip(ages) { name, age ->
    Person(name, age)
  }
```

A Map uses keys to provide fast access to its values. By building a Map with age as the key, we can quickly look up groups of people by age. The library function groupBy() is one way to create such a Map:

```
// BuildingMaps/GroupBy.kt
import buildingmaps.*
import atomictest.eq

fun main() {
  val map: Map<Int, List<Person>> =
    people().groupBy(Person::age)
  map[15] eq listOf(Person("Arthricia", 15))
  map[21] eq listOf(
    Person("Alice", 21),
    Person("Charlie", 21),
    Person("Franz", 21))
  map[22] eq null
  map[25] eq listOf(
    Person("Bob", 25),
    Person("Bill", 25))
  map[33] eq listOf(Person("Revolio", 33))
  map[42] eq listOf(
    Person("Birdperson", 42),
    Person("Crocubot", 42))
}
```

groupBy()'s parameter produces a Map where each key connects to a List of elements. Here, all people of the same age are selected by the age key.

You can produce the same groups using the filter() function, but groupBy() is preferable because it only performs the grouping once. With filter() you must repeat the grouping for each new key:

```
// BuildingMaps/GroupByVsFilter.kt
import buildingmaps.*
import atomictest.eq

fun main() {
  val groups =
    people().groupBy { it.name.first() }
  // groupBy() produces map-speed access:
  groups['A'] eq listOf(Person("Alice", 21),
    Person("Arthricia", 15))
  groups['Z'] eq null

  // Must repeat filter() for each character:
```

```
  people().filter {
    it.name.first() == 'A'
  } eq listOf(Person("Alice", 21),
    Person("Arthricia", 15))
  people().filter {
    it.name.first() == 'F'
  } eq listOf(Person("Franz", 21))

  people().partition {
    it.name.first() == 'A'
  } eq Pair(
    listOf(Person("Alice", 21),
      Person("Arthricia", 15)),
    listOf(Person("Bob", 25),
      Person("Bill", 25),
      Person("Birdperson", 42),
      Person("Charlie", 21),
      Person("Crocubot", 42),
      Person("Franz", 21),
      Person("Revolio", 33)))
}
```

Here, `groupBy()` groups `people()` by their first character, selected by `first()`. We can also use `filter()` to produce the same result by repeating the lambda code for each character.

If you only need two groups, the `partition()` function is more direct because it divides the contents into two lists based on a predicate. `groupBy()` is appropriate when you need more than two resulting groups.

`associateWith()` allows you to take a list of keys and build a `Map` by associating each of these keys with a value created by its parameter (here, the lambda):

```
// BuildingMaps/AssociateWith.kt
import buildingmaps.*
import atomictest.eq

fun main() {
  val map: Map<Person, String> =
    people().associateWith { it.name }
  map eq mapOf(
    Person("Alice", 21) to "Alice",
    Person("Arthricia", 15) to "Arthricia",
    Person("Bob", 25) to "Bob",
    Person("Bill", 25) to "Bill",
    Person("Birdperson", 42) to "Birdperson",
    Person("Charlie", 21) to "Charlie",
    Person("Crocubot", 42) to "Crocubot",
    Person("Franz", 21) to "Franz",
    Person("Revolio", 33) to "Revolio")
}
```

`associateBy()` reverses the order of association produced by `associateWith()`—the selector (the lambda in the following example) becomes the key:

```
// BuildingMaps/AssociateBy.kt
import buildingmaps.*
import atomictest.eq

fun main() {
  val map: Map<String, Person> =
    people().associateBy { it.name }
  map eq mapOf(
    "Alice" to Person("Alice", 21),
    "Arthricia" to Person("Arthricia", 15),
    "Bob" to Person("Bob", 25),
    "Bill" to Person("Bill", 25),
    "Birdperson" to Person("Birdperson", 42),
    "Charlie" to Person("Charlie", 21),
    "Crocubot" to Person("Crocubot", 42),
    "Franz" to Person("Franz", 21),
    "Revolio" to Person("Revolio", 33))
}
```

`associateBy()` must be used with a unique selection key and returns a `Map` that pairs each unique key to the single element selected by that key.

```
// BuildingMaps/AssociateByUnique.kt
import buildingmaps.*
import atomictest.eq

fun main() {
  // associateBy() fails when the key isn't
  // unique -- values disappear:
  val ages = people().associateBy { it.age }
  ages eq mapOf(
    21 to Person("Franz", 21),
    15 to Person("Arthricia", 15),
    25 to Person("Bill", 25),
    42 to Person("Crocubot", 42),
    33 to Person("Revolio", 33))
}
```

If multiple values are selected by the predicate, as in ages, only the last one appears in the generated Map.

getOrElse() tries to look up a value in a Map. Its associated lambda computes a default value when a key is not present. Because it's a lambda, we compute the default key only when necessary:

```
// BuildingMaps/GetOrPut.kt
import atomictest.eq

fun main() {
  val map = mapOf(1 to "one", 2 to "two")
  map.getOrElse(0) { "zero" } eq "zero"

  val mutableMap = map.toMutableMap()
  mutableMap.getOrPut(0) { "zero" } eq
    "zero"
  mutableMap eq "{1=one, 2=two, 0=zero}"
}
```

getOrPut() works on a MutableMap. If a key is present it simply returns the associated value. If the key isn't found, it computes the value, puts it into the map and returns that value.

Many Map operations duplicate ones in List. For example, you can filter() or map() the contents of a Map. You can filter keys and values separately:

```kotlin
// BuildingMaps/FilterMap.kt
import atomictest.eq

fun main() {
  val map = mapOf(1 to "one",
    2 to "two", 3 to "three", 4 to "four")

  map.filterKeys { it % 2 == 1 } eq
    "{1=one, 3=three}"

  map.filterValues { it.contains('o') } eq
    "{1=one, 2=two, 4=four}"

  map.filter { entry ->
    entry.key % 2 == 1 &&
      entry.value.contains('o')
  } eq "{1=one}"
}
```

All three functions `filter()`, `filterKeys()` and `filterValues()` produce a new map containing only the elements that satisfy the predicate. `filterKeys()` applies its predicate to the keys, and `filterValues()` applies its predicate to the values.

Applying Operations to Maps

To `map()` a `Map` sounds like a tautology, like saying "salt is salty." The word *map* represents two distinct ideas:

- Transforming a collection
- The key-value data structure

In many programming languages, the word *map* is used for both concepts. For clarity, we say *transform a map* when applying `map()` to a `Map`.

Here we demonstrate `map()`, `mapKeys()` and `mapValues()`:

```kotlin
// BuildingMaps/TransformingMap.kt
import atomictest.eq

fun main() {
  val even = mapOf(2 to "two", 4 to "four")

  even.map {                              // [1]
    "${it.key}=${it.value}"
  } eq listOf("2=two", "4=four")

  even.map { (key, value) ->              // [2]
    "$key=$value"
  } eq listOf("2=two", "4=four")

  even.mapKeys { (num, _) -> -num }       // [3]
    .mapValues { (_, str) -> "minus $str" } eq
    mapOf(-2 to "minus two",
      -4 to "minus four")

  even.map { (key, value) ->
    -key to "minus $value"
  }.toMap() eq mapOf(-2 to "minus two",   // [4]
    -4 to "minus four")
}
```

- **[1]** Here, map() takes a predicate with a Map.Entry argument. We access its contents as it.key and it.value.
- **[2]** You can also use a ***destructuring declaration*** to place the entry contents into key and value.
- **[3]** If a parameter isn't used, an underscore (_) avoids compiler complaints. mapKeys() and mapValues() return a new map, with all keys or values transformed accordingly.
- **[4]**, map() returns a list of pairs, so to produce a Map we use the explicit conversion toMap().

Functions like any() and all() can also be applied to Maps:

```
// BuildingMaps/SimilarOperation.kt
import atomictest.eq

fun main() {
  val map = mapOf(1 to "one",
    -2 to "minus two")
  map.any { (key, _) -> key < 0 } eq true
  map.all { (key, _) -> key < 0 } eq false
  map.maxByOrNull { it.key }?.value eq "one"
}
```

`any()` checks whether any of the entries in a `Map` satisfy the given predicate, while `all()` is `true` only if all entries in the `Map` satisfy the predicate.

`maxByOrNull()` finds the maximum entry based on the given criteria. There may not be a maximum entry, so the result is nullable.

Exercises and solutions can be found at www.AtomicKotlin.com.

Sequences

> A Kotlin Sequence is like a List, but you can *only* iterate through a Sequence—you cannot index into a Sequence. This restriction produces very efficient chained operations.

Kotlin Sequences are termed *streams* in other functional languages. Kotlin had to choose a different name to maintain interoperability with the Java 8 Stream library.

Operations on Lists are performed *eagerly*—they always happen right away. When chaining List operations, the first result must be produced before starting the next operation. Here, each filter(), map() and any() operation is applied to every element in list:

```
// Sequences/EagerEvaluation.kt
import atomictest.eq

fun main() {
  val list = listOf(1, 2, 3, 4)

  list.filter { it % 2 == 0 }
    .map { it * it }
    .any { it < 10 } eq true

  // Equivalent to:
  val mid1 = list.filter { it % 2 == 0 }
  mid1 eq listOf(2, 4)
  val mid2 = mid1.map { it * it }
  mid2 eq listOf(4, 16)
  mid2.any { it < 10 } eq true
}
```

Eager evaluation is intuitive and straightforward, but can be suboptimal. In EagerEvaluation.kt, it would make more sense to stop after encountering the first element that satisfies the any(). For a long sequence, this optimization might be much faster than evaluating every element and then searching for a single match.

Eager evaluation is sometimes called *horizontal evaluation*:

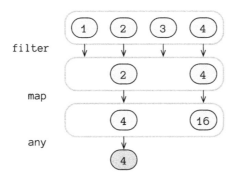

Horizontal Evaluation

The first line contains the initial list contents. Each following line shows the results from the previous operation. Before the next operation is performed, all elements on the current horizontal level are processed.

The alternative to eager evaluation is *lazy evaluation*: a result is computed only when needed. Performing lazy operations on sequences is sometimes called *vertical evaluation*:

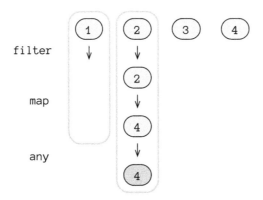

Vertical Evaluation

With lazy evaluation, an operation is performed on an element only when that element's associated result is requested. If the final result of a calculation is found before processing the last element, no further elements are processed.

Converting `List`s to `Sequence`s using `asSequence()` enables lazy evaluation. All

List operations except indexing are also available for Sequences, so you can usually make this single change and gain the benefits of lazy evaluation.

The following example shows the above diagrams converted into code. We perform the identical chain of operations, first on a List, then on a Sequence. The output shows where each operation is called:

```
// Sequences/EagerVsLazyEvaluation.kt
package sequences
import atomictest.*

fun Int.isEven(): Boolean {
  trace("$this.isEven()")
  return this % 2 == 0
}

fun Int.square(): Int {
  trace("$this.square()")
  return this * this
}

fun Int.lessThanTen(): Boolean {
  trace("$this.lessThanTen()")
  return this < 10
}

fun main() {
  val list = listOf(1, 2, 3, 4)
  trace(">>> List:")
  trace(
    list
      .filter(Int::isEven)
      .map(Int::square)
      .any(Int::lessThanTen)
  )
  trace(">>> Sequence:")
  trace(
    list.asSequence()
      .filter(Int::isEven)
      .map(Int::square)
      .any(Int::lessThanTen)
  )
```

```
  trace eq """
    >>> List:
    1.isEven()
    2.isEven()
    3.isEven()
    4.isEven()
    2.square()
    4.square()
    4.lessThanTen()
    true
    >>> Sequence:
    1.isEven()
    2.isEven()
    2.square()
    4.lessThanTen()
    true
  """
}
```

The only difference between the two approaches is the addition of the asSequence() call, but more elements are processed for the List code than the Sequence code.

Calling either filter() or map() on a Sequence produces another Sequence. Nothing happens until you ask for a result from a calculation. Instead, the new Sequence stores all information about postponed operations and will perform those operations only when needed:

```
// Sequences/NoComputationYet.kt
import atomictest.eq
import sequences.*

fun main() {
  val r = listOf(1, 2, 3, 4)
    .asSequence()
    .filter(Int::isEven)
    .map(Int::square)
  r.toString().substringBefore("@") eq
    "kotlin.sequences.TransformingSequence"
}
```

Converting r to a String does not produce the results we want, but just the identifier for the object (including the @ address of the object in memory, which we remove using the standard library substringBefore()). The TransformingSequence just holds the operations but does not perform them.

There are two categories of Sequence operations: *intermediate* and *terminal*. Intermediate operations return another Sequence as a result. filter() and map() are intermediate operations. Terminal operations return a non-Sequence. To do this, a terminal operation executes all stored computations. In the previous examples, any() is a terminal operation because it takes a Sequence and returns a Boolean. In the following example, toList() is terminal because it converts the Sequence to a List, running all stored operations in the process:

```
// Sequences/TerminalOperations.kt
import sequences.*
import atomictest.*

fun main() {
  val list = listOf(1, 2, 3, 4)
  trace(list.asSequence()
    .filter(Int::isEven)
    .map(Int::square)
    .toList())
  trace eq """
    1.isEven()
    2.isEven()
    2.square()
    3.isEven()
    4.isEven()
    4.square()
    [4, 16]
  """
}
```

Because a Sequence stores the operations, it can call those operations in any order, resulting in lazy evaluation.

The following example uses the standard library function generateSequence() to produce an infinite sequence of natural numbers. The first argument is the initial element in the sequence, followed by a lambda defining how the next element is calculated from the previous element:

```
// Sequences/GenerateSequence1.kt
import atomictest.eq

fun main() {
  val naturalNumbers =
    generateSequence(1) { it + 1 }
  naturalNumbers.take(3).toList() eq
    listOf(1, 2, 3)
  naturalNumbers.take(10).sum() eq 55
}
```

Collections are a known size, discoverable through their size property. Sequences are treated as if they are infinite. Here, we decide how many elements we want using take(), followed by a terminal operation (toList() or sum()).

There's an overloaded version of generateSequence() that doesn't require the first parameter, only a lambda that returns the next element in the Sequence. When there are no more elements, it returns null. The following example generates a Sequence until the "termination flag" XXX appears in its input:

```
// Sequences/GenerateSequence2.kt
import atomictest.*

fun main() {
  val items = mutableListOf(
    "first", "second", "third", "XXX", "4th"
  )
  val seq = generateSequence {
    items.removeAt(0).takeIf { it != "XXX" }
  }
  seq.toList() eq "[first, second, third]"
  capture {
    seq.toList()
  } eq "IllegalStateException: This " +
    "sequence can be consumed only once."
}
```

removeAt(0) removes and produces the zeroth element from the List. takeIf() returns the receiver (the String produced by removeAt(0)) if it satisfies the given predicate, and null if the predicate fails (when the String is "XXX").

You can only iterate once through a Sequence. Further attempts produce an exception. To make multiple passes through a Sequence, first convert it to some type of Collection.

Here's an implementation for takeIf(), defined using a generic T so it can work with any type of argument:

```
// Sequences/DefineTakeIf.kt
package sequences
import atomictest.eq

fun <T> T.takeIf(
  predicate: (T) -> Boolean
): T? {
  return if (predicate(this)) this else null
}

fun main() {
  "abc".takeIf { it != "XXX" } eq "abc"
  "XXX".takeIf { it != "XXX" } eq null
}
```

Here, generateSequence() and takeIf() produce a decreasing sequence of numbers:

```
// Sequences/NumberSequence2.kt
import atomictest.eq

fun main() {
  generateSequence(6) {
    (it - 1).takeIf { it > 0 }
  }.toList() eq listOf(6, 5, 4, 3, 2, 1)
}
```

An ordinary if expression can always be used instead of takeIf(), but introducing an extra identifier can make the if expression clumsy. The takeIf() version is more functional, especially if it's used as a part of a chain of calls.

Exercises and solutions can be found at www.AtomicKotlin.com.

Local Functions

You can define functions anywhere—even inside other functions.

Named functions defined within other functions are called *local functions*. Local functions reduce duplication by extracting repetitive code. At the same time, they are only visible within the surrounding function, so they don't "pollute your namespace." Here, even though `log()` is defined just like any other function, it's *nested* inside `main()`:

```
// LocalFunctions/LocalFunctions.kt
import atomictest.eq

fun main() {
  val logMsg = StringBuilder()
  fun log(message: String) =
    logMsg.appendLine(message)
  log("Starting computation")
  val x = 42  // Imitate computation
  log("Computation result: $x")
  logMsg.toString() eq """
    Starting computation
    Computation result: 42
  """
}
```

Local functions are *closures*: they capture `vars` or `vals` from the surrounding environment that would otherwise have to be passed as additional parameters. `log()` uses `logMsg`, which is defined in its outer scope. This way, you don't repeatedly pass `logMsg` into `log()`.

You can create local extension functions:

```
// LocalFunctions/LocalExtensions.kt
import atomictest.eq

fun main() {
  fun String.exclaim() = "$this!"
  "Hello".exclaim() eq "Hello!"
  "Hallo".exclaim() eq "Hallo!"
  "Bonjour".exclaim() eq "Bonjour!"
  "Ciao".exclaim() eq "Ciao!"
}
```

exclaim() is available only inside main().

Here is a demonstration class and example values for use in this atom:

```
// LocalFunctions/Session.kt
package localfunctions

class Session(
  val title: String,
  val speaker: String
)

val sessions = listOf(Session(
  "Kotlin Coroutines", "Roman Elizarov"))

val favoriteSpeakers = setOf("Roman Elizarov")
```

You can refer to a local function using a function reference:

```
// LocalFunctions/LocalFunctionReference.kt
import localfunctions.*
import atomictest.eq

fun main() {
  fun interesting(session: Session): Boolean {
    if (session.title.contains("Kotlin") &&
      session.speaker in favoriteSpeakers) {
      return true
    }
    // ... more checks
    return false
```

```
  }
  sessions.any(::interesting) eq true
}
```

`interesting()` is only used once, so we might be inclined to define it as a lambda. As you will see later in this atom, the `return` expressions within `interesting()` complicate the task of turning it into a lambda. We can avoid this complication with an *anonymous function*. Like local functions, anonymous functions are defined within other functions—however, an anonymous function has no name. Anonymous functions are conceptually similar to lambdas but use the `fun` keyword. Here's `LocalFunctionReference.kt` rewritten using an anonymous function:

```
// LocalFunctions/InterestingSessions.kt
import localfunctions.*
import atomictest.eq

fun main() {
  sessions.any(
    fun(session: Session): Boolean {    // [1]
      if (session.title.contains("Kotlin") &&
        session.speaker in favoriteSpeakers) {
        return true
      }
      // ... more checks
      return false
    }) eq true
}
```

- **[1]** An anonymous function looks like a regular function without a function name. Here, the anonymous function is passed as an argument to `sessions.any()`.

If a lambda becomes too complicated and hard to read, replace it with a local function or an anonymous function.

Labels

Here, `forEach()` acts upon a lambda containing a `return`:

```
// LocalFunctions/ReturnFromFun.kt
import atomictest.eq

fun main() {
  val list = listOf(1, 2, 3, 4, 5)
  val value = 3
  var result = ""
  list.forEach {
    result += "$it"
    if (it == value) {
      result eq "123"
      return                   // [1]
    }
  }
  result eq "Never gets here"  // [2]
}
```

A `return` expression exits a function defined using `fun` (that is, not a lambda). In line **[1]** this means returning from `main()`. Line **[2]** is never called and you see no output.

To return *only* from a lambda, and not from the surrounding function, use a *labeled return*:

```
// LocalFunctions/LabeledReturn.kt
import atomictest.eq

fun main() {
  val list = listOf(1, 2, 3, 4, 5)
  val value = 3
  var result = ""
  list.forEach {
    result += "$it"
    if (it == value) return@forEach
  }
  result eq "12345"
}
```

Here, the label is the name of the function that called the lambda. The labeled return expression `return@forEach` tells it to return *only* to the name `forEach`.

You can create a label by preceding the lambda with `label@`, where `label` can be any name:

```
// LocalFunctions/CustomLabel.kt
import atomictest.eq

fun main() {
  val list = listOf(1, 2, 3, 4, 5)
  val value = 3
  var result = ""
  list.forEach tag@{                  // [1]
    result += "$it"
    if (it == value) return@tag       // [2]
  }
  result eq "12345"
}
```

- **[1]** This lambda is labeled `tag`.
- **[2]** `return@tag` returns from the lambda, not from `main()`.

Let's replace the anonymous function in `InterestingSessions.kt` with a lambda:

```
// LocalFunctions/ReturnInsideLambda.kt
import localfunctions.*
import atomictest.eq

fun main() {
  sessions.any { session ->
    if (session.title.contains("Kotlin") &&
      session.speaker in favoriteSpeakers) {
      return@any true
    }
    // ... more checks
    false
  } eq true
}
```

We must `return` to a label so it exits only the lambda and not `main()`.

Manipulating Local Functions

You can store a lambda or an anonymous function in a `var` or `val`, then use that identifier to call the function. To store a local function, use a function reference (see ***Member References***).

In the following example, `first()` creates an anonymous function, `second()` uses a lambda, and `third()` returns a reference to a local function. `fourth()` achieves the same effect as `third()` but uses a more compact expression body. `fifth()` produces the same effect using a lambda:

```
// LocalFunctions/ReturningFunc.kt
package localfunctions
import atomictest.eq

fun first(): (Int) -> Int {
  val func = fun(i: Int) = i + 1
  func(1) eq 2
  return func
}

fun second(): (String) -> String {
  val func2 = { s: String -> "$s!" }
  func2("abc") eq "abc!"
  return func2
}

fun third(): () -> String {
  fun greet() = "Hi!"
  return ::greet
}

fun fourth() = fun() = "Hi!"

fun fifth() = { "Hi!" }

fun main() {
  val funRef1: (Int) -> Int = first()
  val funRef2: (String) -> String = second()
  val funRef3: () -> String = third()
  val funRef4: () -> String = fourth()
  val funRef5: () -> String = fifth()

  funRef1(42) eq 43
  funRef2("xyz") eq "xyz!"
  funRef3() eq "Hi!"
  funRef4() eq "Hi!"
  funRef5() eq "Hi!"
```

```
  first()(42) eq 43
  second()("xyz") eq "xyz!"
  third()() eq "Hi!"
  fourth()() eq "Hi!"
  fifth()() eq "Hi!"
}
```

`main()` first verifies that calling each function does indeed return a function reference of the expected type. Each `funRef` is then called with an appropriate argument. Finally, each function is called and then the returned function reference is immediately called by adding an appropriate argument list. For example, calling `first()` returns a function, so we call *that* function by appending the argument list `(42)`.

Exercises and solutions can be found at www.AtomicKotlin.com.

Folding Lists

> `fold()` combines all elements of a list, in order, to generate a single result.

A common exercise is to implement operations such as `sum()` or `reverse()` using `fold()`. Here, `fold()` sums a sequence:

```
// FoldingLists/SumViaFold.kt
import atomictest.eq

fun main() {
  val list = listOf(1, 10, 100, 1000)
  list.fold(0) { sum, n ->
    sum + n
  } eq 1111
}
```

`fold()` takes the initial value (its argument, 0 in this case) and successively applies the operation (expressed here as a lambda) to combine the current accumulated value with each element. `fold()` first adds 0 (the initial value) and 1 to get 1. That becomes the sum, which is then added to the 10 to get 11, which becomes the new sum. The operation is repeated for two more elements: 100 and 1000. This produces 111 and 1111. The `fold()` will stop when there is nothing else in the list, returning the final sum of 1111. Of course, `fold()` doesn't really know it's doing a "sum"—the choice of identifier name was ours, to make it easier to understand.

To illuminate the steps in a `fold()`, here's SumViaFold.kt using an ordinary for loop:

```
// FoldingLists/FoldVsForLoop.kt
import atomictest.eq

fun main() {
  val list = listOf(1, 10, 100, 1000)
  var accumulator = 0
  val operation =
    { sum: Int, i: Int -> sum + i }
  for (i in list) {
    accumulator = operation(accumulator, i)
  }
  accumulator eq 1111
}
```

`fold()` accumulates values by successively applying `operation` to combine the current element with the accumulator value.

Although `fold()` is an important concept and the only way to accumulate values in pure functional languages, you may sometimes still use an ordinary `for` loop in Kotlin.

`foldRight()` processes elements starting from right to left, as opposed to `fold()` which processes the elements from left to right. This example demonstrates the difference:

```
// FoldingLists/FoldRight.kt
import atomictest.eq

fun main() {
  val list = listOf('a', 'b', 'c', 'd')
  list.fold("*") { acc, elem ->
    "($acc) + $elem"
  } eq "(((*) + a) + b) + c) + d"
  list.foldRight("*") { elem, acc ->
    "$elem + ($acc)"
  } eq "a + (b + (c + (d + (*))))"
}
```

`fold()` first applies the operation to `a`, as we can see in `(*) + a`, while `foldRight()` first processes the right-hand element `d`, and processes `a` last. `fold()` and `foldRight()` take an explicit accumulator value as the first argument, followed by a lambda.

Sometimes the first element of the List can act as an initial value. reduce() and reduceRight() behave like fold() and foldRight() but use the first and last element, respectively, as the initial value:

```
// FoldingLists/ReduceAndReduceRight.kt
import atomictest.eq

fun main() {
  val chars = "A B C D E".split(" ")
  chars.fold("*") { acc, e -> "$acc $e" } eq
    "* A B C D E"
  chars
    .foldRight("*") { e, acc -> "$acc $e" } eq
    "* E D C B A"
  chars.reduce { acc, e -> "$acc $e" } eq
    "A B C D E"
  chars.reduceRight { e, acc -> "$acc $e" } eq
    "E D C B A"
}
```

runningFold() and runningReduce() produce a List containing all the intermediate steps of the process. The final value in the List is the result of the fold() or reduce():

```
// FoldingLists/RunningFold.kt
import atomictest.eq

fun main() {
  val list = listOf(11, 13, 17, 19)
  list.fold(7) { sum, n ->
    sum + n
  } eq 67
  list.runningFold(7) { sum, n ->
    sum + n
  } eq "[7, 18, 31, 48, 67]"
  list.reduce { sum, n ->
    sum + n
  } eq 60
  list.runningReduce { sum, n ->
    sum + n
  } eq "[11, 24, 41, 60]"
}
```

runningFold() first stores the initial value (7), then stores each intermediate result. runningReduce() keeps track of each sum value.

Exercises and solutions can be found at www.AtomicKotlin.com.

Recursion

> *Recursion* is the programming technique of calling a function within that same function. *Tail recursion* is an optimization that can be explicitly applied to some recursive functions.

A recursive function uses the result of the previous recursive call. Factorials are a common example—`factorial(n)` multiplies all numbers from 1 to n, and can be defined like this:

- `factorial(1)` is `1`
- `factorial(n)` is `n * factorial(n - 1)`

`factorial()` is recursive because it uses the result from the same function applied to its modified argument. Here's a recursive implementation of `factorial()`:

```
// Recursion/Factorial.kt
package recursion
import atomictest.eq

fun factorial(n: Long): Long {
  if (n <= 1) return 1
  return n * factorial(n - 1)
}

fun main() {
  factorial(5) eq 120
  factorial(17) eq 355687428096000
}
```

While this is easy to read, it's expensive. When calling a function, the information about that function and its arguments are stored in a *call stack*. You see the call stack when an exception is thrown and Kotlin displays the *stack trace*:

```
// Recursion/CallStack.kt
package recursion

fun illegalState() {
  // throw IllegalStateException()
}

fun fail() = illegalState()

fun main() {
  fail()
}
```

If you uncomment the line containing the exception, you'll see the following:

```
Exception in thread "main" java.lang.IllegalStateException
  at recursion.CallStackKt.illegalState(CallStack.kt:5)
  at recursion.CallStackKt.fail(CallStack.kt:8)
  at recursion.CallStackKt.main(CallStack.kt:11)
```

The stack trace displays the state of the call stack at the moment the exception is thrown. For CallStack.kt, the call stack consists of only three functions:

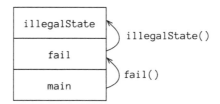

The Call Stack

We start in main(), which calls fail(). The fail() call is added to the call stack along with its arguments. Next, fail() calls illegalState(), which is also added to the call stack.

When you call a recursive function, each recursive invocation adds a frame to the call stack. This can easily produce a StackOverflowError, which means that your call stack became too large and exhausted the available memory.

Programmers commonly cause StackOverflowErrors by forgetting to terminate the chain of recursive calls—this is *infinite recursion*:

```
// Recursion/InfiniteRecursion.kt
package recursion

fun recurse(i: Int): Int = recurse(i + 1)

fun main() {
  // println(recurse(1))
}
```

If you uncomment the line in `main()`, you'll see a stacktrace with many duplicate calls:

```
Exception in thread "main" java.lang.StackOverflowError
at recursion.InfiniteRecursionKt.recurse(InfiniteRecursion.kt:4)
at recursion.InfiniteRecursionKt.recurse(InfiniteRecursion.kt:4)
...
at recursion.InfiniteRecursionKt.recurse(InfiniteRecursion.kt:4)
```

The recursive function keeps calling itself (with a different argument each time), and fills up the call stack:

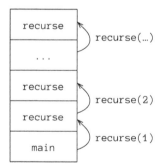

Infinite Recursion

Infinite recursion always ends with a `StackOverflowError`.

Let's sum the integers up to a given number, recursively defining `sum(n)` as n + sum(n - 1):

```
// Recursion/RecursionLimits.kt
package recursion
import atomictest.eq

fun sum(n: Long): Long {
  if (n == 0L) return 0
  return n + sum(n - 1)
}

fun main() {
  sum(2) eq 3
  sum(1000) eq 500500
  // sum(100_000) eq 500050000      // [1]
  (1..100_000L).sum() eq 5000050000 // [2]
}
```

This recursion quickly becomes expensive. If you uncomment line **[1]**, you'll discover that it takes far too long to complete, and all those recursive calls overflow the stack. If `sum(100_000)` still works on your machine, try a bigger number.

Calling `sum(100_000)` causes a `StackOverflowError` by adding `100_000` `sum()` function calls to the call stack. For comparison, line **[2]** uses the `sum()` library function to add the numbers within the range, and this does not fail.

To avoid a `StackOverflowError`, you can use an iterative solution instead of recursion:

```
// Recursion/Iteration.kt
package iteration
import atomictest.eq

fun sum(n: Long): Long {
  var accumulator = 0L
  for (i in 1..n) {
    accumulator += i
  }
  return accumulator
}

fun main() {
  sum(10000) eq 50005000
  sum(100000) eq 5000050000
}
```

There's no risk of a StackOverflowError because we only make a single sum() call and the result is calculated in a for loop. Although the iterative solution is straightforward, it must use the mutable state variable accumulator to store the changing value, and functional programming attempts to avoid mutation.

To prevent call stack overflows, functional languages (including Kotlin) use a technique called *tail recursion*, also known as *tail-call optimization*. The goal of tail recursion is to reduce the size of the call stack. In the sum() example, the call stack becomes a single function call, just as it did in Iteration.kt:

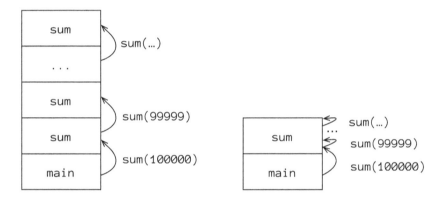

Regular Recursion vs. Tail Recursion

To produce tail recursion, use the tailrec keyword. Under the right conditions, this converts recursive calls into iteration, eliminating call-stack overhead. This is a compiler optimization, but it won't work for just any recursive call.

To use tailrec successfully, recursion must be the final operation, which means there can be no extra calculations on the result of the recursive call before it is returned. For example, if we simply put tailrec before the fun for sum() in RecursionLimits.kt, Kotlin produces the following warning messages:

- *A function is marked as tail-recursive but no tail calls are found*
- *Recursive call is not a tail call*

The problem is that n is combined with the result of the recursive sum() call *before* returning that result. For tailrec to be successful, the result of the recursive call must be returned without doing anything to it during the return. This often requires some work in rearranging the function. For sum(), a successful tailrec looks like this:

```
// Recursion/TailRecursiveSum.kt
package tailrecursion
import atomictest.eq

private tailrec fun sum(
  n: Long,
  accumulator: Long
): Long =
  if (n == 0L) accumulator
  else sum(n - 1, accumulator + n)

fun sum(n: Long) = sum(n, 0)

fun main() {
  sum(2) eq 3
  sum(10000) eq 50005000
  sum(100000) eq 5000050000
}
```

By including the `accumulator` parameter, the addition happens during the recursive call and you don't do anything to the result except return it. The `tailrec` keyword is now successful, because the code was rewritten to delegate all activities to the recursive call. In addition, `accumulator` becomes an immutable value, eliminating the complaint we had for `Iteration.kt`.

`factorial()` is a common example for demonstrating tail recursion, and is one of the exercises for this atom. Another example is the Fibonacci sequence, where each new Fibonacci number is the sum of the previous two. The first two numbers are `0` and `1`, which produces the following sequence: `0, 1, 1, 2, 3, 5, 8, 13, 21` ... This can be expressed recursively:

```
// Recursion/VerySlowFibonacci.kt
package slowfibonacci
import atomictest.eq

fun fibonacci(n: Long): Long {
  return when (n) {
    0L -> 0
    1L -> 1
    else ->
      fibonacci(n - 1) + fibonacci(n - 2)
  }
}

fun main() {
  fibonacci(0) eq 0
  fibonacci(22) eq 17711
  // Very time-consuming:
  // fibonacci(50) eq 12586269025
}
```

This implementation is terribly inefficient because the previously-calculated results are not reused. Thus, the number of operations grows exponentially:

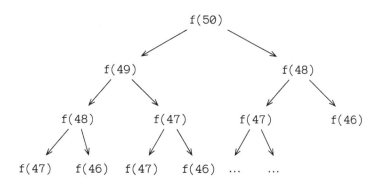

Inefficient Computation of Fibonacci Numbers

When computing the 50th Fibonacci number, we first compute the 49th and 48th numbers independently, which means we compute the 48th number twice. The 46th number is computed as many as 4 times, and so on.

Using tail recursion, the calculations become dramatically more efficient:

```
// Recursion/Fibonacci.kt
package recursion
import atomictest.eq

fun fibonacci(n: Int): Long {
  tailrec fun fibonacci(
    n: Int,
    current: Long,
    next: Long
  ): Long {
    if (n == 0) return current
    return fibonacci(
      n - 1, next, current + next)
  }
  return fibonacci(n, 0L, 1L)
}

fun main() {
  (0..8).map { fibonacci(it) } eq
    "[0, 1, 1, 2, 3, 5, 8, 13, 21]"
  fibonacci(22) eq 17711
  fibonacci(50) eq 12586269025
}
```

We could avoid the local `fibonacci()` function using default arguments. However, default arguments imply that the user can put other values in those defaults, which produce incorrect results. Because the auxiliary `fibonacci()` function is a local function, we don't expose the additional parameters, and you can *only* call `fibonacci(n)`.

`main()` shows the first eight elements of the Fibonacci sequence, the result for 22, and finally the 50th Fibonacci number that is now produced very quickly.

Exercises and solutions can be found at www.AtomicKotlin.com.

Section V: Object-Oriented Programming

... inheritance is a very flexible mechanism. It's possible and in fact fairly common to misuse it, but that's not a reason to distrust it systematically as seems to have become the fashion.—**Bertrand Meyer**

Interfaces

> An *interface* describes the concept of a type. It is a prototype for all classes that *implement* the interface.

It describes *what* a class should do, but not *how* it should do it. An interface provides a form, but generally no implementation. It specifies an object's actions without detailing how those actions are performed. The interface describes the mission or goal of an entity, versus a class that contains implementation details.

One dictionary definition says that an interface is "The place at which independent and often unrelated systems meet and act on or communicate with each other." Thus, an interface is a means of communication between different parts of a system.

An *Application Programming Interface* (API) is a set of clearly defined communication paths between various software components. In object-oriented programming, the API of an object is the set of public members it uses to interact with other objects.

Code using a particular interface only knows what functions can be called for that interface. The interface establishes a "protocol" between classes. (Some object-oriented languages have a keyword called *protocol* to do the same thing.)

To create an interface, use the `interface` keyword instead of the `class` keyword. When defining a class that implements an interface, follow the class name with a : (colon) and the name of the interface:

```
// Interfaces/Computer.kt
package interfaces
import atomictest.*

interface Computer {
  fun prompt(): String
  fun calculateAnswer(): Int
}

class Desktop : Computer {
  override fun prompt() = "Hello!"
  override fun calculateAnswer() = 11
}

class DeepThought : Computer {
  override fun prompt() = "Thinking..."
  override fun calculateAnswer() = 42
}

class Quantum : Computer {
  override fun prompt() = "Probably..."
  override fun calculateAnswer() = -1
}

fun main() {
  val computers = listOf(
    Desktop(), DeepThought(), Quantum()
  )
  computers.map { it.calculateAnswer() } eq
    "[11, 42, -1]"
  computers.map { it.prompt() } eq
    "[Hello!, Thinking..., Probably...]"
}
```

Computer *declares* prompt() and calculateAnswer() but provides no implementations. A class that implements the interface must provide bodies for all the declared functions, making those functions *concrete*. In main() you see that different implementations of an interface express different behaviors via their function definitions.

When implementing a member of an interface, you must use the override modifier. override tells Kotlin you are intentionally using the same name that appears in the interface (or base class)—that is, you aren't accidentally overriding.

An interface can declare properties. These must be overridden in all classes implementing that interface:

```
// Interfaces/PlayerInterface.kt
package interfaces
import atomictest.eq

interface Player {
  val symbol: Char
}

class Food : Player {
  override val symbol = '.'
}

class Robot : Player {
  override val symbol get() = 'R'
}

class Wall(override val symbol: Char) : Player

fun main() {
  listOf(Food(), Robot(), Wall('|')).map {
    it.symbol
  } eq "[., R, |]"
}
```

Each subclass overrides the `symbol` property in a different way:

- `Food` directly replaces the `symbol` value.
- `Robot` has a custom getter that returns the value (see *Property Accessors*).
- `Wall` overrides `symbol` inside the constructor argument list (see *Constructors*)

An enumeration can implement an `interface`:

```
// Interfaces/Hotness.kt
package interfaces
import atomictest.*

interface Hotness {
  fun feedback(): String
}

enum class SpiceLevel : Hotness {
  Mild {
    override fun feedback() =
      "It adds flavor!"
  },
  Medium {
    override fun feedback() =
      "Is it warm in here?"
  },
  Hot {
    override fun feedback() =
      "I'm suddenly sweating a lot."
  },
  Flaming {
    override fun feedback() =
      "I'm in pain. I am suffering."
  }
}

fun main() {
  SpiceLevel.values().map { it.feedback() } eq
    "[It adds flavor!, " +
    "Is it warm in here?, " +
    "I'm suddenly sweating a lot., " +
    "I'm in pain. I am suffering.]"
}
```

The compiler ensures that each `enum` element provides a definition for `feedback()`.

SAM Conversions

The *Single Abstract Method* (SAM) interface comes from Java, where they call member functions "methods." Kotlin has a special syntax for defining SAM interfaces:

`fun interface`. Here we show SAM interfaces with different parameter lists:

```
// Interfaces/SAM.kt
package interfaces

fun interface ZeroArg {
  fun f(): Int
}

fun interface OneArg {
  fun g(n: Int): Int
}

fun interface TwoArg {
  fun h(i: Int, j: Int): Int
}
```

When you say `fun interface`, the compiler ensures there is only a single member function.

You can implement a SAM interface in the ordinary verbose way, or by passing it a lambda; the latter is called a *SAM conversion*. In a SAM conversion, the lambda becomes the implementation for the single method in the interface. Here we show both ways to implement the three interfaces:

```
// Interfaces/SAMImplementation.kt
package interfaces
import atomictest.eq

class VerboseZero : ZeroArg {
  override fun f() = 11
}

val verboseZero = VerboseZero()

val samZero = ZeroArg { 11 }

class VerboseOne : OneArg {
  override fun g(n: Int) = n + 47
}

val verboseOne = VerboseOne()
```

```
val samOne = OneArg { it + 47 }

class VerboseTwo : TwoArg {
  override fun h(i: Int, j: Int) = i + j
}

val verboseTwo = VerboseTwo()

val samTwo =  TwoArg { i, j -> i + j }

fun main() {
  verboseZero.f() eq 11
  samZero.f() eq 11
  verboseOne.g(92) eq 139
  samOne.g(92) eq 139
  verboseTwo.h(11, 47) eq 58
  samTwo.h(11, 47) eq 58
}
```

Comparing the "verbose" implementations to the "sam" implementations you can see that SAM conversions produce much more succinct syntax for a commonly-used idiom, and you aren't forced to define a class to create a single object.

You can pass a lambda where a SAM interface is expected, without first wrapping it into an object:

```
// Interfaces/SAMConversion.kt
package interfaces
import atomictest.trace

fun interface Action {
  fun act()
}

fun delayAction(action: Action) {
  trace("Delaying...")
  action.act()
}

fun main() {
  delayAction { trace("Hey!") }
```

```
    trace eq "Delaying... Hey!"
}
```

In `main()` we pass a lambda instead of an object that implements the `Action` interface. Kotlin automatically creates an `Action` object from this lambda.

Exercises and solutions can be found at www.AtomicKotlin.com.

Complex Constructors

For code to work correctly, objects must be properly initialized.

A constructor is a special function that creates a new object. In *Constructors*, we saw simple constructors that only initialize their arguments. Using var or val in the parameter list makes those parameters properties, accessible from outside the object:

```
// ComplexConstructors/SimpleConstructor.kt
package complexconstructors
import atomictest.eq

class Alien(val name: String)

fun main() {
  val alien = Alien("Pencilvester")
  alien.name eq "Pencilvester"
}
```

In these cases, we don't write constructor code—Kotlin does it for us. For more customization, add constructor code in the class body. Code inside the init section is executed during object creation:

```
// ComplexConstructors/InitSection.kt
package complexconstructors
import atomictest.eq

private var counter = 0

class Message(text: String) {
  private val content: String
  init {
    counter += 10
    content = "[$counter] $text"
  }
  override fun toString() = content
```

```
}
fun main() {
  val m1 = Message("Big ba-da boom!")
  m1 eq "[10] Big ba-da boom!"
  val m2 = Message("Bzzzzt!")
  m2 eq "[20] Bzzzzt!"
}
```

Constructor parameters are accessible inside the `init` section even if they aren't marked as properties using `var` or `val`.

Although defined as `val`, `content` is not initialized at the point of definition. In this case, Kotlin ensures that initialization occurs at one (and only one) point during construction. Either reassigning `content` or forgetting to initialize it produces an error message.

- -

A constructor is the combination of its constructor parameter list—initialized before entering the class body—and the `init` section(s), executed during object creation. Kotlin allows multiple `init` sections, which are executed in definition order. However, in a large and complex class, spreading out the `init` sections may produce maintenance issues for programmers who are accustomed to a single `init` section.

Exercises and solutions can be found at www.AtomicKotlin.com.

Secondary Constructors

When you require several ways to construct an object, named and default arguments are usually the easiest approach. Sometimes, however, you must create multiple overloaded constructors.

The constructor is "overloaded" because you're making different ways to create objects of the same class. In Kotlin, overloaded constructors are called *secondary constructors*. The constructor parameter list (directly after the class name) combined with property initializations and the `init` block is called the *primary constructor*.

To create a secondary constructor, use the `constructor` keyword followed by a parameter list that's distinct from all other primary and secondary parameter lists. Within a secondary constructor, the `this` keyword calls either the primary constructor or another secondary constructor:

```
// SecondaryConstructors/WithSecondary.kt
package secondaryconstructors
import atomictest.*

class WithSecondary(i: Int) {
  init {
    trace("Primary: $i")
  }
  constructor(c: Char) : this(c - 'A') {
    trace("Secondary: '$c'")
  }
  constructor(s: String) :
    this(s.first()) {            // [1]
    trace("Secondary: \"$s\"")
  }
  /* Doesn't compile without a call
     to the primary constructor:
  constructor(f: Float) {        // [2]
    trace("Secondary: $f")
  }
```

```
    */
}
fun main() {
  fun sep() = trace("-".repeat(10))
  WithSecondary(1)
  sep()
  WithSecondary('D')
  sep()
  WithSecondary("Last Constructor")
  trace eq """
    Primary: 1
    ----------
    Primary: 3
    Secondary: 'D'
    ----------
    Primary: 11
    Secondary: 'L'
    Secondary: "Last Constructor"
  """
}
```

Calling another constructor from a secondary constructor (using `this`) must happen before additional constructor logic, because the constructor body may depend on those other initializations. Thus it precedes the constructor body.

The argument list determines the constructor to call. `WithSecondary(1)` matches the primary constructor, `WithSecondary('D')` matches the first secondary constructor, and `WithSecondary("Last Constructor")` matches the second secondary constructor. The `this()` call in **[1]** matches the first secondary constructor, and you can see the chain of calls in the output.

The primary constructor must always be called, either directly or through a call to a secondary constructor. Otherwise, Kotlin generates a compile-time error, as in **[2]**. Thus, all common initialization logic that can be shared between constructors should be placed in the primary constructor.

An `init` section is not required when using secondary constructors:

```
// SecondaryConstructors/GardenItem.kt
package secondaryconstructors
import atomictest.eq
import secondaryconstructors.Material.*

enum class Material {
  Ceramic, Metal, Plastic
}

class GardenItem(val name: String) {
  var material: Material = Plastic
  constructor(
    name: String, material: Material    // [1]
  ) : this(name) {                       // [2]
    this.material = material             // [3]
  }
  constructor(
    material: Material
  ) : this("Strange Thing", material)    // [4]
  override fun toString() = "$material $name"
}

fun main() {
  GardenItem("Elf").material eq Plastic
  GardenItem("Snowman").name eq "Snowman"
  GardenItem("Gazing Ball", Metal) eq    // [5]
    "Metal Gazing Ball"
  GardenItem(material = Ceramic) eq
    "Ceramic Strange Thing"
}
```

- **[1]** Only the parameters of the primary constructor can be declared as properties via `val` or `var`.
- **[2]** You cannot declare a return type for a secondary constructor.
- **[3]** The `material` parameter has the same name as a property, so we disambiguate it using `this`.
- **[4]** The secondary constructor body is optional (although you must still include an explicit `this()` call).

When calling the first secondary constructor in line **[5]**, the property `material` is assigned twice. First, the `Plastic` value is assigned during the call to the primary constructor (in [2]) and initialization of all the class properties, then it's changed to the material parameter at [3].

The GardenItem class can be simplified using default arguments, replacing the secondary constructors with a single primary constructor.

Exercises and solutions can be found at www.AtomicKotlin.com.

Inheritance

Inheritance is a mechanism for creating a new class by reusing and modifying an existing class.

Objects store data in properties and perform actions via member functions. Each object occupies a unique place in storage so one object's properties can have different values from every other object. An object also belongs to a category called a class, which determines the form (properties and functions) for its objects. Thus, an object looks like the class that formed it.

Creating and debugging a class can require extensive work. What if you want to make a class that's similar to an existing class, but with some variations? It seems wasteful to build a new class from scratch. Object-oriented languages provide a mechanism for reuse called *inheritance*.

Inheritance follows the concept of biological inheritance. You say, "I want to make a new class from an existing class, but with some additions and modifications."

The syntax for inheritance is similar to implementing an interface. To inherit a new class `Derived` from an existing class `Base`, use a `:` (colon):

```
// Inheritance/BasicInheritance.kt
package inheritance

open class Base

class Derived : Base()
```

The subsequent atom explains the reason for the parentheses after `Base` during inheritance.

The terms *base class* and *derived class* (or *parent class* and *child class*, or *superclass* and *subclass*) are often used to describe the inheritance relationship.

The base class must be `open`. A non-open class doesn't allow inheritance—it is *closed* by default. This differs from most other object-oriented languages. In Java, for example, a class is automatically inheritable unless you explicitly forbid inheritance by declaring that class to be `final`. Although Kotlin allows it, the `final` modifier is redundant because every class is effectively `final` by default:

```
// Inheritance/OpenAndFinalClasses.kt
package inheritance

// This class can be inherited:
open class Parent

class Child : Parent()

// Child is not open, so this fails:
// class GrandChild : Child()

// This class can't be inherited:
final class Single

// The same as using 'final':
class AnotherSingle
```

Kotlin forces you to clarify your intent by using the `open` keyword to specify that a class is designed for inheritance.

In the following example, `GreatApe` is a base class, and has two properties with fixed values. The derived classes `Bonobo`, `Chimpanzee` and `BonoboB` are new types that are identical to their parent class:

```
// Inheritance/GreatApe.kt
package inheritance.ape1
import atomictest.eq

open class GreatApe {
  val weight = 100.0
  val age = 12
}

open class Bonobo : GreatApe()
class Chimpanzee : GreatApe()
class BonoboB : Bonobo()

fun GreatApe.info() = "wt: $weight age: $age"
```

```
fun main() {
  GreatApe().info() eq "wt: 100.0 age: 12"
  Bonobo().info() eq "wt: 100.0 age: 12"
  Chimpanzee().info() eq "wt: 100.0 age: 12"
  BonoboB().info() eq "wt: 100.0 age: 12"
}
```

`info()` is an extension for `GreatApe`, so naturally you can call it on a `GreatApe`. But you can also call `info()` on a `Bonobo`, a `Chimpanzee`, or a `BonoboB`! Even though the latter three are distinct types, Kotlin happily accepts them as if they were the *same type* as `GreatApe`. This works at any level of inheritance—`BonoboB` is two inheritance levels away from `GreatApe`.

Inheritance guarantees that anything inheriting from `GreatApe` *is* a `GreatApe`. All code that acts upon objects of the derived classes knows that `GreatApe` is at their core, so any functions and properties in `GreatApe` will also be available in its child classes.

Inheritance enables you to write a single piece of code (the `info()` function) that works not just with one class, but also with every class that inherits that class. Thus, inheritance creates opportunities for code simplification and reuse.

`GreatApe.kt` is a bit *too* simple because all the classes are identical. Inheritance gets interesting when you start *overriding* functions, which means redefining a function from a base class to do something different in a derived class.

Let's look at another version of `GreatApe.kt`. This time we include member functions that are modified in the subclasses:

```
// Inheritance/GreatApe2.kt
package inheritance.ape2
import atomictest.eq

open class GreatApe {
  protected var energy = 0
  open fun call() = "Hoo!"
  open fun eat() {
    energy += 10
  }
  fun climb(x: Int) {
```

```kotlin
    energy -= x
  }
  fun energyLevel() = "Energy: $energy"
}

class Bonobo : GreatApe() {
  override fun call() = "Eep!"
  override fun eat() {
    // Modify the base-class var:
    energy += 10
    // Call the base-class version:
    super.eat()
  }
  // Add a function:
  fun run() = "Bonobo run"
}

class Chimpanzee : GreatApe() {
  // New property:
  val additionalEnergy = 20
  override fun call() = "Yawp!"
  override fun eat() {
    energy += additionalEnergy
    super.eat()
  }
  // Add a function:
  fun jump() = "Chimp jump"
}

fun talk(ape: GreatApe): String {
  // ape.run()  // Not an ape function
  // ape.jump() // Nor this
  ape.eat()
  ape.climb(10)
  return "${ape.call()} ${ape.energyLevel()}"
}

fun main() {
  // Cannot access 'energy':
  // GreatApe().energy
  talk(GreatApe()) eq "Hoo! Energy: 0"
  talk(Bonobo()) eq "Eep! Energy: 10"
```

```
  talk(Chimpanzee()) eq "Yawp! Energy: 20"
}
```

Every `GreatApe` has a `call()`. They store energy when they `eat()` and they expend energy when they `climb()`.

As described in **Constraining Visibility**, the derived class can't access the `private` members of the base class. Sometimes the creator of the base class would like to take a particular member and grant access to derived classes but not to the world in general. That's what `protected` does: `protected` members are closed to the outside world, but can be accessed or overridden in subclasses.

If we declare energy as `private`, it won't be possible to change it whenever `GreatApe` is used, which is good, but we also can't access it in subclasses. Making it `protected` allows us to keep it accessible to subclasses but invisible to the outside world.

`call()` is defined the same way in `Bonobo` and `Chimpanzee` as it is in `GreatApe`. It has no parameters and type inference determines that it returns a `String`.

Both `Bonobo` and `Chimpanzee` should have different behaviors for `call()` than `GreatApe`, so we want to change their definitions of `call()`. If you create an identical function signature in a derived class as in a base class, you substitute the behavior defined in the base class with your new behavior. This is called *overriding*.

When Kotlin sees an identical function signature in the derived class as in the base class, it decides that you've made a mistake, called an *accidental override*. If you write a function that has the same name as a function in the base class, you get an error message saying you forgot the `override` keyword. Kotlin assumes you've unintentionally chosen the same name, parameters and return type *unless* you use the `override` keyword (which you first saw in **Constructors**) to say "yes, I mean to do this." The `override` keyword also helps when reading the code, so you don't have to compare signatures to notice the overrides.

Kotlin imposes an additional constraint when overriding functions. Just as you cannot inherit from a base class unless that base class is `open`, you cannot `override` a function from a base class unless that function is defined as `open` in the base class. `climb()` and `energyLevel()` are not `open`, so they cannot be overridden. Inheritance and overriding cannot be accomplished in Kotlin without clear intentions.

It's especially interesting to take a Bonobo or a Chimpanzee and treat it as an ordinary GreatApe. Inside talk(), call() produces the correct behavior in each case. talk() somehow knows the exact type of the object and produces the appropriate variation of call(). This is *polymorphism*.

Inside talk(), you can only call GreatApe member functions because talk()'s parameter is a GreatApe. Even though Bonobo defines run() and Chimpanzee defines jump(), neither function is part of GreatApe.

Often when you override a function, you want to call the base-class version of that function (for one thing, to reuse the code), as seen in the overrides for eat(). This produces a conundrum: If you simply call eat(), you call the same function you're currently inside (as we've seen in *Recursion*). To call the base-class version of eat(), use the super keyword, short for "superclass."

Exercises and solutions can be found at www.AtomicKotlin.com.

Base Class Initialization

When a class inherits another class, Kotlin guarantees that both classes are properly initialized.

Kotlin creates valid objects by ensuring that constructors are called:

- Constructors for member objects.
- Constructors for new objects added in the derived class.
- The constructor for the base class.

In the *Inheritance* examples, the base classes didn't have constructor parameters. If a base class *does* have constructor parameters, a derived class must provide those arguments during construction.

Here's the first `GreatApe` example, rewritten with constructor parameters:

```
// BaseClassInit/GreatApe3.kt
package baseclassinit
import atomictest.eq

open class GreatApe(
  val weight: Double,
  val age: Int
)

open class Bonobo(weight: Double, age: Int) :
  GreatApe(weight, age)

class Chimpanzee(weight: Double, age: Int) :
  GreatApe(weight, age)

class BonoboB(weight: Double, age: Int) :
  Bonobo(weight, age)

fun GreatApe.info() = "wt: $weight age: $age"
```

```
fun main() {
  GreatApe(100.0, 12).info() eq
    "wt: 100.0 age: 12"
  Bonobo(110.0, 13).info() eq
    "wt: 110.0 age: 13"
  Chimpanzee(120.0, 14).info() eq
    "wt: 120.0 age: 14"
  BonoboB(130.0, 15).info() eq
    "wt: 130.0 age: 15"
}
```

When inheriting from GreatApe, you must pass the necessary constructor arguments to the GreatApe base class, otherwise you'll get a compile-time error message.

After Kotlin creates memory for your object, it calls the base-class constructor first, then the constructor for the next-derived class, and so on until it reaches the most-derived constructor. This way, all constructor calls can rely on the validity of all the sub-objects created before them. Indeed, those are the only things it knows about; a Bonobo knows it inherits from GreatApe and the Bonobo constructor can call functions in the GreatApe class, but a GreatApe cannot know whether it's a Bonobo or a Chimpanzee, or call functions specific to those subclasses.

When inheriting from a class you must provide arguments to the base-class constructor after the base class name. This calls the base-class constructor during object construction:

```
// BaseClassInit/NoArgConstructor.kt
package baseclassinit

open class SuperClass1(val i: Int)
class SubClass1(i: Int) : SuperClass1(i)

open class SuperClass2
class SubClass2 : SuperClass2()
```

When there are no base-class constructor parameters, Kotlin still requires empty parentheses after the base class name, to call that constructor without arguments.

If there are secondary constructors in the base class you may call one of those instead:

```kotlin
// BaseClassInit/House.kt
package baseclassinit
import atomictest.eq

open class House(
  val address: String,
  val state: String,
  val zip: String
) {
  constructor(fullAddress: String) :
    this(fullAddress.substringBefore(", "),
      fullAddress.substringAfter(", ")
        .substringBefore(" "),
      fullAddress.substringAfterLast(" "))
  val fullAddress: String
    get() = "$address, $state $zip"
}

class VacationHouse(
  address: String,
  state: String,
  zip: String,
  val startMonth: String,
  val endMonth: String
) : House(address, state, zip) {
  override fun toString() =
    "Vacation house at $fullAddress " +
    "from $startMonth to $endMonth"
}

class TreeHouse(
  val name: String
) : House("Tree Street, TR 00000") {
  override fun toString() =
    "$name tree house at $fullAddress"
}

fun main() {
  val vacationHouse = VacationHouse(
    address = "8 Target St.",
    state = "KS",
    zip = "66632",
```

```
      startMonth = "May",
      endMonth = "September")
  vacationHouse eq
    "Vacation house at 8 Target St., " +
    "KS 66632 from May to September"
  TreeHouse("Oak") eq
    "Oak tree house at Tree Street, TR 00000"
}
```

When `VacationHouse` inherits from `House` it passes the appropriate arguments to the primary `House` constructor. It also adds its own parameters `startMonth` and `endMonth`—you aren't limited by the number, type or order of the parameters in the base class. Your only responsibility is to provide the correct arguments in the call to the base-class constructor.

You call an overloaded base-class constructor by passing the matching constructor arguments in the base-class constructor call. You see this in the definitions of `VacationHouse` and `TreeHouse`. Each calls a different base-class constructor.

Inside a secondary constructor of a derived class you can either call the base-class constructor or a different derived-class constructor:

```
// BaseClassInit/OtherConstructors.kt
package baseclassinit
import atomictest.eq

open class Base(val i: Int)

class Derived : Base {
  constructor(i: Int) : super(i)
  constructor() : this(9)
}

fun main() {
  val d1 = Derived(11)
  d1.i eq 11
  val d2 = Derived()
  d2.i eq 9
}
```

To call the base-class constructor, use the `super` keyword, passing the constructor arguments as if it is a function call. Use `this` to call another constructor of the same class.

Exercises and solutions can be found at www.AtomicKotlin.com.

Abstract Classes

An *abstract class* is like an ordinary class except one or more functions or properties is incomplete: a function lacks a definition or a property is declared without initialization. An interface is like an abstract class but without *state*.

You must use the abstract modifier to mark class members that have missing definitions. A class containing abstract functions or properties must also be marked abstract. Try removing any of the abstract modifiers below and see what message you get:

```
// Abstract/AbstractKeyword.kt
package abstractclasses

abstract class WithProperty {
  abstract val x: Int
}

abstract class WithFunctions {
  abstract fun f(): Int
  abstract fun g(n: Double)
}
```

WithProperty *declares* x with no initialization value (a *declaration* describes something without providing a *definition* to create storage for a value or code for a function). If there isn't an initializer, Kotlin requires references to be abstract, and expects the abstract modifier on the class. Without an initializer, Kotlin cannot infer the type, so it also requires type information for an abstract reference.

WithFunctions declares f() and g() but provides no function definitions, again forcing you to add the abstract modifier to the functions and the containing class. If you don't give a return type for the function, as with g(), Kotlin assumes it returns Unit.

Abstract functions and properties must somehow exist (be made *concrete*) in the class that you ultimately create from the abstract class.

All functions and properties declared in an interface are abstract by default, which makes an interface similar to an abstract class. When an interface contains a function or property declaration, the `abstract` modifier is redundant and can be removed. These two interfaces are equivalent:

```
// Abstract/Redundant.kt
package abstractclasses

interface Redundant {
  abstract val x: Int
  abstract fun f(): Int
  abstract fun g(n: Double)
}

interface Removed {
  val x: Int
  fun f(): Int
  fun g(n: Double)
}
```

The difference between interfaces and abstract classes is that an abstract class can contain *state*, while an interface cannot. State is the data stored inside properties. In the following, the state of `IntList` consists of the values stored in the properties `name` and `list`.

```
// Abstract/StateOfAClass.kt
package abstractstate
import atomictest.eq

class IntList(val name: String) {
  val list = mutableListOf<Int>()
}

fun main() {
  val ints = IntList("numbers")
  ints.name eq "numbers"
  ints.list += 7
  ints.list eq listOf(7)
}
```

An interface may declare properties, but actual data is only stored in classes that implement the interface. An interface isn't allowed to store values in its properties:

```
// Abstract/NoStateInInterfaces.kt
package abstractclasses

interface IntList {
  val name: String
  // Doesn't compile:
  // val list = listOf(0)
}
```

Both interfaces and abstract classes can contain functions with implementations. You can call other abstract members from such functions:

```
// Abstract/Implementations.kt
package abstractclasses
import atomictest.eq

interface Parent {
  val ch: Char
  fun f(): Int
  fun g() = "ch = $ch; f() = ${f()}"
}

class Actual(
  override val ch: Char        // [1]
): Parent {
  override fun f() = 17        // [2]
}

class Other : Parent {
  override val ch: Char        // [3]
    get() = 'B'
  override fun f() = 34        // [4]
}

fun main() {
  Actual('A').g() eq "ch = A; f() = 17" // [5]
  Other().g() eq "ch = B; f() = 34"     // [6]
}
```

`Parent` declares an abstract property `ch` and an abstract function `f()` that must be overridden in any implementing classes. Lines **[1]**-**[4]** show different implementations of these members in subclasses.

`Parent.g()` uses abstract members that have no definitions at the point where `g()` is defined. Interfaces and abstract classes guarantee that all abstract properties and functions are implemented before any objects can be created—and you can't call a member function unless you've got an object. Lines **[5]** and **[6]** call different implementations of `ch` and `f()`.

Because an interface can contain function implementations, it can also contain custom property accessors if the corresponding property doesn't change state:

```
// Abstract/PropertyAccessor.kt
package abstractclasses
import atomictest.eq

interface PropertyAccessor {
  val a: Int
    get() = 11
}

class Impl : PropertyAccessor

fun main() {
  Impl().a eq 11
}
```

You might wonder why we need interfaces when abstract classes are more powerful. To understand the importance of "a class without state," let's look at the concept of multiple inheritance, which Kotlin doesn't support. In Kotlin, a class can only inherit from a single base class:

```
// Abstract/NoMultipleInheritance.kt
package multipleinheritance1

open class Animal
open class Mammal : Animal()
open class AquaticAnimal : Animal()

// More than one base class doesn't compile:
// class Dolphin : Mammal(), AquaticAnimal()
```

Trying to compile the commented code produces an error: *Only one class may appear in a supertype list.*

Java works the same way. The original Java designers decided that C++ multiple inheritance was a bad idea. The main complexity and dissatisfaction at that time came from multiple *state* inheritance. The rules managing inheritance of multiple states are complicated and can easily cause confusion and surprising behavior. Java added an elegant solution to this problem by introducing interfaces, which can't contain state. Java forbids multiple state inheritance, but allows multiple interface inheritance, and Kotlin follows this design:

```
// Abstract/MultipleInterfaceInheritance.kt
package multipleinheritance2

interface Animal
interface Mammal: Animal
interface AquaticAnimal: Animal

class Dolphin : Mammal, AquaticAnimal
```

Just like classes, interfaces can inherit from each other.

When inheriting from several interfaces, it's possible to simultaneously override two or more functions with the same signature (the name combined with the parameters and return type). If function or property signatures collide, you must resolve the collisions by hand, as seen in `class C`:

```
// Abstract/InterfaceCollision.kt
package collision
import atomictest.eq

interface A {
  fun f() = 1
  fun g() = "A.g"
  val n: Double
    get() = 1.1
}

interface B {
  fun f() = 2
  fun g() = "B.g"
  val n: Double
    get() = 2.2
}

class C : A, B {
  override fun f() = 0
  override fun g() = super<A>.g()
  override val n: Double
    get() = super<A>.n + super<B>.n
}

fun main() {
  val c = C()
  c.f() eq 0
  c.g() eq "A.g"
  c.n eq 3.3
}
```

The functions f() and g() and the property n have identical signatures in interfaces A and B, so Kotlin doesn't know what to do and produces an error message if you don't resolve the issue (try individually commenting the definitions in C). Member functions and properties can be overridden with new definitions as in f(), but functions can also access the base versions of themselves using the super keyword, specifying the base class in angle brackets, as in the definition of C.g() and C.n.

Collisions where the identifier is the same but the type is different are not allowed in Kotlin and cannot be resolved.

Exercises and solutions can be found at www.AtomicKotlin.com.

Upcasting

Taking an object reference and treating it as a reference to its base type is called *upcasting*. The term *upcast* refers to the way inheritance hierarchies are traditionally represented with the base class at the top and derived classes fanning out below.

Inheriting and adding new member functions is the practice in Smalltalk, one of the first successful object-oriented languages. In Smalltalk, everything is an object and the only way to create a class is to inherit from an existing class, often adding new member functions. Smalltalk heavily influenced Java, which also requires everything to be an object.

Kotlin frees us from these constraints. We have stand-alone functions so everything doesn't need to be contained within classes. Extension functions allow us to add functionality without inheritance. Indeed, requiring the open keyword for inheritance makes it a very conscious and intentional choice, not something to use all the time.

More precisely, it narrows inheritance to a very specific use, an abstraction that allows us to write code that can be reused across multiple classes within a single hierarchy. The ***Polymorphism*** atom explores these mechanics, but first you must understand upcasting.

Consider some Shapes that can be drawn and erased:

```kotlin
// Upcasting/Shapes.kt
package upcasting

interface Shape {
  fun draw(): String
  fun erase(): String
}

class Circle : Shape {
  override fun draw() = "Circle.draw"
  override fun erase() = "Circle.erase"
}

class Square : Shape {
  override fun draw() = "Square.draw"
  override fun erase() = "Square.erase"
  fun color() = "Square.color"
}

class Triangle : Shape {
  override fun draw() = "Triangle.draw"
  override fun erase() = "Triangle.erase"
  fun rotate() = "Triangle.rotate"
}
```

The show() function accepts any Shape:

```kotlin
// Upcasting/Drawing.kt
package upcasting
import atomictest.*

fun show(shape: Shape) {
  trace("Show: ${shape.draw()}")
}

fun main() {
  listOf(Circle(), Square(), Triangle())
    .forEach(::show)
  trace eq """
    Show: Circle.draw
    Show: Square.draw
    Show: Triangle.draw
```

```
"""
}
```

In main(), show() is called with three different types: Circle, Square, and Triangle. The show() parameter is of the base class Shape, so show() accepts all three types. Each of those types is treated as a basic Shape—we say that the specific types are *upcast* to the basic type.

We typically draw a diagram for this hierarchy with the base class at the top:

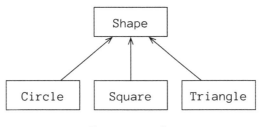

Shape Hierarchy

When we pass a Circle, Square, or Triangle as an argument of type Shape in show(), we cast *up* this inheritance hierarchy. In the process of upcasting, we lose the specific information about whether an object is of type Circle, Square, or Triangle. In each case, it becomes nothing more than a Shape object.

Treating a specific type as a more general type is the entire point of inheritance. The mechanics of inheritance exist solely to fulfill the goal of upcasting to the base type. Because of this abstraction ("everything is a Shape"), we can write a single show() function instead of writing one for every type of element. Upcasting is a way to reuse code for objects.

Indeed, in virtually every case where there's inheritance without upcasting, inheritance is being misused—it's unnecessary, and it makes the code needlessly complicated. This misuse is the reason for the maxim:

> *Prefer composition to inheritance.*

If the point of inheritance is the ability to substitute a derived type for a base type, what happens to the extra member functions: color() in Square and rotate() in Triangle?

Substitutability, also called the *Liskov Substitution Principle*, says that, after upcasting, the derived type can be treated *exactly* like the base type—no more and no less. This means that any member functions added to the derived class are, in effect, "trimmed off." They still exist, but because they are not part of the base-class interface, they are unavailable within show():

```
// Upcasting/TrimmedMembers.kt
package upcasting
import atomictest.*

fun trim(shape: Shape) {
  trace(shape.draw())
  trace(shape.erase())
  // Doesn't compile:
  // shape.color()    // [1]
  // shape.rotate()   // [2]
}

fun main() {
  trim(Square())
  trim(Triangle())
  trace eq """
    Square.draw
    Square.erase
    Triangle.draw
    Triangle.erase
  """
}
```

You can't call color() in line **[1]** because the Square instance was upcast to a Shape, and you can't call rotate() in line **[2]** because the Triangle instance is also upcast to a Shape. The only member functions available are the ones that are common to *all* Shapes—those defined in the base type Shape.

The same logic applies when you *directly* assign a subtype of Shape to a general Shape. The specified type determines the available members:

```
// Upcasting/Assignment.kt
import upcasting.*

fun main() {
  val shape1: Shape = Square()
  val shape2: Shape = Triangle()
  // Doesn't compile:
  // shape1.color()
  // shape2.rotate()
}
```

After an upcast, you can only call members of the base type.

Exercises and solutions can be found at www.AtomicKotlin.com.

Polymorphism

Polymorphism is an ancient Greek term meaning "many forms." In programming, polymorphism means an object or its members have multiple implementations.

Consider a simple hierarchy of `Pet` types. The `Pet` class says that all `Pet`s can `speak()`. `Dog` and `Cat` override the `speak()` member function:

```
// Polymorphism/Pet.kt
package polymorphism
import atomictest.eq

open class Pet {
  open fun speak() = "Pet"
}

class Dog : Pet() {
  override fun speak() = "Bark!"
}

class Cat : Pet() {
  override fun speak() = "Meow"
}

fun talk(pet: Pet) = pet.speak()

fun main() {
  talk(Dog()) eq "Bark!"     // [1]
  talk(Cat()) eq "Meow"      // [2]
}
```

Notice the `talk()` function parameter. When passing a `Dog` or a `Cat` to `talk()`, the specific type is forgotten and becomes a plain `Pet`—both `Dog`s and `Cat`s are *upcast* to `Pet`. The objects are now treated as plain `Pet`s so shouldn't the output for both lines **[1]** and **[2]** be `"Pet"`?

talk() doesn't know the exact type of Pet it receives. Despite that, when you call speak() through a reference to the base-class Pet, the correct subclass implementation is called, and you get the desired behavior.

Polymorphism occurs when a parent class reference contains a child class instance. When you call a member on that parent class reference, polymorphism produces the correct overridden member from the child class.

Connecting a function call to a function body is called *binding*. Ordinarily, you don't think much about binding because it happens statically, at compile time. With polymorphism, the same operation must behave differently for different types—but the compiler cannot know in advance which function body to use. The function body must be determined dynamically, at runtime, using *dynamic binding*. Dynamic binding is also called *late binding* or *dynamic dispatch*. Only at runtime can Kotlin determine the exact speak() function to call. Thus we say that the binding for the polymorphic call pet.speak() occurs dynamically.

Consider a fantasy game. Each Character in the game has a name and can play(). We combine Fighter and Magician to build specific characters:

```
// Polymorphism/FantasyGame.kt
package polymorphism
import atomictest.*

abstract class Character(val name: String) {
  abstract fun play(): String
}

interface Fighter {
  fun fight() = "Fight!"
}

interface Magician {
  fun doMagic() = "Magic!"
}

class Warrior :
  Character("Warrior"), Fighter {
  override fun play() = fight()
}
```

```kotlin
open class Elf(name: String = "Elf") :
  Character(name), Magician {
  override fun play() = doMagic()
}

class FightingElf :
  Elf("FightingElf"), Fighter {
  override fun play() =
    super.play() + fight()
}

fun Character.playTurn() =                // [1]
  trace(name + ": " + play())             // [2]

fun main() {
  val characters: List<Character> = listOf(
    Warrior(), Elf(), FightingElf()
  )
  characters.forEach { it.playTurn() } // [3]
  trace eq """
    Warrior: Fight!
    Elf: Magic!
    FightingElf: Magic!Fight!
  """
}
```

In `main()`, each object is upcast to `Character` as it is placed into the `List`. The trace shows that calling `playTurn()` on each `Character` in the `List` produces different output.

`playTurn()` is an extension function on the base type `Character`. When called in line **[3]**, it is *statically* bound, which means the exact function to be called is determined at compile time. In line **[3]**, the compiler determines that there is only one `playTurn()` function implementation—the one defined on line **[1]**.

When the compiler analyzes the `play()` function call on line **[2]**, it doesn't know which function implementation to use. If the `Character` is an `Elf`, it must call `Elf`'s `play()`. If the `Character` is a `FightingElf`, it must call `FightingElf`'s `play()`. It might also need to call a function from an as-yet-undefined subclass. The function binding differs from invocation to invocation. At compile time, the only certainty is that `play()` on line **[2]** is a member function of one of the `Character` subclasses.

The specific subclass can only be known at runtime, based on the actual Character type.

-

Dynamic binding isn't free. The additional logic that determines the runtime type slightly impacts performance compared to static binding. To force clarity, Kotlin defaults to closed classes and member functions. To inherit and override, you must be explicit.

A language feature such as the when statement can be learned in isolation. Polymorphism cannot—it only works in concert, as part of the larger picture of class relationships. To use object-oriented techniques effectively, you must expand your perspective to include not just members of an individual class, but also the commonality among classes and their relationships with each other.

Exercises and solutions can be found at www.AtomicKotlin.com.

Composition

One of the most compelling arguments for object-oriented programming is code reuse.

You may first think of "reuse" as "copying code." Copying seems like an easy solution, but it doesn't work very well. As time passes, your needs evolve. Applying changes to code that's been copied is a maintenance nightmare. Did you find all the copies? Did you make the changes the same way for each copy? Reused code can be changed in just one place.

In object-oriented programming you reuse code by creating new classes, but instead of creating them from scratch, you use existing classes that someone has already built and debugged. The trick is to use the classes without soiling the existing code.

Inheritance is one way to achieve this. Inheritance creates a new class as a *type of* an existing class. You add code to the form of the existing class without modifying the original. Inheritance is a cornerstone of object-oriented programming.

You can also choose a more straightforward approach, by creating objects of existing classes *inside* your new class. This is called *composition*, because the new class is composed of objects of existing classes. You're reusing the *functionality* of the code, not its form.

Composition is used frequently in this book. Composition is often overlooked because it seems so simple—you just put an object inside a class.

Composition is a *has-a* relationship. "A house *is a* building and *has a* kitchen" can be expressed like this:

```
// Composition/House1.kt
package composition1

interface Building
interface Kitchen

interface House: Building {
  val kitchen: Kitchen
}
```

Inheritance describes an *is-a* relationship, and it's often helpful to read the description aloud: "A house is a building." That sounds right, doesn't it? When the is-a relationship makes sense, inheritance usually makes sense.

If your house has two kitchens, composition yields an easy solution:

```
// Composition/House2.kt
package composition2

interface Building
interface Kitchen

interface House: Building {
  val kitchen1: Kitchen
  val kitchen2: Kitchen
}
```

To allow any number of kitchens, use composition with a collection:

```
// Composition/House3.kt
package composition3

interface Building
interface Kitchen

interface House: Building {
  val kitchens: List<Kitchen>
}
```

We spend time and effort understanding inheritance because it's more complex, and that complexity might give the impression that it's somehow more important. On the contrary:

Prefer composition to inheritance.

Composition produces simpler designs and implementations. This doesn't mean you should avoid inheritance. It's just that we tend to get bound up in more complicated relationships. The maxim *prefer composition to inheritance* is a reminder to step back, look at your design, and wonder whether you can simplify it with composition. The ultimate goal is to properly apply your tools and produce a good design.

Composition appears trivial, but is powerful. When a class grows and becomes responsible for different unrelated things, composition helps pull them apart. Use composition to simplify the complicated logic of a class.

Choosing Between Composition and Inheritance

Both composition and inheritance put subobjects inside your new class—composition has explicit subobjects while inheritance has implicit subobjects. When do you choose one over the other?

Composition provides the functionality of an existing class, but not its interface. You embed an object to use its features in your new class, but the user sees the interface you've defined for that new class rather than the interface of the embedded object. To hide the object completely, embed it privately:

```
// Composition/Embedding.kt
package composition

class Features {
  fun f1() = "feature1"
  fun f2() = "feature2"
}

class Form {
  private val features = Features()
  fun operation1() =
    features.f2() + features.f1()
  fun operation2() =
    features.f1() + features.f2()
}
```

The Features class provides implementations for the operations of Form, but the client programmer who uses Form has no access to features—indeed, the user is effectively unaware of *how* Form is implemented. This means that if you find a better way to implement Form, you can remove features and change to the new approach without any impact on code that calls Form.

If Form inherited Features, the client programmer could expect to upcast Form to Features. The inheritance relationship is then part of Form—the connection is explicit. If you change this, you'll break code that relies upon that connection.

Sometimes it makes sense to allow the class user to directly access the composition of your new class; that is, to make the member objects public. This is relatively safe, assuming the member objects use appropriate implementation hiding. For some systems, this approach can make the interface easier to understand. Consider a Car:

```
// Composition/Car.kt
package composition
import atomictest.*

class Engine {
  fun start() = trace("Engine start")
  fun stop() = trace("Engine stop")
}

class Wheel {
  fun inflate(psi: Int) =
    trace("Wheel inflate($psi)")
}

class Window(val side: String) {
  fun rollUp() =
    trace("$side Window roll up")
  fun rollDown() =
    trace("$side Window roll down")
}

class Door(val side: String) {
  val window = Window(side)
  fun open() = trace("$side Door open")
  fun close() = trace("$side Door close")
}
```

```
class Car {
  val engine = Engine()
  val wheel = List(4) { Wheel() }
  // Two door:
  val leftDoor = Door("left")
  val rightDoor = Door("right")
}

fun main() {
  val car = Car()
  car.leftDoor.open()
  car.rightDoor.window.rollUp()
  car.wheel[0].inflate(72)
  car.engine.start()
  trace eq """
    left Door open
    right Window roll up
    Wheel inflate(72)
    Engine start
  """
}
```

The composition of a Car is part of the analysis of the problem, and not simply part of the underlying implementation. This assists the client programmer's understanding of how to use the class and requires less code complexity for the creator of the class.

When you inherit, you create a custom version of an existing class. This takes a general-purpose class and specializes it for a particular need. In this example, it would make no sense to compose a Car using an object of a Vehicle class—a Car doesn't *contain* a Vehicle, it *is* a Vehicle. The is-a relationship is expressed with inheritance, and the has-a relationship is expressed with composition.

The cleverness of polymorphism can make it can seem that everything ought to be inherited. This will burden your designs. In fact, if you choose inheritance first when you're using an existing class to build a new class, things can become needlessly complicated. A better approach is to try composition first, especially when it's not obvious which approach works best.

Exercises and solutions can be found at www.AtomicKotlin.com.

Inheritance & Extensions

Inheritance is sometimes used to add functions to a class as a way to reuse it for a new purpose. This can lead to code that is difficult to understand and maintain.

Suppose someone has created a `Heater` class along with functions that act upon a `Heater`:

```
// InheritanceExtensions/Heater.kt
package inheritanceextensions
import atomictest.eq

open class Heater {
  fun heat(temperature: Int) =
    "heating to $temperature"
}

fun warm(heater: Heater) {
  heater.heat(70) eq "heating to 70"
}
```

For the sake of argument, imagine that `Heater` is far more complex than this, and that there are many adjunct functions such as `warm()`. We don't want to modify this library—we want to reuse it as-is.

If what we actually want is an HVAC (Heating, Ventilation and Air Conditioning) system, we can inherit `Heater` and add a `cool()` function. The existing `warm()` function, and all other functions that act upon a `Heater`, still work with our new HVAC type—which would not be true if we had used composition:

```
// InheritanceExtensions/InheritAdd.kt
package inheritanceextensions
import atomictest.eq

class HVAC : Heater() {
  fun cool(temperature: Int) =
    "cooling to $temperature"
}

fun warmAndCool(hvac: HVAC) {
  hvac.heat(70) eq "heating to 70"
  hvac.cool(60) eq "cooling to 60"
}

fun main() {
  val heater = Heater()
  val hvac = HVAC()
  warm(heater)
  warm(hvac)
  warmAndCool(hvac)
}
```

This seems practical: Heater didn't do everything we wanted, so we inherited HVAC from Heater and tacked on another function.

As you saw in **Upcasting**, object-oriented languages have a mechanism to deal with member functions added during inheritance: the added functions are trimmed off during upcasting and are unavailable to the base class. This is the *Liskov Substitution Principle*, aka "Substitutability," which says functions that accept a base class must be able to use objects of derived classes without knowing it. Substitutability is why warm() still works on an HVAC.

Although modern OO programming *allows* the addition of functions during inheritance, this can be a "code smell"—it appears to be reasonable and expedient but can lead you into trouble. Just because it seems to work doesn't mean it's a good idea. In particular, it might negatively impact a later maintainer of the code (which might be you). This kind of problem is called *technical debt*.

Adding functions during inheritance can be useful when the new class is rigorously treated as a base class throughout your system, ignoring the fact that it has its own bases. In **Type Checking** you'll see more examples where adding functions during inheritance can be a viable technique.

What we really wanted when creating the HVAC class was a Heater class with an added cool() function so it works with warmAndCool(). This is exactly what an extension function does, without inheritance:

```
// InheritanceExtensions/ExtensionFuncs.kt
package inheritanceextensions2
import inheritanceextensions.Heater
import atomictest.eq

fun Heater.cool(temperature: Int) =
  "cooling to $temperature"

fun warmAndCool(heater: Heater) {
  heater.heat(70) eq "heating to 70"
  heater.cool(60) eq "cooling to 60"
}

fun main() {
  val heater = Heater()
  warmAndCool(heater)
}
```

Instead of inheriting to extend the base class interface, extension functions extend the base class interface directly, without inheritance.

If we had control over the Heater library, we could design it differently, to be more flexible:

```
// InheritanceExtensions/TemperatureDelta.kt
package inheritanceextensions
import atomictest.*

class TemperatureDelta(
  val current: Double,
  val target: Double
)

fun TemperatureDelta.heat() {
  if (current < target)
    trace("heating to $target")
```

```
}
fun TemperatureDelta.cool() {
  if (current > target)
    trace("cooling to $target")
}

fun adjust(deltaT: TemperatureDelta) {
  deltaT.heat()
  deltaT.cool()
}

fun main() {
  adjust(TemperatureDelta(60.0, 70.0))
  adjust(TemperatureDelta(80.0, 60.0))
  trace eq """
    heating to 70.0
    cooling to 60.0
  """
}
```

In this approach, we control the temperature by choosing among multiple strategies. We could also have made `heat()` and `cool()` member functions instead of extension functions.

Interface by Convention

An extension function can be thought of as creating an interface containing a single function:

```
// InheritanceExtensions/Convention.kt
package inheritanceextensions

class X

fun X.f() {}

class Y

fun Y.f() {}

fun callF(x: X) = x.f()

fun callF(y: Y) = y.f()

fun main() {
  val x = X()
  val y = Y()
  x.f()
  y.f()
  callF(x)
  callF(y)
}
```

Both X and Y now appear to have a member function called f(), but we don't get polymorphic behavior so we must overload callF() to make it work for both types.

This "interface by convention" is used extensively in the Kotlin libraries, especially when dealing with collections. Although these are predominantly Java collections, the Kotlin library turns them into functional-style collections by adding a large number of extension functions. For example, on virtually any collection-like object, you can expect to find map() and reduce(), among many others. Because the programmer comes to expect this convention, it makes programming easier.

The Kotlin standard library Sequence interface contains a single member function. The other Sequence functions are all extensions[34]—there are well over one hundred. Initially, this approach was used for compatibility with Java collections, but now it's part of the Kotlin philosophy: Create a simple interface containing only the methods that define its essence, then create all auxiliary operations as extensions.

---

[34] https://kotlinlang.org/api/latest/jvm/stdlib/kotlin.sequences/

The *Adapter* Pattern

A library often defines a type and provides functions that accept parameters of that type and/or return that type:

```
// InheritanceExtensions/UsefulLibrary.kt
package usefullibrary

interface LibType {
  fun f1()
  fun f2()
}

fun utility1(lt: LibType) {
  lt.f1()
  lt.f2()
}

fun utility2(lt: LibType) {
  lt.f2()
  lt.f1()
}
```

To use this library, you must somehow convert your existing class to LibType. Here, we inherit from an existing MyClass to produce MyClassAdaptedForLib, which implements LibType and can thus be passed to the functions in UsefulLibrary.kt:

```
// InheritanceExtensions/Adapter.kt
package inheritanceextensions
import usefullibrary.*
import atomictest.*

open class MyClass {
  fun g() = trace("g()")
  fun h() = trace("h()")
}

fun useMyClass(mc: MyClass) {
  mc.g()
  mc.h()
}
```

```
class MyClassAdaptedForLib :
  MyClass(), LibType {
  override fun f1() = h()
  override fun f2() = g()
}

fun main() {
  val mc = MyClassAdaptedForLib()
  utility1(mc)
  utility2(mc)
  useMyClass(mc)
  trace eq "h() g() g() h() g() h()"
}
```

Although this does extend a class during inheritance, the new member functions are used *only* for the purpose of adapting to UsefulLibrary. Everywhere else, objects of MyClassAdaptedForLib can be treated as MyClass objects, as in the call to useMyClass(). There's no code that uses the extended MyClassAdaptedForLib where users of the base class must know about the derived class.

Adapter.kt relies on MyClass being open for inheritance. What if you don't control MyClass and it's not open? Fortunately, adapters can also be built using composition. Here, we add a MyClass field inside MyClassAdaptedForLib:

```
// InheritanceExtensions/ComposeAdapter.kt
package inheritanceextensions2
import usefullibrary.*
import atomictest.*

class MyClass { // Not open
  fun g() = trace("g()")
  fun h() = trace("h()")
}

fun useMyClass(mc: MyClass) {
  mc.g()
  mc.h()
}

class MyClassAdaptedForLib : LibType {
```

```
  val field = MyClass()
  override fun f1() = field.h()
  override fun f2() = field.g()
}

fun main() {
  val mc = MyClassAdaptedForLib()
  utility1(mc)
  utility2(mc)
  useMyClass(mc.field)
  trace eq "h() g() g() h() g() h()"
}
```

This is not quite as clean as Adapter.kt—you must explicitly access the MyClass object as seen in the call to useMyClass(mc.field). But it still handily solves the problem of adapting to a library.

Extension functions seem like they might be very useful for creating adapters. Unfortunately, you cannot implement an interface by collecting extension functions.

Members versus Extensions

There are cases where you are forced to use member functions rather than extensions. If a function must access a private member, you have no choice but to make it a member function:

```
// InheritanceExtensions/PrivateAccess.kt
package inheritanceextensions
import atomictest.eq

class Z(var i: Int = 0) {
  private var j = 0
  fun increment() {
    i++
    j++
  }
}

fun Z.decrement() {
  i--
```

```
  // j -- // Cannot access
}
```

The member function `increment()` can manipulate `j`, but the extension function `decrement()` doesn't have access to `j` because `j` is `private`.

The most significant limitation to extension functions is that they cannot be overridden:

```
// InheritanceExtensions/NoExtOverride.kt
package inheritanceextensions
import atomictest.*

open class Base {
  open fun f() = "Base.f()"
}

class Derived : Base() {
  override fun f() = "Derived.f()"
}

fun Base.g() = "Base.g()"
fun Derived.g() = "Derived.g()"

fun useBase(b: Base) {
  trace("Received ${b::class.simpleName}")
  trace(b.f())
  trace(b.g())
}

fun main() {
  useBase(Base())
  useBase(Derived())
  trace eq """
    Received Base
    Base.f()
    Base.g()
    Received Derived
    Derived.f()
    Base.g()
  """
}
```

The `trace` output shows that polymorphism works with the member function `f()` but not the extension function `g()`.

When a function doesn't need overriding and you have adequate access to the members of a class, you can define it as either a member function or an extension function—a stylistic choice that should maximize code clarity.

A member function reflects the essence of a type; you can't imagine the type without that function. Extension functions indicate "auxiliary" or "convenience" operations that support or utilize the type, but are not necessarily essential to that type's existence. Including auxiliary functions inside a type makes it harder to reason about, while defining some functions as extensions keeps the type clean and simple.

Consider a `Device` interface. The `model` and `productionYear` properties are intrinsic to `Device` because they describe key features. Functions like `overpriced()` and `outdated()` can be defined either as members of the interface or as extension functions. Here they are member functions:

```
// InheritanceExtensions/DeviceMembers.kt
package inheritanceextensions1
import atomictest.eq

interface Device {
  val model: String
  val productionYear: Int
  fun overpriced() = model.startsWith("i")
  fun outdated() = productionYear < 2050
}

class MyDevice(
  override val model: String,
  override val productionYear: Int
): Device

fun main() {
  val gadget: Device =
    MyDevice("my first phone", 2000)
  gadget.outdated() eq true
  gadget.overpriced() eq false
}
```

If we assume `overpriced()` and `outdated()` will not be overridden in subclasses, they can be defined as extensions:

```
// InheritanceExtensions/DeviceExtensions.kt
package inheritanceextensions2
import atomictest.eq

interface Device {
  val model: String
  val productionYear: Int
}

fun Device.overpriced() =
  model.startsWith("i")

fun Device.outdated() =
  productionYear < 2050

class MyDevice(
  override val model: String,
  override val productionYear: Int
): Device

fun main() {
  val gadget: Device =
    MyDevice("my first phone", 2000)
  gadget.outdated() eq true
  gadget.overpriced() eq false
}
```

Interfaces that only contain descriptive members are easier to comprehend and reason about, so the Device interface in the second example is probably a better choice. Ultimately, however, it's a design decision.

- -

Languages like C++ and Java allow inheritance unless you specifically disallow it. Kotlin assumes that you *won't* be using inheritance—it actively prevents inheritance and polymorphism unless they are intentionally allowed using the open keyword. This provides insight into Kotlin's orientation:

> *Often, functions are all you need. Sometimes objects are very useful. Objects are one tool among many, but they're not for everything.*

If you're pondering how to use inheritance in a particular situation, consider whether you need inheritance at all, and apply the maxim *Prefer extension functions and composition to inheritance* (modified from the book Design Patterns[35]).

Exercises and solutions can be found at www.AtomicKotlin.com.

---

[35] https://en.wikipedia.org/wiki/Design_Patterns

Class Delegation

Both composition and inheritance place subobjects inside your new class. With composition the subobject is explicit and with inheritance it is implicit.

Composition uses the functionality of an embedded object but does not expose its interface. For a class to reuse an existing implementation *and* implement its interface, you have two options: inheritance and *class delegation*.

Class delegation is midway between inheritance and composition. Like composition, you place a member object in the class you're building. Like inheritance, class delegation exposes the interface of the subobject. In addition, you can upcast to the member type. For code reuse, class delegation makes composition as powerful as inheritance.

How would you achieve this without language support? Here, a spaceship needs a control module:

```kotlin
// ClassDelegation/SpaceShipControls.kt
package classdelegation

interface Controls {
  fun up(velocity: Int): String
  fun down(velocity: Int): String
  fun left(velocity: Int): String
  fun right(velocity: Int): String
  fun forward(velocity: Int): String
  fun back(velocity: Int): String
  fun turboBoost(): String
}

class SpaceShipControls : Controls {
  override fun up(velocity: Int) =
    "up $velocity"
  override fun down(velocity: Int) =
```

```
    "down $velocity"
  override fun left(velocity: Int) =
    "left $velocity"
  override fun right(velocity: Int) =
    "right $velocity"
  override fun forward(velocity: Int) =
    "forward $velocity"
  override fun back(velocity: Int) =
    "back $velocity"
  override fun turboBoost() = "turbo boost"
}
```

If we want to expand the functionality of the controls or adjust some commands, we might try inheriting from SpaceShipControls. This doesn't work because SpaceShipControls is not open.

To expose the member functions in Controls, you can create an instance of SpaceShipControls as a property and explicitly delegate all the exposed member functions to that instance:

```
// ClassDelegation/ExplicitDelegation.kt
package classdelegation
import atomictest.eq

class ExplicitControls : Controls {
  private val controls = SpaceShipControls()
  // Delegation by hand:
  override fun up(velocity: Int) =
    controls.up(velocity)
  override fun back(velocity: Int) =
    controls.back(velocity)
  override fun down(velocity: Int) =
    controls.down(velocity)
  override fun forward(velocity: Int) =
    controls.forward(velocity)
  override fun left(velocity: Int) =
    controls.left(velocity)
  override fun right(velocity: Int) =
    controls.right(velocity)
  // Modified implementation:
  override fun turboBoost(): String =
    controls.turboBoost() + "... boooooost!"
```

```
}
fun main() {
  val controls = ExplicitControls()
  controls.forward(100) eq "forward 100"
  controls.turboBoost() eq
    "turbo boost... boooooost!"
}
```

The functions are forwarded to the underlying `controls` object, and the resulting interface is the same as if you had used regular inheritance. You can also provide implementation changes, as with `turboBoost()`.

Kotlin automates the process of class delegation, so instead of writing explicit function implementations as in `ExplicitDelegation.kt`, you specify an object to use as a delegate.

To delegate to a class, place the `by` keyword after the interface name, followed by the member property to use as the delegate:

```
// ClassDelegation/BasicDelegation.kt
package classdelegation

interface AI
class A : AI

class B(val a: A) : AI by a
```

Read this as "class `B` implements interface `AI` *by* using the `a` member object." You can only delegate to interfaces, so you can't say `A by a`. The delegate object (`a`) must be a constructor argument.

`ExplicitDelegation.kt` can now be rewritten using `by`:

```kotlin
// ClassDelegation/DelegatedControls.kt
package classdelegation
import atomictest.eq

class DelegatedControls(
  private val controls: SpaceShipControls =
    SpaceShipControls()
): Controls by controls {
  override fun turboBoost(): String =
    "${controls.turboBoost()}... boooooost!"
}

fun main() {
  val controls = DelegatedControls()
  controls.forward(100) eq "forward 100"
  controls.turboBoost() eq
    "turbo boost... boooooost!"
}
```

When Kotlin sees the by keyword, it generates code similar to what we wrote for ExplicitDelegation.kt. After delegation, the functions of the member object are accessible via the outer object, but without writing all that extra code.

Kotlin doesn't support multiple class inheritance, but you can simulate it using class delegation. In general, multiple inheritance is used to combine classes that have completely different functionality. For example, suppose you want to produce a button by combining a class that draws a rectangle on the screen with a class that manages mouse events:

```kotlin
// ClassDelegation/ModelingMI.kt
package classdelegation
import atomictest.eq

interface Rectangle {
  fun paint(): String
}

class ButtonImage(
  val width: Int,
  val height: Int
): Rectangle {
```

```kotlin
  override fun paint() =
    "painting ButtonImage($width, $height)"
}

interface MouseManager {
  fun clicked(): Boolean
  fun hovering(): Boolean
}

class UserInput : MouseManager {
  override fun clicked() = true
  override fun hovering() = true
}

// Even if we make the classes open, we
// get an error because only one class may
// appear in a supertype list:
// class Button : ButtonImage(), UserInput()

class Button(
  val width: Int,
  val height: Int,
  var image: Rectangle =
    ButtonImage(width, height),
  private var input: MouseManager = UserInput()
): Rectangle by image, MouseManager by input

fun main() {
  val button = Button(10, 5)
  button.paint() eq
    "painting ButtonImage(10, 5)"
  button.clicked() eq true
  button.hovering() eq true
  // Can upcast to both delegated types:
  val rectangle: Rectangle = button
  val mouseManager: MouseManager = button
}
```

The class Button implements two interfaces: Rectangle and MouseManager. It can't inherit from implementations of both ButtonImage and UserInput, but it can delegate to both of them.

Notice that the definition for `image` in the constructor argument list is both `public` and a `var`. This allows the client programmer to dynamically replace the `ButtonImage`.

The last two lines in `main()` show that a `Button` can be upcast to both of its delegated types. This was the goal of multiple inheritance, so delegation effectively solves the need for multiple inheritance.

- -

Inheritance can be constraining. For example, you cannot inherit a class when the superclass is not `open`, or if your new class is already extending another class. Class delegation releases you from these and other limitations.

Use class delegation with care. Among the three choices—inheritance, composition and class delegation—try composition first. It's the simplest approach and solves the majority of use cases. Inheritance is necessary when you need a hierarchy of types, to create relationships between those types. Class delegation can work when those options don't.

Exercises and solutions can be found at www.AtomicKotlin.com.

Downcasting

Downcasting discovers the specific type of a previously-upcast object.

Upcasts are always safe because the base class cannot have a bigger interface than the derived class. Every base-class member is guaranteed to exist and is therefore safe to call. Although object-oriented programming is primarily focused on upcasting, there are situations where downcasting can be a useful and expedient approach.

Downcasting happens at runtime, and is also called *run-time type identification* (RTTI).

Consider a class hierarchy where the base type has a narrower interface than the derived types. If you upcast an object to the base type, the compiler no longer knows the specific type. In particular, it cannot know what extended functions are safe to call:

```
// DownCasting/NarrowingUpcast.kt
package downcasting

interface Base {
  fun f()
}

class Derived1 : Base {
  override fun f() {}
  fun g() {}
}

class Derived2 : Base {
  override fun f() {}
  fun h() {}
}

fun main() {
  val b1: Base = Derived1() // Upcast
```

```
  b1.f()      // Part of Base
  // b1.g()   // Not part of Base
  val b2: Base = Derived2() // Upcast
  b2.f()      // Part of Base
  // b2.h()   // Not part of Base
}
```

To solve this problem, there must be some way to guarantee that a downcast is correct, so you don't accidentally cast to the wrong type and call a non-existent member.

Smart Casts

Smart casts in Kotlin are automatic downcasts. The is keyword checks whether an object is a particular type. Any code within the scope of that check assumes that it *is* that type:

```
// DownCasting/IsKeyword.kt
import downcasting.*

fun main() {
  val b1: Base = Derived1() // Upcast
  if(b1 is Derived1)
    b1.g() // Within scope of "is" check
  val b2: Base = Derived2() // Upcast
  if(b2 is Derived2)
    b2.h() // Within scope of "is" check
}
```

If b1 is of type Derived1, you can call g(). If b2 is of type Derived2, you can call h().

Smart casts are especially useful inside when expressions that use is to search for the type of the when argument. In main(), each specific type is first upcast to a Creature, then passed to what():

```
// DownCasting/Creature.kt
package downcasting
import atomictest.eq

interface Creature

class Human : Creature {
  fun greeting() = "I'm Human"
}

class Dog : Creature {
  fun bark() = "Yip!"
}

class Alien : Creature {
  fun mobility() = "Three legs"
}

fun what(c: Creature): String =
  when (c) {
    is Human -> c.greeting()
    is Dog -> c.bark()
    is Alien -> c.mobility()
    else -> "Something else"
  }

fun main() {
  val c: Creature = Human()
  what(c) eq "I'm Human"
  what(Dog()) eq "Yip!"
  what(Alien()) eq "Three legs"
  class Who : Creature
  what(Who()) eq "Something else"
}
```

In main(), upcasting happens when assigning a Human to Creature, passing a Dog to what(), passing an Alien to what(), and passing a Who to what().

Class hierarchies are traditionally drawn with the base class at the top and derived classes fanning down below it. what() takes a previously-upcast Creature and discovers its exact type, thus casting that Creature object *down* the inheritance hierarchy, from the more-general base class to a more-specific derived class.

A `when` expression that produces a value requires an `else` branch to capture all remaining possibilities. In `main()`, the `else` branch is tested using an instance of the local class `Who`.

Each branch of the `when` uses c as if it is the type we checked for: calling `greeting()` if c is `Human`, `bark()` if it's a `Dog` and `mobility()` if it's an `Alien`.

The Modifiable Reference

Automatic downcasts are subject to a special constraint. If the base-class reference to the object is modifiable (a `var`), then there's a possibility that this reference could be assigned to a different object between the instant that the type is detected and the instant when you call specific functions on the downcast object. That is, the specific type of the object might change between type detection and use.

In the following, c is the argument to `when`, and Kotlin insists that this argument be immutable so that it cannot change between the `is` expression and the call made after the `->`:

```
// DownCasting/MutableSmartCast.kt
package downcasting

class SmartCast1(val c: Creature) {
  fun contact() {
    when (c) {
      is Human -> c.greeting()
      is Dog -> c.bark()
      is Alien -> c.mobility()
    }
  }
}

class SmartCast2(var c: Creature) {
  fun contact() {
    when (val c = c) {             // [1]
      is Human -> c.greeting()     // [2]
      is Dog -> c.bark()
      is Alien -> c.mobility()
    }
```

```
    }
}
```

The c constructor argument is a `val` in `SmartCast1` and a `var` in `SmartCast2`. In both cases c is passed into the `when` expression, which uses a series of smart casts.

In **[1]**, the expression `val c = c` looks odd, and only used here for convenience—we don't recommend "shadowing" identifier names in normal code. `val c` creates a new local identifier c that captures the value of the property c. However, the property c is a `var` while the local (shadowed) c is a `val`. Try removing the `val c =`. This means that the c will now be the property, which is a `var`. This produces an error message for line **[2]**:

- *Smart cast to 'Human' is impossible, because 'c' is a mutable property that could have been changed by this time*

`is Dog` and `is Alien` produce similar messages. This is not limited to `when` expressions; there are other situations that can produce the same error message.

The change described in the error message typically happens through *concurrency*, when multiple independent tasks have the opportunity to change c at unpredictable times. (Concurrency is an advanced topic that we do not cover in this book).

Kotlin forces us to ensure that c will not change from the time that the `is` check is performed and the time that c is used as the downcast type. `SmartCast1` does this by making the c property a `val`, and `SmartCast2` does it by introducing the local `val c`.

Similarly, complex expressions cannot be smart-cast because the expression might be re-evaluated. Properties that are `open` for inheritance can't be smart-cast because their value might be overridden in subclasses, so there's no guarantee the value will be the same on the next access.

The `as` Keyword

The `as` keyword forcefully casts a general type to a specific type:

```
// DownCasting/Unsafe.kt
package downcasting
import atomictest.*

fun dogBarkUnsafe(c: Creature) =
  (c as Dog).bark()

fun dogBarkUnsafe2(c: Creature): String {
  c as Dog
  c.bark()
  return c.bark() + c.bark()
}

fun main() {
  dogBarkUnsafe(Dog()) eq "Yip!"
  dogBarkUnsafe2(Dog()) eq "Yip!Yip!"
  (capture {
    dogBarkUnsafe(Human())
  }) contains listOf("ClassCastException")
}
```

dogBarkUnsafe2() shows a second form of as: if you say c as Dog, then c is treated as a Dog throughout the rest of the scope.

A failing as cast throws a ClassCastException. A plain as is called an *unsafe cast*.

When a *safe cast* as? fails, it doesn't throw an exception, but instead returns null. You must then do something reasonable with that null to prevent a later NullPointerException. The Elvis operator (described in *Safe Calls & the Elvis Operator*) is usually the most straightforward approach:

```
// DownCasting/Safe.kt
package downcasting
import atomictest.eq

fun dogBarkSafe(c: Creature) =
  (c as? Dog)?.bark() ?: "Not a Dog"

fun main() {
  dogBarkSafe(Dog()) eq "Yip!"
  dogBarkSafe(Human()) eq "Not a Dog"
}
```

If c is not a Dog, as? produces a null. Thus, (c as? Dog) is a nullable expression and we must use the safe call operator ?. to call bark(). If as? produces a null, then the whole expression (c as? Dog)?.bark() will also produce a null, which the Elvis operator handles by producing "Not a Dog".

Discovering Types in Lists

When used in a predicate, is finds objects of a given type within a List, or any *iterable* (something you can iterate through):

```
// DownCasting/FindType.kt
package downcasting
import atomictest.eq

val group: List<Creature> = listOf(
  Human(), Human(), Dog(), Alien(), Dog()
)

fun main() {
  val dog = group
    .find { it is Dog } as Dog?     // [1]
  dog?.bark() eq "Yip!"             // [2]
}
```

Because group contains Creatures, find() returns a Creature. We want to treat it as a Dog, so we explicitly cast it at the end of line [1]. There might be zero Dogs in group, in which case find() returns a null so we must cast the result to a nullable Dog?. Because dog is nullable, we use the safe call operator in line [2].

You can usually avoid the code in line [1] by using filterIsInstance(), which produces all elements of a specific type:

```
// DownCasting/FilterIsInstance.kt
import downcasting.*
import atomictest.eq

fun main() {
  val humans1: List<Creature> =
    group.filter { it is Human }
  humans1.size eq 2
  val humans2: List<Human> =
    group.filterIsInstance<Human>()
  humans2 eq humans1
}
```

filterIsInstance() is a more readable way to produce the same result as filter(). However, the result types are different: while filter() returns a List of Creature (even though all the resulting elements are Human), filterIsInstance() returns a list of the target type Human. We've also eliminated the nullability issues seen in FindType.kt.

Exercises and solutions can be found at www.AtomicKotlin.com.

Sealed Classes

To constrain a class hierarchy, declare the superclass `sealed`.

Consider a trip taken by travelers using different modes of transportation:

```
// SealedClasses/UnSealed.kt
package withoutsealedclasses
import atomictest.eq

open class Transport

data class Train(
  val line: String
): Transport()

data class Bus(
  val number: String,
  val capacity: Int
): Transport()

fun travel(transport: Transport) =
  when (transport) {
    is Train ->
      "Train ${transport.line}"
    is Bus ->
      "Bus ${transport.number}: " +
      "size ${transport.capacity}"
    else -> "$transport is in limbo!"
  }

fun main() {
  listOf(Train("S1"), Bus("11", 90))
    .map(::travel) eq
    "[Train S1, Bus 11: size 90]"
}
```

Train and Bus each contain different details about their Transport mode.

travel() contains a when expression that discovers the exact type of the transport parameter. Kotlin requires the default else branch, because there might be other subclasses of Transport.

travel() shows downcasting's inherent trouble spot. Suppose you inherit Tram as a new type of Transport. If you do this, travel() continues to compile and run, giving you no clue that you should modify it to detect Tram. If you have many instances of downcasting scattered throughout your code, this becomes a maintenance challenge.

We can improve the situation using the sealed keyword. When defining Transport, replace open class with sealed class:

```
// SealedClasses/SealedClasses.kt
package sealedclasses
import atomictest.eq

sealed class Transport

data class Train(
  val line: String
) : Transport()

data class Bus(
  val number: String,
  val capacity: Int
) : Transport()

fun travel(transport: Transport) =
  when (transport) {
    is Train ->
      "Train ${transport.line}"
    is Bus ->
      "Bus ${transport.number}: " +
      "size ${transport.capacity}"
  }

fun main() {
  listOf(Train("S1"), Bus("11", 90))
    .map(::travel) eq
```

```
    "[Train S1, Bus 11: size 90]"
}
```

All direct subclasses of a `sealed` class must be located in the same file as the base class.

Although Kotlin forces you to exhaustively check all possible types in a `when` expression, the `when` in `travel()` no longer requires an `else` branch. Because `Transport` is `sealed`, Kotlin knows that no additional subclasses of `Transport` exist other than the ones present in this file. The `when` expression is now exhaustive without an `else` branch.

`sealed` hierarchies discover errors when adding new subclasses. When you introduce a new subclass, you must update all the code that uses the existing hierarchy. The `travel()` function in `UnSealed.kt` will continue to work because the `else` branch produces `"$transport is in limbo!"` on unknown types of transportation. However, that's probably not the behavior you want.

A `sealed` class reveals all the places to modify when we add a new subclass such as `Tram`. The `travel()` function in `SealedClasses.kt` won't compile if we introduce the `Tram` class without making additional changes. The `sealed` keyword makes it impossible to ignore the problem, because you get a compilation error.

The `sealed` keyword makes downcasting more palatable, but you should still be suspicious of designs that make excessive use of downcasting. There is often a better and cleaner way to write that code using polymorphism.

sealed **vs.** abstract

Here we show that both `abstract` and `sealed` classes allow identical types of functions, properties, and constructors:

```kotlin
// SealedClasses/SealedVsAbstract.kt
package sealedclasses

abstract class Abstract(val av: String) {
  open fun concreteFunction() {}
  open val concreteProperty = ""
  abstract fun abstractFunction(): String
  abstract val abstractProperty: String
  init {}
  constructor(c: Char) : this(c.toString())
}

open class Concrete() : Abstract("") {
  override fun concreteFunction() {}
  override val concreteProperty = ""
  override fun abstractFunction() = ""
  override val abstractProperty = ""
}

sealed class Sealed(val av: String) {
  open fun concreteFunction() {}
  open val concreteProperty = ""
  abstract fun abstractFunction(): String
  abstract val abstractProperty: String
  init {}
  constructor(c: Char) : this(c.toString())
}

open class SealedSubclass() : Sealed("") {
  override fun concreteFunction() {}
  override val concreteProperty = ""
  override fun abstractFunction() = ""
  override val abstractProperty = ""
}

fun main() {
  Concrete()
  SealedSubclass()
}
```

A sealed class is basically an abstract class with the extra constraint that all direct subclasses must be defined within the same file.

Indirect subclasses of a sealed class can be defined in a separate file:

```
// SealedClasses/ThirdLevelSealed.kt
package sealedclasses

class ThirdLevel : SealedSubclass()
```

`ThirdLevel` doesn't directly inherit from `Sealed` so it doesn't need to reside in `SealedVsAbstract.kt`.

Although a `sealed interface` seems like it would be a useful construct, Kotlin doesn't provide it because Java classes cannot be prevented from implementing the same interface.

Enumerating Subclasses

When a class is `sealed`, you can easily iterate through its subclasses:

```
// SealedClasses/SealedSubclasses.kt
package sealedclasses
import atomictest.eq

sealed class Top
class Middle1 : Top()
class Middle2 : Top()
open class Middle3 : Top()
class Bottom3 : Middle3()

fun main() {
  Top::class.sealedSubclasses
    .map { it.simpleName } eq
    "[Middle1, Middle2, Middle3]"
}
```

Creating a class generates a *class object*. You can access properties and member functions of that class object to discover information, and to create and manipulate objects of that class. `::class` produces a class object, so `Top::class` produces the class object for `Top`.

One of the properties of class objects is `sealedSubclasses`, which expects that `Top` is a `sealed` class (otherwise it produces an empty list). `sealedSubclasses` produces all the class objects of those subclasses. Notice that only the immediate subclasses of `Top` appear in the result.

The `toString()` for a class object is slightly verbose. We produce the class name alone by using the `simpleName` property.

`sealedSubclasses` uses *reflection*, which requires that the dependency `kotlin-reflection.jar` be in the classpath. Reflection is a way to dynamically discover and use characteristics of a class.

`sealedSubclasses` can be an important tool when building polymorphic systems. It can ensure that new classes will automatically be included in all appropriate operations. Because it discovers the subclasses at runtime, however, it may have a performance impact on your system. If you are having speed issues, be sure to use a profiler to discover whether `sealedSubclasses` might be the problem (as you learn to use a profiler, you'll discover that performance problems are usually *not* where you guess them to be).

Exercises and solutions can be found at www.AtomicKotlin.com.

Type Checking

In Kotlin you can easily act on an object based on its type. Normally this activity is the domain of polymorphism, so *type checking* enables interesting design choices.

Traditionally, type checking is used for special cases. For example, the majority of insects can fly, but there are a tiny number that cannot. It doesn't make sense to burden the Insect interface with the few insects that are unable to fly, so in basic() we use type checking to pick those out:

```
// TypeChecking/Insects.kt
package typechecking
import atomictest.eq

interface Insect {
  fun walk() = "$name: walk"
  fun fly() = "$name: fly"
}

class HouseFly : Insect

class Flea : Insect {
  override fun fly() =
    throw Exception("Flea cannot fly")
  fun crawl() = "Flea: crawl"
}

fun Insect.basic() =
  walk() + " " +
  if (this is Flea)
    crawl()
  else
    fly()

interface SwimmingInsect: Insect {
```

```kotlin
  fun swim() = "$name: swim"
}

interface WaterWalker: Insect {
  fun walkWater() =
    "$name: walk on water"
}

class WaterBeetle : SwimmingInsect
class WaterStrider : WaterWalker
class WhirligigBeetle :
  SwimmingInsect, WaterWalker

fun Insect.water() =
  when(this) {
    is SwimmingInsect -> swim()
    is WaterWalker -> walkWater()
    else -> "$name: drown"
  }

fun main() {
  val insects = listOf(
    HouseFly(), Flea(), WaterStrider(),
    WaterBeetle(), WhirligigBeetle()
  )
  insects.map { it.basic() } eq
    "[HouseFly: walk HouseFly: fly, " +
    "Flea: walk Flea: crawl, " +
    "WaterStrider: walk WaterStrider: fly, " +
    "WaterBeetle: walk WaterBeetle: fly, " +
    "WhirligigBeetle: walk " +
    "WhirligigBeetle: fly]"
  insects.map { it.water() } eq
    "[HouseFly: drown, Flea: drown, " +
    "WaterStrider: walk on water, " +
    "WaterBeetle: swim, " +
    "WhirligigBeetle: swim]"
}
```

There are also a very small number of insects that can walk on water or swim underwater. Again, it doesn't make sense to put those special-case behaviors in the base class to support such a small fraction of types. Instead, `Insect.water()`

contains a when expression that selects those subtypes for special behavior and assumes standard behavior for everything else.

Selecting a few isolated types for special treatment is the typical use case for type checking. Notice that adding new types to the system doesn't impact the existing code (unless a new type also requires special treatment).

To simplify the code, name produces the type of the object pointed to by the this under question:

```
// TypeChecking/AnyName.kt
package typechecking

val Any.name
  get() = this::class.simpleName
```

name takes an Any and gets the associated class reference using ::class, then produces the simpleName of that class.

Now consider a variation of the "shape" example:

```
// TypeChecking/TypeCheck1.kt
package typechecking
import atomictest.eq

interface Shape {
  fun draw(): String
}

class Circle : Shape {
  override fun draw() = "Circle: Draw"
}

class Square : Shape {
  override fun draw() = "Square: Draw"
  fun rotate() = "Square: Rotate"
}

fun turn(s: Shape) = when(s) {
  is Square -> s.rotate()
  else -> ""
}
```

```
fun main() {
  val shapes = listOf(Circle(), Square())
  shapes.map { it.draw() } eq
    "[Circle: Draw, Square: Draw]"
  shapes.map { turn(it) } eq
    "[, Square: Rotate]"
}
```

There are several reasons why you might add `rotate()` to `Square` instead of `Shape`:

- The `Shape` interface is out of your control, so you cannot modify it.
- Rotating `Square` seems like a special case that shouldn't burden and/or complicate the `Shape` interface.
- You're just trying to quickly solve a problem by adding `Square` and you don't want to take the trouble of putting `rotate()` in `Shape` and implementing it in all the subtypes.

There are certainly situations when this solution doesn't negatively impact your design, and Kotlin's `when` produces clean and straightforward code.

If, however, you must evolve your system by adding more types, it begins to get messy:

```
// TypeChecking/TypeCheck2.kt
package typechecking
import atomictest.eq

class Triangle : Shape {
  override fun draw() = "Triangle: Draw"
  fun rotate() = "Triangle: Rotate"
}

fun turn2(s: Shape) = when(s) {
  is Square -> s.rotate()
  is Triangle -> s.rotate()
  else -> ""
}

fun main() {
  val shapes =
```

```
    listOf(Circle(), Square(), Triangle())
  shapes.map { it.draw() } eq
    "[Circle: Draw, Square: Draw, " +
    "Triangle: Draw]"
  shapes.map { turn(it) } eq
    "[, Square: Rotate, ]"
  shapes.map { turn2(it) } eq
    "[, Square: Rotate, Triangle: Rotate]"
}
```

The polymorphic call in shapes.map { it.draw() } adapts to the new Triangle class without any changes or errors. Also, Kotlin disallows Triangle unless it implements draw().

The original turn() doesn't break when we add Triangle, but it also doesn't produce the result we want. turn() must become turn2() to generate the desired behavior.

Suppose your system begins to accumulate more functions like turn(). The Shape logic is now distributed across all these functions, rather than being centralized within the Shape hierarchy. If you add more new types of Shape, you must search for every function containing a when that switches on a Shape type, and modify it to include the new case. If you miss any of these functions, the compiler won't catch it.

turn() and turn2() exhibit what is often called *type-check coding*, which means testing for every type in your system. (If you are only looking for one or a few special types it is not usually considered type-check coding).

In traditional object-oriented languages, type-check coding is usually considered an antipattern because it invites the creation of one or more pieces of code that must be vigilantly maintained and updated whenever you add or change types in your system. Polymorphism, on the other hand, encapsulates those changes into the types that you add or modify, and those changes are then transparently propagated through your system.

The problem only occurs when the system needs to evolve by adding more Shape types. If that's not how your system evolves, you won't encounter the issue. If it is a problem it doesn't usually happen suddenly, but becomes steadily more difficult as your system evolves.

We shall see that Kotlin significantly mitigates this problem through the use of `sealed` classes. The solution isn't perfect, but type checking becomes a much more reasonable design choice.

Type Checking in Auxiliary Functions

The essence of a `BeverageContainer` is that it holds and delivers beverages. It seems to make sense to treat recycling as an auxiliary function:

```
// TypeChecking/BeverageContainer.kt
package typechecking
import atomictest.eq

interface BeverageContainer {
  fun open(): String
  fun pour(): String
}

class Can : BeverageContainer {
  override fun open() = "Pop Top"
  override fun pour() = "Can: Pour"
}

open class Bottle : BeverageContainer {
  override fun open() = "Remove Cap"
  override fun pour() = "Bottle: Pour"
}

class GlassBottle : Bottle()
class PlasticBottle : Bottle()

fun BeverageContainer.recycle() =
  when(this) {
    is Can -> "Recycle Can"
    is GlassBottle -> "Recycle Glass"
    else -> "Landfill"
  }

fun main() {
  val refrigerator = listOf(
```

```
    Can(), GlassBottle(), PlasticBottle()
  )
  refrigerator.map { it.open() } eq
    "[Pop Top, Remove Cap, Remove Cap]"
  refrigerator.map { it.recycle() } eq
    "[Recycle Can, Recycle Glass, " +
    "Landfill]"
}
```

By defining `recycle()` as an auxiliary function it captures the different recycling behaviors in a single place, rather than having them distributed throughout the `BeverageContainer` hierarchy by making `recycle()` a member function.

Acting on types with `when` is clean and straightforward, but the design is still problematic. When you add a new type, `recycle()` quietly uses the `else` clause. Because of this, necessary changes to type-checking functions like `recycle()` might be missed. What we'd like is for the compiler to tell us that we've forgotten a type check, just as it does when we implement an interface or inherit an `abstract` class and it tells us we've forgotten to override a function.

`sealed` classes provide a significant improvement here. Making `Shape` a `sealed` class means that the `when` in `turn()` (after removing the `else`) requires that each type be checked. Interfaces cannot be `sealed` so we must rewrite `Shape` into a class:

```
// TypeChecking/TypeCheck3.kt
package typechecking3
import atomictest.eq
import typechecking.name

sealed class Shape {
  fun draw() = "$name: Draw"
}

class Circle : Shape()

class Square : Shape() {
  fun rotate() = "Square: Rotate"
}

class Triangle : Shape() {
  fun rotate() = "Triangle: Rotate"
```

```
}

fun turn(s: Shape) = when(s) {
  is Circle -> ""
  is Square -> s.rotate()
  is Triangle -> s.rotate()
}

fun main() {
  val shapes = listOf(Circle(), Square())
  shapes.map { it.draw() } eq
    "[Circle: Draw, Square: Draw]"
  shapes.map { turn(it) } eq
    "[, Square: Rotate]"
}
```

If we add a new Shape, the compiler tells us to add a new type-check path in turn().

But let's look at what happens when we try to apply sealed to the BeverageContainer problem. In the process, we create additional Can and Bottle subtypes:

```
// TypeChecking/BeverageContainer2.kt
package typechecking2
import atomictest.eq

sealed class BeverageContainer {
  abstract fun open(): String
  abstract fun pour(): String
}

sealed class Can : BeverageContainer() {
  override fun open() = "Pop Top"
  override fun pour() = "Can: Pour"
}

class SteelCan : Can()
class AluminumCan : Can()

sealed class Bottle : BeverageContainer() {
  override fun open() = "Remove Cap"
  override fun pour() = "Bottle: Pour"
}
```

```kotlin
class GlassBottle : Bottle()
sealed class PlasticBottle : Bottle()
class PETBottle : PlasticBottle()
class HDPEBottle : PlasticBottle()

fun BeverageContainer.recycle() =
  when(this) {
    is Can -> "Recycle Can"
    is Bottle -> "Recycle Bottle"
  }

fun BeverageContainer.recycle2() =
  when(this) {
    is Can -> when(this) {
      is SteelCan -> "Recycle Steel"
      is AluminumCan -> "Recycle Aluminum"
    }
    is Bottle -> when(this) {
      is GlassBottle -> "Recycle Glass"
      is PlasticBottle -> when(this) {
        is PETBottle -> "Recycle PET"
        is HDPEBottle -> "Recycle HDPE"
      }
    }
  }

fun main() {
  val refrigerator = listOf(
    SteelCan(), AluminumCan(),
    GlassBottle(),
    PETBottle(), HDPEBottle()
  )
  refrigerator.map { it.open() } eq
    "[Pop Top, Pop Top, Remove Cap, " +
    "Remove Cap, Remove Cap]"
  refrigerator.map { it.recycle() } eq
    "[Recycle Can, Recycle Can, " +
    "Recycle Bottle, Recycle Bottle, " +
    "Recycle Bottle]"
  refrigerator.map { it.recycle2() } eq
    "[Recycle Steel, Recycle Aluminum, " +
```

```
    "Recycle Glass, " +
    "Recycle PET, Recycle HDPE]"
}
```

The intermediate classes `Can` and `Bottle` must also be `sealed` for this approach to work.

As long as the classes are direct subclasses of `BeverageContainer`, the compiler guarantees that the `when` in `recycle()` is exhaustive. But subclasses like `GlassBottle` and `AluminumCan` are not checked. To solve the problem we must explicitly include the nested `when` expressions seen in `recycle2()`, at which point the compiler *does* require exhaustive type checks (try commenting one of the specific `Can` or `Bottle` types to verify this).

To create a robust type-checking solution you must rigorously use `sealed` at each intermediate level of the class hierarchy, while ensuring that each level of subclasses has a corresponding nested `when`. In this case, if you add a new subtype of `Can` or `Bottle` the compiler ensures that `recycle2()` tests for each subtype.

Although not as clean as polymorphism, this is a significant improvement over prior object-oriented languages, and allows you to choose whether to write a polymorphic member function or auxiliary function. Notice that this problem only occurs when you have multiple levels of inheritance.

For comparison, let's rewrite `BeverageContainer2.kt` by bringing `recycle()` into `BeverageContainer`, which can again be an `interface`:

```
// TypeChecking/BeverageContainer3.kt
package typechecking3
import atomictest.eq
import typechecking.name

interface BeverageContainer {
  fun open(): String
  fun pour() = "$name: Pour"
  fun recycle(): String
}

abstract class Can : BeverageContainer {
  override fun open() = "Pop Top"
}
```

```kotlin
class SteelCan : Can() {
  override fun recycle() = "Recycle Steel"
}

class AluminumCan : Can() {
  override fun recycle() = "Recycle Aluminum"
}

abstract class Bottle : BeverageContainer {
  override fun open() = "Remove Cap"
}

class GlassBottle : Bottle() {
  override fun recycle() = "Recycle Glass"
}

abstract class PlasticBottle : Bottle()

class PETBottle : PlasticBottle() {
  override fun recycle() = "Recycle PET"
}

class HDPEBottle : PlasticBottle() {
  override fun recycle() = "Recycle HDPE"
}

fun main() {
  val refrigerator = listOf(
    SteelCan(), AluminumCan(),
    GlassBottle(),
    PETBottle(), HDPEBottle()
  )
  refrigerator.map { it.open() } eq
    "[Pop Top, Pop Top, Remove Cap, " +
    "Remove Cap, Remove Cap]"
  refrigerator.map { it.recycle() } eq
    "[Recycle Steel, Recycle Aluminum, " +
    "Recycle Glass, " +
    "Recycle PET, Recycle HDPE]"
}
```

By making `Can` and `Bottle` abstract classes, we force their subclasses to override `recycle()` in the same way that the compiler forces each type to be checked inside `recycle2()` in `BeverageContainer2.kt`.

Now the behavior of `recycle()` is distributed among the classes, which might be fine—it's a design decision. If you decide that recycling behavior changes often and you'd like to have it all in one place, then using the auxiliary type-checked `recycle2()` from `BeverageContainer2.kt` might be a better choice for your needs, and Kotlin's features make that reasonable.

Exercises and solutions can be found at www.AtomicKotlin.com.

Nested Classes

Nested classes enable more refined structures within your objects.

A nested class is simply a class within the namespace of the outer class. The implication is that the outer class "owns" the nested class. This feature is not essential, but nesting a class can clarify your code. Here, `Plane` is nested within `Airport`:

```
// NestedClasses/Airport.kt
package nestedclasses
import atomictest.eq
import nestedclasses.Airport.Plane

class Airport(private val code: String) {
  open class Plane {
    // Can access private properties:
    fun contact(airport: Airport) =
      "Contacting ${airport.code}"
  }
  private class PrivatePlane : Plane()
  fun privatePlane(): Plane = PrivatePlane()
}

fun main() {
  val denver = Airport("DEN")
  var plane = Plane()                    // [1]
  plane.contact(denver) eq "Contacting DEN"
  // Can't do this:
  // val privatePlane = Airport.PrivatePlane()
  val frankfurt = Airport("FRA")
  plane = frankfurt.privatePlane()
  // Can't do this:
  // val p = plane as PrivatePlane       // [2]
  plane.contact(frankfurt) eq "Contacting FRA"
}
```

In `contact()`, the nested class `Plane` has access to the `private` property code in the `airport` argument, whereas an ordinary class would not have this access. Other than that, `Plane` is simply a class inside the `Airport` namespace.

Creating a `Plane` object does not require an `Airport` object, but if you create it outside the `Airport` class body, you must ordinarily qualify the constructor call in **[1]**. By importing `nestedclasses.Airport.Plane` we avoid this qualification.

A nested class can be `private`, as with `PrivatePlane`. Making it `private` means that `PrivatePlane` is completely invisible outside the body of `Airport`, so you cannot call the `PrivatePlane` constructor outside of `Airport`. If you define and return a `PrivatePlane` from a member function, as seen in `privatePlane()`, the result must be upcast to a `public` type (assuming it extends a `public` type), and cannot be downcast to the `private` type, as seen in **[2]**.

Here's an example of nesting where `Cleanable` is a base class for both the enclosing class `House` and all the nested classes. `clean()` goes through a `List` of parts and calls `clean()` for each one, producing a kind of recursion:

```
// NestedClasses/NestedHouse.kt
package nestedclasses
import atomictest.*

abstract class Cleanable(val id: String) {
  open val parts: List<Cleanable> = listOf()
  fun clean(): String {
    val text = "$id clean"
    if (parts.isEmpty()) return text
    return "${parts.joinToString(
      " ", "(", ")",
      transform = Cleanable::clean)} $text\n"
  }
}

class House : Cleanable("House") {
  override val parts = listOf(
    Bedroom("Master Bedroom"),
    Bedroom("Guest Bedroom")
  )
  class Bedroom(id: String) : Cleanable(id) {
    override val parts =
```

```
      listOf(Closet(), Bathroom())
    class Closet : Cleanable("Closet") {
      override val parts =
        listOf(Shelf(), Shelf())
      class Shelf : Cleanable("Shelf")
    }
    class Bathroom : Cleanable("Bathroom") {
      override val parts =
        listOf(Toilet(), Sink())
      class Toilet : Cleanable("Toilet")
      class Sink : Cleanable("Sink")
    }
  }
}

fun main() {
  House().clean() eq """
  (((Shelf clean Shelf clean) Closet clean
   (Toilet clean Sink clean) Bathroom clean
  ) Master Bedroom clean
   ((Shelf clean Shelf clean) Closet clean
   (Toilet clean Sink clean) Bathroom clean
  ) Guest Bedroom clean
  ) House clean
  """
}
```

Notice the multiple levels of nesting. For example, `Bedroom` contains `Bathroom` which contains `Toilet` and `Sink`.

Local Classes

Classes that are nested inside functions are called *local* classes:

```
// NestedClasses/LocalClasses.kt
package nestedclasses

fun localClasses() {
  open class Amphibian
  class Frog : Amphibian()
  val amphibian: Amphibian = Frog()
}
```

`Amphibian` looks like a candidate to be an `interface` rather than an `open class`. However, local interfaces are not allowed.

Local open classes should be rare; if you need one, what you're trying to make is probably significant enough to create a regular class.

`Amphibian` and `Frog` are invisible outside `localClasses()`, so you can't return them from the function. To return objects of local classes, you must upcast them to a class or interface defined *outside* the function:

```
// NestedClasses/ReturnLocal.kt
package nestedclasses

interface Amphibian

fun createAmphibian(): Amphibian {
  class Frog : Amphibian
  return Frog()
}

fun main() {
  val amphibian = createAmphibian()
  // amphibian as Frog
}
```

`Frog` is still invisible outside `createAmphibian()`—in `main()`, you cannot cast `amphibian` to a `Frog` because `Frog` isn't available, so Kotlin reports the attempt to use `Frog` as an "unresolved reference."

Classes Inside Interfaces

Classes can be nested within interfaces:

```
// NestedClasses/WithinInterface.kt
package nestedclasses
import atomictest.eq

interface Item {
  val type: Type
  data class Type(val type: String)
}

class Bolt(type: String) : Item {
  override val type = Item.Type(type)
}

fun main() {
  val items = listOf(
    Bolt("Slotted"), Bolt("Hex")
  )
  items.map(Item::type) eq
    "[Type(type=Slotted), Type(type=Hex)]"
}
```

In `Bolt`, the `val type` must be overridden and assigned using the qualified class name `Item.Type`.

Nested Enumerations

Enumerations are classes, so they can be nested inside other classes:

```
// NestedClasses/Ticket.kt
package nestedclasses
import atomictest.eq
import nestedclasses.Ticket.Seat.*

class Ticket(
  val name: String,
  val seat: Seat = Coach
) {
  enum class Seat {
    Coach,
    Premium,
```

```
    Business,
    First
  }
  fun upgrade(): Ticket {
    val newSeat = values()[
      (seat.ordinal + 1)
        .coerceAtMost(First.ordinal)
    ]
    return Ticket(name, newSeat)
  }
  fun meal() = when(seat) {
    Coach -> "Bag Meal"
    Premium -> "Bag Meal with Cookie"
    Business -> "Hot Meal"
    First -> "Private Chef"
  }
  override fun toString() = "$seat"
}

fun main() {
  val tickets = listOf(
    Ticket("Jerry"),
    Ticket("Summer", Premium),
    Ticket("Squanchy", Business),
    Ticket("Beth", First)
  )
  tickets.map(Ticket::meal) eq
    "[Bag Meal, Bag Meal with Cookie, " +
    "Hot Meal, Private Chef]"
  tickets.map(Ticket::upgrade) eq
    "[Premium, Business, First, First]"
  tickets eq
    "[Coach, Premium, Business, First]"
  tickets.map(Ticket::meal) eq
    "[Bag Meal, Bag Meal with Cookie, " +
    "Hot Meal, Private Chef]"
}
```

upgrade() adds one to the ordinal value of the seat, then uses the library function coerceAtMost() to ensure the new value does not exceed First.ordinal before indexing into values() to produce the new Seat type. Following functional programming principles, upgrading a Ticket produces a new Ticket rather than modifying the old one.

`meal()` uses `when` to test every type of `Seat` and this suggests we could use polymorphism instead.

Enumerations cannot be nested within functions, and cannot inherit from other classes (including other enumerations).

Interfaces can contain nested enumerations. `FillIt` is a game-like simulation that fills a square grid with randomly-chosen X and O marks:

```
// NestedClasses/FillIt.kt
package nestedclasses
import nestedclasses.Game.State.*
import nestedclasses.Game.Mark.*
import kotlin.random.Random
import atomictest.*

interface Game {
  enum class State { Playing, Finished }
  enum class Mark { Blank, X ,O }
}

class FillIt(
  val side: Int = 3, randomSeed: Int = 0
): Game {
  val rand = Random(randomSeed)
  private var state = Playing
  private val grid =
    MutableList(side * side) { Blank }
  private var player = X
  fun turn() {
    val blanks = grid.withIndex()
      .filter { it.value == Blank }
    if(blanks.isEmpty()) {
      state = Finished
    } else {
      grid[blanks.random(rand).index] = player
      player = if (player == X) O else X
    }
  }
  fun play() {
    while(state != Finished)
```

```
      turn()
  }
  override fun toString() =
    grid.chunked(side).joinToString("\n")
}

fun main() {
  val game = FillIt(8, 17)
  game.play()
  game eq """
  [O, X, O, X, O, X, X, X]
  [X, O, O, O, O, O, X, X]
  [O, O, X, O, O, O, X, X]
  [X, O, O, O, O, O, X, O]
  [X, X, O, O, X, X, X, O]
  [X, X, O, O, X, X, O, X]
  [O, X, X, O, O, O, X, O]
  [X, O, X, X, X, O, X, X]
  """
}
```

For testability, we seed a Random object with randomSeed to produce identical output each time the program runs. Each element of grid is initialized with Blank. In turn(), we first find all cells containing Blank, along with their indices. If there are no more Blank cells then the simulation is complete. Otherwise, we use random() with our seeded generator to select one of the Blank cells. Because we used withIndex() earlier, we must select the index property to produce the location of the cell we want to change.

To display the List in the form of a two-dimensional grid, toString() uses the chunked() library function to break the List into pieces, each of length side, then joins these together with newlines.

Try experimenting with FillIt using different sides and randomSeeds.

Exercises and solutions can be found at www.AtomicKotlin.com.

Objects

The object keyword defines something that looks roughly like a class. However, you can't create instances of an object—there's only one. This is sometimes called the *Singleton* pattern.

An object is a way to combine functions and properties that logically belong together, but this combination either doesn't require multiple instances, or you want to explicitly prevent multiple instances. You never create an instance of an object—there's only one and it's available once the object has been defined:

```
// Objects/ObjectKeyword.kt
package objects
import atomictest.eq

object JustOne {
  val n = 2
  fun f() = n * 10
  fun g() = this.n * 20   // [1]
}

fun main() {
  // val x = JustOne() // Error
  JustOne.n eq 2
  JustOne.f() eq 20
  JustOne.g() eq 40
}
```

Here, you can't say JustOne() to create a new instance of a class JustOne. That's because the object keyword defines the structure and creates the object at the same time. In addition, it places the elements inside the object's namespace. If you only want the object to be visible within the current file, you can make it private.

- [1] The this keyword refers to the single object instance.

You cannot provide a parameter list for an object.

Naming conventions are slightly different when using object. Typically, when we create an instance of a class, we lower-case the first letter of the instance name. When you create an object, however, Kotlin defines the class *and* creates a single instance of that class. We capitalize the first letter of the object name because it also represents a class.

An object can inherit from a regular class or interface:

```
// Objects/ObjectInheritance.kt
package objects
import atomictest.eq

open class Paint(val color: String) {
  open fun apply() = "Applying $color"
}

object Acrylic: Paint("Blue") {
  override fun apply() =
    "Acrylic, ${super.apply()}"
}

interface PaintPreparation {
  fun prepare(): String
}

object Prepare: PaintPreparation {
  override fun prepare() = "Scrape"
}

fun main() {
  Prepare.prepare() eq "Scrape"
  Paint("Green").apply() eq "Applying Green"
  Acrylic.apply() eq "Acrylic, Applying Blue"
}
```

There's only a single instance of an object, so that instance is shared across all code that uses it. Here's an object in its own package:

```
// Objects/GlobalSharing.kt
package objectsharing

object Shared {
  var i: Int = 0
}
```

We can now use Shared in a different package:

```
// Objects/Share1.kt
package objectshare1
import objectsharing.Shared

fun f() {
  Shared.i += 5
}
```

And within a third package:

```
// Objects/Share2.kt
package objectshare2
import objectsharing.Shared
import objectshare1.f
import atomictest.eq

fun g() {
  Shared.i += 7
}

fun main() {
  f()
  g()
  Shared.i eq 12
}
```

You can see from the results that Shared is the same object in all packages, which makes sense because object creates a single instance. If you make Shared private, it's not available in the other files.

objects can't be placed inside functions, but they can be nested inside other objects or classes (as long as those classes are not themselves nested within other classes):

```
// Objects/ObjectNesting.kt
package objects
import atomictest.eq

object Outer {
  object Nested {
    val a = "Outer.Nested.a"
  }
}

class HasObject {
  object Nested {
    val a = "HasObject.Nested.a"
  }
}

fun main() {
  Outer.Nested.a eq "Outer.Nested.a"
  HasObject.Nested.a eq "HasObject.Nested.a"
}
```

There's another way to put an object inside a class: a companion object, which you'll see in the *Companion Objects* atom.

Exercises and solutions can be found at www.AtomicKotlin.com.

Inner Classes

Inner classes are like nested classes, but an object of an inner class maintains a reference to the outer class.

An `inner` class has an implicit link to the outer class. In the following example, `Hotel` is like `Airport` from ***Nested Classes***, but it uses `inner` classes. Note that `reception` is part of `Hotel`, but `callReception()`, which is a member of the nested class `Room`, accesses `reception` without qualification:

```
// InnerClasses/Hotel.kt
package innerclasses
import atomictest.eq

class Hotel(private val reception: String) {
  open inner class Room(val id: Int = 0) {
    // Uses 'reception' from outer class:
    fun callReception() =
      "Room $id Calling $reception"
  }
  private inner class Closet : Room()
  fun closet(): Room = Closet()
}

fun main() {
  val nycHotel = Hotel("311")
  // You need an outer object to
  // create an instance of the inner class:
  val room = nycHotel.Room(319)
  room.callReception() eq
    "Room 319 Calling 311"
  val sfHotel = Hotel("0")
  val closet = sfHotel.closet()
  closet.callReception() eq "Room 0 Calling 0"
}
```

Because `Closet` inherits the inner class `Room`, `Closet` must also be an `inner` class. Nested classes cannot inherit from `inner` classes.

`Closet` is `private`, so it is only visible within the scope of `Hotel`.

An `inner` object keeps a reference to its associated outer object. Thus, when creating an `inner` object you must first have an outer object. You cannot create a `Room` object without a `Hotel` object, as you see with `nycHotel.Room()`.

`inner data` classes are not allowed.

Qualified `this`

One of the benefits of classes is the `this` reference. You don't have to explicitly say "the current object" when you access a property or member function.

With a simple class, the meaning of `this` is obvious, but with an `inner` class, `this` could refer to either the `inner` object or an outer object. To resolve this issue, Kotlin provides the *qualified `this`* syntax: `this` followed by `@` and the name of the target class.

Consider three levels of classes: an outer class `Fruit` containing an `inner` class `Seed`, which itself contains an `inner` class `DNA`:

```
// InnerClasses/QualifiedThis.kt
package innerclasses
import atomictest.eq
import typechecking.name

class Fruit { // Implicit label @Fruit
  fun changeColor(color: String) =
    "Fruit $color"
  fun absorbWater(amount: Int) {}
  inner class Seed { // Implicit label @Seed
    fun changeColor(color: String) =
      "Seed $color"
    fun germinate() {}
    fun whichThis() {
      // Defaults to the current class:
      this.name eq "Seed"
```

```kotlin
      // To clarify, you can redundantly
      // qualify the default this:
      this@Seed.name  eq "Seed"
      // Must explicitly access Fruit:
      this@Fruit.name  eq "Fruit"
      // Cannot access a further-inner class:
      // this@DNA.name
    }
    inner class DNA { // Implicit label @DNA
      fun changeColor(color: String) {
        // changeColor(color) // Recursive
        this@Seed.changeColor(color)
        this@Fruit.changeColor(color)
      }
      fun plant() {
        // Call outer-class functions
        // Without qualification:
        germinate()
        absorbWater(10)
      }
      // Extension function:
      fun Int.grow() { // Implicit label @grow
        // Default is the Int.grow() receiver:
        this.name eq "Int"
        // Redundant qualification:
        this@grow.name  eq "Int"
        // You can still access everything:
        this@DNA.name  eq "DNA"
        this@Seed.name  eq "Seed"
        this@Fruit.name  eq "Fruit"
      }
      // Extension functions on outer classes:
      fun Seed.plant() {}
      fun Fruit.plant() {}
      fun whichThis() {
        // Defaults to the current class:
        this.name eq "DNA"
        // Redundant qualification:
        this@DNA.name  eq "DNA"
        // The others must be explicit:
        this@Seed.name  eq "Seed"
        this@Fruit.name  eq "Fruit"
```

```
      }
    }
  }
}

// Extension function:
fun Fruit.grow(amount: Int) {
  absorbWater(amount)
  // Calls Fruit's version of changeColor():
  changeColor("Red") eq "Fruit Red"
}

// Inner-class extension function:
fun Fruit.Seed.grow(n: Int) {
  germinate()
  // Calls Seed's version of changeColor():
  changeColor("Green") eq "Seed Green"
}

// Inner-class extension function:
fun Fruit.Seed.DNA.grow(n: Int) = n.grow()

fun main() {
  val fruit = Fruit()
  fruit.grow(4)
  val seed = fruit.Seed()
  seed.grow(9)
  seed.whichThis()
  val dna = seed.DNA()
  dna.plant()
  dna.grow(5)
  dna.whichThis()
  dna.changeColor("Purple")
}
```

`Fruit`, `Seed` and `DNA` all have functions called `changeColor()`, but there's no overriding—this is not an inheritance relationship. Because they have the same name and signature, the only way to distinguish them is with a qualified `this`, as you see in `DNA`'s `changeColor()`. Inside `plant()`, functions in either of the two outer classes can be called without qualification if there are no name collisions.

Even though it's an extension function, `grow()` can still access all the objects in the outer class. `grow()` can be called anywhere the `Fruit.Seed.DNA` implicit receiver is available; for example, inside an extension function for `DNA`.

Inner Class Inheritance

An inner class can inherit another inner class from a *different* outer class. Here, `Yolk` in `BigEgg` is derived from `Yolk` in `Egg`:

```
// InnerClasses/InnerClassInheritance.kt
package innerclasses
import atomictest.*

open class Egg {
  private var yolk = Yolk()
  open inner class Yolk {
    init { trace("Egg.Yolk()") }
    open fun f() { trace("Egg.Yolk.f()") }
  }
  init { trace("New Egg()") }
  fun insertYolk(y: Yolk) { yolk = y }
  fun g() { yolk.f() }
}

class BigEgg : Egg() {
  inner class Yolk : Egg.Yolk() {
    init { trace("BigEgg.Yolk()") }
    override fun f() {
      trace("BigEgg.Yolk.f()")
    }
  }
  init { insertYolk(Yolk()) }
}

fun main() {
  BigEgg().g()
  trace eq """
    Egg.Yolk()
    New Egg()
    Egg.Yolk()
    BigEgg.Yolk()
```

```
    BigEgg.Yolk.f()
"""
}
```

`BigEgg.Yolk` explicitly names `Egg.Yolk` as its base class, and overrides its `f()` member function. The function `insertYolk()` allows `BigEgg` to upcast one of its own `Yolk` objects into the `yolk` reference in `Egg`, so when `g()` calls `yolk.f()`, the overridden version of `f()` is used. The second call to `Egg.Yolk()` is the base-class constructor call of the `BigEgg.Yolk` constructor. You can see that the overridden version of `f()` is used when `g()` is called.

As a review of object construction, study the `trace` output until it makes sense.

Local & Anonymous Inner Classes

Classes defined inside member functions are called *local inner classes*. These can also be created anonymously, using an *object expression*, or using a **SAM conversion**. In all cases, the `inner` keyword is not used, but is implied:

```
// InnerClasses/LocalInnerClasses.kt
package innerclasses
import atomictest.eq

fun interface Pet {
  fun speak(): String
}

object CreatePet {
  fun home() = " home!"
  fun dog(): Pet {
    val say = "Bark"
    // Local inner class:
    class Dog : Pet {
      override fun speak() = say + home()
    }
    return Dog()
  }
  fun cat(): Pet {
    val emit = "Meow"
```

```kotlin
    // Anonymous inner class:
    return object: Pet {
      override fun speak() = emit + home()
    }
  }
  fun hamster(): Pet {
    val squeak = "Squeak"
    // SAM conversion:
    return Pet { squeak + home() }
  }
}

fun main() {
  CreatePet.dog().speak() eq "Bark home!"
  CreatePet.cat().speak() eq "Meow home!"
  CreatePet.hamster().speak() eq "Squeak home!"
}
```

A local inner class has access to other elements in the function as well as elements in the outer-class object, thus say, emit, squeak and home() are available within speak().

You can identify an anonymous inner class because it uses an object expression, which you see in cat(). It returns an object of a class inherited from Pet that overrides speak(). Anonymous inner classes are smaller and more straightforward and do not create a named class that will only be used in one place. Even more compact is a **SAM conversion**, as seen in hamster().

Because inner classes keep a reference to the outer-class object, local inner classes can access all members of the enclosing class:

```kotlin
// InnerClasses/CounterFactory.kt
package innerclasses
import atomictest.*

fun interface Counter {
  fun next(): Int
}

object CounterFactory {
  private var count = 0
  fun new(name: String): Counter {
    // Local inner class:
    class Local : Counter {
      init { trace("Local()") }
      override fun next(): Int {
        // Access local identifiers:
        trace("$name $count")
        return count++
      }
    }
    return Local()
  }
  fun new2(name: String): Counter {
    // Instance of an anonymous inner class:
    return object: Counter {
      init { trace("Counter()") }
      override fun next(): Int {
        trace("$name $count")
        return count++
      }
    }
  }
  fun new3(name: String): Counter {
    trace("Counter()")
    return Counter { // SAM conversion
      trace("$name $count")
      count++
    }
  }
}

fun main() {
```

```
    fun test(counter: Counter) {
      (0..3).forEach { counter.next() }
    }
    test(CounterFactory.new("Local"))
    test(CounterFactory.new2("Anon"))
    test(CounterFactory.new3("SAM"))
    trace eq """
      Local() Local 0 Local 1 Local 2 Local 3
      Counter() Anon 4 Anon 5 Anon 6 Anon 7
      Counter() SAM 8 SAM 9 SAM 10 SAM 11
    """
}
```

A Counter keeps track of a count and returns the next Int value. new(), new2() and new3() each create a different implementation of the Counter interface. new() returns an instance of a named inner class, new2() returns an instance of an anonymous inner class, and new3() uses a *SAM conversion* to create an anonymous object. All the resulting Counter objects have implicit access to the elements of the outer object, thus they are inner classes and not just nested classes. You can see from the output that count in CounterFactory is shared by all Counter objects.

SAM conversions are limited—for example, they do not support init clauses.

- -

In Kotlin, files can contain multiple top-level classes and functions. Because of this, there's rarely a need for local classes, so if you do need them they should be basic and straightforward. For example, it's reasonable to create a simple data class that's only used inside a function. If a local class becomes complex, you should probably take it out of the function and make it a regular class.

Exercises and solutions can be found at www.AtomicKotlin.com.

Companion Objects

Member functions act on particular instances of a class. Some functions aren't "about" an object, so they don't need to be tied to that object.

Functions and fields inside `companion objects` are about the class. Regular class elements can access the elements of the companion object, but the companion object elements cannot access the regular class elements.

As you saw in **Objects**, it's possible to define a regular `object` inside a class, but that doesn't provide an association between the `object` and the class. In particular, you're forced to explicitly name the nested `object` when you refer to its members. If you define a companion object inside a class, its elements become transparently available to that class:

```
// CompanionObjects/CompanionObject.kt
package companionobjects
import atomictest.eq

class WithCompanion {
  companion object {
    val i = 3
    fun f() = i * 3
  }
  fun g() = i + f()
}

fun WithCompanion.Companion.h() = f() * i

fun main() {
  val wc = WithCompanion()
  wc.g() eq 12
  WithCompanion.i eq 3
  WithCompanion.f() eq 9
  WithCompanion.h() eq 27
}
```

Outside the class, you access members of the companion object using the class name, as in `WithCompanion.i` and `WithCompanion.f()`. Other members of the class can access the companion object elements without qualification, as you see in the definition of `g()`.

`h()` is an extension function to the companion object.

If a function doesn't require access to private class members, you can choose to define it at file scope rather than putting it in a companion object.

Only one companion object is allowed per class. For clarity, you can give the companion object a name:

```
// CompanionObjects/NamingCompanionObjects.kt
package companionobjects
import atomictest.eq

class WithNamed {
  companion object Named {
    fun s() = "from Named"
  }
}

class WithDefault {
  companion object {
    fun s() = "from Default"
  }
}

fun main() {
  WithNamed.s() eq "from Named"
  WithNamed.Named.s() eq "from Named"
  WithDefault.s() eq "from Default"
  // The default name is "Companion":
  WithDefault.Companion.s() eq "from Default"
}
```

Even when you name the companion object you can still access its elements without using the name. If you don't give the companion object a name, Kotlin assigns it the name `Companion`.

If you create a property inside a companion object, it produces a single piece of storage for that field, shared with all instances of the associated class:

```
// CompanionObjects/ObjectProperty.kt
package companionobjects
import atomictest.eq

class WithObjectProperty {
  companion object {
    private var n: Int = 0 // Only one
  }
  fun increment() = ++n
}

fun main() {
  val a = WithObjectProperty()
  val b = WithObjectProperty()
  a.increment() eq 1
  b.increment() eq 2
  a.increment() eq 3
}
```

The tests in main() show that n has only a single piece of storage, no matter how many instances of WithObjectProperty are created. a and b both access the same memory for n.

increment() shows that you can access private members of the companion object from its surrounding class.

When a function is *only* accessing properties in the companion object, it makes sense to move that function inside the companion object:

```
// CompanionObjects/ObjectFunctions.kt
package companionobjects
import atomictest.eq

class CompanionObjectFunction {
  companion object {
    private var n: Int = 0
    fun increment() = ++n
  }
}

fun main() {
  CompanionObjectFunction.increment() eq 1
```

```
  CompanionObjectFunction.increment() eq 2
}
```

You no longer need a `CompanionObjectFunction` instance to call `increment()`.

Suppose you'd like to keep a count of every object you create, to give each one a unique readable identifier:

```
// CompanionObjects/ObjectCounter.kt
package companionobjects
import atomictest.eq

class Counted {
  companion object {
    private var count = 0
  }
  private val id = count++
  override fun toString() = "#$id"
}

fun main() {
  List(4) { Counted() } eq "[#0, #1, #2, #3]"
}
```

A companion object can be an instance of a class defined elsewhere:

```
// CompanionObjects/CompanionInstance.kt
package companionobjects
import atomictest.*

interface ZI {
  fun f(): String
  fun g(): String
}

open class ZIOpen : ZI {
  override fun f() = "ZIOpen.f()"
  override fun g() = "ZIOpen.g()"
}

class ZICompanion {
  companion object: ZIOpen()
```

```
  fun u() = trace("${f()} ${g()}")
}

class ZICompanionInheritance {
  companion object: ZIOpen() {
    override fun g() =
      "ZICompanionInheritance.g()"
    fun h() = "ZICompanionInheritance.h()"
  }
  fun u() = trace("${f()} ${g()} ${h()}")
}

class ZIClass {
  companion object: ZI {
    override fun f() = "ZIClass.f()"
    override fun g() = "ZIClass.g()"
  }
  fun u() = trace("${f()} ${g()}")
}

fun main() {
  ZIClass.f()
  ZIClass.g()
  ZIClass().u()
  ZICompanion.f()
  ZICompanion.g()
  ZICompanion().u()
  ZICompanionInheritance.f()
  ZICompanionInheritance.g()
  ZICompanionInheritance().u()
  trace eq """
    ZIClass.f() ZIClass.g()
    ZIOpen.f() ZIOpen.g()
    ZIOpen.f()
    ZICompanionInheritance.g()
    ZICompanionInheritance.h()
  """
}
```

`ZICompanion` uses a `ZIOpen` object as its companion object, and `ZICompanion-Inheritance` creates a `ZIOpen` object *while* overriding and extending `ZIOpen`. `ZIClass` shows that you can implement an interface while creating the companion object.

If the class you want to use as a companion object is not open, you cannot use it directly as we did above. However, if that class implements an interface you can still use it via *Class Delegation*:

```
// CompanionObjects/CompanionDelegation.kt
package companionobjects
import atomictest.*

class ZIClosed : ZI {
  override fun f() = "ZIClosed.f()"
  override fun g() = "ZIClosed.g()"
}

class ZIDelegation {
  companion object: ZI by ZIClosed()
  fun u() = trace("${f()} ${g()}")
}

class ZIDelegationInheritance {
  companion object: ZI by ZIClosed() {
    override fun g() =
      "ZIDelegationInheritance.g()"
    fun h() =
      "ZIDelegationInheritance.h()"
  }
  fun u() = trace("${f()} ${g()} ${h()}")
}

fun main() {
  ZIDelegation.f()
  ZIDelegation.g()
  ZIDelegation().u()
  ZIDelegationInheritance.f()
  ZIDelegationInheritance.g()
  ZIDelegationInheritance().u()
  trace eq """
    ZIClosed.f() ZIClosed.g()
    ZIClosed.f()
    ZIDelegationInheritance.g()
    ZIDelegationInheritance.h()
```

        """
}
```

`ZIDelegationInheritance` shows that you can take the non-open class `ZIClosed`, delegate it, then override and extend *that delegate*. Delegation forwards the methods of an interface to the instance that provides an implementation. Even if the class of that instance is `final`, we can still override and add methods to the delegation receiver.

Here's a small brain-teaser:

```
// CompanionObjects/DelegateAndExtend.kt
package companionobjects
import atomictest.eq

interface Extended: ZI {
  fun u(): String
}

class Extend : ZI by Companion, Extended {
  companion object: ZI {
    override fun f() = "Extend.f()"
    override fun g() = "Extend.g()"
  }
  override fun u() = "${f()} ${g()}"
}

private fun test(e: Extended): String {
  e.f()
  e.g()
  return e.u()
}

fun main() {
  test(Extend()) eq "Extend.f() Extend.g()"
}
```

In `Extend`, the `ZI` interface is implemented using its own `companion object`, which has the default name `Companion`. But we are also implementing the `Extended` interface, which is the `ZI` interface plus an extra function `u()`. The `ZI` portion of `Extended` is already implemented, via `Companion`, so we only need to override the
```

additional function u() to complete Extend. Now an Extend object can be upcast to Extended as the argument to test().

A common use for a companion object is controlling object creation—this is the *Factory Method* pattern. Suppose you'd like to only allow the creation of Lists of Numbered2 objects, and not individual Numbered2 objects:

```
// CompanionObjects/CompanionFactory.kt
package companionobjects
import atomictest.eq

class Numbered2
private constructor(private val id: Int) {
  override fun toString() = "#$id"
  companion object Factory {
    fun create(size: Int) =
      List(size) { Numbered2(it) }
  }
}

fun main() {
  Numbered2.create(0) eq "[]"
  Numbered2.create(5) eq
    "[#0, #1, #2, #3, #4]"
}
```

The Numbered2 constructor is private. This means there's only one way to create an instance—via the create() factory function. A factory function can sometimes solve problems that regular constructors cannot.

Constructors in companion objects are initialized when the enclosing class is instantiated for the first time in a program:

```
// CompanionObjects/Initialization.kt
package companionobjects
import atomictest.*

class CompanionInit {
  companion object {
    init {
      trace("Companion Constructor")
    }
  }
}

fun main() {
  trace("Before")
  CompanionInit()
  trace("After 1")
  CompanionInit()
  trace("After 2")
  CompanionInit()
  trace("After 3")
  trace eq """
    Before
    Companion Constructor
    After 1
    After 2
    After 3
  """
}
```

You can see from the output that the companion object is constructed only once, the first time a `CompanionInit()` object is created.

Exercises and solutions can be found at www.AtomicKotlin.com.

Section VI: Preventing Failure

If debugging is the process of removing software bugs, then programming must be the process of putting them in.—**Edsger Dijkstra**

Exception Handling

> Failure is always a possibility.

Kotlin finds basic errors when it analyzes your program. Errors that cannot be detected at compile time must be dealt with at runtime. In ***Exceptions***, you learned to throw exceptions. In this atom, we *catch* exceptions.

Historically, failures were often disastrous. For example, programs written in the C language would simply stop working, lose their data, and potentially crash the operating system.

Improved error handling is a powerful way to increase code reliability. Error handling is especially important when creating reusable program components. To create a robust system, each component must be robust. With consistent error handling, components can reliably communicate problems to client code.

Modern applications often use concurrency, and a concurrent program must survive non-critical exceptions. A server, for example, should recover when an open session is terminated via an exception.

Exceptions conflate three activities:

1. Error reporting
2. Recovery
3. Resource cleanup

Let's consider each one.

Reporting

Standard library exceptions are often adequate. For more specific exception handling, you can inherit new exception types from `Exception` or a subtype:

```
// ExceptionHandling/DefiningExceptions.kt
package exceptionhandling
import atomictest.*

class Exception1(
  val value: Int
): Exception("wrong value: $value")

open class Exception2(
  description: String
): Exception(description)

class Exception3(
  description: String
): Exception2(description)

fun main() {
  capture {
    throw Exception1(13)
  } eq "Exception1: wrong value: 13"
  capture {
    throw Exception3("error")
  } eq "Exception3: error"
}
```

A `throw` expression, as in `main()`, requires an instance of a `Throwable` subtype. To define new exception types, inherit `Exception` (which extends `Throwable`). Both `Exception1` and `Exception2` inherit `Exception`, while `Exception3` inherits `Exception2`.

Recovery

The ambition of exception handling is recovery. This means that you fix the problem, return the program to a stable state, and resume execution. Recovery often includes *logging* information about the error.

Quite often, recovery isn't possible. An exception might represent an unrecoverable program failure, either a coding error or something uncontrollable in the environment.

When an exception is thrown, the exception-handling mechanism looks for an appropriate place to continue execution. An exception keeps moving out to higher levels, from `function1()` that threw the exception, to `function2()` that calls `function1()`, to `function3()` that calls `function2()`, and so on until reaching `main()`. A matching handler *catches* the exception. This stops the search and runs that handler. If the program never finds a matching handler, it terminates with a console stack trace.

```
// ExceptionHandling/Stacktrace.kt
package stacktrace
import exceptionhandling.Exception1

fun function1(): Int =
  throw Exception1(-52)

fun function2() = function1()

fun function3() = function2()

fun main() {
//  function3()
}
```

Uncommenting the call to `function3()` produces the following stack trace:

```
Exception in thread "main" exceptionhandling.Exception1: wrong value: -\
52
  at stacktrace.StacktraceKt.function1(Stacktrace.kt:6)
  at stacktrace.StacktraceKt.function2(Stacktrace.kt:8)
  at stacktrace.StacktraceKt.function3(Stacktrace.kt:10)
  at stacktrace.StacktraceKt.main(Stacktrace.kt:13)
  at stacktrace.StacktraceKt.main(Stacktrace.kt)
```

Any of `function1()`, `function2()` or `function3()` can `catch` the exception and handle it, preventing the exception from terminating the program.

An *exception handler* is the `catch` keyword followed by a parameter list containing the exception you're handling. This is followed by a block of code implementing the recovery.

In the following example, the function `toss()` produces different exceptions for arguments 1-3, otherwise it returns "OK". `test()` contains a complete set of handlers for the `toss()` function:

```
// ExceptionHandling/Handlers.kt
package exceptionhandling
import atomictest.eq

fun toss(which: Int) = when (which) {
  1 -> throw Exception1(1)
  2 -> throw Exception2("Exception 2")
  3 -> throw Exception3("Exception 3")
  else -> "OK"
}

fun test(which: Int): Any? =
  try {
    toss(which)
  } catch (e: Exception1) {
    e.value
  } catch (e: Exception3) {
    e.message
  } catch (e: Exception2) {
    e.message
  }

fun main() {
  test(0) eq "OK"
  test(1) eq 1
  test(2) eq "Exception 2"
  test(3) eq "Exception 3"
}
```

When you call `toss()` you must `catch` all relevant `toss()` exceptions, allowing non-relevant exceptions to "bubble up" and be caught elsewhere.

The entire `try-catch` in `test()` is a single expression: it returns either the last expression of the `try` body or the last expression of the `catch` clause matching an exception. If no `catch` handles the exception, that exception is thrown further up the stack. If uncaught, it generates a stack trace.

Because `Exception3` extends `Exception2`, an `Exception3` is handled as an `Exception2` if `Exception2`'s `catch` appears in the sequence of handlers before `Exception3`'s `catch`:

```
// ExceptionHandling/Hierarchy.kt
package exceptionhandling
import atomictest.eq

fun testCatchOrder(which: Int) =
  try {
    toss(which)
  } catch (e: Exception2) {    // [1]
    "Handler for Exception2 got ${e.message}"
  } catch (e: Exception3) {    // [2]
    "Handler for Exception3 got ${e.message}"
  }

fun main() {
  testCatchOrder(2) eq
    "Handler for Exception2 got Exception 2"
  testCatchOrder(3) eq
    "Handler for Exception2 got Exception 3"
}
```

The catch-clause order means an Exception3 is caught by line **[1]**, despite the more specific type of exception handler in line **[2]**.

Exception Subtypes

In testCode(), an incorrect code argument throws an IllegalArgumentException:

```
// ExceptionHandling/LibraryException.kt
package exceptionhandling
import atomictest.*

fun testCode(code: Int) {
  if (code <= 1000) {
    throw IllegalArgumentException(
      "'code' must be > 1000: $code")
  }
}

fun main() {
  try {
```

```
    // A1 is 161 in base-16 (hex) notation:
    testCode("A1".toInt(16))
  } catch (e: IllegalArgumentException) {
    e.message eq
      "'code' must be > 1000: 161"
  }
  try {
    testCode("0".toInt(1))
  } catch (e: IllegalArgumentException) {
    e.message eq
      "radix 1 was not in valid range 2..36"
  }
}
```

An `IllegalArgumentException` is thrown by both `testCode()` and the library function `toInt(radix)`. This results in the somewhat confusing error messages in `main()`. The problem is that we are using the same exception to represent two different issues. We solve it by throwing a new exception type called `IncorrectInputException` for our error:

```
// ExceptionHandling/NewException.kt
package exceptionhandling
import atomictest.eq

class IncorrectInputException(
  message: String
): Exception(message)

fun checkCode(code: Int) {
  if (code <= 1000) {
    throw IncorrectInputException(
      "Code must be > 1000: $code")
  }
}

fun main() {
  try {
    checkCode("A1".toInt(16))
  } catch (e: IncorrectInputException) {
    e.message eq "Code must be > 1000: 161"
  } catch (e: IllegalArgumentException) {
    "Produces error" eq "if it gets here"
```

```
  }
  try {
    checkCode("1".toInt(1))
  } catch (e: IncorrectInputException) {
    "Produces error" eq "if it gets here"
  } catch (e: IllegalArgumentException) {
    e.message eq
      "radix 1 was not in valid range 2..36"
  }
}
```

Now each issue has its own handler.

Resist creating too many exception types. As a rule of thumb, use different exception types to distinguish different handling schemes, and use different constructor parameters to provide details for a particular handling scheme.

Resource Cleanup

When failure is inevitable, automatic resource cleanup helps other parts of the program to continue running safely.

`finally` ensures resource cleanup during exception handling. A `finally` clause always runs, regardless of whether you leave a `try` block normally or exceptionally:

```
// ExceptionHandling/TryFinally.kt
package exceptionhandling
import atomictest.*

fun checkValue(value: Int) {
  try {
    trace(value)
    if (value <= 0)
      throw IllegalArgumentException(
        "value must be positive: $value")
  } finally {
    trace("In finally clause for $value")
  }
}
```

```kotlin
fun main() {
  listOf(10, -10).forEach {
    try {
      checkValue(it)
    } catch (e: IllegalArgumentException) {
      trace("In catch clause for main()")
      trace(e.message)
    }
  }
  trace eq """
    10
    In finally clause for 10
    -10
    In finally clause for -10
    In catch clause for main()
    value must be positive: -10
  """
}
```

`finally` works even with intermediate `catch` clauses. For example, suppose a switch must be turned off when you're done with it:

```kotlin
// ExceptionHandling/GuaranteedCleanup.kt
package exceptionhandling
import atomictest.eq

data class Switch(
  var on: Boolean = false,
  var result: String = "OK"
)

fun testFinally(i: Int): Switch {
  val sw = Switch()
  try {
    sw.on = true
    when (i) {
      0 -> throw IllegalStateException()
      1 -> return sw                    // [1]
    }
  } catch (e: IllegalStateException) {
    sw.result = "exception"
  } finally {
```

```
    sw.on = false
  }
  return sw
}

fun main() {
  testFinally(0) eq
    "Switch(on=false, result=exception)"
  testFinally(1) eq
    "Switch(on=false, result=OK)"    // [2]
  testFinally(2) eq
    "Switch(on=false, result=OK)"
}
```

Even if we `return` inside a `try` (**[1]**), the `finally` clause still runs (**[2]**). Whether `testFinally()` completes normally or with an exception, the `finally` clause always executes.

Exception Handling in AtomicTest

This book uses AtomicTest's `capture()` to ensure that expected exceptions are thrown. `capture()` takes a function argument and returns a `CapturedException` object containing the exception class and error message:

```
// ExceptionHandling/CaptureImplementation.kt
package exceptionhandling
import atomictest.CapturedException

fun capture(f:() -> Unit): CapturedException =
  try {                                  // [1]
    f()
    CapturedException(null,
      "<Error>: Expected an exception") // [2]
  } catch (e: Throwable) {                // [3]
    CapturedException(e::class,          // [4]
      if (e.message != null) ": ${e.message}"
      else "")
  }
```

```
fun main() {
  capture {
    throw Exception("!!!")
  } eq "Exception: !!!"              // [5]
  capture {
    1
  } eq "<Error>: Expected an exception"
}
```

capture() calls its function argument f within a try block ([1]), handling all possible exceptions by catching Throwable ([3]). If no exception is thrown, the CapturedException message indicates that an exception was expected ([2]). If an exception is caught, the returned CapturedException contains the exception class and a message ([4]). A CapturedException can be compared to a String using eq ([5]).

Ordinarily you won't catch Throwable, but will process each specific exception type.

Guidelines

Recovering from exceptions turns out to be remarkably rare, considering that recovery was the original intent. The primary purpose of exceptions in Kotlin is to discover program bugs, not recovery. Catching exceptions in ordinary Kotlin code is thus a "code smell."

Here are guidelines for programming with exceptions in Kotlin:

1. **Logic Errors**: These are bugs in your code. Either don't catch them at all (and produce a stack trace), or catch them at the top level of your application and report the bugs, possibly restarting the affected operation.
2. **Data Errors**: These are errors from bad data that the programmer cannot control. The application must somehow deal with the problem without blaming it on program logic. For example, we've used String.toInt() this atom, which throws an exception for an inappropriate String. It also has a companion String.toIntOrNull() that produces a null upon failure so you can use it in an expression such as val n = string.toIntOrNull() ?: default.

    The Kotlin library is designed around dealing with a bad result by returning a null instead of throwing an exception. Operations that are expected to occasionally fail will usually have an "OrNull" version that you can use instead of the exception version.

3. ***Check instructions*** test for logic errors. These produce exceptions when they find a bug, but they look like function calls so you don't explicitly throw exceptions in your code.

4. **Input/Output Errors**: These are external conditions that you can't control and you can't ignore. However, using the "OrNull" approach rapidly obscures the understandability of the code. More importantly, you often *can* recover from I/O errors, typically by retrying the operation. Thus, I/O operations in Kotlin throw exceptions, so you'll have code in your applications that handle those and attempt to recover from them.

Exercises and solutions can be found at www.AtomicKotlin.com.

Check Instructions

Check instructions assert that constraints are satisfied. They are commonly used to validate function arguments and results.

Check instructions discover programming errors by expressing non-obvious requirements. They can also act as documentation for future readers of that code. You'll usually find check instructions at the beginning of a function, to ensure that the arguments are legitimate, and at the end, to check the function's calculations.

Check instructions typically throw exceptions when they fail. You can usually use check instructions instead of explicitly throwing exceptions. Check instructions are easier to write and think about, and produce more comprehensible code. Use them whenever possible to test and illuminate your programs.

`require()`

Design By Contract[36] *preconditions* guarantee initialization constraints. Kotlin's `require()` is normally used to validate function arguments, so it typically appears at the beginning of function bodies. These tests cannot be checked at compile time. Preconditions are relatively easy to include in your code, but sometimes they can be turned into **unit tests**.

Consider a numerical field representing a month on the Julian calendar. You know this value must always be in the range 1..12. A precondition reports an error if the value falls outside that range:

---

[36] https://en.wikipedia.org/wiki/Design_by_contract

```
// CheckInstructions/JulianMonth.kt
package checkinstructions
import atomictest.*

data class Month(val monthNumber: Int) {
  init {
    require(monthNumber in 1..12) {
      "Month out of range: $monthNumber"
    }
  }
}

fun main() {
  Month(1) eq "Month(monthNumber=1)"
  capture { Month(13) } eq
    "IllegalArgumentException: " +
    "Month out of range: 13"
}
```

We perform the `require()` inside the constructor. `require()` throws an IllegalArgumentException if its condition isn't satisfied. You can always use `require()` instead of throwing IllegalArgumentException.

The second parameter for `require()` is a lambda that produces a String. If the String requires construction, that overhead doesn't occur unless `require()` fails.

When the arguments for `Quadratic.kt` from *Summary 2* are inappropriate, it throws IllegalArgumentException. We can simplify the code using `require()`:

```
// CheckInstructions/QuadraticRequire.kt
package checkinstructions
import kotlin.math.sqrt
import atomictest.*

class Roots(
  val root1: Double,
  val root2: Double
)

fun quadraticZeroes(
  a: Double,
  b: Double,
```

```
    c: Double
): Roots {
  require(a != 0.0) { "a is zero" }
  val underRadical = b * b - 4 * a * c
  require(underRadical >= 0) {
    "Negative underRadical: $underRadical"
  }
  val squareRoot = sqrt(underRadical)
  val root1 = (-b - squareRoot) / (2 * a)
  val root2 = (-b + squareRoot) / (2 * a)
  return Roots(root1, root2)
}

fun main() {
  capture {
    quadraticZeroes(0.0, 4.0, 5.0)
  } eq "IllegalArgumentException: " +
    "a is zero"
  capture {
    quadraticZeroes(3.0, 4.0, 5.0)
  } eq "IllegalArgumentException: " +
    "Negative underRadical: -44.0"
  val roots = quadraticZeroes(1.0, 2.0, -8.0)
  roots.root1 eq -4.0
  roots.root2 eq 2.0
}
```

This code is much clearer and cleaner than the original Quadratic.kt.

The following DataFile class allows us to work with files regardless of whether the examples run in the IDE via the AtomicKotlin course or in the standalone build for the book. All DataFile objects store their files in the targetDir subdirectory:

```
// CheckInstructions/DataFile.kt
package checkinstructions
import atomictest.eq
import java.io.File
import java.nio.file.Paths

val targetDir = File("DataFiles")

class DataFile(val fileName: String) :
  File(targetDir, fileName) {
  init {
    if (!targetDir.exists())
      targetDir.mkdir()
  }
  fun erase() { if (exists()) delete() }
  fun reset(): File {
    erase()
    createNewFile()
    return this
  }
}

fun main() {
  DataFile("Test.txt").reset() eq
    Paths.get("DataFiles", "Test.txt")
      .toString()
}
```

A `DataFile` manipulates the underlying file in the operating system to write and read that file. The base class for `DataFile` is `java.io.File`, which is one of the oldest classes in the Java library; it appeared in the first version of the language, back when they thought it was a great idea to use the same class (`File`) to represent both files *and* directories. Kotlin effortlessly inherits `File`, despite its antiquity.

During construction, we create `targetDir` if it doesn't exist. The `erase()` function deletes the file, while `reset()` deletes the file and creates a new, empty file.

The Java standard library `Paths` class contains only an overloaded `get()`. The version of `get()` we want takes any number of `Strings` and builds a `Path` object, representing a directory path that is independent of the operating system.

Opening a file often has a number of preconditions, usually involving file paths, naming, and contents. Consider a function that opens and reads a file with a name beginning with `file_`. Using `require()`, we verify that the file name is correct and that the file exists and is not empty:

```
// CheckInstructions/GetTrace.kt
package checkinstructions
import atomictest.*

fun getTrace(fileName: String): List<String> {
  require(fileName.startsWith("file_")) {
    "$fileName must start with 'file_'"
  }
  val file = DataFile(fileName)
  require(file.exists()) {
    "$fileName doesn't exist"
  }
  val lines = file.readLines()
  require(lines.isNotEmpty()) {
    "$fileName is empty"
  }
  return lines
}

fun main() {
  DataFile("file_empty.txt").writeText("")
  DataFile("file_wubba.txt").writeText(
    "wubba lubba dub dub")
  capture {
    getTrace("wrong_name.txt")
  } eq "IllegalArgumentException: " +
    "wrong_name.txt must start with 'file_'"
  capture {
    getTrace("file_nonexistent.txt")
  } eq "IllegalArgumentException: " +
    "file_nonexistent.txt doesn't exist"
  capture {
    getTrace("file_empty.txt")
  } eq "IllegalArgumentException: " +
    "file_empty.txt is empty"
  getTrace("file_wubba.txt") eq
    "[wubba lubba dub dub]"
}
```

We've been using the two-parameter version of require(), but there's also a single-parameter version that produces a default message:

```
// CheckInstructions/SingleArgRequire.kt
package checkinstructions
import atomictest.*

fun singleArgRequire(arg: Int): Int {
  require(arg > 5)
  return arg
}

fun main() {
  capture {
    singleArgRequire(5)
  } eq "IllegalArgumentException: " +
    "Failed requirement."
  singleArgRequire(6) eq 6
}
```

The failure message is not as explicit as the two-parameter version, but in some cases it is sufficient.

requireNotNull()

requireNotNull() tests its first argument and returns that argument if it is not null. Otherwise, it produces an IllegalArgumentException.

Upon success, requireNotNull()'s argument is automatically smart-cast to a non-nullable type. Thus, you usually don't need requireNotNull()'s return value:

```
// CheckInstructions/RequireNotNull.kt
package checkinstructions
import atomictest.*

fun notNull(n: Int?): Int {
  requireNotNull(n) {            // [1]
    "notNull() argument cannot be null"
  }
  return n * 9                   // [2]
}

fun main() {
  val n: Int? = null
  capture {
    notNull(n)
  } eq "IllegalArgumentException: " +
    "notNull() argument cannot be null"
  capture {
    requireNotNull(n)            // [3]
  } eq "IllegalArgumentException: " +
    "Required value was null."
  notNull(11) eq 99
}
```

- **[2]** Notice that n no longer requires a null check, because the call to requireNotNull() has made it non-nullable.

As with require(), there's a two-parameter version with a message you can craft yourself (**[1]**), and a single-parameter version with a default message (**[3]**). Because requireNotNull() tests for a specific issue (nullity), the single-parameter version is more useful than it is with require().

check()

A design-by-contract *postcondition* tests the results of a function. Postconditions are important for long, complex functions where you might not trust the results. Whenever you can describe constraints on the results of a function, it's wise to express them as a postcondition.

`check()` is identical to `require()` except that it throws `IllegalStateException`. It is typically used at the *end* of a function, to verify that the results (or the fields in the function's object) are valid—that things haven't somehow gotten into a bad state.

Suppose a complex function writes to a file, and you are unsure whether all execution paths will create that file. Adding a postcondition at the end of the function helps ensure correctness:

```
// CheckInstructions/Postconditions.kt
package checkinstructions
import atomictest.*

val resultFile = DataFile("Results.txt")

fun createResultFile(create: Boolean) {
  if (create)
    resultFile.writeText("Results\n# ok")
  // ... other execution paths
  check(resultFile.exists()) {
    "${resultFile.name} doesn't exist!"
  }
}

fun main() {
  resultFile.erase()
  capture {
    createResultFile(false)
  } eq "IllegalStateException: " +
    "Results.txt doesn't exist!"
  createResultFile(true)
}
```

Assuming your preconditions ensure valid arguments, a postcondition failure almost always indicates a programming error. For this reason, you'll see postconditions less often because, once the programmer is convinced the code is correct, the postcondition can be commented or removed if it impacts performance. Of course, it's always best to leave such tests in place so problems caused by future code changes are immediately detected. One way to do this is by moving postconditions into ***unit tests***.

assert()

To avoid commenting and uncommenting `check()` statements, `assert()` allows you to enable and disable `assert()` checks.

`assert()` comes from Java. Assertions are disabled by default, and are only engaged if you explicitly turn them on using a command-line flag. In Kotlin, this flag is `-ea`.

We recommend using `require()` and `check()`, which are always available without special configuration.

Exercises and solutions can be found at www.AtomicKotlin.com.

The Nothing Type

A Nothing return type indicates a function that never returns

This is usually a function that always throws an exception.

Here's a function that produces an infinite loop (avoid these)—because it never returns, its return type is Nothing:

```
// NothingType/InfiniteLoop.kt
package nothingtype

fun infinite(): Nothing {
  while (true) {}
}
```

Nothing is a built-in Kotlin type with no instances.

A practical example is the built-in TODO(), which has a return type of Nothing and throws NotImplementedError:

```
// NothingType/Todo.kt
package nothingtype
import atomictest.*

fun later(s: String): String = TODO("later()")

fun later2(s: String): Int = TODO()

fun main() {
  capture {
    later("Hello")
  } eq "NotImplementedError: " +
    "An operation is not implemented: later()"
  capture {
    later2("Hello!")
  } eq "NotImplementedError: " +
    "An operation is not implemented."
}
```

Both `later()` and `later2()` return non-`Nothing` types even though `TODO()` returns `Nothing`. `Nothing` is compatible with any type.

`later()` and `later2()` compile successfully. If you call either one, an exception reminds you to write implementations. `TODO()` is a useful tool for "sketching" a code framework to verify that everything fits together before filling in the details.

In the following, `fail()` always throws an `Exception` so it returns `Nothing`. Notice that a call to `fail()` is more readable and compact than explicitly throwing an exception:

```
// NothingType/Fail.kt
package nothingtype
import atomictest.*

fun fail(i: Int): Nothing =
  throw Exception("fail($i)")

fun main() {
  capture {
    fail(1)
  } eq "Exception: fail(1)"
  capture {
    fail(2)
  } eq "Exception: fail(2)"
}
```

`fail()` allows you to easily change the error-handling strategy. For example, you can change the exception type or log an additional message before throwing an exception.

This throws a `BadData` exception if the argument is not a `String`:

```
// NothingType/CheckObject.kt
package nothingtype
import atomictest.*

class BadData(m: String) : Exception(m)

fun checkObject(obj: Any?): String =
  if (obj is String)
    obj
  else
    throw BadData("Needs String, got $obj")

fun test(checkObj: (obj: Any?) -> String) {
  checkObj("abc") eq "abc"
  capture {
    checkObj(null)
  } eq "BadData: Needs String, got null"
  capture {
    checkObj(123)
  } eq "BadData: Needs String, got 123"
}

fun main() {
  test(::checkObject)
}
```

checkObject()'s return type is the return type of the if expression. Kotlin treats a throw as type Nothing, and Nothing can be assigned to any type. In checkObject(), String takes priority over Nothing, so the type of the if expression is String.

We can rewrite checkObject() using a *safe cast and an Elvis operator*. checkObject2() casts obj to a String if it can be cast, otherwise it throws an exception:

```
// NothingType/CheckObject2.kt
package nothingtype

fun failWithBadData(obj: Any?): Nothing =
  throw BadData("Needs String, got $obj")

fun checkObject2(obj: Any?): String =
  (obj as? String) ?: failWithBadData(obj)

fun main() {
  test(::checkObject2)
}
```

When given a plain `null` with no additional type information, the compiler infers a nullable `Nothing`:

```
// NothingType/ListOfNothing.kt
import atomictest.eq

fun main() {
  val none: Nothing? = null

  var nullableString: String? = null    // [1]
  nullableString = "abc"
  nullableString = none                 // [2]
  nullableString eq null

  val nullableInt: Int? = none          // [3]
  nullableInt eq null

  val listNone: List<Nothing?> = listOf(null)
  val ints: List<Int?> = listOf(null)   // [4]
  ints eq listNone
}
```

You can assign both `null` and `none` to a `var` or `val` of a nullable type, such as `nullableString` or `nullableInt`. This is allowed because the type of both `null` and `none` is `Nothing?` (nullable `Nothing`). In the same way that an expression of the `Nothing` type (for example, `fail()`) can be interpreted as "any type," an expression of the `Nothing?` type, such as `null`, can be interpreted as "any nullable type." Assignments to different nullable types are shown in lines **[1]**, **[2]** and **[3]**.

`listNone` is initialized with a `List` containing only the `null` value. The compiler infers this to be `List<Nothing?>`. For this reason, you must explicitly specify the element type (**[4]**) that you want to store in the `List` when you initialize it with only `null`.

Exercises and solutions can be found at www.AtomicKotlin.com.

Resource Cleanup

> Using `try-finally` blocks for resource cleanup is tedious and error-prone. Kotlin's library functions manage cleanup for you.

As you learned in ***Exception Handling***, the `finally` clause cleans up resources regardless of how the `try` block exits. But what if an exception can happen while closing a resource? You end up with another `try` inside the `finally` clause. On top of that, if one exception is thrown inside a `try` and another while closing the resource, the latter shouldn't conceal the former. Ensuring proper cleanup becomes very messy.

To reduce this complexity, Kotlin's `use()` guarantees proper cleanup of closeable resources, liberating you from handwritten cleanup code.

`use()` works with any object that implements Java's `AutoCloseable` interface. It executes the code within the block, then calls `close()` on the object, regardless of how you exit the block—either normally (including via `return`), or through an exception.

`use()` rethrows all exceptions, so you must still deal with those exceptions.

Predefined classes that work with `use()` are found in the Java documentation for `AutoCloseable`. For example, to read lines from a `File` we apply `use()` to a `BufferedReader`. `DataFile` from ***Check Instructions*** inherits `java.io.File`:

```
// ResourceCleanup/AutoCloseable.kt
import atomictest.eq
import checkinstructions.DataFile

fun main() {
  DataFile("Results.txt")
    .bufferedReader()
    .use { it.readLines().first() } eq
    "Results"
}
```

useLines() opens a File object, extracts all its lines, and passes those lines to a target function (typically a lambda):

```
// ResourceCleanup/UseLines.kt
import atomictest.eq
import checkinstructions.DataFile

fun main() {
  DataFile("Results.txt").useLines {
    it.filter { "#" in it }.first()     // [1]
  } eq "# ok"
  DataFile("Results.txt").useLines { lines ->
    lines.filter { line ->              // [2]
      "#" in line
    }.first()
  } eq "# ok"
}
```

- **[1]** The left-hand it refers to the collection of lines in the file, while the right-hand it refers to each individual line. To reduce confusion, avoid writing code with two different nearby its.
- **[2]** Named arguments prevent confusion from too many its.

Everything happens within the useLines() lambda; outside the lambda the file contents are unavailable unless you explicitly return them. As it closes the file, useLines() returns the result of the lambda.

forEachLine() makes it easy to apply an action to each line in a file:

```
// ResourceCleanup/ForEachLine.kt
import checkinstructions.DataFile
import atomictest.*

fun main() {
  DataFile("Results.txt").forEachLine {
    if (it.startsWith("#"))
      trace("$it")
  }
  trace eq "# ok"
}
```

The lambda in forEachLine() returns Unit, which means that anything you do with the lines must be achieved through side effects. In functional programming, we prefer returning results over side effects, and thus useLines() is a more functional approach than forEachLine(). However, forEachLine() is a quick solution for simple utilities.

You can create your own class that works with use() by implementing the Auto-Closeable interface, which contains only the close() function:

```
// ResourceCleanup/Usable.kt
package resourcecleanup
import atomictest.*

class Usable() : AutoCloseable {
  fun func() = trace("func()")
  override fun close() = trace("close()")
}

fun main() {
  Usable().use { it.func() }
  trace eq "func() close()"
}
```

use() ensures resource cleanup at the point the resource is created, rather than forcing you to write cleanup code when you're finished with the resource.

Exercises and solutions can be found at www.AtomicKotlin.com.

Logging

Logging captures information from a running program.

For example, an installation program might log:

- The steps taken during setup.
- The directories for file storage.
- Startup values for the program.

A web server might log the origin address and status of each request.

Logging is also helpful during debugging. Without logging, you might decipher the behavior of a program using `println()` statements. This can be helpful in the absence of a debugger (such as the one built into IntelliJ IDEA). However, once you decide the program is working properly, you'll probably take the `println()` statements out. Later, if you run into more bugs, you might put them back in. In contrast, logging can be dynamically enabled when you need it, and turned off otherwise.

For some failures you can only report the issue. A program that recovers from some types of errors (as shown in **Exception Handling**) can log details about those errors for later analysis. In a web application, for example, you don't terminate the program if something goes wrong. Logging captures these events, giving programmers and administrators a way to discover the problems. Meanwhile, the application continues running.

We use an open-source logging package designed for Kotlin called Kotlin-logging[37], which has the feel and simplicity of Kotlin. There are other logging packages to choose from.

You must create a logger before using it. You'll almost always want to create it at file scope so it's available to all components in that file:

---
[37] https://github.com/MicroUtils/kotlin-logging

```
// Logging/BasicLogging.kt
package logging
import mu.KLogging

private val log = KLogging().logger

fun main() {
  val msg = "Hello, Kotlin Logging!"
  log.trace(msg)
  log.debug(msg)
  log.info(msg)
  log.warn(msg)
  log.error(msg)
}
```

`main()` shows the different *logging levels*: `trace()`, `debug()` and `info()` capture behavioral information, while `warn()` and `error()` indicate problems.

Start-up configuration determines the logging levels that are actually reported. This can be modified during execution. Operators of long-running applications can change the logging level without restarting the program (which is often unacceptable).

Logging libraries have a rather odd history. People were dissatisfied with the original logging library distributed with Java, so they created other libraries. In an attempt to unify logging, designers began developing common logging interfaces. Acknowledging that organizations may be invested in existing logging libraries, those interfaces were created as *facades* for multiple different logging libraries. Later, other programmers created (presumably improved) facades over *those* facades. Utilizing a logging system often means choosing a facade, then choosing one or more underlying implementations.

The Kotlin-logging library is a facade over the Simple Logging Facade for Java (SLF4J)[38], which is an abstraction over multiple logging frameworks. You choose the framework that meets your needs—although it is more likely that the operations group in your company will make that decision, as they are the ones that usually manage logging and analyze the resulting log files.

For this example we use `slf4j-simple` as our implementation. This comes as part of SLF4J and thus we are not required to install or configure an additional library—

---

[38]https://www.slf4j.org/

some libraries have an annoying amount of setup complexity. `slf4j-simple` sends its output to the console error stream. When you run the program, you see:

```
[main] INFO mu.KLogging - Hello, Kotlin Logging!
[main] WARN mu.KLogging - Hello, Kotlin Logging!
[main] ERROR mu.KLogging - Hello, Kotlin Logging!
```

`trace()` and `debug()` produce no output because the default configuration doesn't report those levels. To get different reporting levels, change your logging configuration. Logging configuration varies depending on the logging package you're using, so we don't talk about it here.

Logging implementations that log to files often manage those log files by automatically discarding the oldest parts when files get too large. There are additional tools designed to read and analyze log files. The practice of logging can require fairly involved research.

For basic problems, the work of installing, configuring, and using a logging system might tempt you back to `println()` statements. Fortunately, there are easier strategies.

The quick-and-dirty approach is to define a global function. This can easily be disabled when you don't need it:

```
// Logging/SimpleLoggingStrategy.kt
package logging
import checkinstructions.DataFile

val logFile = // Reset ensures an empty file:
  DataFile("simpleLogFile.txt").reset()

fun debug(msg: String) =
  System.err.println("Debug: $msg")
// To disable:
// fun debug(msg: String) = Unit

fun trace(msg: String) =
  logFile.appendText("Trace: $msg\n")

fun main() {
  debug("Simple Logging Strategy")
```

```
  trace("Line 1")
  trace("Line 2")
  println(logFile.readText())
}
/* Sample Output:
Debug: Simple Logging Strategy
Trace: Line 1
Trace: Line 2
*/
```

`debug()` sends its output to the console error stream. `trace()` sends its output to a log file.

You can also create your own simple logging class:

```
// Logging/AtomicLog.kt
package atomiclog
import checkinstructions.DataFile

class Logger(fileName: String) {
  val logFile = DataFile(fileName).reset()
  private fun log(type: String, msg: String) =
    logFile.appendText("$type: $msg\n")
  fun trace(msg: String) = log("Trace", msg)
  fun debug(msg: String) = log("Debug", msg)
  fun info(msg: String) = log("Info", msg)
  fun warn(msg: String) = log("Warn", msg)
  fun error(msg: String) = log("Error", msg)
  // For basic testing:
  fun report(msg: String) {
    trace(msg)
    debug(msg)
    info(msg)
    warn(msg)
    error(msg)
  }
}
```

You can add support for other features like logging levels and time stamps.

Using the library is straightforward:

```
// Logging/UseAtomicLog.kt
package useatomiclog
import atomiclog.Logger
import atomictest.eq

private val logger = Logger("AtomicLog.txt")

fun main() {
  logger.report("Hello, Atomic Log!")
  logger.logFile.readText() eq """
  Trace: Hello, Atomic Log!
  Debug: Hello, Atomic Log!
  Info: Hello, Atomic Log!
  Warn: Hello, Atomic Log!
  Error: Hello, Atomic Log!
  """
}
```

It's tempting to create yet another logging library. This is probably not a good use of time.

- -

Logging is not as simple as calling library functions—there's a significant run-time component. Logging is typically included in the deliverable product, and operations people must be able to turn logging on and off, dynamically adjust logging levels, and control the logfiles. For long-running programs such as servers, this last issue is particularly important because it includes strategies to prevent logfiles from filling up.

Exercises and solutions can be found at www.AtomicKotlin.com.

Unit Testing

> Unit testing is the practice of creating a correctness test for each aspect of a function. Unit tests rapidly reveal broken code, accelerating development speed.

There's far more to testing than we can cover in this book, so this atom is only a basic introduction.

The "Unit" in "Unit testing" describes a small piece of code, usually a function, that is tested separately and independently. This should not be confused with the unrelated Kotlin `Unit` type.

Unit tests are typically written by the programmer, and run each time you build the project. Because unit tests run so frequently, they must run quickly.

You've been learning about unit testing while reading this book, via the `AtomicTest` library we use to validate the book's code. `AtomicTest` uses the concise `eq` for the most common pattern in unit testing: comparing an expected result with a generated result.

Of the numerous unit test frameworks, JUnit is the most popular for Java. There are also frameworks created specifically for Kotlin. The Kotlin standard library includes `kotlin.test`, which provides a facade for different test libraries. This way you're not limited to using a particular library. `kotlin.test` also contains wrappers for basic assertion functions.

To use `kotlin.test`, you must modify the `dependencies` section of your project's `build.gradle` file to include:

```
testImplementation "org.jetbrains.kotlin:kotlin-test-common"
```

Inside a unit test, the programmer calls various assertion functions that validate the expected behavior of the function under test. Assertion functions include `assertEquals()`, which compares the actual value against an expected value, and `assertTrue()`, which tests its first argument, a Boolean expression. In this example, the unit tests are the functions with names beginning with the word `test`:

```
// UnitTesting/NoFramework.kt
package unittesting
import kotlin.test.assertEquals
import kotlin.test.assertTrue
import atomictest.*

fun fortyTwo() = 42

fun testFortyTwo(n: Int = 42) {
  assertEquals(
    expected = n,
    actual = fortyTwo(),
    message = "Incorrect,")
}

fun allGood(b: Boolean = true) = b

fun testAllGood(b: Boolean = true) {
  assertTrue(allGood(b), "Not good")
}

fun main() {
  testFortyTwo()
  testAllGood()
  capture {
    testFortyTwo(43)
  } contains
    listOf("expected:", "<43>",
      "but was", "<42>")
  capture {
    testAllGood(false)
  } contains listOf("Error", "Not good")
}
```

In `main()`, you can see that a failing assertion function produces an `Assertion-Error`—this means the unit test has failed, signaling the problem to the programmer.

`kotlin.test` contains an assortment of functions that have names starting with `assert`:

- `assertEquals()`, `assertNotEquals()`
- `assertTrue()`, `assertFalse()`

- `assertNull()`, `assertNotNull()`
- `assertFails()`, `assertFailsWith()`

Similar functions are typically included in every unit test framework, but the names and parameter order can be different. For example, the `message` parameter in `assertEquals()` might be first or last. Also, it's easy to mix up `expected` and `actual`—using named arguments avoids this problem.

The `expect()` function in `kotlin.test` runs a block of code and compares that result with the expected value:

```
fun <T> expect(
  expected: T,
  message: String?,
  block: () -> T
) {
  assertEquals(expected, block(), message)
}
```

Here's `testFortyTwo()` rewritten using `expect()`:

```
// UnitTesting/UsingExpect.kt
package unittesting
import atomictest.*
import kotlin.test.*

fun testFortyTwo2(n: Int = 42) {
  expect(n, "Incorrect,") { fortyTwo() }
}

fun main() {
  testFortyTwo2()
  capture {
    testFortyTwo2(43)
  } contains
    listOf("expected:",
      "<43> but was:", "<42>")
  assertFails { testFortyTwo2(43) }
  capture {
    assertFails { testFortyTwo2() }
  } contains
    listOf("Expected an exception",
```

```
      "to be thrown",
      "but was completed successfully.")
  assertFailsWith<AssertionError> {
    testFortyTwo2(43)
  }
  capture {
    assertFailsWith<AssertionError> {
      testFortyTwo2()
    }
  } contains
    listOf("Expected an exception",
      "to be thrown",
      "but was completed successfully.")
}
```

It's important to add tests for corner cases. If a function produces an error under certain conditions, this should be verified with a unit test (as AtomicTest's capture() does). assertFails() and assertFailsWith() ensure that the exception is thrown. assertFailsWith() also checks the type of the exception.

Test Frameworks

A typical test framework contains a collection of assertion functions and a mechanism to run tests and display results. Most test runners show results with green for success and red for failure.

This atom uses JUnit5 as the underlying library for kotlin.test. To include it in a project, the dependencies section of your build.gradle should look like this:

```
testImplementation "org.jetbrains.kotlin:kotlin-test"
testImplementation "org.jetbrains.kotlin:kotlin-test-junit"
testImplementation "org.jetbrains.kotlin:kotlin-test-junit5"
testImplementation "org.junit.jupiter:junit-jupiter:$junit_version"
```

If you're using a different library, you can find setup details in that framework's instructions.

kotlin.test provides facades for the most commonly used functions. Assertions are delegated to the appropriate functions in the underlying test framework. In the `org.junit.jupiter.api.Assertions` class, for example, `assertEquals()` calls `Assertions.assertEquals()`.

Kotlin supports *annotations* for definitions and expressions. An annotation is the `@` sign followed by the annotation name, and indicates special treatment for the annotated element. The `@Test` annotation converts a regular function into a test function. We can test `fortyTwo()` and `allGood()` using the `@Test` annotation:

```
// Tests/unittesting/SampleTest.kt
package unittesting
import kotlin.test.*

class SampleTest {
  @Test
  fun testFortyTwo() {
    expect(42, "Incorrect,") { fortyTwo() }
  }
  @Test
  fun testAllGood() {
    assertTrue(allGood(), "Not good")
  }
}
```

`kotlin.test` uses a `typealias` to create a facade for the `@Test` annotation:

```
typealias Test = org.junit.jupiter.api.Test
```

This tells the compiler to substitute the `@org.junit.jupiter.api.Test` annotation for `@Test`.

A test class usually contains multiple unit tests. Ideally, each unit test only verifies a single behavior. This quickly guides you to the problem if a test fails when introducing new functionality.

`@Test` functions can be run:

- Independently
- As part of a class
- Together with all tests defined for the application

IntelliJ IDEA allows you to rerun only the failed tests.

Consider a simple state machine with three states: On, Off and Paused. The functions start(), pause(), resume() and finish() control the state machine. resume() is valuable because resuming a paused machine is significantly cheaper and/or faster than starting a machine.

```
// UnitTesting/StateMachine.kt
package unittesting
import unittesting.State.*

enum class State { On, Off, Paused }

class StateMachine {
  var state: State = Off
    private set
  private fun transition(
    new: State, current: State = On
  ) {
    if(new == Off && state != Off)
      state = Off
    else if(state == current)
      state = new
  }
  fun start() = transition(On, Off)
  fun pause() = transition(Paused, On)
  fun resume() = transition(On, Paused)
  fun finish() = transition(Off)
}
```

These operations are ignored:

- resume() or finish() on a machine that is Off.
- pause() or start() on a Paused machine.

To test StateMachine, we create a property sm inside the test class. The test runner creates a fresh StateMachineTest object for each different test:

```
// Tests/unittesting/StateMachineTest.kt
package unittesting
import kotlin.test.*

class StateMachineTest {
  val sm = StateMachine()
  @Test
  fun start() {
    sm.start()
    assertEquals(State.On, sm.state)
  }
  @Test
  fun `pause and resume`() {
    sm.start()
    sm.pause()
    assertEquals(State.Paused, sm.state)
    sm.resume()
    assertEquals(State.On, sm.state)
    sm.pause()
    assertEquals(State.Paused, sm.state)
  }
  // ...
}
```

Normally, Kotlin only allows letters and digits for function names. However, if you put a function name inside backticks, you can use any characters (including whitespace). This means you can create function names that are sentences describing their tests, such as `pause and resume`. This produces more useful error information.

An essential goal of unit testing is to simplify the gradual development of complicated software. After introducing each new piece of functionality, a developer not only adds new tests to check its correctness but also runs all the existing tests to make sure that the prior functionality still works. You feel safer when introducing new changes, and the system is more predictable and stable.

In the process of fixing a new bug, you create additional unit tests for this and similar cases, so you don't make the same mistakes in the future.

If you use a continuous integration (CI) server such as Teamcity[39], all available tests run automatically and you're notified if something breaks.

---

[39] https://www.jetbrains.com/teamcity/

Consider a class with several properties:

```
// UnitTesting/Learner.kt
package unittesting

enum class Language {
  Kotlin, Java, Go, Python, Rust, Scala
}

data class Learner(
  val id: Int,
  val name: String,
  val surname: String,
  val language: Language
)
```

It's often helpful to add utility functions for manufacturing test data, especially when you must create many objects with the same default values during testing. Here, makeLearner() creates objects with default values:

```
// Tests/unittesting/LearnerTest.kt
package unittesting
import unittesting.Language.*
import kotlin.test.*

fun makeLearner(
  id: Int,
  language: Language = Kotlin,          // [1]
  name: String = "Test Name $id",
  surname: String = "Test Surname $id"
) = Learner(id, name, surname, language)

class LearnerTest {
  @Test
  fun `single Learner`() {
    val learner = makeLearner(10, Java)
    assertEquals("Test Name 10", learner.name)
  }
  @Test
  fun `multiple Learners`() {
    val learners = (1..9).map(::makeLearner)
    assertTrue(
```

```
        learners.all { it.language == Kotlin })
    }
}
```

Adding default arguments to `Learner` that are only for testing introduces unnecessary complexity and potential confusion. `makeLearner()` is easier and cleaner when producing test instances, and it eliminates redundant code.

The order of `makeLearner()`'s parameters simplifies its usage. In this case, we expect to specify a non-default `lang` more often than changing default test values for `name` and `surname`, so the `lang` parameter is second (**[1]**).

Mocking and Integration Tests

A system that depends on other components complicates the creation of isolated tests. Rather than introducing dependencies on real components, programmers often use a practice called *mocking*.

A mock replaces a real entity with a fake one during testing. Databases are commonly mocked to preserve the integrity of the stored data. The mock can implement the same interface as the real one, or it can be created using mocking libraries such as MockK[40].

It's vital to test separate pieces of functionality independently—that's what unit tests do. It's also essential to ensure that different parts of the system work when combined with each other—that's what *integration tests* do. Unit tests are "inward-directed" while integration tests are "outward-directed".

Testing Inside IntelliJ IDEA

IntelliJ IDEA and Android Studio support creating and running unit tests.

To create a test, right-click (control-click on a Mac) the class or function you want to test and select "Generate…" from the pop-up menu. From the "Generate" menu, choose "Test…". A second approach is to open the list of "intention actions"[41], and select "Create Test"[42].

---

[40] https://github.com/mockk/mockk
[41] https://www.jetbrains.com/help/idea/intention-actions.html
[42] https://www.jetbrains.com/help/idea/create-tests.html

Select JUnit5 as the "Testing library". If a message appears saying "JUnit5 library not found in the module," push the "Fix" button next to the message. The "Destination package" should be `unittesting`. The result will end up in another directory (always separate tests from main code). The Gradle default is the `src/test/kotlin` folder, but you can choose a different destination.

Check the boxes next to the functions you want tested. You can automatically navigate from the source code to the corresponding test class and back; for details see the documentation[43].

Once the test framework code is generated, you can modify it to suit your needs. For the examples and exercises in this atom, replace:

```
import org.junit.Test
import org.junit.Assert.*
```

with:

```
import kotlin.test.*
```

When running tests within IntelliJ IDEA, you may get an error message like "test events were not received." This is because IDEA's default configuration assumes you are running your tests externally, using Gradle. To fix it so you can run your tests inside IDEA, start at the file menu:

```
File | Settings | Build, Execution, Deployment | Build Tools | Gradle
```

On that page you'll see a drop-down titled "Run tests using:" which is set to "Gradle (Default)". Change this to "IntelliJ IDEA" and your tests will run correctly.

Exercises and solutions can be found at www.AtomicKotlin.com.

---

[43]https://www.jetbrains.com/help/idea/create-tests.html#test-code-navigation

Section VII: Power Tools

Any fool can write code that a computer can understand. Good programmers write code that humans can understand.—**Martin Fowler**

Extension Lambdas

An extension lambda is like an extension function. It defines a lambda instead of a function.

Here, va and vb yield the same result:

```
// ExtensionLambdas/Vanbo.kt
package extensionlambdas
import atomictest.eq

val va: (String, Int) -> String = { str, n ->
  str.repeat(n) + str.repeat(n)
}

val vb: String.(Int) -> String = {
  this.repeat(it) + repeat(it)
}

fun main() {
  va("Vanbo", 2) eq "VanboVanboVanboVanbo"
  "Vanbo".vb(2) eq "VanboVanboVanboVanbo"
  vb("Vanbo", 2) eq "VanboVanboVanboVanbo"
  // "Vanbo".va(2) // Doesn't compile
}
```

va is an ordinary lambda like the ones you've seen throughout this book. It takes two parameters, a String and an Int, and returns a String. The lambda body also has two parameters, followed by the requisite arrow: str, n ->.

vb moves the String parameter outside the parentheses and uses extension function syntax: String.(Int). Just like an *extension function*, the object of the type being extended (String, in this case), becomes the *receiver*, and can be accessed using this.

The first call in vb uses the explicit form this.repeat(it). The second call omits the this to produce repeat(it). Like any lambda, if you have only one parameter (Int, in this case), it refers to that parameter.

In main(), the call to va() is just what you'd expect from the lambda type declaration (String, Int) -> String—two arguments in a traditional function call. vb() is an extension so it can be called using the extension form "Vanbo".vb(2). vb() can *also* be called using the traditional form vb("Vanbo", 2). va() cannot be called using the extension form.

When you first see an extension lambda, it can seem like the String.(Int) part is what you should focus on. But String is not being extended by the parameter list (Int)—it is being extended by the entire lambda: String.**(Int) -> String**

The Kotlin documentation usually refers to extension lambdas as *function literals with receiver*. The term *function literal* encompasses both lambdas and anonymous functions. The term *lambda with receiver* is often used synonymously for *extension lambda*, to emphasize that it's a lambda with the receiver as an additional implicit parameter.

Like an extension function, an extension lambda can have multiple parameters:

```
// ExtensionLambdas/Parameters.kt
package extensionlambdas
import atomictest.eq

val zero: Int.() -> Boolean = {
  this == 0
}

val one: Int.(Int) -> Boolean = {
  this % it == 0
}

val two: Int.(Int, Int) -> Boolean = {
  arg1, arg2 ->
    this % (arg1 + arg2) == 0
}

val three: Int.(Int, Int, Int) -> Boolean = {
  arg1, arg2, arg3 ->
    this % (arg1 + arg2 + arg3) == 0
}

fun main() {
```

```
  0.zero() eq true
  10.one(10) eq true
  20.two(10, 10) eq true
  30.three(10, 10, 10) eq true
}
```

In one( ), it is used instead of naming the parameter. If this produces unclear syntax, it's better to use explicit parameter names.

We've been demonstrating extension lambdas by defining vals, but they more commonly appear as function parameters, as in f2( ):

```
// ExtensionLambdas/FunctionParameters.kt
package extensionlambdas

class A {
  fun af() = 1
}

class B {
  fun bf() = 2
}

fun f1(lambda: (A, B) -> Int) =
  lambda(A(), B())

fun f2(lambda: A.(B) -> Int) =
  A().lambda(B())

fun lambdas() {
  f1 { aa, bb -> aa.af() + bb.bf() }
  f2 { af() + it.bf() }
}
```

In main( ), notice the more succinct syntax in the lambda provided to f2( ).

If your extension lambda returns Unit, the result produced by the lambda body is ignored:

```
// ExtensionLambdas/LambdaUnitReturn.kt
package extensionlambdas

fun unitReturn(lambda: A.() -> Unit) =
  A().lambda()

fun nonUnitReturn(lambda: A.() -> String) =
  A().lambda()

fun lambdaUnitReturn () {
  unitReturn {
    "Unit ignores the return value" +
    "So it can be anything ..."
  }
  unitReturn { 1 } // ... of any type ...
  unitReturn { }   // ... or nothing
  nonUnitReturn {
    "Must return the proper type"
  }
  // nonUnitReturn { } // Not an option
}
```

You can pass an extension lambda to a function that expects an ordinary lambda, as long as the parameter lists conform to each other:

```
// ExtensionLambdas/Transform.kt
package extensionlambdas
import atomictest.eq

fun String.transform1(
  n: Int, lambda: (String, Int) -> String
) = lambda(this, n)

fun String.transform2(
  n: Int, lambda: String.(Int) -> String
) = lambda(this, n)

val duplicate: String.(Int) -> String = {
  repeat(it)
}

val alternate: String.(Int) -> String = {
```

```
    toCharArray()
      .filterIndexed { i, _ -> i % it == 0 }
      .joinToString("")
}

fun main() {
  "hello".transform1(5, duplicate)
    .transform2(3, alternate) eq "hleolhleo"
  "hello".transform2(5, duplicate)
    .transform1(3, alternate) eq "hleolhleo"
}
```

transform1() expects an ordinary lambda while transform2() expects an extension lambda. In main(), the extension lambdas duplicate and alternate are passed to both transform1() and transform2(). The this receiver inside the extension lambdas duplicate and alternate becomes the first String argument when either lambda is passed to transform1().

Using :: we can pass a function reference when an extension lambda is expected:

```
// ExtensionLambdas/FuncReferences.kt
package extensionlambdas
import atomictest.eq

fun Int.d1(f: (Int) -> Int) = f(this) * 10

fun Int.d2(f: Int.() -> Int) = f() * 10

fun f1(n: Int) = n + 3
fun Int.f2() = this + 3

fun main() {
  74.d1(::f1) eq 770
  74.d2(::f1) eq 770
  74.d1(Int::f2) eq 770
  74.d2(Int::f2) eq 770
}
```

A reference to an extension function has the same type as an extension lambda: Int::f2 has the type Int.() -> Int.

In the call 74.d1(Int::f2) we pass an extension function to d1() which does not declare an extension lambda parameter.

Polymorphism works with both ordinary extension functions (`Base.g()`) and extension lambdas (the `Base.h()` parameter):

```
// ExtensionLambdas/ExtensionPolymorphism.kt
package extensionlambdas
import atomictest.eq

open class Base {
  open fun f() = 1
}

class Derived : Base() {
  override fun f() = 99
}

fun Base.g() = f()

fun Base.h(xl: Base.() -> Int) = xl()

fun main() {
  val b: Base = Derived() // Upcast
  b.g() eq 99
  b.h { f() } eq 99
}
```

You wouldn't expect it *not* to work, but it's always worth testing an assumption by creating an example.

You can use anonymous function syntax (described in **Local Functions**) instead of extension lambdas. Here we use an anonymous extension function:

```
// ExtensionLambdas/AnonymousFunction.kt
package extensionlambdas
import atomictest.eq

fun exec(
  arg1: Int, arg2: Int,
  f: Int.(Int) -> Boolean
) = arg1.f(arg2)

fun main() {
  exec(10, 2, fun Int.(d: Int): Boolean {
```

```
    return this % d == 0
  }) eq true
}
```

In `main()`, the call to `exec()` shows that the anonymous extension function is accepted as an extension lambda.

The Kotlin standard library contains a number of functions that work with extension lambdas. For example, a `StringBuilder` is a modifiable object that produces an immutable `String` when you call `toString()`. In contrast, the more modern `buildString()` accepts an extension lambda. It creates its own `StringBuilder` object, applies the extension lambda to that object, then calls `toString()` to produce the result:

```
// ExtensionLambdas/StringCreation.kt
package extensionlambdas
import atomictest.eq

private fun messy(): String {
  val built = StringBuilder()      // [1]
  built.append("ABCs: ")
  ('a'..'x').forEach { built.append(it) }
  return built.toString()          // [2]
}

private fun clean() = buildString {
  append("ABCs: ")
  ('a'..'x').forEach { append(it) }
}

private fun cleaner() =
  ('a'..'x').joinToString("", "ABCs: ")

fun main() {
  messy() eq "ABCs: abcdefghijklmnopqrstuvwx"
  messy() eq clean()
  clean() eq cleaner()
}
```

In `messy()` we repeat the name `built` multiple times. We must also create a `String-Builder` (**[1]**) and produce the result (**[2]**). Using `buildString()` in `clean()`, you don't need to create and manage the receiver for the append() calls, which makes everything much more succinct.

cleaner() shows that, if you look, you can sometimes find a more direct solution that skips the builder altogether.

There are standard library functions similar to buildString() that use extension lambdas to produce initialized, read-only Lists and Maps:

```
// ExtensionLambdas/ListsAndMaps.kt
@file:OptIn(ExperimentalStdlibApi::class)
package extensionlambdas
import atomictest.eq

val characters: List<String> = buildList {
  add("Chars:")
  ('a'..'d').forEach { add("$it") }
}

val charmap: Map<Char, Int> = buildMap {
  ('A'..'F').forEachIndexed { n, ch ->
    put(ch, n)
  }
}

fun main() {
  characters eq "[Chars:, a, b, c, d]"
  //   characters eq characters2
  charmap eq "{A=0, B=1, C=2, D=3, E=4, F=5}"
}
```

Inside the extension lambdas, the List and Map are mutable, but the results of buildList and buildMap are read-only Lists and Maps.

Writing Builders Using Extension Lambdas

Hypothetically, you can create constructors to produce all necessary object configurations. Sometimes the number of possibilities makes this messy and impractical. The *Builder* pattern has several benefits:

1. It creates objects in a multi-step process. This can sometimes be helpful when object construction is complex.
2. It produces different object variations using the same basic construction code.
3. It separates common construction code from specialized code, making it easier to write and read the code for individual object variations.

Implementing builders using extension lambdas provides an additional benefit, which is the creation of a *Domain-Specific Language* (DSL). The goal of a DSL is syntax that is comfortable and sensible to a user who is a domain expert rather than a programming expert. This allows that user to produce working solutions knowing only a small subset of the surrounding language—while at the same time benefiting from the structure and safety of that language.

For example, consider a system that captures actions and ingredients for preparing different kinds of sandwiches. We can use classes to model the pieces of a `Recipe`:

```kotlin
// ExtensionLambdas/Sandwich.kt
package sandwich
import atomictest.eq

open class Recipe : ArrayList<RecipeUnit>()

open class RecipeUnit {
  override fun toString() =
    "${this::class.simpleName}"
}

open class Operation : RecipeUnit()
class Toast : Operation()
class Grill : Operation()
class Cut : Operation()

open class Ingredient : RecipeUnit()
class Bread : Ingredient()
class PeanutButter : Ingredient()
class GrapeJelly : Ingredient()
class Ham : Ingredient()
class Swiss : Ingredient()
class Mustard : Ingredient()

open class Sandwich : Recipe() {
```

```kotlin
  fun action(op: Operation): Sandwich {
    add(op)
    return this
  }
  fun grill() = action(Grill())
  fun toast() = action(Toast())
  fun cut() = action(Cut())
}

fun sandwich(
  fillings: Sandwich.() -> Unit
): Sandwich {
  val sandwich = Sandwich()
  sandwich.add(Bread())
  sandwich.toast()
  sandwich.fillings()
  sandwich.cut()
  return sandwich
}

fun main() {
  val pbj = sandwich {
    add(PeanutButter())
    add(GrapeJelly())
  }
  val hamAndSwiss = sandwich {
    add(Ham())
    add(Swiss())
    add(Mustard())
    grill()
  }
  pbj eq "[Bread, Toast, PeanutButter, " +
    "GrapeJelly, Cut]"
  hamAndSwiss eq "[Bread, Toast, Ham, " +
    "Swiss, Mustard, Grill, Cut]"
}
```

sandwich() captures the basic ingredients and operations to produce any Sandwich (here, we assume all sandwiches are toasted, but in the exercises you'll see how to make that optional). The fillings extension lambda allows the caller to configure the Sandwich in numerous different ways, but without requiring a constructor for each configuration.

The syntax seen in main() shows how this system might be used as a DSL—the user only needs to understand the syntax of creating a Sandwich by calling sandwich() and providing the ingredients and operations inside the curly braces.

Exercises and solutions can be found at www.AtomicKotlin.com.

Scope Functions

Scope functions create a temporary scope wherein you can access an object without using its name.

Scope functions exist only to make your code more concise and readable. They do not provide additional abilities.

There are five scope functions: `let()`, `run()`, `with()`, `apply()`, and `also()`. They are designed to work with a lambda and do not require an `import`. They differ in the way you access the *context object*, using either `it` or `this`, and in what they return. `with()` uses a different calling syntax than the others. Here you can see the differences:

```kotlin
// ScopeFunctions/Differences.kt
package scopefunctions
import atomictest.eq

data class Tag(var n: Int = 0) {
  var s: String = ""
  fun increment() = ++n
}

fun main() {
  // let(): Access object with 'it'
  // Returns last expression in lambda
  Tag(1).let {
    it.s = "let: ${it.n}"
    it.increment()
  } eq 2

  // let() with named lambda argument:
  Tag(2).let { tag ->
    tag.s = "let: ${tag.n}"
    tag.increment()
  } eq 3
```

```
// run(): Access object with 'this'
// Returns last expression in lambda
Tag(3).run {
  s = "run: $n" // Implicit 'this'
  increment()   // Implicit 'this'
} eq 4

// with(): Access object with 'this'
// Returns last expression in lambda
with(Tag(4)) {
  s = "with: $n"
  increment()
} eq 5

// apply(): Access object with 'this'
// Returns modified object
Tag(5).apply {
  s = "apply: $n"
  increment()
} eq "Tag(n=6)"

// also(): Access object with 'it'
// Returns modified object
Tag(6).also {
  it.s = "also: ${it.n}"
  it.increment()
} eq "Tag(n=7)"

// also() with named lambda argument:
Tag(7).also { tag ->
  tag.s = "also: ${tag.n}"
  tag.increment()
} eq "Tag(n=8)"
}
```

There are multiple scope functions because they satisfy different combinations of needs:

- Scope functions that access the context object using this (run(), with() and apply()) produce the cleanest syntax within their scope block.

- Scope functions that access the context object using `it` (`let()` and `also()`) allow you to provide a named lambda argument.
- Scope functions that produce the last expression in their lambda (`let()`, `run()` and `with()`) are for creating results.
- Scope functions that return the modified context object (`apply()` and `also()`) are for chaining expressions together.

`with()` is a regular function and `run()` is an extension function; otherwise they are identical. Prefer `run()` for call chains and when the receiver is nullable.

Here's a summary of scope function characteristics:

	`this` Context	`it` Context
Produces last expression	`with`, `run`	`let`
Produces receiver	`apply`	`also`

You can apply a scope function to a nullable receiver using the *safe access operator* `?.`, which only calls the scope function if the receiver is not `null`:

```
// ScopeFunctions/AndNullability.kt
package scopefunctions
import atomictest.eq
import kotlin.random.Random

fun gets(): String? =
  if (Random.nextBoolean()) "str!" else null

fun main() {
  gets()?.let {
    it.removeSuffix("!") + it.length
  }?.eq("str4")
}
```

In `main()`, if `gets()` produces a non-`null` result then `let` is invoked. The non-nullable receiver of `let` becomes the non-nullable `it` inside the lambda.

Applying the safe access operator to the context object `null`-checks the entire scope, as seen in **[1]**-**[4]** in the following. Otherwise, each call within the scope must be individually `null`-checked:

```kotlin
// ScopeFunctions/Gnome.kt
package scopefunctions

class Gnome(val name: String) {
  fun who() = "Gnome: $name"
}

fun whatGnome(gnome: Gnome?) {
  gnome?.let { it.who() }       // [1]
  gnome.let { it?.who() }
  gnome?.run { who() }          // [2]
  gnome.run { this?.who() }
  gnome?.apply { who() }        // [3]
  gnome.apply { this?.who() }
  gnome?.also { it.who() }      // [4]
  gnome.also { it?.who() }
  // No help for nullability:
  with(gnome) { this?.who() }
}
```

When you use the safe access operator on `let()`, `run()`, `apply()` or `also()`, the entire scope is ignored for a `null` context object:

```kotlin
// ScopeFunctions/NullGnome.kt
package scopefunctions
import atomictest.*

fun whichGnome(gnome: Gnome?) {
  trace(gnome?.name)
  gnome?.let { trace(it.who()) }
  gnome?.run { trace(who()) }
  gnome?.apply { trace(who()) }
  gnome?.also { trace(it.who()) }
}

fun main() {
  whichGnome(Gnome("Bob"))
  whichGnome(null)
  trace eq """
    Bob
    Gnome: Bob
    Gnome: Bob
```

```
    Gnome: Bob
    Gnome: Bob
    null
  """
}
```

The trace shows that when whichGnome() receives a null argument, no scope functions execute.

Attempting to retrieve an object from a Map has a nullable result because there's no guarantee it will find an entry for that key. Here we show the different scope functions applied to the result of a Map lookup:

```
// ScopeFunctions/MapLookup.kt
package scopefunctions
import atomictest.*

data class Plumbus(var id: Int)

fun display(map: Map<String, Plumbus>) {
  trace("displaying $map")
  val pb1: Plumbus = map["main"]?.let {
    it.id += 10
    it
  } ?: return
  trace(pb1)

  val pb2: Plumbus? = map["main"]?.run {
    id += 9
    this
  }
  trace(pb2)

  val pb3: Plumbus? = map["main"]?.apply {
    id += 8
  }
  trace(pb3)

  val pb4: Plumbus? = map["main"]?.also {
    it.id += 7
  }
  trace(pb4)
```

```
}
fun main() {
  display(mapOf("main" to Plumbus(1)))
  display(mapOf("none" to Plumbus(2)))
  trace eq """
    displaying {main=Plumbus(id=1)}
    Plumbus(id=11)
    Plumbus(id=20)
    Plumbus(id=28)
    Plumbus(id=35)
    displaying {none=Plumbus(id=2)}
  """
}
```

Although `with()` can be forced into this example, the results are too ugly to consider.

In the `trace` you see that each `Plumbus` object is created during the first call to `display()` in `main()`, but none are created during the second call. Look at the definition of pb1 and recall *the Elvis operator*. If the expression to the left of `?:` is not `null`, it becomes the result and is assigned to pb1. But if that expression is `null`, the right side of `?:` becomes the result, which is `return` so `display()` returns before completing the initialization of pb1, and thus none of the values pb1-pb4 are created.

Scope functions work with nullable types in chained calls:

```
// ScopeFunctions/NameTag.kt
package scopefunctions
import atomictest.trace

val functions = listOf(
  fun(name: String?) {
    name
      ?.takeUnless { it.isBlank() }
      ?.let { trace("$it in let") }
  },
  fun(name: String?) {
    name
      ?.takeUnless { it.isBlank() }
      ?.run { trace("$this in run") }
  },
```

```
  fun(name: String?) {
    name
      ?.takeUnless { it.isBlank() }
      ?.apply { trace("$this in apply") }
  },
  fun(name: String?) {
    name
      ?.takeUnless { it.isBlank() }
      ?.also { trace("$it in also") }
  },
)

fun main() {
  functions.forEach { it(null) }
  functions.forEach { it("  ") }
  functions.forEach { it("Yumyulack") }
  trace eq """
    Yumyulack in let
    Yumyulack in run
    Yumyulack in apply
    Yumyulack in also
  """
}
```

`functions` is a `List` of function references that are applied by the `forEach` calls in `main()`, using `it` together with function-call syntax. Each function in `functions` uses a different scope function. The `forEach` calls to `it(null)` and `it(" ")` are effectively ignored, so we only display non-null, non-blank input.

When nesting scope functions, multiple `this` or `it` objects can be available in a given context. Sometimes it's difficult to know which object is selected:

```
// ScopeFunctions/Nesting.kt
package scopefunctions
import atomictest.eq

fun nesting(s: String, i: Int): String =
  with(s) {
    with(i) {
      toString()
    }
  } +
  s.let {
    i.let {
      it.toString()
    }
  } +
  s.run {
    i.run {
      toString()
    }
  } +
  s.apply {
    i.apply {
      toString()
    }
  } +
  s.also {
    i.also {
      it.toString()
    }
  }

fun main() {
  nesting("X", 7) eq "777XX"
}
```

In all cases, the call to toString() is applied to Int because the "closest" this or it is the Int implicit receiver. apply() and also() return the modified object s instead of the result of the calculation. As scope functions are intended to improve readability, nesting scope functions is a questionable practice.

None of the scope functions provide **resource cleanup** the way that use() does:

```
// ScopeFunctions/Blob.kt
package scopefunctions
import atomictest.*

data class Blob(val id: Int) : AutoCloseable {
  override fun toString() = "Blob($id)"
  fun show() { trace("$this")}
  override fun close() = trace("Close $this")
}

fun main() {
  Blob(1).let { it.show() }
  Blob(2).run { show() }
  with(Blob(3)) { show() }
  Blob(4).apply { show() }
  Blob(5).also { it.show() }
  Blob(6).use { it.show() }
  Blob(7).use { it.run { show() } }
  Blob(8).apply { show() }.also { it.close() }
  Blob(9).also { it.show() }.apply { close() }
  Blob(10).apply { show() }.use {  }
  trace eq """
    Blob(1)
    Blob(2)
    Blob(3)
    Blob(4)
    Blob(5)
    Blob(6)
    Close Blob(6)
    Blob(7)
    Close Blob(7)
    Blob(8)
    Close Blob(8)
    Blob(9)
    Close Blob(9)
    Blob(10)
    Close Blob(10)
  """
}
```

Although use() looks similar to let() and also(), use() does not allow anything to be returned from its lambda. This prevents expression chaining or producing results.

Without `use()`, `close()` is not called for any of the scope functions. To use a scope function and guarantee cleanup, place the scope function inside the `use()` lambda as in `Blob(7)`. `Blob(8)` and `Blob(9)` show how to explicitly call `close()`, and how to use `apply()` and `also()` interchangeably.

`Blob(10)` uses `apply()` and the result is passed into `use()`, which calls `close()` at the end of its lambda.

Scope Functions are Inlined

Normally, passing a lambda as an argument stores the lambda code in an auxiliary object, adding a small bit of runtime overhead compared to a regular function call. This overhead is usually not a concern, considering the benefits of lambdas (readability and code structure). In addition, the JVM contains numerous optimizations that often compensate for the overhead.

Any performance cost, no matter how small, produces recommendations to "use a feature with care." All runtime overhead is eliminated by defining the scope functions as `inline`. This way, scope functions can be used without hesitation.

When the compiler sees an `inline` function call, it substitutes the function body for the function call, replacing all parameters with actual arguments.

Inlining works well for small functions, where function-call overhead can be a significant portion of the entire call. As functions get larger, the cost of the call shrinks in comparison to the time required by the entire call, diminishing the value of inlining. At the same time, the resulting bytecode increases because the entire function body is inserted at each call site.

When an inlined function takes a lambda argument, the compiler inlines the lambda body together with the function body. Thus, no additional classes or objects are created to pass the lambda to the function. (This only works when the lambda is called directly, or passed to another `inline` function).

Although you can apply it to any function, `inline` is intended for either inlining lambda bodies or creating **reified generics**. You can find more information about inline functions here[44].

Exercises and solutions can be found at www.AtomicKotlin.com.

---
[44]https://kotlinlang.org/docs/reference/inline-functions.html

Creating Generics

> Generic code works with types that are "specified later."

Ordinary classes and functions work with specific types. If you want code to work across more types, this rigidity can be overconstraining.

Polymorphism is an object-oriented generalization tool. You write a function that takes a base-class object as a parameter, then call that function with an object of any class derived from that base class—including classes that haven't yet been created. Now your function is more general, and useful in more places.

A single hierarchy can be too limiting because you must inherit *from that hierarchy* to produce an object that fits your function parameter. If a function parameter is an interface instead of a class, the limitations are loosened to include anything that implements that interface. This gives the client programmer the option of implementing an interface in combination with an existing class—that is, to *adapt* an existing class to fit the function. Used this way, interfaces can cut across class hierarchies.

Sometimes even an interface is too restrictive because it forces you to work with only that interface. Your code can be even more general if it works with "some unspecified type," rather than a particular interface or class. That "unspecified type" is a *generic type parameter*.

Creating generic types and functions is a fairly complex topic, much of which is outside the scope of this book. This atom attempts to give you just enough background so you aren't surprised when you come across generic concepts and keywords. If you want to get serious about writing generic types and functions you'll need to study more advanced resources.

Any

Any is the root of the Kotlin class hierarchy. Every Kotlin class has Any as a superclass. One way to work with unspecified types is by passing Any arguments, and this can sometimes confuse the issue of when to use generics. If Any works, it's the simpler solution, and simpler is generally better.

There are two ways to use Any. The first, and most straightforward approach, is when you only need to operate on an Any, and nothing more. This is extremely limiting—Any has only three member functions: equals(), hashCode() and toString(). There are also extension functions, but these cannot perform any direct operations on the type. For example, apply() only applies its function argument to the Any.

If you know the type of the Any, you can cast it and perform type-specific operations. Because this involves run-time type information (as shown in **Downcasting**), you risk a runtime error if you pass the wrong type to your function (there's also a slight performance impact). Sometimes this is justified to gain the benefit of eliminating code duplication.

For example, suppose three types each have the ability to communicate. They come from different libraries so you can't just put them in the same hierarchy, and they have different function names for communicating:

```
// CreatingGenerics/Speakers.kt
package creatinggenerics
import atomictest.eq

class Person {
  fun speak() = "Hi!"
}

class Dog {
  fun bark() = "Ruff!"
}

class Robot {
  fun communicate() = "Beep!"
}

fun talk(speaker: Any) = when (speaker) {
  is Person -> speaker.speak()
  is Dog -> speaker.bark()
  is Robot -> speaker.communicate()
  else -> "Not a talker" // Or exception
}
```

```
fun main() {
  talk(Person()) eq "Hi!"
  talk(Dog()) eq "Ruff!"
  talk(Robot()) eq "Beep!"
  talk(11) eq "Not a talker"
}
```

The `when` expression discovers the type of the `speaker` and calls the appropriate function. If you don't think `talk()` will ever need to work with additional types, this is a tolerable solution. Otherwise, it requires you to modify `talk()` for each new type you add, and to rely on runtime information to discover when you miss something.

Defining Generics

Duplicated code is a candidate for conversion into a generic function or type. You do this by adding angle brackets (`<>`) containing one or more generic placeholders. Here, the generic placeholder `T` represents the unknown type:

```
// CreatingGenerics/DefiningGenerics.kt
package creatinggenerics

fun <T> gFunction(arg: T): T = arg

class GClass<T>(val x: T) {
  fun f(): T = x
}

class GMemberFunction {
  fun <T> f(arg: T): T = arg
}

interface GInterface<T> {
  val x: T
  fun f(): T
}

class GImplementation<T>(
```

```
    override val x: T
) : GInterface<T> {
  override fun f(): T = x
}

class ConcreteImplementation
  : GInterface<String> {
  override val x: String
    get() = "x"
  override fun f() = "f()"
}

fun basicGenerics() {
  gFunction("Yellow")
  gFunction(1)
  gFunction(Dog()).bark()         // [1]
  gFunction<Dog>(Dog()).bark()

  GClass("Cyan").f()
  GClass(11).f()
  GClass(Dog()).f().bark()        // [2]
  GClass<Dog>(Dog()).f().bark()

  GMemberFunction().f("Amber")
  GMemberFunction().f(111)
  GMemberFunction().f(Dog()).bark()   // [3]
  GMemberFunction().f<Dog>(Dog()).bark()

  GImplementation("Cyan").f()
  GImplementation(11).f()
  GImplementation(Dog()).f().bark()

  ConcreteImplementation().f()
  ConcreteImplementation().x
}
```

basicGenerics() shows that each generic handles different types:

- gFunction() takes a parameter of type T and returns a T result.
- GClass stores a T. Its member function f() returns a T.
- GMemberFunction parameterizes a member function *within* the class, rather than parameterizing the entire class.

- You can also define an `interface` with generic parameters as shown in `GInterface`. An implementation of `GInterface` can either redefine a type parameter as in `GImplementation`, or provide a specific type argument, as in `ConcreteImplementation`.

Notice in **[1]**, **[2]** and **[3]** that we are able to call `bark()` on the result, because that result emerges as type `Dog`.

Consider **[1]**, **[2]** and **[3]**, and the lines immediately following them. The type `T` is determined by type inference for **[1]**, **[2]** and **[3]**. Sometimes this is not possible if a generic or its invocation is too complex to be parsed by the compiler. In this case you must specify the type(s) using the syntax shown in the lines immediately following **[1]**, **[2]** and **[3]**.

Preserving Type Information

As you will see later in this atom, code *within* generic classes and functions can't know the type of `T`—this is called *erasure*. Generics can be thought of as a way to preserve type information for the return value. This way, you don't have to write code to explicitly check and cast a return value to the desired type.

A common use of generic code is for containers that hold other objects. Consider a `CarCrate` class that acts as a trivial collection by holding and producing a single element of type `Car`:

```
// CreatingGenerics/CarCrate.kt
package creatinggenerics
import atomictest.eq

class Car {
  override fun toString() = "Car"
}

class CarCrate(private var c: Car) {
  fun put(car: Car) { c = car }
  fun get(): Car = c
}

fun main() {
```

```
  val cc = CarCrate(Car())
  val car: Car = cc.get()
  car eq "Car"
}
```

When we call `cc.get()`, the result comes back as type `Car`. We'd like to make this tool available to more objects than just `Car`s, so we generify this class as `Crate<T>`:

```
// CreatingGenerics/Crate.kt
package creatinggenerics
import atomictest.eq

open class Crate<T>(private var contents: T) {
  fun put(item: T) { contents = item }
  fun get(): T = contents
}

fun main() {
  val cc = Crate(Car())
  val car: Car = cc.get()
  car eq "Car"
}
```

`Crate<T>` ensures that you can only `put()` a `T` into the `Crate`, and when you call `get()` on that `Crate`, the result comes back as type `T`.

We can make a version of `map()` for `Crate` by defining a generic extension function:

```
// CreatingGenerics/MapCrate.kt
package creatinggenerics
import atomictest.eq

fun <T, R> Crate<T>.map(f:(T) -> R): List<R> =
  listOf(f(get()))

fun main() {
  Crate(Car()).map { it.toString() + "x" } eq
    "[Carx]"
}
```

`map()` returns the `List` of results produced by applying `f()` to each element in the input sequence. Because `Crate` only contains a single element, the result is always a

`List` of one element. There are two generic arguments: `T` for the input value and `R` for the result, allowing `f()` to produce a result type that is different from the input type.

Type Parameter Constraints

A *type parameter constraint* says that the generic argument type must be inherited from the constraint. `<T: Base>` means that `T` must be of type `Base` or something derived from `Base`. This section shows that using constraints is different from a non-generic type that inherits `Base`.

Consider a type hierarchy that models different items and ways to dispose of them:

```
// CreatingGenerics/Disposable.kt
package creatinggenerics
import atomictest.eq

interface Disposable {
  val name: String
  fun action(): String
}

class Compost(override val name: String) :
  Disposable {
    override fun action() = "Add to composter"
  }

interface Transport : Disposable

class Donation(override val name: String) :
  Transport {
    override fun action() = "Call for pickup"
  }

class Recyclable(override val name: String) :
  Transport {
    override fun action() = "Put in bin"
  }

class Landfill(override val name: String) :
```

```
  Transport {
    override fun action() = "Put in dumpster"
  }
val items = listOf(
  Compost("Orange Peel"),
  Compost("Apple Core"),
  Donation("Couch"),
  Donation("Clothing"),
  Recyclable("Plastic"),
  Recyclable("Metal"),
  Recyclable("Cardboard"),
  Landfill("Trash"),
)

val recyclables =
  items.filterIsInstance<Recyclable>()
```

Using a constraint, we can access properties and functions of the constrained type within a generic function:

```
// CreatingGenerics/Constrained.kt
package creatinggenerics
import atomictest.eq

fun <T: Disposable> nameOf(disposable: T) =
  disposable.name

// As an extension:
fun <T: Disposable> T.name() = name

fun main() {
  recyclables.map { nameOf(it) } eq
    "[Plastic, Metal, Cardboard]"
  recyclables.map { it.name() } eq
    "[Plastic, Metal, Cardboard]"
}
```

We cannot access name without the constraint.

This achieves the same result without generics:

```
// CreatingGenerics/NonGenericConstraint.kt
package creatinggenerics
import atomictest.eq

fun nameOf2(disposable: Disposable) =
  disposable.name

fun Disposable.name2() = name

fun main() {
  recyclables.map { nameOf2(it) } eq
    "[Plastic, Metal, Cardboard]"
  recyclables.map { it.name2() } eq
    "[Plastic, Metal, Cardboard]"
}
```

Why use a constraint instead of ordinary polymorphism? The answer is in the return type. With generics, the return type can be exact, rather than being upcast to the base type:

```
// CreatingGenerics/SameReturnType.kt
package creatinggenerics
import kotlin.random.Random

private val rnd = Random(47)

fun List<Disposable>.aRandom(): Disposable =
  this[rnd.nextInt(size)]

fun <T: Disposable> List<T>.bRandom(): T =
  this[rnd.nextInt(size)]

fun <T> List<T>.cRandom(): T =
  this[rnd.nextInt(size)]

fun sameReturnType() {
  val a: Disposable = recyclables.aRandom()
  val b: Recyclable = recyclables.bRandom()
  val c: Recyclable = recyclables.cRandom()
}
```

Without generics, aRandom() can only produce a base-class Disposable, while both bRandom() and cRandom() produce a Recyclable. bRandom() never accesses any elements of T, therefore its constraint is pointless and it ends up being the same as cRandom(), which doesn't use a constraint.

The only time you need constraints is if you require *both* of the following:

1. Access a function or property.
2. Preserve the type when returning it.

```
// CreatingGenerics/Constraints.kt
package creatinggenerics
import kotlin.random.Random

private val rnd = Random(47)

// Accesses action() but can't
// return the exact type:
fun List<Disposable>.inexact(): Disposable {
  val d: Disposable = this[rnd.nextInt(size)]
  d.action()
  return d
}

// Can't access action() without a constraint:
fun <T> List<T>.noAccess(): T {
  val d: T = this[rnd.nextInt(size)]
  // d.action()
  return d
}

// Access action() and return the exact type:
fun <T: Disposable> List<T>.both(): T {
  val d: T = this[rnd.nextInt(size)]
  d.action()
  return d
}

fun constraints() {
  val i: Disposable = recyclables.inexact()
  val n: Recyclable = recyclables.noAccess()
  val b: Recyclable = recyclables.both()
}
```

`inexact()` is an extension to `List<Disposable>`, which allows it to access `action()`, but it is not generic so it can only return the base type `Disposable`. As a generic, `noAccess()` is able to return the exact type of `T`, but without a constraint it cannot access `action()`. Only when you add the constraint on `T` in `both()` are you able to access `action()` *and* return the exact type `T`.

Type Erasure

Java compatibility is an essential part of Kotlin. In Java, generics were not part of the original language—they were added years later, after large bodies of code had been written. Forcing generics into Java without breaking existing code required a crucial compromise: the generic types are only available during compilation but are not preserved at runtime—the types are *erased*. This *erasure* affects Kotlin.

Let's pretend erasure doesn't happen:

```
// CreatingGenerics/Erasure.kt
package creatinggenerics

fun main() {
  val strings = listOf("a", "b", "c")
  val all: List<Any> = listOf(1, 2, "x")
  useList(strings)
  useList(all)
}

fun useList(list: List<Any>) {
  // if (list is List<String>) {}  // [1]
}
```

Uncomment line **[1]** and you'll see the following error: "Cannot check for instance of erased type: List<String>". You can't test for the generic type at runtime because the type information has been erased.

If erasure *didn't* happen, the list might look like this, assuming additional type information is placed at the end of the list (it does **not** work this way!):

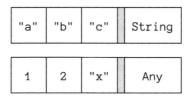

Reified Generics

Because generic types are erased, type information is *not* stored in the `List`. Instead, both `strings` and `all` are just `List`s, with no additional type information:

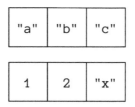

Erased Generics

You cannot guess type information from the `List` contents without analyzing all elements. Checking only the first element from the second list leads you to incorrectly assume that it's a `List<Int>`.

The Kotlin designers decided to follow Java and use erasure, for two reasons:

1. Java compatibility.
2. Overhead. Storing generic type information significantly increases the memory occupied by a generic `List` or `Map`. For example, a standard `Map` consists of many `Map.Entry` objects, and `Map.Entry` is a generic class. Thus, if generics were reified everywhere by default, each key and value of every `Map.Entry` would contain additional type information.

Reification of Function Type Arguments

Type information is also erased for generic function calls, which means you can't do much with a generic parameter inside a function.

To retain type information for function arguments, add the `reified` keyword. Consider a function `a()` that requires class information to perform its task:

```
// CreatingGenerics/ReificationA.kt
package creatinggenerics
import kotlin.reflect.KClass

fun <T: Any> a(kClass: KClass<T>) {
  // Uses KClass<T>
}
```

When we call a() inside a second generic function b(), we would like to use type information for the generic argument:

```
// CreatingGenerics/ReificationB.kt
package creatinggenerics

// Doesn't compile because of erasure:
// fun <T: Any> b() = a(T::class)
```

The type information for T is erased when this code runs, so b() won't compile. You can't access the class of the generic type parameter inside the function body.

The Java solution is to pass type information into the function by hand:

```
// CreatingGenerics/ReificationC.kt
package creatinggenerics
import kotlin.reflect.KClass

fun <T: Any> c(kClass: KClass<T>) = a(kClass)

class K

val kc = c(K::class)
```

Passing explicit type information *should* be redundant because the compiler knows the type of T, and could silently pass it for you. This is effectively what the reified keyword does.

To use reified, the function must also be inline:

```
// CreatingGenerics/ReificationD.kt
package creatinggenerics

inline fun <reified T: Any> d() = a(T::class)

val kd = d<K>()
```

d() produces the same effect as c(), but d() doesn't require the class reference as an argument.

reified tells the compiler to preserve the information about the corresponding type argument. The type information is now available at runtime so you can access it inside the function body.

Reification allows the use of is with a generic parameter type:

```
// CreatingGenerics/CheckType.kt
package creatinggenerics
import atomictest.eq

inline fun <reified T> check(t: Any) = t is T
// fun <T> check1(t: Any) = t is T      // [1]

fun main() {
  check<String>("1") eq true
  check<Int>("1") eq false
}
```

- [1] Without reified, the type information is erased so you can't check whether a given element is an instance of T.

In the following example, select() produces the name of each Disposable item of a particular subtype. It uses reified combined with a constraint:

```
// CreatingGenerics/Select.kt
package creatinggenerics
import atomictest.eq

inline fun <reified T : Disposable> select() =
  items.filterIsInstance<T>().map { it.name }

fun main() {
  select<Compost>() eq
    "[Orange Peel, Apple Core]"
  select<Donation>() eq "[Couch, Clothing]"
  select<Recyclable>() eq
    "[Plastic, Metal, Cardboard]"
  select<Landfill>() eq "[Trash]"
}
```

The library function `filterIsInstance()` is itself defined using the `reified` keyword.

Variance

Combining generics and inheritance produces two dimensions of change. If you have a `Container<T>` and you want to assign it to a `Container<U>` where `T` and `U` have an inheritance relationship, you must place constraints upon `Container` using the `in` or `out` *variance annotations*, depending on how you want to use `Container`.

Here are three versions of a `Box` container: a basic `Box<T>`, one using `<in T>` and one using `<out T>`:

```
// CreatingGenerics/InAndOutBoxes.kt
package variance

class Box<T>(private var contents: T) {
  fun put(item: T) { contents = item }
  fun get(): T = contents
}

class InBox<in T>(private var contents: T) {
  fun put(item: T) { contents = item }
}

class OutBox<out T>(private var contents: T) {
  fun get(): T = contents
}
```

`in T` means that member functions of the class can only accept arguments of type T, but cannot return values of type T. That is, T objects can be placed *into* an InBox, but cannot come out.

`out T` means that member functions can return T objects, but cannot accept arguments of type T—you cannot place T objects into an OutBox.

Why do we need these constraints? Consider this hierarchy:

```
// CreatingGenerics/Pets.kt
package variance

open class Pet
class Cat : Pet()
class Dog : Pet()
```

Cat and Dog are both subtypes of Pet. Is there a subtyping relation between Box<Cat> and Box<Pet>? It seems like we should be able to assign, for example, a Box of Cat to a Box of Pet or to a Box of Any (because Any is a supertype of everything):

```
// CreatingGenerics/BoxAssignment.kt
package variance

val catBox = Box<Cat>(Cat())
// val petBox: Box<Pet> = catBox
// val anyBox: Box<Any> = catBox
```

If Kotlin allowed this, petBox would have put(item: Pet). Dog is also a Pet, so this would allow you to put a Dog into catBox, violating the "cat-ness" of that Box.

Worse, anyBox would have put(item: Any), so you could put an Any into catBox—the container would have no type safety at all.

If we prevent the use of put(), the assignments are safe because no one can put a Dog into an OutBox<Cat>. The compiler allows us to assign an OutBox<Cat> to an OutBox<Pet> or to an OutBox<Any>, because the out annotation prevents them from having put() functions:

```
// CreatingGenerics/OutBoxAssignment.kt
package variance

val outCatBox: OutBox<Cat> = OutBox(Cat())
val outPetBox: OutBox<Pet> = outCatBox
val outAnyBox: OutBox<Any> = outCatBox

fun getting() {
  val cat: Cat = outCatBox.get()
  val pet: Pet = outPetBox.get()
  val any: Any = outAnyBox.get()
}
```

With no put(), we cannot place a Dog into an OutBox<Cat>, so its "cat-ness" is preserved.

Without a get(), an InBox<Any> can be assigned to an InBox<Pet>, an InBox<Cat> or an InBox<Dog>:

```
// CreatingGenerics/InBoxAssignment.kt
package variance

val inBoxAny: InBox<Any> = InBox(Any())
val inBoxPet: InBox<Pet> = inBoxAny
val inBoxCat: InBox<Cat> = inBoxAny
val inBoxDog: InBox<Dog> = inBoxAny

fun main() {
  inBoxAny.put(Any())
  inBoxAny.put(Pet())
  inBoxAny.put(Cat())
  inBoxAny.put(Dog())

  inBoxPet.put(Pet())
  inBoxPet.put(Cat())
  inBoxPet.put(Dog())

  inBoxCat.put(Cat())
  inBoxDog.put(Dog())
}
```

It is safe to put() an Any, Pet, Cat or Dog into an InBox<Any>, while you can only put() a Pet, Cat or Dog into an InBox<Pet>. inBoxCat and inBoxDog will only accept Cats and Dogs, respectively. These are the behaviors we expect for boxes that have those type parameters, and the compiler enforces it.

Here's a summary of the subtyping relationships for Box, OutBox and InBox:

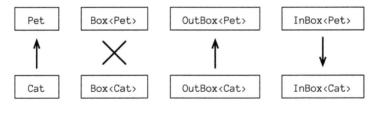

Variance

- Box<T> is *invariant*. This means that neither Box<Cat> nor Box<Pet> is a subtype of the other, so neither can be assigned to the other.
- OutBox<out T> is *covariant*. This means that OutBox<Cat> is a subtype of

OutBox<Pet>. When you upcast an OutBox<Cat> to an OutBox<Pet>, it varies in the *same* way as upcasting a Cat to a Pet.
- InBox<in T> is *contravariant*. This means that InBox<Pet> is a subtype of InBox<Cat>. When you upcast an InBox<Pet> to an InBox<Cat>, it varies in the *opposite* way as upcasting a Cat to a Pet.

A read-only List from the Kotlin standard library is covariant. You can assign a List<Cat> to a List<Pet>. A MutableList is invariant because it contains an add():

```
// CreatingGenerics/CovariantList.kt
package variance

fun main() {
  val catList: List<Cat> = listOf(Cat())
  val petList: List<Pet> = catList
  var mutablePetList: MutableList<Pet> =
    mutableListOf(Cat())
  mutablePetList.add(Dog())
  // Type mismatch:
  // mutablePetList =
  //    mutableListOf<Cat>(Cat())   // [1]
}
```

- **[1]** If this assignment worked, we could violate the "cat-ness" of the mutableListOf<Cat> by adding a Dog.

Functions can have *covariant return types*. This means that an overriding function can return a type that's more specific than the function it overrides:

```
// CreatingGenerics/CovariantReturnTypes.kt
package variance

interface Parent
interface Child : Parent

interface X {
  fun f(): Parent
}

interface Y : X {
  override fun f(): Child
}
```

Notice how the overridden f() in Y returns a Child, while f() in X returns a Parent.

This subsection has only been a light introduction to the topic of *variance*.

- -

Repeated code is a candidate for generic types or functions. This atom only provides a basic grasp of the ideas—if you need deeper understanding you must find it in a more advanced treatment.

Exercises and solutions can be found at www.AtomicKotlin.com.

Operator Overloading

In the context of computer programming, *overloading* means "adding extra meaning to something that already exists."

Operator overloading allows you to take an operator like + and give it meaning for your new type, or extra meaning for an existing type.

Operator overloading has a tumultuous past. It was popularized in C++, but because C++ had no garbage collection, writing overloaded operators was difficult. As a result, the early Java designers deemed operator overloading "bad" and didn't allow it in Java, even though Java's garbage collection would have made it relatively easy. The simplicity of operator overloading when supported by garbage collection was demonstrated in the Python language, which constrained you to a limited (familiar) set of operators, as did C++. Scala then experimented with allowing you to invent your own operators, causing some programmers to abuse this feature and create incomprehensible code. Kotlin learned from these languages, and has simplified the process of operator overloading but restricts your choices to a reasonable and familiar set of operators. In addition, the rules of operator precedence cannot be changed.

We'll create a small class Num and add an overloaded + as an extension function. To overload an operator you use the operator keyword before fun, followed by the special predefined function name for that operator. For example, the special function name for the + operator is plus():

```
// OperatorOverloading/Num.kt
package operatoroverloading
import atomictest.eq

data class Num(val n: Int)

operator fun Num.plus(rval: Num) =
  Num(n + rval.n)

fun main() {
  Num(4) + Num(5) eq Num(9)
  Num(4).plus(Num(5)) eq Num(9)
}
```

If you were defining a normal (non-operator) function for use between two operands, you'd use the `infix` keyword, but operators are already `infix`. Because `plus()` is an ordinary function, you can also call it in the conventional way.

When you define an operator as a member function, you can access `private` elements in a class that an extension function cannot:

```
// OperatorOverloading/MemberOperator.kt
package operatoroverloading
import atomictest.eq

data class Num2(private val n: Int) {
  operator fun plus(rval: Num2) =
    Num2(n + rval.n)
}

// Cannot access 'n': it is private in 'Num2':
// operator fun Num2.minus(rval: Num2) =
//   Num2(n - rval.n)

fun main() {
  Num2(4) + Num2(5) eq Num2(9)
}
```

In some contexts it's helpful to create special meaning for an operator. Here, we model a `Molecule` with a `+` that attaches it to another `Molecule`. The `attached` property is the link between `Molecules`:

```
// OperatorOverloading/Molecule.kt
package operatoroverloading
import atomictest.eq

data class Molecule(
  val id: Int = idCount++,
  var attached: Molecule? = null
) {
  companion object {
    private var idCount = 0
  }
  operator fun plus(other: Molecule) {
    attached = other
  }
}

fun main() {
  val m1 = Molecule()
  val m2 = Molecule()
  m1 + m2                                  // [1]
  m1 eq "Molecule(id=0, attached=" +
    "Molecule(id=1, attached=null))"
}
```

- [1] Reads like a familiar math expression, but to the person using the model it might be an especially meaningful syntax.

This example is incomplete; if you add the line m2 + m1, then try to display m2, you'll get a stack overflow (can you fix the problem?).

Equality

Invoking == (equality) or != (inequality) calls the equals() member function. data classes automatically redefine equals() to compare the stored data, but if you don't redefine equals() for non-data classes, the default version compares references rather than contents:

```kotlin
// OperatorOverloading/DefaultEquality.kt
package operatoroverloading
import atomictest.eq

class A(val i: Int)
data class D(val i: Int)

fun main() {
  // Normal class:
  val a = A(1)
  val b = A(1)
  val c = a
  (a == b) eq false
  (a == c) eq true
  // Data class:
  val d = D(1)
  val e = D(1)
  (d == e) eq true
}
```

a and b refer to different objects in memory, so the references are different and a == b is false, even though the two objects store identical data. a and c refer to the same object in memory, so comparing them produces true. Because the data class D automatically generates an equals() that looks at the contents of D, d == e produces true.

equals() is the only operator that cannot be an extension function; it must be overridden as a member function. When defining your own equals(), you are overriding the default equals(other: Any?). Notice that the type of other is Any? rather than the specific type of your class. This allows you to compare your type with other types, which means you must choose the types allowed for comparison:

```
// OperatorOverloading/DefiningEquality.kt
package operatoroverloading
import atomictest.eq

class E(var v: Int) {
  override fun equals(other: Any?) = when {
    this === other -> true            // [1]
    other !is E -> false              // [2]
    else -> v == other.v              // [3]
  }
  override fun hashCode(): Int = v
  override fun toString() = "E($v)"
}

fun main() {
  val a = E(1)
  val b = E(2)
  (a == b) eq false     // a.equals(b)
  (a != b) eq true      // !a.equals(b)
  // Reference equality:
  (E(1) === E(1)) eq false
}
```

- **[1]** This is an optimization: if `other` refers to the same object in memory, the result is automatically `true`. The triple equality symbol `===` tests for reference equality.
- **[2]** This determines that the type of `other` must be the same as the current type. For `E` to be compared to other types, add further match expressions.
- **[3]** This compares the stored data. At this point the compiler knows that `other` is of type `E`, so we can access `other.v` without a cast.

When overriding `equals()` you should also override `hashCode()`. This is a complex topic, but the basic rule is that if two objects are equal, they must produce the same `hashCode()` value. Standard data structures like `Map` and `Set` will fail without this rule. Things get even more complicated with an `open` class because you must compare an instance with all possible subclasses. You can learn more about the concept of hashing in Wikipedia[45].

---

[45]https://en.wikipedia.org/wiki/Hash_function

Defining a proper equals() and hashCode() is beyond the scope of this book—what we do here illustrates the concept and works for our simple example but won't work for more complicated cases. This complexity is the reason that data classes create their own equals() and hashCode(). If you must define your own equals() and hashCode(), we recommend automatically generating them using IntelliJ IDEA or Android Studio with the action Generate -> equals and hashCode[46].

When you compare nullable objects using ==, Kotlin enforces null-checking. This can be achieved using either if or the Elvis operator:

```
// OperatorOverloading/EqualsForNullable.kt
package operatoroverloading
import atomictest.eq

fun equalsWithIf(a: E?, b: E?) =
  if (a === null)
    b === null
  else
    a == b

fun equalsWithElvis(a: E?, b: E?) =
  a?.equals(b) ?: (b === null)

fun main() {
  val x: E? = null
  val y = E(0)
  val z: E? = null
  (x == y) eq false
  (x == z) eq true
  equalsWithIf(x, y) eq false
  equalsWithIf(x, z) eq true
  equalsWithElvis(x, y) eq false
  equalsWithElvis(x, z) eq true
}
```

equalsWithIf() first checks to see if the reference a is null, in which case the only way the two can be equal is if the reference b is also null. If a is not a null reference, the member equals() is used to compare the two. equalsWithElvis() achieves the same effect, but more succinctly using both ?. and ?:.

---

[46]https://www.jetbrains.com/help/idea/generating-code.html#generate-equals-hashcode

Arithmetic operators

We can define basic arithmetic operators as extensions to `class E`:

```
// OperatorOverloading/ArithmeticOperators.kt
package operatoroverloading
import atomictest.eq

// Unary operators:
operator fun E.unaryPlus() = E(v)
operator fun E.unaryMinus() = E(-v)
operator fun E.not() = this

// Increment/decrement:
operator fun E.inc() = E(v + 1)
operator fun E.dec() = E(v - 1)

fun unary(a: E) {
  +a                // unaryPlus()
  -a                // unaryMinus()
  !a                // not()

  var b = a
  b++               // inc() (must be var)
  b--               // dec() (must be var)
}

// Binary operators:
operator fun E.plus(e: E) = E(v + e.v)
operator fun E.minus(e: E) = E(v - e.v)
operator fun E.times(e: E) = E(v * e.v)
operator fun E.div(e: E) = E(v / e.v)
operator fun E.rem(e: E) = E(v % e.v)

fun binary(a: E, b: E) {
  a + b             // a.plus(b)
  a - b             // a.minus(b)
  a * b             // a.times(b)
  a / b             // a.div(b)
  a % b             // a.rem(b)
}
```

```
// Augmented assignment:
operator fun E.plusAssign(e: E) { v += e.v }
operator fun E.minusAssign(e: E) { v - e.v }
operator fun E.timesAssign(e: E) { v *= e.v }
operator fun E.divAssign(e: E) { v /= e.v }
operator fun E.remAssign(e: E) { v %= e.v }

fun assignment(a: E, b: E) {
  a += b            // a.plusAssign(b)
  a -= b            // a.minusAssign(b)
  a *= b            // a.timesAssign(b)
  a /= b            // a.divAssign(b)
  a %= b            // a.remAssign(b)
}

fun main() {
  val two = E(2)
  val three = E(3)
  two + three eq E(5)
  two * three eq E(6)
  val thirteen = E(13)
  thirteen / three eq E(4)
  thirteen % three eq E(1)
  val one = E(1)
  one += three * three
  one eq E(10)
}
```

When writing an extension, remember that the properties and functions of the extended type are implicitly available. In the definition of unaryPlus(), for example, the v in E(v) is the v property from the E that's being extended.

Note that x += e can be resolved to either x = x.plus(e) if x is a var or to x.plusAssign(e) if x is val and the corresponding plusAssign() member is available. If both options work, the compiler emits an error indicating that it can't choose.

The parameter can be of a different type than the type the operator extends. Here, the + operator extension for E takes an Int parameter:

```
// OperatorOverloading/DifferentTypes.kt
package operatoroverloading
import atomictest.eq

operator fun E.plus(i: Int) = E(v + i)

fun main() {
  E(1) + 10 eq E(11)
}
```

Operator precedence is fixed, and is identical for both built-in types and custom types. For example, multiplication has a higher precedence than addition, and both have higher precedence than equality; thus 1 + 2 * 3 == 7 is true. You can find the operator precedence table in the documentation[47].

Sometimes when you mix arithmetic and programming operators, the result isn't obvious. Here, we combine + and the Elvis operator:

```
// OperatorOverloading/ConfusingPrecedence.kt
package operatoroverloading
import atomictest.eq

fun main() {
  val x: Int? = 1
  val y: Int = 2
  val sum = x ?: 0 + y
  sum eq 1
  (x ?: 0) + y eq 3      // [1]
  x ?: (0 + y) eq 1      // [2]
}
```

In sum, + has higher precedence than the Elvis operator ?: so the result is 1 ?: (0 + 2) == 1. This might be not what the programmer intended. When mixing different operations where precedence is not obvious, we recommend adding parentheses as in lines **[1]** and **[2]**.

Comparison

All comparison operations <, >, <=, >= are automatically available when you define compareTo():

[47]https://kotlinlang.org/docs/reference/grammar.html#expressions

```
// OperatorOverloading/Comparison.kt
package operatoroverloading
import atomictest.eq

operator fun E.compareTo(e: E): Int =
  v.compareTo(e.v)

fun main() {
  val a = E(2)
  val b = E(3)
  (a < b) eq true      // a.compareTo(b) < 0
  (a > b) eq false     // a.compareTo(b) > 0
  (a <= b) eq true     // a.compareTo(b) <= 0
  (a >= b) eq false    // a.compareTo(b) >= 0
}
```

compareTo() must return an Int indicating:

- 0 if the elements are equal.
- A positive value if the first element (the receiver) is bigger than the second (the argument).
- A negative value if the first element is smaller than the second.

Ranges and Containers

rangeTo() overloads the .. operator for creating ranges, while contains() indicates whether a value is within a range:

```
// OperatorOverloading/Ranges.kt
package operatoroverloading
import atomictest.eq

data class R(val r: IntRange) { // Range
  override fun toString() = "R($r)"
}

operator fun E.rangeTo(e: E) = R(v..e.v)

operator fun R.contains(e: E): Boolean =
```

```
  e.v in r

fun main() {
  val a = E(2)
  val b = E(3)
  val r = a..b         // a.rangeTo(b)
  (a in r) eq true     // r.contains(a)
  (a !in r) eq false   // !r.contains(a)
  r eq R(2..3)
}
```

Container Access

Overloading `contains()` allows you to check whether a value is `in` a container, while `get()` and `set()` support reading and assigning elements in a container using square brackets:

```
// OperatorOverloading/ContainerAccess.kt
package operatoroverloading
import atomictest.eq

data class C(val c: MutableList<Int>) {
  override fun toString() = "C($c)"
}

operator fun C.contains(e: E) = e.v in c

operator fun C.get(i: Int): E = E(c[i])

operator fun C.set(i: Int, e: E) {
  c[i] = e.v
}

fun main() {
  val c = C(mutableListOf(2, 3))
  (E(2) in c) eq true    // c.contains(E(2))
  (E(4) in c) eq false   // c.contains(E(4))
  c[1] eq E(3)           // c.get(1)
  c[1] = E(4)            // c.set(2, E(4))
```

```
  c eq C(mutableListOf(2, 4))
}
```

In IntelliJ IDEA or Android Studio you can navigate [48] to a declaration of a function or a class from its usage. This also works with operators: you can put the cursor on `..` then navigate to its definition to see which operator function is called.

Invoke

Placing parentheses after an object generates a call to invoke(), so the invoke() operator makes an object look like a function. You can define invoke() with any number of parameters:

```
// OperatorOverloading/Invoke.kt
package operatoroverloading
import atomictest.eq

class Func {
  operator fun invoke() = "invoke()"
  operator fun invoke(i: Int) = "invoke($i)"
  operator fun invoke(i: Int, j: String) =
    "invoke($i, $j)"
  operator fun invoke(
    i: Int, j: String, k: Double
  ) = "invoke($i, $j, $k)"
}

fun main() {
  val f = Func()
  f() eq "invoke()"
  f(22) eq "invoke(22)"
  f(22, "Hi") eq "invoke(22, Hi)"
  f(22, "Three", 3.1416) eq
    "invoke(22, Three, 3.1416)"
}
```

You can also define invoke() with vararg to work with any number of arguments of the same type (see ***Variable Argument Lists***).

---

[48]https://www.jetbrains.com/help/idea/navigating-through-the-source-code.html#go_to_declaration

invoke() can be defined as an extension function. Here, it's an extension for String, taking a function as a parameter and calling that function on the String:

```
// OperatorOverloading/StringInvoke.kt
package operatoroverloading
import atomictest.eq

operator fun String.invoke(
  f: (s: String) -> String
) = f(this)

fun main() {
  "mumbling" { it.uppercase() } eq
    "MUMBLING"
}
```

Because the lambda is the final invoke() argument, it can be called without parentheses.

If you have a function reference, you can use it to call the function directly using parentheses or via invoke():

```
// OperatorOverloading/InvokeFunctionType.kt
package operatoroverloading
import atomictest.eq

fun main() {
  val func: (String) -> Int = { it.length }
  func("abc") eq 3
  func.invoke("abc") eq 3

  val nullableFunc: ((String) -> Int)? = null
  if (nullableFunc != null) {
    nullableFunc("abc")
  }
  nullableFunc?.invoke("abc")   // [1]
}
```

- [1] If a function reference is nullable, you can combine invoke() and safe access.

The most common use for a custom invoke() is when creating DSLs.

Function Names in Backticks

Kotlin allows spaces, certain nonstandard characters, and reserved words in a function name by placing that function name inside backticks:

```
// OperatorOverloading/Backticks.kt
package operatoroverloading

fun `A long name with spaces`() = Unit

fun `*how* is this working?`() = Unit

fun `'when' is a keyword`() = Unit

// fun `Illegal characters :<>`() = Unit

fun main() {
  `A long name with spaces`()
  `*how* is this working?`()
  `'when' is a keyword`()
}
```

This can be particularly helpful for *Unit Testing* because you can create readable test names that include details about those tests. It also simplifies interactions with Java code.

You can easily create incomprehensible code:

```
// OperatorOverloading/Swearing.kt
package operatoroverloading
import atomictest.eq

infix fun String.`#!%`(s: String) =
  "$this Rowzafrazaca $s"

fun main() {
  "howdy" `#!%` "Ma'am!" eq
    "howdy Rowzafrazaca Ma'am!"
}
```

Kotlin accepts this code, but what does it mean to the reader? Because code is read much more than it is written, you should make your programs as understandable as possible.

- -

Operator overloading is not an essential feature, but is an excellent example of how a language is more than just a way to manipulate the underlying computer. The challenge is crafting the language to provide better ways to express your abstractions, so humans have an easier time understanding the code without getting bogged down in needless detail. It's possible to define operators in ways that obscure meaning, so tread carefully.

Everything is syntactic sugar. Toilet paper is syntactic sugar, and I still want it.— **Barry Hawkins**

Exercises and solutions can be found at www.AtomicKotlin.com.

Using Operators

In practice you rarely overload operators—usually only when you create your own library.

However, you regularly *use* overloaded operators, often without noticing. For example, the Kotlin standard library defines numerous operators that improve your experience with collections. Here's some familiar code seen from a new angle:

```
// UsingOperators/NewAngle.kt
import atomictest.eq

fun main() {
  val list = MutableList(10) { 'a' + it }
  list[7] eq 'h' // operator get()
  list.get(8) eq 'i' // Explicit call
  list[9] = 'x' // operator set()
  list.set(9, 'x') // Explicit call
  list[9] eq 'x'
  ('d' in list) eq true // operator contains()
  list.contains('e') eq true // Explicit call
}
```

Accessing list elements using square brackets calls the overloaded operators `get()` and `set()`, while `in` calls `contains()`.

Calling `+=` on a mutable collection modifies it, while calling `+` returns a new collection containing the old elements together with the new element:

```
// UsingOperators/OperatorPlus.kt
import atomictest.eq

fun main() {
  val mutableList = mutableListOf(1, 2, 3)
  mutableList += 4  // operator plusAssign()
  mutableList.plusAssign(5) // Explicit
  mutableList eq "[1, 2, 3, 4, 5]"
  mutableList + 99 eq "[1, 2, 3, 4, 5, 99]"
  mutableList eq "[1, 2, 3, 4, 5]"
  val list = listOf(1)  // Read-only
  val newList = list + 2  // operator plus()
  list eq "[1]"
  newList eq "[1, 2]"
  val another = list.plus(3)  // Explicit
  another eq "[1, 3]"
}
```

Calling += on a read-only collection probably doesn't produce what you expect:

```
// UsingOperators/Unexpected.kt
import atomictest.eq

fun main() {
  var list = listOf(1, 2)
  list += 3  // Probably unexpected
  list eq "[1, 2, 3]"
}
```

In a mutable collection, a += b calls plusAssign() to modify a. However, plusAssign() is not available for read-only collections, so Kotlin rewrites a += b into a = a + b. This calls plus(), which doesn't change the collection, but rather creates a new one and assigns the result to the var list reference. The net effect is that a += b still produces the result we expect for a—at least for simple types like Int.

```
// UsingOperators/ReadOnlyAndPlus.kt
import atomictest.eq

fun main() {
  var list = listOf(1, 2)
  val initial = list
  list += 3
  list eq "[1, 2, 3]"
  list = list.plus(4)
  list eq "[1, 2, 3, 4]"
  initial eq "[1, 2]"
}
```

The last line shows that the `initial` collection remains unchanged. Creating a new collection for every added element probably isn't your intent. The problem doesn't arise if you use `val` for `list` instead of `var` because calling `+=` won't compile. This is one more reason to use `val` by default—only use `var` when necessary.

`compareTo()` was introduced as a standalone extension function in *Operator Overloading*. However, you get greater benefits if your class implements the `Comparable` interface and overrides its `compareTo()`:

```
// UsingOperators/CompareTo.kt
package usingoperators
import atomictest.eq

data class Contact(
  val name: String,
  val mobile: String
): Comparable<Contact> {
  override fun compareTo(
    other: Contact
  ): Int = name.compareTo(other.name)
}

fun main() {
  val alice = Contact("Alice", "0123456789")
  val bob = Contact("Bob", "9876543210")
  val carl = Contact("Carl", "5678901234")
  (alice < bob) eq true
  (alice <= bob) eq true
  (alice > bob) eq false
```

```
    (alice >= bob) eq false
    val contacts = listOf(bob, carl, alice)
    contacts.sorted() eq
      listOf(alice, bob, carl)
    contacts.sortedDescending() eq
      listOf(carl, bob, alice)
}
```

Any two Comparables can be compared using <, <=, > and >= (note that == and != are not included). Kotlin doesn't require the operator modifier when overriding compareTo() because it has already been defined as an operator in the Comparable interface.

Implementing Comparable also enables features like sortability, and creating a range of instances without redefining the .. operator. You can then check to see if a value is in that range:

```
// UsingOperators/ComparableRange.kt
package usingoperators
import atomictest.eq

class F(val i: Int): Comparable<F> {
  override fun compareTo(other: F) =
    i.compareTo(other.i)
}

fun main() {
  val range = F(1)..F(7)
  (F(3) in range) eq true
  (F(9) in range) eq false
}
```

Prefer implementing Comparable. Only define compareTo() as an extension function when using a class you have no control over.

Destructuring Operators

Another group of operators you don't typically define is the componentN() functions (component1(), component2() etc.), used for *Destructuring Declarations*. In main(), Kotlin quietly generates calls to component1() and component2() for the destructuring assignment:

```
// UsingOperators/DestructuringDuo.kt
package usingoperators
import atomictest.*

class Duo(val x: Int, val y: Int) {
  operator fun component1(): Int {
    trace("component1()")
    return x
  }
  operator fun component2(): Int {
    trace("component2()")
    return y
  }
}

fun main() {
  val (a, b) = Duo(1, 2)
  a eq 1
  b eq 2
  trace eq "component1() component2()"
}
```

The same approach works with Maps, which use an Entry type containing component1() and component2() member functions:

```
// UsingOperators/DestructuringMap.kt
import atomictest.eq

fun main() {
  val map = mapOf("a" to 1)
  for ((key, value) in map) {
    key eq "a"
    value eq 1
  }
  // The Destructuring assignment becomes:
  for (entry in map) {
    val key = entry.component1()
    val value = entry.component2()
    key eq "a"
    value eq 1
  }
}
```

You can use destructuring declarations with any `data class` because `componentN()` functions are automatically generated:

```
// UsingOperators/DestructuringData.kt
package usingoperators
import atomictest.eq

data class Person(
  val name: String,
  val age: Int
) {
  // Compiler generates:
  // fun component1() = name
  // fun component2() = age
}

fun main() {
  val person = Person("Alice", 29)
  val (name, age) = person
  // The Destructuring assignment becomes:
  val name_ = person.component1()
  val age_ = person.component2()
  name eq "Alice"
  age eq 29
  name_ eq "Alice"
  age_ eq 29
}
```

Kotlin generates a `componentN()` function for each property.

Exercises and solutions can be found at www.AtomicKotlin.com.

Property Delegation

A property can delegate its accessor logic.

You connect a property to a delegate with the `by` keyword:

```
val/var property by delegate
```

The delegate's class must contain a `getValue()` function if the property is a `val` (read only) or `getValue()` and `setValue()` functions if the property is a `var` (read/write). First consider the read-only case:

```
// PropertyDelegation/BasicRead.kt
package propertydelegation
import atomictest.eq
import kotlin.reflect.KProperty

class Readable(val i: Int) {
  val value: String by BasicRead()
}

class BasicRead {
  operator fun getValue(
    r: Readable,
    property: KProperty<*>
  ) = "getValue: ${r.i}"
}

fun main() {
  val x = Readable(11)
  val y = Readable(17)
  x.value eq "getValue: 11"
  y.value eq "getValue: 17"
}
```

`value` in `Readable` is delegated to a `BasicRead` object. `getValue()` takes a `Readable` parameter that allows it to access the `Readable`—when you say `by` it binds the `BasicRead` to the whole `Readable` object. Notice that `getValue()` accesses `i` in `Readable`.

Because `getValue()` returns a `String`, the type of `value` must also be `String`.

The second `getValue()` parameter `property` is of the special type `KProperty`, and this provides reflective information about the delegated property.

If the delegated property is a `var`, it must handle both reading and writing, so the delegate class requires both `getValue()` and `setValue()`:

```
// PropertyDelegation/BasicReadWrite.kt
package propertydelegation
import atomictest.eq
import kotlin.reflect.KProperty

class ReadWriteable(var i: Int) {
  var msg = ""
  var value: String by BasicReadWrite()
}

class BasicReadWrite {
  operator fun getValue(
    rw: ReadWriteable,
    property: KProperty<*>
  ) = "getValue: ${rw.i}"
  operator fun setValue(
    rw: ReadWriteable,
    property: KProperty<*>,
    s: String
  ) {
    rw.i = s.toIntOrNull() ?: 0
    rw.msg = "setValue to ${rw.i}"
  }
}

fun main() {
  val x = ReadWriteable(11)
  x.value eq "getValue: 11"
  x.value = "99"
  x.msg eq "setValue to 99"
  x.value eq "getValue: 99"
}
```

The first two setValue() parameters are the same as getValue(), and the third is the value on the right side of the =, which is what we want to set. Both getValue() and setValue() must agree on the type that is read and written, which in this case is String (the type of value in ReadWriteable).

Notice that setValue() accesses i in ReadWriteable, and also msg.

BasicRead.kt and BasicReadWrite.kt do not implement an interface. A class can be used as a delegate if it simply conforms to the convention of having the necessary function(s) with the necessary signature(s). However, you can also implement the ReadOnlyProperty interface, as seen here in BasicRead2:

```
// PropertyDelegation/BasicRead2.kt
package propertydelegation
import atomictest.eq
import kotlin.properties.ReadOnlyProperty
import kotlin.reflect.KProperty

class Readable2(val i: Int) {
  val value: String by BasicRead2()
  // SAM conversion:
  val value2: String by
  ReadOnlyProperty { _, _ -> "getValue: $i" }
}

class BasicRead2 :
  ReadOnlyProperty<Readable2, String> {
  override operator fun getValue(
    thisRef: Readable2,
    property: KProperty<*>
  ) = "getValue: ${thisRef.i}"
}

fun main() {
  val x = Readable2(11)
  val y = Readable2(17)
  x.value eq "getValue: 11"
  x.value2 eq "getValue: 11"
  y.value eq "getValue: 17"
  y.value2 eq "getValue: 17"
}
```

Implementing ReadOnlyProperty communicates to the reader that BasicRead2 can be used as a delegate and ensures a proper getValue() definition.

Because ReadOnlyProperty has only a single member function (and it has been defined as a fun interface in the standard library), value2 is defined much more succinctly using a *SAM conversion*.

BasicReadWrite.kt can be modified to implement ReadWriteProperty, ensuring proper getValue() and setValue() definitions:

```
// PropertyDelegation/BasicReadWrite2.kt
package propertydelegation
import atomictest.eq
import kotlin.properties.ReadWriteProperty
import kotlin.reflect.KProperty

class ReadWriteable2(var i: Int) {
  var msg = ""
  var value: String by BasicReadWrite2()
}

class BasicReadWrite2 :
  ReadWriteProperty<ReadWriteable2, String> {
  override operator fun getValue(
    rw: ReadWriteable2,
    property: KProperty<*>
  ) = "getValue: ${rw.i}"
  override operator fun setValue(
    rw: ReadWriteable2,
    property: KProperty<*>,
    s: String
  ) {
    rw.i = s.toIntOrNull() ?: 0
    rw.msg = "setValue to ${rw.i}"
  }
}

fun main() {
  val x = ReadWriteable2(11)
  x.value eq "getValue: 11"
  x.value = "99"
  x.msg eq "setValue to 99"
```

```
  x.value eq "getValue: 99"
}
```

Thus, a delegate class must contain either or both of the following functions, which are called when the delegated property is accessed:

1. For reading:

   ```
   operator fun getValue(thisRef: T, property: KProperty<*>): V
   ```

2. For writing:

   ```
   setValue(thisRef: T, property: KProperty<*>, value: V)
   ```

If the delegated property is a val, only the first function is required and ReadOnlyProperty can be implemented using a **SAM conversion**.

The parameters are:

- thisRef: T points to the delegate object, where T is the type of that delegate. If you don't want to use thisRef in the function, you can effectively disable it by using Any? for T.
- property: KProperty<*> provides information about the property itself. The most commonly-used is name, which produces the field name of the delegated property.
- value is the value stored by setValue() into the delegated property. V is the type of that property.

getValue() and setValue() can either be defined by convention, or written as implementations of ReadOnlyProperty or ReadWriteProperty.

To enable access to private elements, nest the delegate class:

```
// PropertyDelegation/Accessibility.kt
package propertydelegation
import atomictest.eq
import kotlin.properties.ReadOnlyProperty
import kotlin.reflect.KProperty

class Person(
  private val first: String,
  private val last: String
) {
  val name by      // SAM conversion:
  ReadOnlyProperty<Person, String> { _, _ ->
    "$first $last"
  }
}

fun main() {
  val alien = Person("Floopy", "Noopers")
  alien.name eq "Floopy Noopers"
}
```

Assuming adequate access to the elements in the delegating class, getValue() and setValue() can be written as extension functions:

```
// PropertyDelegation/Add.kt
package propertydelegation2
import atomictest.eq
import kotlin.reflect.KProperty

class Add(val a: Int, val b: Int) {
  val sum by Sum()
}

class Sum

operator fun Sum.getValue(
  thisRef: Add,
  property: KProperty<*>
) = thisRef.a + thisRef.b

fun main() {
  val addition = Add(144, 12)
```

```
    addition.sum eq 156
}
```

This way you can use an existing class that you are unable to modify or inherit and still delegate a property with it.

Here, when you set the value of the property, the number stored is the Fibonacci number for that value, using the `fibonacci()` function from the *Recursion* atom:

```
// PropertyDelegation/FibonacciProperty.kt
package propertydelegation
import kotlin.properties.ReadWriteProperty
import kotlin.reflect.KProperty
import recursion.fibonacci
import atomictest.eq

class Fibonacci :
  ReadWriteProperty<Any?, Long> {
  private var current: Long = 0
  override operator fun getValue(
    thisRef: Any?,
    property: KProperty<*>
  ) = current
  override operator fun setValue(
    thisRef: Any?,
    property: KProperty<*>,
    value: Long
  ) {
    current = fibonacci(value.toInt())
  }
}

fun main() {
  var fib by Fibonacci()
  fib eq 0L
  fib = 22L
  fib eq 17711L
  fib = 90L
  fib eq 2880067194370816120L
}
```

`fib` in `main()` is a *local delegated property*—it's defined inside a function rather than a class. A delegated property can also be defined at file scope.

`ReadWriteProperty`'s first generic argument can be `Any?` because we never use it to access anything inside `Fibonacci`, which would require specific type information. Instead we manipulate the `current` property as we can in any member function.

In most of the examples we've seen so far, the first parameter of `getValue()` and `setValue()` are of a specific type. Those delegates were tied to that specific type. Sometimes it is possible to create a general-purpose delegate by ignoring the first type as `Any?`. For example, suppose we'd like to store each delegated `String` property in a text file named for that property:

```
// PropertyDelegation/FileDelegate.kt
package propertydelegation
import kotlin.properties.ReadWriteProperty
import kotlin.reflect.KProperty
import checkinstructions.DataFile

class FileDelegate :
  ReadWriteProperty<Any?, String> {
  override fun getValue(
    thisRef: Any?,
    property: KProperty<*>
  ): String {
    val file =
      DataFile(property.name + ".txt")
    return if (file.exists())
      file.readText()
    else ""
  }
  override fun setValue(
    thisRef: Any?,
    property: KProperty<*>,
    value: String
  ) {
    DataFile(property.name + ".txt")
      .writeText(value)
  }
}
```

This delegate only needs to interact with the file, and doesn't need anything through `thisRef`. We ignore `thisRef` by typing it as `Any?`, because `Any?` has no interesting operations. We *are* interested in `property.name`, which is the name of the field.

Now we can automatically create a file associated with each property and store that property's data in that file:

```
// PropertyDelegation/Configuration.kt
package propertydelegation
import checkinstructions.DataFile
import atomictest.eq

class Configuration {
  var user by FileDelegate()
  var id by FileDelegate()
  var project by FileDelegate()
}

fun main() {
  val config = Configuration()
  config.user = "Luciano"
  config.id = "Ramalho47"
  config.project = "MyLittlePython"
  DataFile("user.txt").readText() eq "Luciano"
  DataFile("id.txt").readText() eq "Ramalho47"
  DataFile("project.txt").readText() eq
    "MyLittlePython"
}
```

Because it can ignore the surrounding type, `FileDelegate` is reusable.

Exercises and solutions can be found at www.AtomicKotlin.com.

Property Delegation Tools

The standard library contains special property delegation operations.

`Map` is one of the few types in the Kotlin library that is preconfigured to be used as a delegated property. A single `Map` can be used to store all the properties in a class. Each property identifier becomes a `String` key for the map, and the property's type is captured in the associated value:

```
// DelegationTools/CarService.kt
package propertydelegation
import atomictest.eq

class Driver(
  map: MutableMap<String, Any?>
) {
  var name: String by map
  var age: Int by map
  var id: String by map
  var available: Boolean by map
  var coord: Pair<Double, Double> by map
}

fun main() {
  val info = mutableMapOf<String, Any?>(
    "name" to "Bruno Fiat",
    "age" to 22,
    "id" to "X97C111",
    "available" to false,
    "coord" to Pair(111.93, 1231.12)
  )
  val driver = Driver(info)
  driver.available eq false
  driver.available = true
  info eq "{name=Bruno Fiat, age=22, " +
    "id=X97C111, available=true, " +
```

```
    "coord=(111.93, 1231.12)}"
}
```

Notice that the original `Map` info is modified when setting `driver.available = true`. This works because the Kotlin standard library contains `Map` extension functions `getValue()` and `setValue()` that enable property delegation. These simplified versions show how they work:

```
// DelegationTools/MapAccessors.kt
package delegationtools
import kotlin.reflect.KProperty

operator fun MutableMap<String, Any>.getValue(
  thisRef: Any?, property: KProperty<*>
): Any? {
  return this[property.name]
}

operator fun MutableMap<String, Any>.setValue(
  thisRef: Any?, property: KProperty<*>,
  value: Any
) {
  this[property.name] = value
}
```

To see the actual library definitions, put the cursor on the `by` keyword in IntelliJ IDEA or Android Studio and invoke "Go to Declaration"[49].

`Delegates.observable()` observes modifications of a mutable property. Here, we trace old and new values:

---

[49]https://www.jetbrains.com/help/idea/navigating-through-the-source-code.html#go_to_declaration

```
// DelegationTools/Team.kt
package delegationtools
import kotlin.properties.Delegates.observable
import atomictest.eq

class Team {
  var msg = ""
  var captain: String by observable("<0>") {
    prop, old, new ->
      msg += "${prop.name} $old to $new "
  }
}

fun main() {
  val team = Team()
  team.captain = "Adam"
  team.captain = "Amanda"
  team.msg eq "captain <0> to Adam " +
    "captain Adam to Amanda"
}
```

`observable()` takes two arguments:

1. The initial value for the property; `"<0>"` in this case.
2. A function which is the action to perform when the property is modified. Here, we use a lambda. The function arguments are the property being changed, the current value of that property, and the value it's being changed to.

`Delegates.vetoable()` allows you to prevent a change to a property if the new property value doesn't satisfy the given predicate. Here, `aName()` insists that the team captain's name begin with the letter "A":

```kotlin
// DelegationTools/TeamWithTraditions.kt
package delegationtools
import atomictest.*
import kotlin.properties.Delegates
import kotlin.reflect.KProperty

fun aName(
  property: KProperty<*>,
  old: String,
  new: String
) = if (new.startsWith("A")) {
  trace("$old -> $new")
  true
} else {
  trace("Name must start with 'A'")
  false
}

interface Captain {
  var captain: String
}

class TeamWithTraditions : Captain {
  override var captain: String
    by Delegates.vetoable("Adam", ::aName)
}

class TeamWithTraditions2 : Captain {
  override var captain: String
    by Delegates.vetoable("Adam") {
      _, old, new ->
        if (new.startsWith("A")) {
          trace("$old -> $new")
          true
        } else {
          trace("Name must start with 'A'")
          false
        }
    }
}

fun main() {
```

```
  listOf(
    TeamWithTraditions(),
    TeamWithTraditions2()
  ).forEach {
    it.captain = "Amanda"
    it.captain = "Bill"
    it.captain eq "Amanda"
  }
  trace eq """
    Adam -> Amanda
    Name must start with 'A'
    Adam -> Amanda
    Name must start with 'A'
  """
}
```

Delegates.vetoable() takes two arguments: the initial value for the property, and an onChange() function, which is ::aName in this example. onChange() takes three arguments: property: KProperty<*>, the old value currently held by the property, and the new value being placed in the property. The function returns a Boolean indicating whether the change is successful or prevented.

TeamWithTraditions2 defines Delegates.vetoable() using a lambda instead of the function aName().

The remaining tool in properties.Delegates is notNull(), which produces a property that must be initialized before it can be read:

```
// DelegationTools/NeverNull.kt
package delegationtools
import atomictest.*
import kotlin.properties.Delegates

class NeverNull {
  var nn: Int by Delegates.notNull()
}

fun main() {
  val non = NeverNull()
  capture {
    non.nn
  } eq "IllegalStateException: Property " +
```

```
    "nn should be initialized before get."
  non.nn = 11
  non.nn eq 11
}
```

Trying to read non.nn before nn has been assigned a value produces an exception. After nn has been assigned, you can successfully read it.

Exercises and solutions can be found at www.AtomicKotlin.com.

Lazy Initialization

So far, you've learned two ways to initialize properties.

1. Store the initial value at the point of definition, or in the constructor.
2. Define a custom getter that computes the property for each access.

This atom explores a third use case: costly initialization that you might not need right away, or ever. For example:

- Complex and time-consuming calculations
- Network requests
- Database access

This can produce two problems:

1. Long application start-up time.
2. Performing unnecessary work for a property that is never used, or that can have delayed access.

This happens frequently enough that Kotlin includes a built-in solution. A `lazy` property is initialized when it's first used, rather than when it's created. If we never use a `lazy` property, it never performs that expensive initialization.

The concept of `lazy` properties isn't unique to Kotlin. Laziness can be implemented within other languages, whether or not they provide direct support. Kotlin provides a consistent, recognizable idiom for such properties using ***property delegation***. With a `lazy` property, by is followed by a call to `lazy()`:

```
val lazyProperty by lazy { initializer }
```

`lazy()` takes a lambda containing the initialization logic. As usual, the last expression in the lambda becomes the result, which is assigned to the property:

```
// LazyInitialization/LazySyntax.kt
package lazyinitialization
import atomictest.*

val idle: String by lazy {
  trace("Initializing 'idle'")
  "I'm never used"
}

val helpful: String by lazy {
  trace("Initializing 'helpful'")
  "I'm helping!"
}

fun main() {
  trace(helpful)
  trace eq """
    Initializing 'helpful'
    I'm helping!
  """
}
```

The `idle` property isn't initialized because it's never accessed.

Notice that both `helpful` and `idle` are `val`s. Without `lazy` initialization, you'd be forced to make them `var`s, producing less-reliable code.

We can see all the work that `lazy` initialization does for you by implementing the behavior for an `Int` property without it:

```
// LazyInitialization/LazyInt.kt
package lazyinitialization
import atomictest.*

class LazyInt(val init: () -> Int) {
  private var helper: Int? = null
  val value: Int
    get() {
      if (helper == null)
        helper = init()
      return helper!!
    }
```

```kotlin
}

fun main() {
  val later = LazyInt {
    trace("Initializing 'later'")
    5
  }
  trace("First 'value' access:")
  trace(later.value)
  trace("Second 'value' access:")
  trace(later.value)
  trace eq """
    First 'value' access:
    Initializing 'later'
    5
    Second 'value' access:
    5
  """
}
```

The `value` property doesn't store a value, but instead has a getter that retrieves the value from the `helper` property. This is similar to the code Kotlin generates for `lazy`.

Now we can compare the three ways to initialize a property—at the point of definition, using a getter, and using `lazy` initialization:

```kotlin
// LazyInitialization/PropertyOptions.kt
package lazyinitialization
import atomictest.trace

fun compute(i: Int): Int {
  trace("Compute $i")
  return i
}

object Properties {
  val atDefinition = compute(1)
  val getter
    get() = compute(2)
  val lazyInit by lazy { compute(3) }
  val never by lazy { compute(4) }
}
```

```kotlin
fun main() {
  listOf(
    Properties::atDefinition,
    Properties::getter,
    Properties::lazyInit
  ).forEach {
    trace("${it.name}:")
    trace("${it.get()}")
    trace("${it.get()}")
  }
  trace eq """
    Compute 1
    atDefinition:
    1
    1
    getter:
    Compute 2
    2
    Compute 2
    2
    lazyInit:
    Compute 3
    3
    3
  """
}
```

- `atDefinition` is initialized when you create an instance of `Properties`.
- "Compute 1" appears before "atDefinition:" which shows that initialization happens before any accesses.
- `getter` is computed every time you access it. "Compute 2" appears twice, once for each access to the property.
- The initialization value for `lazyInit` is only calculated the first time it is accessed. Initialization never happens if you don't access that property—notice that "Compute 4" never appears in the trace.

Exercises and solutions can be found at www.AtomicKotlin.com.

Late Initialization

Sometimes you want to initialize properties of your class after it is created, but in a separate member function instead of using `lazy`.

For example, a framework or library might require initialization in a special function. If you extend that library class, you can provide your own implementation of that special function.

Consider a `Bag` interface with a `setUp()` that initializes instances:

```
// LateInitialization/Bag.kt
package lateinitialization

interface Bag {
  fun setUp()
}
```

Suppose we want to reuse a library that creates and manipulates `Bag`s and guarantees that `setUp()` is called. This library requires subclass initialization in `setUp()` instead of in a constructor:

```
// LateInitialization/Suitcase.kt
package lateinitialization
import atomictest.eq

class Suitcase : Bag {
  private var items: String? = null
  override fun setUp() {
    items = "socks, jacket, laptop"
  }
  fun checkSocks(): Boolean =
    items?.contains("socks") ?: false
}

fun main() {
```

```
  val suitcase = Suitcase()
  suitcase.setUp()
  suitcase.checkSocks() eq true
}
```

`Suitcase` initializes `items` by overriding `setUp()`. However, we can't just define `items` as a `String`—if we do that, we must provide a non-null initializer in the constructor. Using a stub value such as an empty `String` is a bad practice because you never know whether it's actually been initialized. `null` indicates that it's not initialized.

Defining `items` as a nullable `String?` means we must check for `null` in all member functions, as in `checkSocks()`. However, we know that the library we're reusing initializes `items` by calling `setUp()`, so the `null` checks should not be necessary.

The `lateinit` property modifier fixes this problem—here, we initialize `items` after creating an instance of `BetterSuitcase`:

```
// LateInitialization/BetterSuitcase.kt
package lateinitialization
import atomictest.eq

class BetterSuitcase : Bag {
  lateinit var items: String
  override fun setUp() {
    items = "socks, jacket, laptop"
  }
  fun checkSocks() = "socks" in items
}

fun main() {
  val suitcase = BetterSuitcase()
  suitcase.setUp()
  suitcase.checkSocks() eq true
}
```

Compare this version of `checkSocks()` with the one in `Suitcase.kt`. `lateinit` means `items` is safely defined as a non-nullable property.

`lateinit` can be used on a property inside the body of a class, a top-level property, or local `var`.

Limitations:

- `lateinit` can only be used on a `var` property, not a `val`.
- The property must be a non-nullable type.
- The property cannot be a primitive type.
- `lateinit` is not allowed for `abstract` properties in an `abstract` class or `interface`.
- `lateinit` is not allowed for properties with a custom `get()` or `set()`.

What happens if you forget to initialize such a property? You won't get compile-time errors or warnings, because the initialization logic might be complex and depend on other properties that Kotlin can't monitor:

```
// LateInitialization/FaultySuitcase.kt
package lateinitialization
import atomictest.*

class FaultySuitcase : Bag {
  lateinit var items: String
  override fun setUp() {}
  fun checkSocks() = "socks" in items
}

fun main() {
  val suitcase = FaultySuitcase()
  suitcase.setUp()
  capture {
    suitcase.checkSocks()
  } eq
    "UninitializedPropertyAccessException" +
    ": lateinit property items " +
    "has not been initialized"
}
```

This runtime exception has enough detail for you to easily discover and fix the problem. Tracking down an error reported by a `null` pointer exception is usually much more difficult.

`isInitialized` tells you whether a `lateinit` property been initialized. The property must be in your current scope, and is accessed using the `::` operator:

```
// LateInitialization/IsInitialized.kt
package lateinitialization
import atomictest.*

class WithLate {
  lateinit var x: String
  fun status() = "${::x.isInitialized}"
}

lateinit var y: String

fun main() {
  trace("${::y.isInitialized}")
  y = "Ready"
  trace("${::y.isInitialized}")
  val withlate = WithLate()
  trace(withlate.status())
  withlate.x = "Set"
  trace(withlate.status())
  trace eq "false true false true"
}
```

Although you can create a local `lateinit var`, you cannot call `isInitialized` on it because references to local `var`s or `val`s are not supported.

Exercises and solutions can be found at www.AtomicKotlin.com.

Appendices

Appendices

Appendix A: AtomicTest

This minimal test framework is used to validate the book examples. It also helps introduce and promote unit testing early in the learning process.

This framework is described in the following atoms:

- *Testing* introduces the framework and describes the eq and neq functions and the trace object.
- *Exceptions* introduces the capture() function.
- *Exception Handling* describes the capture() function implementation.
- *Unit Testing* uses AtomicTest to help introduce the concept of unit testing.

```
// AtomicTest/AtomicTest.kt
package atomictest
import kotlin.math.abs
import kotlin.reflect.KClass

const val ERROR_TAG = "[Error]: "

private fun <L, R> test(
  actual: L,
  expected: R,
  checkEquals: Boolean = true,
  predicate: () -> Boolean
) {
  println(actual)
  if (!predicate()) {
    print(ERROR_TAG)
    println("$actual " +
      (if (checkEquals) "!=" else "==") +
      " $expected")
  }
}

/**
```

```kotlin
 * Compares the string representation
 * of this object with the string `rval`.
 */
infix fun Any.eq(rval: String) {
  test(this, rval) {
    toString().trim() == rval.trimIndent()
  }
}

/**
 * Verifies this object is equal to `rval`.
 */
infix fun <T> T.eq(rval: T) {
  test(this, rval) {
    this == rval
  }
}

/**
 * Verifies this object is != `rval`.
 */
infix fun <T> T.neq(rval: T) {
  test(this, rval, checkEquals = false) {
    this != rval
  }
}

/**
 * Verifies that a `Double` number is equal
 * to `rval` within a positive delta.
 */
infix fun Double.eq(rval: Double) {
  test(this, rval) {
    abs(this - rval) < 0.0000001
  }
}

/**
 * Holds captured exception information:
 */
class CapturedException(
  private val exceptionClass: KClass<*>?,
```

```kotlin
    private val actualMessage: String
) {
  private val fullMessage: String
    get() {
      val className =
        exceptionClass?.simpleName ?: ""
      return className + actualMessage
    }
  infix fun eq(message: String) {
    fullMessage eq message
  }
  infix fun contains(parts: List<String>) {
    if (parts.any { it !in fullMessage }) {
      print(ERROR_TAG)
      println("Actual message: $fullMessage")
      println("Expected parts: $parts")
    }
  }
  override fun toString() = fullMessage
}

/**
 * Captures an exception and produces
 * information about it. Usage:
 *     capture {
 *       // Code that fails
 *     } eq "FailureException: message"
 */
fun capture(f:() -> Unit): CapturedException =
  try {
    f()
    CapturedException(null,
      "$ERROR_TAG Expected an exception")
  } catch (e: Throwable) {
    CapturedException(e::class,
      (e.message?.let { ": $it" } ?: ""))
  }

/**
 * Accumulates output when called as in:
 *     trace("info")
 *     trace(object)
```

```
 * Later compares accumulated to expected:
 *   trace eq "expected output"
 */
object trace {
  private val trc = mutableListOf<String>()
  operator fun invoke(obj: Any?) {
    trc += obj.toString()
  }
  /**
   * Compares trc contents to a multiline
   * `String` by ignoring white space.
   */
  infix fun eq(multiline: String) {
    val trace = trc.joinToString("\n")
    val expected = multiline.trimIndent()
      .replace("\n", " ")
    test(trace, multiline) {
      trace.replace("\n", " ") == expected
    }
    trc.clear()
  }
}
```

Appendix B: Java Interoperability

You can easily call Java code from Kotlin, and Kotlin code from Java.

An essential Kotlin design goal is to create a seamless experience for Java programmers. If you want to slowly migrate to Kotlin, you can easily start by sprinkling bits of Kotlin into your existing Java project. This way you can write new Kotlin code atop your Java base, benefiting from Kotlin language features without being forced to rewrite Java code when it doesn't make sense.

This appendix explores issues and techniques when interfacing between Kotlin and Java.

Calling Java from Kotlin

To use a Java class from Kotlin, import it, create an instance, and call a function, just as you would in Java. Here, we use `java.util.Random()`:

```
// interoperability/Random.kt
import atomictest.eq
import java.util.Random

fun main() {
  val rand = Random(47)
  rand.nextInt(100) eq 58
}
```

As with creating any instance in Kotlin, you don't need Java's new. A class from a Java library works like a native Kotlin class.

JavaBean-style getters and setters in a Java class become properties in Kotlin:

```java
// interoperability/Chameleon.java
package interoperability;
import java.io.Serializable;

public
class Chameleon implements Serializable {
  private int size;
  private String color;
  public int getSize() {
    return size;
  }
  public void setSize(int newSize) {
    size = newSize;
  }
  public String getColor() {
    return color;
  }
  public void setColor(String newColor) {
    color = newColor;
  }
}
```

When working with Java, the package name must be identical (including case) to the directory name. Java package names typically contain only lowercase letters. To conform to this convention, this appendix uses only lowercase letters in the `interoperability` example subdirectory name.

The imported `Chameleon` class works like a Kotlin class with properties:

```
// interoperability/UseBeanClass.kt
import interoperability.Chameleon
import atomictest.eq

fun main() {
  val chameleon = Chameleon()
  chameleon.size = 1
  chameleon.size eq 1
  chameleon.color = "green"
  chameleon.color eq "green"
  chameleon.color = "turquoise"
  chameleon.color eq "turquoise"
}
```

Extension functions are especially helpful when you use an existing Java library that lacks needed member functions. For example, we can add an `adjustToTemperature()` operation to `Chameleon`:

```
// interoperability/ExtensionsToJavaClass.kt
package interop
import interoperability.Chameleon
import atomictest.eq

fun Chameleon.adjustToTemperature(
  isHot: Boolean
) {
  color = if (isHot) "grey" else "black"
}

fun main() {
  val chameleon = Chameleon()
  chameleon.size = 2
  chameleon.size eq 2
  chameleon.adjustToTemperature(isHot = true)
  chameleon.color eq "grey"
}
```

The Kotlin standard library contains many extensions for Java standard library classes such as `List` and `String`.

Calling Kotlin from Java

Kotlin produces libraries that are usable from Java. For the Java programmer, a Kotlin library looks like a Java library.

Because everything in Java is a class, let's start with a Kotlin class containing a property and a function:

```
// interoperability/KotlinClass.kt
package interop

class Basic {
  var property1 = 1
  fun value() = property1 * 10
}
```

If you import this class into Java, it looks like an ordinary Java class:

```
// interoperability/UsingKotlinClass.java
package interoperability;
import interop.Basic;
import static atomictest.AtomicTestKt.eq;

public class UsingKotlinClass {
  public static void main(String[] args) {
    Basic b = new Basic();
    eq(b.getProperty1(), 1);
    b.setProperty1(12);
    eq(b.value(), 120);
  }
}
```

property1 becomes a private field containing JavaBean-style getters and setters. The value() member function becomes a Java method with the same name.

We have also imported AtomicTest, which requires additional ceremony in Java: we must import it using the static keyword and give the package name. eq() can only be called as an ordinary function because Java doesn't support infix notation.

If a Kotlin class is in the same package as Java code, you don't need to import it:

```
// interoperability/KotlinDataClass.kt
package interoperability

data class Staff(
  var name: String,
  var role: String
)
```

data classes generate extra member functions like equals(), hashCode() and toString(), all of which work seamlessly within Java. At the end of main(), we verify the implementations of equals() and hashCode() by placing a Data object into a HashMap, then retrieving it:

```
// interoperability/UseDataClass.java
package interoperability;
import java.util.HashMap;
import static atomictest.AtomicTestKt.eq;

public class UseDataClass {
  public static void main(String[] args) {
    Staff e = new Staff(
      "Fluffy", "Office Manager");
    eq(e.getRole(), "Office Manager");
    e.setName("Uranus");
    e.setRole("Assistant");
    eq(e,
      "Staff(name=Uranus, role=Assistant)");

    // Call copy() from the data class:
    Staff cf = e.copy("Cornfed", "Sidekick");
    eq(cf,
      "Staff(name=Cornfed, role=Sidekick)");

    HashMap<Staff, String> hm =
      new HashMap<>();
    // Employees work as hash keys:
    hm.put(e, "Cheerful");
    eq(hm.get(e), "Cheerful");
  }
}
```

If you use the command line to run Java code that incorporates Kotlin code, you must include kotlin-runtime.jar as a dependency, otherwise you'll get runtime exceptions complaining that some of the library utility classes are not found. IntelliJ IDEA automatically includes `kotlin-runtime.jar`.

Kotlin top-level functions map to `static` methods in a Java class that takes its name from the Kotlin file:

```
// interoperability/TopLevelFunction.kt
package interop

fun hi() = "Hello!"
```

To import, specify the class name generated by Kotlin. This name must also be used when calling the `static` method:

```
// interoperability/CallTopLevelFunction.java
package interoperability;
import interop.TopLevelFunctionKt;
import static atomictest.AtomicTestKt.eq;

public class CallTopLevelFunction {
  public static void main(String[] args) {
    eq(TopLevelFunctionKt.hi(), "Hello!");
  }
}
```

If you don't want to qualify `hi()` with the package name, use `import static` as we do with `AtomicTest`:

```
// interoperability/CallTopLevelFunction2.java
package interoperability;
import static interop.TopLevelFunctionKt.hi;
import static atomictest.AtomicTestKt.eq;

public class CallTopLevelFunction2 {
  public static void main(String[] args) {
    eq(hi(), "Hello!");
  }
}
```

If you don't like the class name generated by Kotlin, you can change it using the `@JvmName` annotation:

```
// interoperability/ChangeName.kt
@file:JvmName("Utils")
package interop

fun salad() = "Lettuce!"
```

Now instead of `ChangeNameKt`, we use `Utils`:

```
// interoperability/MakeSalad.java
package interoperability;
import interop.Utils;
import static atomictest.AtomicTestKt.eq;

public class MakeSalad {
  public static void main(String[] args) {
    eq(Utils.salad(), "Lettuce!");
  }
}
```

You can find further details in the documentation[50].

Adapting Java to Kotlin

One of Kotlin's design goals is to take an existing Java type and adapt it to your needs. This ability is not restricted to library designers—the same logic can be applied to any external code base.

In *Recursion*, we created `Fibonacci.kt` to efficiently produce Fibonacci numbers. That implementation is limited by the size of the `Long` it returns. If you'd like to return larger values, the Java standard library includes the `BigInteger` class. A few lines of code morphs `BigInteger` into something that feels like a native Kotlin class:

---

[50]https://kotlinlang.org/docs/reference/java-to-kotlin-interop.html

```
// interoperability/BigInt.kt
package biginteger
import java.math.BigInteger

fun Int.toBigInteger(): BigInteger =
  BigInteger.valueOf(toLong())

fun String.toBigInteger(): BigInteger =
  BigInteger(this)

operator fun BigInteger.plus(
  other: BigInteger
): BigInteger = add(other)
```

The `toBigInteger()` extension functions converts any `Int` or `String` to a `BigInteger` by calling the `BigInteger` constructor and passing the receiver string as an argument.

Overloading the operator `BigInteger.plus()` allows you to write `number + other`. This makes working with `BigInteger` enjoyable compared to Java's clumsy `number.plus(other)`.

Using `BigInteger`, `Recursion/Fibonacci.kt` easily converts to produce much larger results:

```
// interoperability/BigFibonacci.kt
package interop
import atomictest.eq
import java.math.BigInteger
import java.math.BigInteger.ONE
import java.math.BigInteger.ZERO

fun fibonacci(n: Int): BigInteger {
  tailrec fun fibonacci(
    n: Int,
    current: BigInteger,
    next: BigInteger
  ): BigInteger {
    if (n == 0) return current
    return fibonacci(
      n - 1, next, current + next)    // [1]
  }
```

```
    return fibonacci(n, ZERO, ONE)
}

fun main() {
  (0..7).map { fibonacci(it) } eq
  "[0, 1, 1, 2, 3, 5, 8, 13]"
  fibonacci(22) eq 17711.toBigInteger()
  fibonacci(150) eq
    "9969216677189303386214405760200"
      .toBigInteger()
}
```

All Longs were replaced with BigInteger. In main(), you see both Int and String converted to BigInteger using different toBigInteger() extension properties. In line **[1]** we use the plus operator to find the sum current + next; this is identical to the original version using Long.

fibonacci(150) overflows the Recursion/Fibonacci.kt version, but works fine after the conversion to BigInteger.

Java Checked Exceptions & Kotlin

Java was predominantly patterned after the C++ language, which allowed you to specify the exceptions that a function might throw. The Java designers decided to go one step further and *force* anyone calling that function to catch every specified exception. This seemed like a good idea at the time, and thus was born *checked exceptions*—an experiment that, to our knowledge, has not been repeated in subsequent programming languages.

Here's how Java forces you to catch checked exceptions in the process of opening, reading and closing a file. We only provide the basics to show the checked exceptions; you must actually write more complex code to correctly solve this problem in Java:

```
// interoperability/JavaChecked.java
package interoperability;
import java.io.*;
import java.nio.file.*;
import static atomictest.AtomicTestKt.eq;

public class JavaChecked {
  // Build path to current source file, based
  // on directory where Gradle is invoked:
  static Path thisFile = Paths.get(
    "DataFiles", "file_wubba.txt");
  public static void main(String[] args) {
    BufferedReader source = null;
    try {
      source = new BufferedReader(
        new FileReader(thisFile.toFile()));
    } catch(FileNotFoundException e) {
      // Recover from file-open error
    }
    try {
      String first = source.readLine();
      eq(first, "wubba lubba dub dub");
    } catch(IOException e) {
      // Recover from read() error
    }
    try {
      source.close();
    } catch(IOException e) {
      // Recover from close() error
    }
  }
}
```

Each of the above operations involves checked exceptions and must be placed inside a `try` block or Java produces compile-time errors for uncaught exceptions.

The only reason to `catch` an exception is if you can somehow recover from the problem. If it's not something you can fix, there's no point in writing a `catch` clause for that exception—just let it become an error report. In the above examples, recovery from the errors seems dubious, but you're still forced to write the `try-catch` blocks.

Let's rewrite this example in Kotlin:

```
// interoperability/KotlinChecked.kt
import atomictest.eq
import java.io.File

fun main() {
  File("DataFiles/file_wubba.txt")
    .readLines()[0] eq
    "wubba lubba dub dub"
}
```

Kotlin allows us to reduce the operation to a single line of code because it adds extension functions to the Java `File` class. At the same time, Kotlin eliminates the checked exceptions. If we wanted, we could surround intermediate operations with `try-catch` blocks, but Kotlin does not enforce checked exceptions. This provides error reporting without compelling you to write the additional noisy code.

Java libraries often use checked exceptions in situations that are outside the programmer's control and are typically unrecoverable. In these cases, it's best to catch the exception at the top level and restart the process, if possible. Requiring all intermediate levels to pass the exception only adds cognitive overhead when trying to understand the code.

If you're writing Kotlin code that is called from Java and you must specify a checked exception, Kotlin provides the `@Throws` annotation to give this information to the Java caller:

```
// interoperability/AnnotateThrows.kt
package interop
import java.io.IOException

@Throws(IOException::class)
fun hasCheckedException() {
  throw IOException()
}
```

Here's how `hasCheckedException()` is called from Java:

```
// interoperability/CatchChecked.java
package interoperability;
import interop.AnnotateThrowsKt;
import java.io.IOException;
import static atomictest.AtomicTestKt.eq;

public class CatchChecked {
  public static void main(String[] args) {
    try {
      AnnotateThrowsKt.hasCheckedException();
    } catch(IOException e) {
      eq(e, "java.io.IOException");
    }
  }
}
```

If you don't handle the exception, the Java compiler issues an error message.

Although Kotlin includes language support for exception handling, it tends to emphasize error reporting and reserves exception handling for those rare situations where you can actually recover from a problem (almost exclusively I/O operations).

Nullable Types & Java

Kotlin ensures that *pure* Kotlin code has no `null` errors, but when you call into Java, you have no such guarantees. In the following Java code, `get()` sometimes returns `null`:

```
// interoperability/JTool.java
package interoperability;

public class JTool {
  public static JTool get(String s) {
    if(s == null) return null;
    return new JTool();
  }
  public String method() {
    return "Success";
  }
}
```

To use `JTool` within Kotlin, you must know how `get()` behaves. You have three choices, shown here in the definitions of a, b and c:

```
// interoperability/PlatformTypes.kt
package interop
import interoperability.JTool
import atomictest.eq

object KotlinCode {
  val a: JTool? = JTool.get("")  // [1]
  val b: JTool = JTool.get("")   // [2]
  val c = JTool.get("")          // [3]
}

fun main() {
  with(KotlinCode) {
    a?.method() eq "Success"     // [4]
    b.method() eq "Success"
    c.method() eq "Success"      // [5]
    ::a.returnType eq
      "interoperability.JTool?"
    ::b.returnType eq
      "interoperability.JTool"
    ::c.returnType eq
      "interoperability.JTool!"  // [6]
  }
}
```

- **[1]** Specify the type as nullable.
- **[2]** Specify the type as non-nullable.
- **[3]** Use type inference.

The `with()` in `main()` allows us to refer to a, b and c without the `KotlinCode` qualification. Because the identifiers are inside an `object`, we can use member reference syntax and the `returnType` property to determine their types.

To initialize a, b and c, we pass a non-`null` `String` to `get()`, so a, b and c all end up with non-`null` references and each one can successfully call `method()`.

- **[4]** Because a is nullable, it must use `?.` during member function calls.

- **[5]** c behaves like a non-nullable reference and can be dereferenced without any additional checks.
- **[6]** Notice that c returns neither a nullable type nor a non-nullable type, but something entirely different: JTool!.

Type! is Kotlin's *platform type*, and has no notation—you can't write it into your code. It is used whenever Kotlin must infer a type outside its domain.

If a type comes from Java, accessing it can produce a null pointer exception (NPE). Here's what happens when JTool.get() returns a null reference:

```
// interoperability/NPEOnPlatformType.kt
import interoperability.JTool
import atomictest.*

fun main() {
  val xn: JTool? = JTool.get(null)   // [1]
  xn?.method() eq null

  val yn = JTool.get(null)           // [2]
  yn?.method() eq null               // [3]
  capture {
    yn.method()                      // [4]
  } contains listOf("NullPointerException")

  capture {
    val zn: JTool = JTool.get(null)  // [5]
  } eq "NullPointerException: " +
    "get(null) must not be null"
}
```

When you call a Java method like JTool.get() inside Kotlin, its return value (unless annotated as explained in the next section) is a platform type, which in this case is JTool!.

- **[1]** Because xn is of the nullable type JTool?, it can successfully receive a null. Assigning to a nullable type is safe, because Kotlin forces you to test for null using ?. when calling method().
- **[2]** At the point of definition, yn successfully receives the null without complaint because Kotlin infers it to be the platform type JTool!.

- [3] You can dereference yn by using a safe-access call ?., which in this case returns null.
- [4] However, using ?. is not required. You can simply dereference yn. In this case you get a NullPointerException without any helpful message.
- [5] Assigning to a non-nullable type can produce an NPE. Kotlin checks for nullity at the point of assignment. The initialization of zn fails because the declared type JTool promises that zn is not nullable, but it receives a null which produces a NullPointerException, this time with a helpful message.

The exception message contains detailed information about the expression that produced the null: NullPointerException: get(null) must not be null. Even though it's a runtime exception, the comprehensive error message makes the problem much easier than fixing a regular NPE.

A platform type contains the *least* amount of information available for that type. In this case, it only tells you that the type is JTool. It might or might not be nullable—when using an inferred platform type you simply don't know.

You can't explicitly declare a platform type (e.g. JTool!). You can only observe a platform type in error messages, or when you display the inferred type as in PlatformTypes.kt, or by checking the type within the IDE.

When working on a mixed Kotlin and Java project, you may or may not have control over the Java code base. When using an external Java library, you can't modify the source code, so you must work with platform types.

Platform types provide seamless Java interoperability, and maintain the consistency of type inference. However, don't rely on them. The proper strategy when calling un-annotated Java code is to avoid type inference, and instead understand whether or not the code you are calling can produce nulls.

Nullability Annotations

If you control the Java code base, you can add *nullability annotations* to the Java code and avoid subtle NPE errors. @Nullable and @NotNull tell Kotlin to treat a Java type as nullable or non-nullable, respectively. Here we add Kotlin nullability annotations to JTool.java:

```
// interoperability/AnnotatedJTool.java
package interoperability;
import org.jetbrains.annotations.NotNull;
import org.jetbrains.annotations.Nullable;

public class AnnotatedJTool {
  @Nullable
  public static JTool
  getUnsafe(@Nullable String s) {
    if(s == null) return null;
    return getSafe(s);
  }
  @NotNull
  public static JTool
  getSafe(@NotNull String s) {
    return new JTool();
  }
  public String method() {
    return "Success";
  }
}
```

Applying an annotation to a Java parameter affects only that parameter. Applying an annotation in front of a Java method modifies the return type.

When you call getUnsafe() and getSafe() in Kotlin, Kotlin treats the AnnotatedJTool member functions as native Kotlin nullable or non-nullable:

```
// interoperability/AnnotatedJava.kt
package interop
import interoperability.AnnotatedJTool
import atomictest.eq

object KotlinCode2 {
  val a = AnnotatedJTool.getSafe("")
  // Doesn't compile:
  // val b = AnnotatedJTool.getSafe(null)
  val c = AnnotatedJTool.getUnsafe("")
  val d = AnnotatedJTool.getUnsafe(null)
}

fun main() {
```

```
  with(KotlinCode2) {
    ::a.returnType eq
      "interoperability.JTool"
    ::c.returnType eq
      "interoperability.JTool?"
    ::d.returnType eq
      "interoperability.JTool?"
  }
}
```

`@NotNull JTool` is transformed to Kotlin's non-nullable type `JTool`, and the annotated `@Nullable JTool` is transformed to Kotlin's `JTool?`. You can see this in the types shown in `main()` for `a`, `c`, and `d`.

You can't pass a nullable argument when a non-nullable argument is expected, even if it's a Java type annotated with `@NotNull`, so Kotlin won't compile `AnnotatedJTool.getSafe(null)`.

Different kinds of nullability annotations are supported, using different names:
- `@Nullable` and `@CheckForNull` are specified by the JSR-305 standard.
- `@Nullable` and `@NonNull` are used in Android.
- `@Nullable` and `@NotNull` are supported by JetBrains tools.
- There are others. You can find the full list in the Kotlin documentation[51].

Kotlin detects default nullability annotations for a Java package or class, as specified in the JSR-305 standard. If it's `@NotNull` by default, you should explicitly specify only `@Nullable` annotations. If it's `@Nullable` by default, you should explicitly specify only `@NotNull` annotations. The documentation[52] contains the technical details for choosing the default annotation.

If you develop mixed Kotlin and Java projects, your applications will be safer if you use nullability annotations in your Java code.

Collections & Java

This book doesn't require Java knowledge. However, when you write code in Kotlin for the Java Virtual Machine (JVM), it's helpful to be familiar with the Java standard collections library, because Kotlin uses it to create its own collections.

---
[51]https://kotlinlang.org/docs/java-interop.html#nullability-annotations
[52]https://kotlinlang.org/docs/java-interop.html#jsr-305-support

The Java collections library is a set of classes and interfaces that implement collection data structures, such as lists, sets and maps. These data structures usually have clear and simple interfaces, but for speed may have complicated implementations.

New languages typically create their own collections library from scratch. For example, the Scala language has its own collections library which in many ways surpasses the Java collections library, but also makes it more challenging to mix Scala and Java.

Kotlin's collections library is intentionally *not* rewritten from scratch. Instead, it consists of improvements atop the Java collections library. For example, when you create a mutable `List`, you're actually using Java's `ArrayList`:

```
// interoperability/HiddenArrayList.kt
import atomictest.eq

fun main() {
  val list = mutableListOf(1, 2, 3)
  list.javaClass.name eq
    "java.util.ArrayList"
}
```

For seamless interoperability with Java code, Kotlin uses the interfaces from the Java standard library, and often the same implementations. This produces three benefits:

1. Kotlin code can easily mix with Java code. No additional conversion is required when passing Kotlin collections to Java code.
2. Years of performance tuning in the Java standard library is automatically available to Kotlin programmers.
3. The standard library included with a Kotlin application is small, because it uses Java collections rather than defining its own. The Kotlin standard library consists primarily of extension functions that improve the Java collections.

Kotlin also fixes a design problem. In Java all collection interfaces are mutable. For example, `java.util.List` has methods `add()` and `remove()` that modify the `List`. As we've shown throughout this book, mutability is the source of a significant number of programming problems. Thus, in Kotlin, the default `Collection` type is read-only:

```
// interoperability/ReadOnlyByDefault.kt
package interop

data class Animal(val name: String)

interface Zoo {
  fun viewAnimals(): Collection<Animal>
}

fun visitZoo(zoo: Zoo) {
  val animals = zoo.viewAnimals()
  // Compile-time error:
  // animals.add(Animal("Grumpy Cat"))
}
```

Read-only collections are safer and more bug-free because they prevent accidental modification.

Java provides a partial solution for collection immutability: when returning a collection you can place it inside a special wrapper that throws an exception for any attempt to modify the underlying collection. This doesn't produce static type checking, but can still prevent subtle bugs. However, you must remember to wrap the collection to make it read-only, whereas in Kotlin you must be explicit when you *want* a mutable collection.

Kotlin has separate interfaces for mutable and read-only collections:

- Collection/MutableCollection
- List/MutableList
- Set/MutableSet
- Map/MutableMap

These duplicate the interfaces from the Java standard library:

- java.util.Collection
- java.util.List
- java.util.Set
- java.util.Map

In Kotlin, as in Java, Collection is a supertype for both List and Set. MutableCollection extends Collection and is a supertype of MutableList and MutableSet. Here's the basic structure:

```
// interoperability/CollectionStructure.kt
package collectionstructure

interface Collection<E>
interface List<E>: Collection<E>
interface Set<E>: Collection<E>
interface Map<K, V>
interface MutableCollection<E>
interface MutableList<E>:
  List<E>, MutableCollection<E>
interface MutableSet<E>:
  Set<E>, MutableCollection<E>
interface MutableMap<K, V>: Map<K, V>
```

For simplicity, we show only the names and not the full declarations from the Kotlin standard library.

Kotlin mutable collections match their Java counterparts. If you compare `MutableCollection` from `kotlin.collections` with `java.util.List`, you'll see that they declare the same member functions (*methods*, in Java terminology). Kotlin's `Collection`, `List`, `Set` and `Map` also duplicate Java's interfaces, but without any mutation methods.

Both `kotlin.collections.List` and `kotlin.collections.MutableList` are visible from Java as `java.util.List`. These interfaces are special: they exist only in Kotlin, but at the bytecode level they are both replaced with Java's `List`.

A Kotlin `List` can be cast to a Java `List`:

```
// interoperability/JavaList.kt
import atomictest.eq

fun main() {
  val list = listOf(1, 2, 3)
  (list is java.util.List<*>) eq true
}
```

This code produces a warning:

- *This class shouldn't be used in Kotlin.*
- *Use kotlin.collections.List or kotlin.collections.MutableList instead.*

This is a reminder to use Kotlin's interfaces, not Java's, when programming in Kotlin.

Keep in mind that read-only is not the same as immutable. A collection cannot be changed using a read-only reference, but it can still change:

```
// interoperability/ReadOnlyCollections.kt
import atomictest.eq

fun main() {
  val mutable = mutableListOf(1, 2, 3)
  // Read-only reference to a mutable list:
  val list: List<Int> = mutable
  mutable += 4
  // list has changed:
  list eq "[1, 2, 3, 4]"
}
```

Here, the read-only `list` references a `MutableList`, which can then be changed by manipulating `mutable`. Because all Java collections are mutable, Java code can modify a read-only Kotlin collection, even if you pass it via a read-only reference.

Kotlin collections don't produce full safety, but provide a good compromise between having a better library and maintaining compatibility with Java.

Java Primitive Types

In Kotlin, you call a constructor to create an object, but in Java you must use `new` to produce an object. `new` places the resulting object on the heap. Such types are called *reference types*.

Creating objects on the heap can be inefficient for basic types such as numbers. For these types, Java falls back on the approach taken by C and C++: Instead of creating the variable using `new`, a non-reference "automatic" variable is created that holds the value directly. Automatic variables are placed on the stack, making them much more efficient. Such types get special treatment by the JVM and are called *primitive types*.

There are a fixed number of primitive types: `boolean`, `int`, `long`, `char`, `byte`, `short`, `float` and `double`. Primitive types always contain a non-null value, and they can't be used as generic arguments. If you need to store `null` or use such types as generic arguments, you can use the corresponding reference type defined in the Java standard library, such as `java.lang.Boolean` or `java.lang.Integer`. These types are often called *wrapper types* or *boxed types* to emphasize that they only wrap the primitive value and store it on the heap.

```java
// interoperability/JavaWrapper.java
package interoperability;
import java.util.*;

public class JavaWrapper {
  public static void main(String[] args) {
    // Primitive type
    int i = 10;
    // Wrapper types
    Integer iOrNull = null;
    List<Integer> list = new ArrayList<>();
  }
}
```

Java distinguishes between reference types and primitive types, but Kotlin does not. You use the same type `Int` both for defining an integer `var`/`val` or using it as a generic argument. At the JVM level, Kotlin employs the same primitive type support. When possible, Kotlin replaces `Int` with a primitive `int` in the bytecode. A nullable `Int?` or `Int` used as a generic argument can only be represented using the wrapper type:

```
// interoperability/KotlinWrapper.kt
package interop

fun main() {
  // Generates a primitive int:
  val i = 10
  // Generates wrapper types:
  val iOrNull: Int? = null
  val list: List<Int> = listOf(1, 2, 3)
}
```

You normally don't need to think much about whether primitives or wrappers are generated by the Kotlin compiler, but it's useful to know how it's implemented on the JVM.

-

The documentation[53] explains more about the nuances of Kotlin/Java interoperability.

---

[53]https://kotlinlang.org/docs/java-interop.html

Lightning Source UK Ltd.
Milton Keynes UK
UKHW050731140122
397142UK00006B/454